From Union to Empire

Essays in the Jeffersonian Tradition

From Union to Empire
Essays in the Jeffersonian Tradition

Clyde N. Wilson

The Foundation
for
American Education

Columbia, South Carolina

The paper in this book meets the guidelines for permanence
and durability of the Committee on Production Guidelines for
Book Longevity of the Council on Library Resources.

Library of Congress Cataloging-in-Publication Data

Wilson, Clyde Norman.
    From Union to Empire: Essays in the Jeffersonian tradi-
    tion / Clyde N. Wilson.
        p. cm.
    Includes bibliographical references.
    ISBN 0-9623842-1-6
        1. Conservatism—United States—History. 2. Jefferson,
Thomas, 1743–1826—Political and social views. I. Title.

JC573.2.U6 W548 2002
320.52'0973—dc21
2002004659

Published in the United States by
THE FOUNDATION FOR AMERICAN EDUCATION
Post Office Box 11851
Columbia, SC 29211

In memory of Russell, Mel, and Murray.

CONTENTS

✮✮✮

American History
As It Can Be Written

D r. Clyde Wilson is a Christian, a Southerner, an American, an historian, and a conservative. For over three decades he has worked on the definitive edition of *The Papers of John C. Calhoun*, has written on Calhoun and published a collection of Calhoun's most important writings. He has also seen to it that at least a corporal's guard of younger historians, whose work he has supervised at the University of South Carolina, will not fit the standard pattern stamped out nearly everywhere else. I suppose these are the bare essentials. He is also, as his essays demonstrate, a teacher and writer of great merit. His writings—published in *Modern Age*, *Chronicles*, *Telos*, and many other forums—show Professor Wilson off as the kind of conservative who is a stalwart defender of federalism and republicanism, and the liberties associated with them. Such conservatives are few and far between these days.

Wilson mentions having been a "Goldwater Youth." Many of us were such, and we are probably not much the worse for it. Conservatism itself has undergone major changes since then, none for the better. But in those long bygone days, Conservatives—already donning the capital "C"—held forth at length about accumulated wisdom rooted in tradition. The past was all. One might, therefore, have expected some of them to be serious historians. Alas, the truth never quite lived up to the claims, and now the Official Conservatives have thrown history entirely overboard, except as a heap of mere curiosities useful in ephemeral disputations. Instead, they call for world-revolution directed by the United States in "its" (the federal government's) starring role as perfected millennial state—to steal a phrase from Richard Weaver.

That transformation requires some explaining and explanations duly emerge from Wilson's essays, spanning the period 1969 to 2001. One notices a certain radicalization of his views over that time, the outcome of cumulative disillusionment—and rightly so—with the ideas, leadership, and policies of the Official Conservatives and their vehicle, the Republican party. Wilson's views on recent events are systematically connected with his views on the great sweep of American history.

It is the function of history and the role of the historian to help us understand who we are and how we got into to the situation in which we find ourselves. Wilson writes that a historian should be clear about "where he is coming from." Beyond that, his obligations are to do serious research, write honest narrative and analysis, and save his individual views for his concluding sections. This brings us to Wilson the Southerner. He is noteworthy for being one of a vanishing small group of professional historians who do not regard Southern life and history as one dark, Gothic misfortune after another.

Wilson is not content merely to throw the occasional spanner into the enemy's works. Instead, he takes the war to the enemy's doorstep. What comes of this is the creative deployment of a Southern perspective on American history—one that yields interesting and important insights. This seemed more than clear to me, some thirty years ago, when I first read in *Modern Age* the essay titled, "The Jeffersonian Conservative Tradition." I knew we would be hearing a lot more from this historian.

The essay just mentioned already contained many of the major themes of Wilson's work. One of them is the search for the essential American political and social order and ideology as these unfolded in the colonial period and became embodied in the "settlement" of the late 18th century. Wilson provides a "Virginia-centric" reading of American history, centering on local self-government in real communities, within which individual liberty was possible. This involves, necessarily, a critique of the established counter-traditions, which pass for American history. He applies the insights thereby gained to the prospects for republican recovery and restoration. In this, he shows a clearheaded grasp of the obstacles, but unlike the Marxists who wish "to analyze the existing situation and take power" (as the phrase goes), he wants to analyze the existing situation in order to *limit* power.

Historical myths, originated and wielded by New England historians and writers as a weapon against their opponents in the South and West, became the received view of American historiography. What is for Wilson the representative American norm, the localist Virginia model, was accordingly downplayed and sidelined as the mere defense of slavery. But neither side of this dialectic can be fully understood without the other.

In Wilson's view, figures from the revolutionary and founding periods have not been understood so much as put to present partisan use, only to be thrown overboard when a more radical generation spots the real, historical man under the myth. He addresses this pattern in several essays on Thomas Jefferson and his changing reputation. Thus, Jefferson, damned by Henry Adams for New England Federalist reasons, praised by Vernon Louis Parrington for Progressive reasons, praised further by New Dealers looking for legitimate ancestors, is now dismissed from the founders' pantheon for not living up to received mythology about him. By contrast, James Madison's stock keeps rising ever higher. Wilson writes that Madison, "because of his superficiality, lends himself the most readily to modernization and liberalization. That is why he is called 'The Father of the Constitution'" (p.p. 66-67).

Centralists have raised a series of made-to-order U.S. nationalisms on the ruins of the decentralized republican societies. At the heart of these phantasms is the flexible Constitution, whose meaning is never stable for more than a decade or so. It is no surprise, therefore, that Wilson is a critic of the Constitution itself.

The Federalists—often mistaken for conservatives—were "tinkerers." Their constitutional handiwork was "innovative, speculative, and antitraditional" (p. 4). It is the *elites* that have been radical in American history—not the people. The majority so feared by the Federalists was "not, in America, a desperate property-less mob, but a restricted electorate of middle class property holders" (p. 5).

New England intellectuals, addled by the decay of their theology and imported historicist notions, took over the writing of American history and championed central power. George Bancroft, Hegelian and democrat, added to the state-centric reading of U.S. history, and modern liberals have carried on the tradition, claiming that the federal union is more democratic, the more powerful and centralized it becomes.

As Wilson reconstructs American history, the essential American tradition is best represented by the Jeffersonian, Jacksonian, secessionist, and Populist line of descent. He makes a good case for the sheer continuity of these movements, whatever the drawbacks of Jackson as a leader, or the Populists as theorists. These struggles represent the old fight of Court vs. Country as it played out in the New World.

The essays bristle with contempt for our vaunted two-party "system"—made possible by the Federalists' tinkering and creating numerous incentives for self-serving behavior by political aspirants. You will find next to no kind words for the Republican Party in Wilson's book. He is of the real republican school and his heroes are such as John Taylor of Caroline and John C. Calhoun.

This somehow brings us back to the conservative movement after World War II. Having accepted much of the standard historical mythology, too many conservatives have sought to find predecessors in the Federalist-Whig-Republican line. This odd construction has systematically misled them, while giving them an extra rationale for becoming part of the Court Party, that is, Big Government Conservatives. But as Wilson has remarked more than once, Northern conservatives never conserved anything. As one of the opposing school, Wilson dedicates this book to "Russell, Mel and Murray," each of whom had a firmer grasp on American history than a truckload of Neo-Conservatives and *Wall Street Journal* editorialists could ever hope to have.

It is hard to do justice to Clyde Wilson's work, and as a preface should simply say something useful about the work in hand, I bring this to a close. Suffice it to say that there is good, powerful writing here, where an understanding of the value of genuine aristocratic leadership is mixed with the practical wisdom of the plain folk of the South. I have long been waiting for a collection of Wilson's essays and, having seen it, I can say that it is well worth careful and repeated reading.

There are even film reviews in this collection. On that note, I can only add that, while the Court Party has gone from success to success under the slogan "Doin' right ain't got no end," nevertheless, Clyde Wilson has "whupped 'em again."

Joseph R. Stromberg
JoAnn B. Rothbard Chair, Ludwig von Mises Institute
Auburn, Alabama
January 23, 2002

Acknowledgments

F rom *Union to Empire: Essays in the Jeffersonian Tradition* gathers together some of my writings about American public things that have appeared in a variety of journals and books over three decades. In a few cases, the articles are longer versions of pieces that had to be abbreviated for space reasons in their original publication. There may be a sentence here and there that is dated, but it seems to me that more often the pieces are a bit prophetic (if overly optimistic) in addressing matters that had not yet shown up for fashionable regimented discussion in the publications of the Manhattan-Beltway pundits. The writings, I like to think, reveal a consistent viewpoint—one that was once the predominant American viewpoint—and one that is still found congenial by a good many worthy folks.

For the satisfying opportunity to collect and publish these occasional writings I am indebted to Mr. Charles Hamel, President of the Foundation for American Education, and Mr. Christopher Sullivan, editor of *Southern Partisan*, without whom the book would not exist. And to Mr. Michael Givens who originally proposed the idea. Also to Mr. Timothy Manning, Jr., who provided indispensable help in preparing the book for the press.

Acknowledgments should be given to the journals and presses that have allowed us to use material previously published by them: *Southern Partisan*; *Chornicles: A Magazine of American Culture*; the Intercollegiate Studies Institute, publisher of *Modern Age* and *Intercollegiate Review*; the Center for Libertarian Studies, publisher of *The Rothbard Rockwell Report* and www.lewrockwell.com; the Ludwig von Mises Institute, publisher of *Free Market* and *Reassessing the Presidency*, edited by John V. Denson; the League of the South Institute for the Study of Southern Culture and History; Liberty Press, Inc.; Transaction Publishers for "From Union to Empire," published in David Gordon, ed., *Secession, State and Liberty*, c. 1998; *National Review* for "George Mason," c. 1970, and "Burkean on the Bench," c. 1972; *The World and I*; *Telos*; and *Crisis*.

Clyde N. Wilson
Carolina, Spring 2003

Chapter One

Agrarian Conservatism

The Jeffersonian Conservative Tradition

A s a movement of thought, the resurgent conservativism of twentieth century America cannot achieve maturity with a properly worked out historical self-image—a documented and convincing picture of what traditions, tendencies, and movements it is heir to. In its earliest stages the conservative resurgence has conceived of itself largely as an extension of the European Burkean and Catholic traditions, because these were the traditions most familiar to the thinkers who first gave systematic expression to anti-Liberalism in this century. While this approach has provided a useful philosophical critique of Liberalism, it has left the history of conservativism on this side of the Atlantic in great ambiguity. Various resolutions of the ambiguity have been essayed, none satisfactory. Some Liberals have drawn the conclusion, not an entirely illogical reading of the ideas of some conservatives, that the American experience has been in toto anticonservative, i.e., antilegitimate and antitraditional in the Burkean sense, and that, therefore, there is and can be no American conservative tradition.[1] Some conservatives have tacitly accepted this view by evading the question of the historical roots of American conservativism. Others have turned to a facile catholicity, linking together such diverse and inimical figures and John Adams and John Randolph, Abraham Lincoln and John C. Calhoun, into a rather eclectic chain of tradition.

In general, however, American conservatives, when they have felt the need to establish their lineage, have accepted the rather conventional and threadbare descriptive framework of liberalism-conservativism already existing in American historiography and popular lore. This conventional description postulates a Federalist-Whig-Republican conservative line on the one hand, and a

---

1. This is the thesis of Professor Louis Hartz's well-known *The Liberal Tradition in America* (New York, 1955).

1

Jeffersonian-Jacksonian-Populist-New Deal liberal line on the other. Conservatives have tended to identify themselves as the heirs of the first and to repudiate the second as the line of twentieth century liberalism.

In thus yielding to the bounds of a hostile dialectic, conservatives have erred. Neither of the chains postulated is a true continuum of any tradition, and the dichotomy they express is a self-serving fabrication of twentieth century social democratic (i.e., Liberal) historians seeking to formulate a false tradition of legitimacy for their own radicalism. Conservatives have damaged their understanding of their own heritage by accepting both the analytical and evaluative framework of Liberals in regard to the history of the United States. If Arthur Schlesinger, Jr., has postulated a Jacksonian Democracy which was a radical, anticapitalist, and undilutedly democratic ancestor of the New Deal, conservatives have responded, not by achieving their own understanding of Jacksonian democracy, but by turning Schlesinger on his head and disapproving Jackson and approving those who opposed him. Conservatives are thus in a position of accepting (and turning inside out) the historical analyses of a school of thinkers whose economic and metaphysical analyses they would not leave unquestioned for an instant.

Before American conservatism achieves a full understanding of what it is and whence it comes, it must achieve its own painstaking, comprehensive, and subtle reevaluation of the political movements of our history. This paper identifies and delineates one possible tradition, properly understood. This formulation will not be accepted, at least at first glance, by most thinkers identifying themselves as conservatives, but it is hoped that it will at least show some of the flaws in the existing understanding and point to questions that need answers.[2]

What should American conservativism seek to conserve? Reducing analysis to the simplest possible terms, it should seek to conserve the structure of society and government that is the most organic, legitimate, and just for the American nation, i.e., the federal and constitutional republic bequeathed to us by that unique event, the American Revolution, a "revolution" which was prudential rather than revolutionary, preservative rather than innovating, legalistic rather than speculative; a revolution for life, liberty, *and property*, made by propertied, principled gentlemen expressing the best of their inherited political wisdom; a war of national independence waged without mass romantic nationalism.

One may, of course, maintain a view of the American Revolution as radical. Such a view comforts two groups—radicals seeking a line of legitimacy for themselves and conservative purists who would reject the American experience altogether. The latter have aptly been described by the *National Review* as indulgers in a Manichean heresy,[3] and indeed they would out-Burke Burke himself. The American who maintains the unique legitimacy of his revolution puts him-

---

2. The conservativism whose ancestry I am seeking to determine here is not some pale reflection of Liberalism of the sort cooked up by Rossiter or Viereck. I refer to the movement which, with various reservations and differences of emphasis, coalesced in support of the candidacy of Barry M. Goldwater in 1964.
3. "Is Conservativism Dead?," April 8, 1969.

self in the company of distinguished European conservatives, of whom Friedrich Gentz, the Prussian adviser of Metternich, was perhaps the most persuasive.[4]

What are the essential elements of the conservative American polity, i.e., the federal and constitutional republic, and who have been, historically, the conservators and who the underminers of these elements? Again reducing analysis to the simplest possible terms, we will define three elements:

Republicanism. The basic form of the government is one in which sovereignty rests in the people as a whole but is expressed in the rule of a qualified majority under the restraint of law. He is the conservator of republicanism who sees to it that the democratic and aristocratic elements remain in proper balance, that the polity does not veer too far toward mobocracy or oligarchy.

Constitutionalism. Law protects the people from the rulers and the individual from the people. The rulers may exercise only the powers specifically delegated to them in the written law. He is the conservator of constitutionalism who favors adherence to the law no matter how powerful the plea of expediency by the ambitious tyrant or the impassioned majority.[5] Senator Goldwater grasped the essence of this element when he described an American conservative as one who is "at war equally with autocrats and with 'democratic' Jacobins."[6]

Federalism. Organically, the American republic is decentralized, i.e., the sovereignty of the people is exercised by them in part as citizens of indestructible states rather than as one undivided nationality. He is the conservator of federalism who sees that sovereignty remains so distributed.

This scheme of the American system has been set forth (with danger of gross over-simplification) so that historic movements may be measured as to how much they tended to conserve or to undermine the fundamental elements. Two warnings should be inserted. First, a religious-moral basis, stemming from the Christian tradition but related to no specific denomination, is assumed. The second warning concerns property and its role as a conservative influence. Property, of course, is an element of consideration in a just and legitimate government. Because of this conservatives have sometimes tended to identify with those historical political groups who seemed to be the conservators of property and against those who seemed to represent the unjust acquisitiveness of no-property. But, in fact, prior to the New Deal there were no significant contests in America between property and no-property. The ordinary form of political conflict was between various forms of property.

Conservatives are aware that the Founding Fathers feared the undermining effects of the propertyless mob on the social order. They are less aware that the Fathers also feared the undermining effects of aggressive and excessive wealth. Thus John Adams was concerned repeatedly with the danger to the republic from

---

4. Gentz's 1800 essay contrasting the American and French Revolution is available from Covenant Publications of Monroe, Louisiana.

5. There are, of course, commanding emergencies in any polity which will require the temporary and limited relaxation of law.

6. *The Conscience of a Conservative*, (Paperback edition; New York, 1960), p. 13.

wealthy and ambitious men (the Roosevelts, Rockefellers, Kennedys, etc.) who he rightly saw would preserve their own inordinate interests by allying themselves with the mob against the great class of middle and upper middle property owners who were the true backbone of the country.[7]

★★★

We are so used to regarding the work of the Philadelphia Convention as noble, final, and indispensible that we have lost sight of the extent to which it was innovative, speculative, and antitraditional, overlooking that the delegates violated their instructions (which were to amend the Articles of Confederation), that several distinguished members refused to sign the Constitution, and that some states ratified in a spirit of reservation and trial rather than of finality.[8]

The organic or natural form of government that emerged from the Revolution, as expressed in the first constitutions of most of the states, embodied a weak form of separation of powers in which the legislative branch was clearly predominant and the independence of the executive and judiciary only partial. Let us turn the usual categories of reference around and consider for a moment the claim of the Anti-Federalists to be conservatives who wanted to preserve this natural and spontaneous outgrowth of the Revolution in which the powers of government were few and such powers as there were diffused among the states and within the states among the most numerous branch of government, the legislature, which was itself checked by diversity of interests, frequent elections, property qualifications, and bicameralism. Let us view the Federalist proponents of the Constitution as innovators who wanted to change to a complicated system of checks and balances which was to a degree abstractly conceived and based upon detached intellectualizing about separation of powers as a supposed virtue of the British Constitution.

The chief concern of the Federalists within the polity was to check a rash majority by erecting powerful independent offices in the executive and judiciary. Somewhat short-sightedly, they believed that these centers of power would always be instruments of restraint. They failed to foresee the true course of events, i.e., that there was no natural reason why the executive and judiciary would remain conservative, and if ever once captured (as in the New Deal) by the passions of the mob or the spirit of rash innovation, the presidency and federal

---

7. "The rich, the well born, and the able acquire an influence among the people that will soon be too much for simple honesty and plain sense," wrote Adams, arguing for the separation of the rich into an upper house of the legislature. The Founding Fathers had in mind the classical example of Julius Caesar.

8. Virginia, with other states, proposed numerous amendments and declared that "the powers granted under the Constitution, being derived from the people of the United States, may be resumed by them, whenever the same shall be perverted to their injury or oppression. . . ."

courts provided impregnable bastions for radical sorties upon the social order. The Federalists can thus be seen as tinkerers who sought to secure conservatism by means of abstractly conceived governmental machinery. Their tinkering has been largely responsible for the successes of anticonservative movements and the seemingly irreversible institutionalism of New Deal Liberalism in the federal courts and bureaucracy.

The Anti-Federalists sought to check the abuse of power by keeping all government weak and leaving the predominance of such power as there was in the legislature which was, by its nature as a representative of diverse interests, a cautious and compromising body. The Anti-Federalists, and the Jeffersonians who succeeded in engrafting the principle of weak government onto the Constitution through the Tenth Amendment, were more accurate in analysis and more conservative in proposal. The Federalists' political speculations (as have those of twentieth century liberals to opposite ends) tended to focus too much upon European society and not enough upon particular American conditions. The unrestrained majority which the Federalists feared was not, in America, a desperate, propertyless mob, but a restricted electorate of middle class property holders. The danger to the constitutional and federal republican polity in America has never come from the majority but rather from ambitious tyrants and alienated intellectual coteries for whom the strong presidency and judiciary are tailormade fortresses.

Suppose that instead of writing a Constitution which erected a powerful central government with a powerful president and courts, the Philadelphia Convention had followed its instructions and had provided amendments for the Articles of Confederation which had tightened the bonds of union and made a more viable federal structure, allowing a degree of separation of powers within a general parliamentary system, without creating an overweening central power. Would that not have been a proper role for conservatives who are by definition disposed to preserve even while reforming? The Federalists introduced into the American polity, theoretically as a check and a balance, a monarchy (presidency) with power far in excess of the monarchy in the British system which was their ostensible model. They carried the principles of division of powers and restraint of innovation to such an extreme that they undermined the legislature.

Can a twentieth century conservative doubt that the government which would have resulted from a reformed Articles would have been more conservative, that it would have been more conducive to the preservation of the constitutional and federal republic against unlimited centralized democracy, and more responsive to the cautious and responsible elements of the polity against the aggressive and fanatical than the present Constitution? The locus of power in such a federal government would be a legislature broadly responsive to the diverse interests of the Union like the present House of Representatives rather than a president and bureaucracy responsive to strategic and untutored blocks of mass opinion or aggressive coteries of ideological fancy.

Indeed, Liberal historians have come to recognize that it was the Federalists who provided them with their powers to reconstruct society by plan and have turned against the Anti-Federalists. In an article which is reminiscent of recent attacks on "radical rightists," a liberal historian portrays the Anti-Federalists as obstructionists with excessive fears of strong governmental powers.[9]

☆☆☆

The party battles of the 1790's which resulted in the triumph of what is known as Jeffersonian Democracy have been seen largely in the terms which the Federalists intended them to be seen. Conservatives today tend to see the Federalists of the period as champions of conservatism, stability, and diluted democracy, and to see the party of Thomas Jefferson (which was also the party of James Madison, John Randolph, and Nathaniel Macon) as a wild-eyed mob imbued with the dangerous principles of French philosophes. This partisan picture from the times is inaccurate and, incidentally, is quite comforting to twentieth century Liberalism. The Jeffersonian party was led by the American group the most truly aristocratic in the best sense, the Virginian planters. It represented the majority conservative agricultural property interests of the country at large against the aggressive commercial property interests of the Northern cities.[10]

The issues of the French Revolution became entwined in the American party battles of the 1790's, but the cleavage had more to do with partisan name-calling, anglophobia, and the sectionality of seafaring interests in America than with ideology. Very few Jeffersonians approved the French Revolution after it passed its milder phases. To one group of American conservatives who were bred to regard Thomas Jefferson as the paramount hero of states rights and constitutionalism, it is shocking to encounter the virulence with which another group of American conservatives attacks Jefferson as the archdemocrat. It is true that as a thinker Jefferson was free ranging. But one is hard put to find genuinely radical acts of Jefferson the statesman. He favored some experimentation with the legal forms of society, but almost entirely in subordinate matters. I would be prepared to maintain in a forum where there is adequate space that none of the tinkering Jefferson did was as fundamental or as harmful as that of John Adams in riding his hobby-horse of checks and balances. Certainly Jefferson was a more truly conservative statesman than that rash innovator, Alexander Hamilton, whom Russell Kirk has rightly described as not qualifying as a conservative.[11]

---

9. Cecilia Kenyon, "Men of Little Faith: the Anti-Federalists on Representative Government," *William and Mary Quarterly*, XII (1955).

10. Although he would not necessarily agree with me in placement of value or in detail, this is in essence the analysis of Professor Henry Paolucci in his *War, Peace, and the Presidency* (New York, 1968), pp. 88-89.

11. *A Program for Conservatives* (Paperback edition; Chicago, 1962), p. 258.

The disagreement between Federalists and Jeffersonians was a matter of mechanism and interest not principle. While Jefferson was optimistic about popular rule in America, I believe it would be difficult to prove that he believed in the unlimited perfectibility of man. Jefferson and the Virginian school of political philosophy which he represented were basically English legalists, not French radicals.[12] The essence of his disagreement with Federalism was summed up in Jefferson's question: "If man cannot be trusted with the government of himself, how can he be trusted with the government of others?" The Federalists, who postulated the imperfectibility of man, also postulated a class of the wise and good (themselves) who were fit to rule, presumtably because inexplicably exempt from the general corruption human nature is heir to. To this Jefferson replied that rulers were as likely to be corrupted as the ruled, therefore the proper response to the fallen nature of man was a government too weak to afford predominant power to any one group of men.

The Jeffersonian stance was the more conservative because it was more truly in keeping with the facts of human nature and the particular conditions of America. Federalism, representing at its worst a single-minded pursuit of one set of property interests at the expense of another, and coupled as it was with a virulent New England chauvinism, was not necessarily an essentially conservative force in its long-range impact. That a rather fanatical and self seeking group of men called Thomas Jefferson a Jacobin does not prove him one, any more than calling Senator Goldwater a fascist proved him one. The Federalist grasp for centralized power symbolized by the Alien and Sedition laws was not an effort by responsible gentlemen to curb an unlicensed mob. Rather it was a threat to the freedom to criticize of other propertied, principled gentlemen who were quite as able to govern as the beneficiaries of the laws. Freedom to criticize the rulers is, after all, an aristocratic, not a democratic right. Conservatives would do well to add to their Madison, Randolph, and Calhoun an acquaintance with that great Jeffersonian thinker, John Taylor of Caroline, who brilliantly laid low the pseudo-aristocratic pretensions of the Federalists, the injustice of their economic system, and the radical dangers of their view of the judiciary, as well as accurately predicted the mobocracy that would ensue from the triumph of their principles.[13]

It is not surprising that the conservative understanding of the phenomenon known as Jacksonian Democracy is defective since the historiography of the subject has constituted a great battleground of contradictory claims. Recently, however, historians, working from both Liberal and conservative biases, have reached

---

12. *Ibid.*, p. 33.
13. Professor Eugene T. Mudge's scholarly and thorough *The Social Philosophy of John Taylor of Caroline* (New York, 1939) provides an introduction to Taylor's difficult works.

agreement on a few points which have not yet penetrated popular lore or conservative thinking. The most important of these points is that the party of Andrew Jackson was not the creator of the phenomenon misnamed Jacksonian Democracy. Both the Democratic Party of Andrew Jackson and the party of those who opposed him were mass democratic political movements which resulted from a spontaneous increase in mass political participation and a spontaneous demand for removal of aristocratic legal restraints from state constitutions in the 1820's and 1830's.

Neither party was clearly more aristocratic and conservative or democratic and radical than the other. Jackson himself was a wealthy cotton planter from middle Tennessee who had always sided with the economically more conservative faction in his state. Many conservative aristocrats like James Fenimore Cooper identified with the Democratic Party. The most virulently levelling people of the time, the New England poor whites of western New York and the Midwest who spawned a hundred isms, were Whigs and Anti-Masons, bitterly opposed to Jacksonians as aristocrats. Nor was there a direct line of continuity from Jeffersonians to Jacksonians and from Federalists to Whigs. Many Federalists became Democrats and many Whigs were former Jeffersonians.[14]

The party situation was much as it has usually been in American history until very recently. Neither party was really ideological in the European sense, and the classes and interests which composed them varied from state to state. Conservatives have tacitly accepted Arthur Schlesinger's portrayal of Jacksonianism as anticapitalist, socialist, when in fact all parties and all Americans of the time except a few intellectual radicals were decidedly capitalist in philosophy. Historians, including both conservatives and honest Liberals, have recently been groping toward a more sophisticated understanding of what was at issue in Jackson's famous Bank War.[15] Though the economic issues, as always, are very complex; simply stated, the picture that emerges is not one of socialists against capitalists, but of Democratic laissez-faire capitalists against Whiggish monopoly capitalists. The impetus against the Bank of the United States came from energetic rising businessmen who wanted expansion, which in their opinion was checked by a government-granted monopoly which profited a few men and one region at the expense of the businessmen and the commerce of other regions. Jackson and his chief supporters had an impeccably conservative

---

14. Lee Benson, *The Concept of Jacksonian Democracy: New York as a Test Case* (Princeton, 1961); Shaw Livermore, *The Twilight of Federalism* (Princeton, 1962); and Richard P. McCormick, *The Second American Party System: Party Formation in the Jacksonian Era* (Chapel Hill, 1966), are recent works of Liberal but capable scholars demonstrating the discontinuity of the first and second party systems and the absense of party-ideological cleavage in the era.

15. A most cogent statement of the newer viewpoint is *Banking and Politics in America: From the Revolution to the Civil War* (Princeton, 1957), by Bray Hammond, a conservatively inclined banker. For a very Liberal historian who reached the same conclusion, in contradiction to Schlesinger, see "Andrew Jackson and the Rise of Liberal Capitalism," in Richard Hofstadter, *The American Political Tradition* (New York, 1948). Another Liberal historian, Richard B. Morris, has entitled an article in refutation of Schlesinger, "Andrew Jackson—Strikebreaker."

predilection for hard money. The Whigs represented the capitalism of manufacturers and national bankers. The Democrats represented the capitalism of state bankers, importers, and agriculturalists.

Though the Jacksonian Party in some respects acted to expand the power of the presidency within the federal government, its general over-all tendency was to weaken the power of government at all levels, particularly the power of the federal government to dispense economic favors such as tariffs, subsidies, and internal improvements. This was the primary issue between the Democratic Party, nationally, and its opponents, the Whigs, and their successors, the Republicans. Aristocrats like James Fenimore Cooper saw the Democratic Party as the truly conservative party—that which was preserving the purity and virtue of the pristine republic in which a representative voted for his convictions rather than for bribes for his constituents; the Whigs, who were, to be sure, conservatives if being in favor of government handouts to business is conservative, he regarded as rather vulgar men on the make whose basic principle (also the basic principle of twentieth century Liberal politics) was to bribe part of the electorate by economic largess distributed by the government at the expense of another part of the electorate.[16]

The basic issue was one of Jacksonian laissez-faire or classical liberalism (as evidenced by the Taney Court's erosion of government-granted business privileges under the contract clause) versus a kind of Whiggish progressivism which proposed that the government take an active economic role in promoting the development and prosperity of the country (as evidenced most cogently by John Quincy Adams's first message to Congress which recommended, among other things, federal construction of roads and canals, a national university, and the passage of laws designed allegedly for the promotion of agriculture, commerce, manufacturing, arts, sciences, and literature). Possibly the Whigs were correct in their desire for tariffs, subsidies, and government-built internal improvements to develop the American countryside. Even so, theirs was not in that regard a conservative stance, not a program which placed preserving the constitutional and federal republic at the top of the list of priorities. A government which dispenses favors to the business classes at the expense of the agricultural classes is only the opposite side of the coin to a government which dispenses favors to labor unions and welfare "clients" at the expense of the business classes.

Despite Arthur Schlesinger's skillful pleading, most of the radicals and reformers who flourished in the Jacksonian era were not Democrats. The abolitionists, working men's parties, woman suffragists, utopian socialists, and adherents of other isms were part of what is known as the era of Jacksonian Democracy, but they were mostly not in the Jacksonian party. The radicals were mostly alienated intellectuals who came, as do twentieth century Liberals, out of the self-appointed, privileged aristocracy of the Eastern Establishment, and who regarded the common sense Jacksonian Democrats of the South and West about

---

16. Cooper's philosophy is set forth in his *American Democrat* of 1838. There is an illuminating foreword by H.L. Mencken in the 1931 Alfred A. Knopf edition.

as the Eastern intellectuals of today regard the common sense conservatives of South and West, as uncouth and contemptible obstacles to the grandiose plans of elite thinkers. The few real radicals of the Democratic Party, the Locofocos of New York who were never a majority among New York Democrats, ended up in the Republican Party by way of Free-Soilism.

There is probably no conservative consensus about the Civil War. I suspect that one will find conservatives dividing over the Civil War along a line which marks off a tacit difference of premises. Those whose conservatism is basically political, who value America because it is a surviving constitutional republic in a revolutionary world, which has fused order and freedom with fair success, will, like Frank Meyer, regret the great body blows delivered by the Republican Party to the constitutional and federal republic in the Civil War and Reconstruction.[17] Those whose conservatism is basically theoretical and nationalistic, who put a transcendent value upon the American states will, like Professor Harry Jaffa, see the Republican Party as the conservative savior of the nation.[18]

The question of whether the Confederate South or the Republican North was the carrier of the American conservative tradition can probably be debated fruitlessly and forever. Possibly a thinker of the stature of Richard Weaver could have produced a synthesis, as seems to have been implied in his movement from Southern Agrarian to admirer of Lincoln. I will only comment that conservative scholars like Dr. Jaffa, in their treatment of the Civil War, tend to make themselves, historiographically, comrades in arms of the ilk of Arthur Schlesinger and Bernard DeVoto; and it seems to me that they are in danger of "drawing up an indictment against a whole people," and of treating the legalistic and tradition-minded rising of the South as if it were the treason of a handful of subversives.

It seems to me impossible to deny that within the North the Democratic Party was the conservative party in the era of Civil War and Reconstruction, if conservatism is defined as a preference for preserving republicanism, federalism, and constitutionalism. Conservatives who are accustomed to thinking of the New Deal Democratic Party tend to read back into history and to assume that the Republican Party has always been the more or less conservative party and the Democratic Party more or less the more radical. The belief, however prevalent, is false. Neither party was anticapitalist, and we should not allow Liberals the comfort of presuming a respectable anticapitalist tradition in this country. The Democratic Party (with the aid of some former Whigs) did yeoman service in the

---

17. Frank S. Meyer, "Lincoln Without Rhetoric," *National Review* (August 24, 1965); "Again on Lincoln," *National Review* (January 25, 1966).
18. Harry V. Jaffa, *Crisis of the House Divided* (Garden City, N.Y., 1959). See also his disagreement with Meyer in *National Review* (September 21, 1965).

Civil War era in hewing to the line of states rights, strict construction of powers, and government noninterference in the economy, i.e., in conserving the constitutional and federal republic, while the Republican Party was embarked upon a program of radicalism in some ways still unprecedented.

There is very little done by Liberals in the twentieth century for which one cannot find some ancestor in the acts of the Republican Party in the nineteenth century. Lincoln's arbitrary exercise of executive power has still not been matched. The great war powers exercised by Wilson and Roosevelt were formally granted them by Congress. Lincoln's were simply seized. In deliberate indifference to the letter and spirit of the Constitution in pursuit of expediencies and passions of the moment, a Great Society Congress can find ample example in the conduct of the Republican Congressional party from 1860 to 1876. In twisting the meaning of the Constitution to serve special interests and ideologies, the Warren Court can find colleagues in many of the Republican justices of the post-Civil War period. The first example of large scale use of FDR's famous tax, spend, and elect formula is the billions voted by the Republican Party for Union war contracts and pensions. The Radicals who formed one wing of the Republican Party are exact psychological and moral ancestors of today's intolerant Liberals.

From the subsidence of the issues of the Civil War as the major issues of politics, i.e., the end of Reconstruction, until the beginning of the New Deal, the Democratic and Republican parties were divided chiefly by sectional, ethnic, and historical considerations, not by class or ideology.[19] Neither party was anticapitalist. The two well-known leftist movements of the time, Populism and Progressivism, drew from both parties. Both parties contained capitalists, professional men, laborers, and farmers. Capitalists who were engaged in manufacturing or types of agriculture which found a protective tariff useful tended to be Republican. Capitalists who were engaged in finance or international trade (like August Belmont), or in types of agriculture harmed by protective tariffs tended to be Democratic. In regard to the three elements of the polity we have defined as worthy of conservative allegiance, the Democratic Party was probably, on the whole, sounder than the Republican party on constitutionalism and federalism. The nativist prejudices of Yankee Protestant Republicans have left an impression that the Democratic Party of "rum, Romanism, and rebellion," was the more demagogic and corrupt, but in fact both parties were demagogic and machine-ridden. They did their demagoguery and corruption with different groups.

---

19. Kevin Phillips, *The Emerging Republican Majority* (New Rochelle, N.Y., 1969), documents this in detail.

The word "populist" is commonly used as an epithet by conservatives and recently also by Liberals, though the exact meaning of the word as used has never been clear. With Populism, as with Jacksonian Democracy, conservatives have tended to accept without question the analysis and evaluation of Liberal historians, merely turning it inside out. Liberal historians, seeking ancestors for New Deal radicalism, have given us our conventional image of Populism. The Liberal distortion has been subtle, and to restore the image to rights requires careful delineation of what Populism was and was not.

On the surface of things, Populists will clearly be seen as nonconservatives. They favored government ownership of railroads; the progressive income tax; direct democracy through recall, referendum, and initiative; and inflation. Considering the context in which these proposals were put forth demonstrates the extremely limited radicalism of the Populists, however. Populism was chiefly a sectional movement. It was not in essence socialist and anticapitalist in the sense that the New Deal was socialist and anticapitalist (although certain real radicals and socialists clung to its fringes). The Populists, it is now recognized, were not wild-eyed, barefoot radicals, but were in fact the respectable businessmen and gentry of certain regions of the country. Populism was precipitated by a belief (whether true or not is debatable) that the arbitrary intervention of the federal government in the economy in favor of certain interests (manufacturers protected by tariffs, particular capitalists who were granted charters as national bankers) had resulted in an inordinate and artificial accumulation of wealth in a few hands and in the Northeastern section of the country at the expense of the legitimate business interests of certain agricultural regions.

The railroads which the Populist sought to regulate were not the creations of rugged private enterprise. In most cases they had been extensively subsidized by federal, state, and local governments through grants of public lands, cash, and tax and tariff concessions. They had engaged in large scale swindling of investors and had been the source of corruption in the legislative process (surely a matter of concern to conservatives). They levied rate discriminations against businessmen in certain locations not justified by economic costs. In other words, the provocation was great and some solution was necessary.

In their fear that a concentration of great wealth in a few hands tended to undermine the Republic the Populists were more in tune with the Founding Fathers than were the "conservative" business interests of the time. The Founding Fathers thought of the leadership of the best in terms of a gentry which made up perhaps 10 percent of the population and owned perhaps half the property. They did not think in terms of a Rockefeller-Morgan oligarchy which made up 1 or 2 percent of the population and owned 90 percent of the real wealth. One who will take the trouble to read the Populists' literature will find that they were concerned as conservative rural Americans about the dangers to the Republic from the hordes of propertyless urban workers as well as from the international bankers.

The initiative, referendum and recall, and the direct election of senators were certainly anticonservative in the structural sense in that they sought to modify republicanism in the direction of direct democracy. There was, however, already a condition of mass democracy; and the Populists believed, perhaps not unreasonably, that a mass democracy dominated by popular will might be sounder than a mass democracy dominated by political machines. The Founding Fathers had intended the republican statesman to be an independent gentleman of conscience who pursued politics as an honor and duty. He had in fact become, to an unforeseen extent, the dependent hack of a political organization, pursuing politics as a vocation. Direct democracy in the Populist program was radical in method but conservative in instinct in that it aimed nostalgically to restore a more honorable relationship between people and representative.[20] Finally, the Populist advocacy of inflation was a product of a period of deflation in which a national debt contracted in wartime greenbacks was being paid off in very hard gold dollars. The Populists in effect desired a restoration of an earlier fiscal status quo, not revolution.

Populism, although less respectable, was also far less fundamentally radical than the Progressivism which followed it and expressed very different discontents. It has become the fashion among Liberal historians to sneer at the Populists who, after all, preferred to think for themselves (however awkwardly) rather than tamely accept the intellectual and moral conventions of the Eastern establishment which were quite as pervasive and quite as false as today. There is a historical kinship of spirit between those who resisted the Eastern establishment in the 1890's and in the 1960's. A chart could be constructed showing a correlation between the areas of the country which strongly supported William Jennings Bryan and Barry Goldwater.

Populism had none of the social worker mentality which characterized Progressivism. Where Populism was the zany but unsentimental faith of outsiders, Progressivism was the fat and saucy self-righteousness of an urbanized, rootless, antitraditional, hypocritically self-serving coterie of upper and middle class intellectuals and pseudo-intellectuals. Progressivism has bequeathed to twentieth century Liberalism its basic style—the posing of emotionally galvanic "problems" to be solved by mass emotional concern leading to governmental action, never mind what action. Like Liberalism, Progressivism assumed that only selfish interests could fail to see the urgency of the "problem" and the wisdom of the "solution" which had caught the Progressive's fancy. As does Liberalism, Progressivism fed upon a murky and artificial "public opinion" which ignored logic, law, tradition, and all genuine analysis in pursuit of its solutions.

---

20. Russell Kirk, *A Program for Conservatives*, pp. 34-35.

Prior to Progressivism the political opinions of most Americans, however bad or wrong, had made sense in their own context, had borne some relation to either common sense observation or inherited prejudice (prejudice being to Burke the wisdom of unlettered men). The opinions of the mass of Progressives were superficial plausibilities induced by that little learning that is a dangerous thing, aggravated by a physical remoteness from the sphere of tangible action. With the seizure of a part of the electorate by the Progressivist mentality, for the first time image became more important than reality. Only then could the American voters reject a sincere and decent William Jennings Bryan or an honest and able William Howard Taft for a dangerous buffoon like Theodore Roosevelt or a coldly self-seeking hypocrite like Woodrow Wilson.

Theodore Roosevelt was in a sense the first practitioner of modern Liberalism, a fact overlooked by conservatives who admire him as an exponent of a strong foreign policy (failing to make William Graham Sumner's distinction between jingoism and a proper nationalism). Theodore Roosevelt, the respectable, privileged Eastern aristocrat and Republican, is the fountainhead of the idea that the federal government, and particularly the president, is responsible for solving all the problems of all the people, regardless of Constitution and justice. He was the first to project an image of a president who takes club in hand and bludgeons a reluctant Congress dominated by vested "interests" into doing the "right thing," an image which he deliberately cultivated for his own aggrandizement. It was TR who gave us the now obtaining rule that a president is elected on his capacity for being a popular celebrity in the mass media rather than his capacity for statesmanship.

★★★

If some forecaster of the 1920's had perceived that a socialist revolution was to come to America in the next decade, he would not automatically have assumed that the Democratic Party would be the vehicle of the revolution. The Republicans, being the predominant party, encompassed greater extremes than did the Democrats and contained probably a greater number of Progressives. Harding and Coolidge were not Progressives but their bourgeois mindlessness and the mass worship they received were as foreign to the American tradition as the New Deal itself.

The Democratic Party, despite the perverting influence of Wilsonism, maintained much of its allegiance to its traditional principles of states rights, strict construction, and laissez-faire, which, as has often been pointed out, were reflected in the 1932 platform. One could make an impressive list of New Dealers who had been Republicans before they came to FDR—including Henry Wallace, Harold Ickes, and Donald Richberg, not to mention such New Deal Republican stalwarts as LaGuardia, LaFollette, and Norris. One could make an equally

14

impressive list of Democratic greats who repudiated the New Deal, including Al Smith, John W. Davis, William G. McAdoo, Lewis Douglas, and Newton D. Baker (some of whom viewed the New Deal as a takeover of the Democratic Party by Republican Progressives), not to mention most of the heretofore predominant Southern wing of the party. There were millions of Democratic voters who continued to be so through the New Deal because of economic interest or because the Republicans offered no attractive opposition, but who never succumbed to Liberal ideology and who fell away in droves when Liberalism began to harden into an elitist establishment. On the other hand, there were millions of nominally Republican voters who were in fact mesmerized by Liberal ideology and began to turn to the Democratic Party in the 1960's.[21]

Through most of American history the conservative force of our society has been the great mass of sensible, productive, and self-respecting lower-middle and middle class citizens with a decent awe for inherited principles. The radical and undermining forces have been the alienated intellectuals and privileged, self-appointed aristocrats cut off from the mainstream of American life, whether Hartford Conventioners, Abolitionists, Progressives, or Liberals, who cared neither for republicanism, constitutionalism, or federalism, but for their own abstract panaceas and their own powers.

Occasionally the radicals have been able to put together enough discontented minorities and befuddled middle class voters who responded to pseudo-intellectualizing rather than common sense, to make an electoral majority, but seldom have the radical and the conservative elements been separated clearly by party. Such a polarization seemed possible for the first time in 1968, when, the Establishment underminers and their allies and dupes, having completely taken over the Democratic Party, were repudiated by a new Jeffersonian coalition of productive citizens who were a majority in forty-four of the fifty states.

(1969)

---

21. I again call on Kevin Phillips's superb documentation of American political tendencies.

Citizens or Subjects?

During the past half century a struggle has been going on to decide whether America will remain a republic or become an empire. Almost every political, cultural, social, and even economic issue that has been fought over is subsumed in this larger struggle. The forces of imperialism have seemed to have history on their side and have almost, but not quite, prevailed. The forces of republicanism are battered but not quite vanquished.

The 1980 elections were the *beginnings* of a last great counteroffensive by the republicans. The war will probably be decided within the next decade. The outcome will determine whether the descendants of the present generation of Americans will be free citizens of a proud republic or merely ciphers in a faceless mass of imperial subjects. The slender hope of avoiding the latter end depends in the short run upon the foresight, morale, and determination of the republicans and in the long run upon the ultimate survivability of American institutions.

An empire is not to be distinguished from a republic by the extent of its overseas commitments or the possession of foreign colonies or the size of its military forces. It is possible, though not necessarily easy, for a people to remain republican while engaging in extensive trade, military campaigning, and even colonization overseas. An empire is differentiated from a republic by the nature of its domestic society and by the purposes which inform its official and public activities.

Nations come into existence when a unique identity is fused by history out of a particular group of people, a particular land, and a particular culture. In unusually fortunate circumstances, a nation emerges with institutions of self-government, institutions in which political power originates within and is widely dispersed among the community—a republican society. Such institutions appeared naturally among the British colonists of North America and were legitimized by the Revolution and the Constitution.

The Founding Fathers knew that republican societies were fragile. History taught them that republics, and particularly large and diverse ones, tended to degenerate into empires. Their best thought and effort were directed at means of enhancing and prolonging the life of those self-governing institutions of which Americans had fortuitously found themselves in possession. The fear or degeneracy loomed so large that how to avoid it was the source of the sharpest disagreements that occurred among the founding generation.

At the heart of their dissensions was the confusion engendered by the paradox of liberty and order. But all agreed that political liberty was a meaningful concept only within an ordered community. Self-government was of value only to one who was indeed self-governed. That is, only a virtuous people could be republican. Virtue was defined according to stern Roman values, with something of the sober English ones thrown in. A society of men who did not govern themselves could not be self-governing. Republicanism was not a benefit bestowed from above, a decree of government that magically guaranteed freedom and equality to all warm bodies. Self-government was a blessing that flowed to people who, both by their efforts and by the kind of people they were, established communities in which self-government became possible and reasonable, communities in which there were moral resources sufficient for the strenuous task of reconciling liberty, order, and popular rule. Men did not become good citizens by having democracy. They had democracy because they were the stuff of good citizens.

Further, a society of men who did not value their self-government enough to make sacrifices for it could not long remain self-governing: sacrifices not only in what was necessary to defend against foreign dangers, but also sacrifices in self-discipline and self-denial of those indulgences and laxities that accumulated to the degeneracy and subversion of republicanism.

The benefit of republicanism, the reason why it justified these sacrifices, indeed, the very definition of self-government, was the superiority of the community to its rulers. In a reversal of the common pattern of mankind, rulers (a necessary evil) became delegates of the community, temporarily assigned to look after the public business, rather than the community existing chiefly as a source of gratification and support to the rulers. The rulers were "responsible," a word used often by the Founding Fathers—"responsible" to the community which designated them and to which they would retire, in time, to share as ordinary citizens in the benefits or burdens following upon their administration. This was the difference between a republic and an empire.

"Responsibility" was an intensely moral concept. Responsibility in the officeholder entailed being under the law, scrupulously staying within the limits of delegated authority, being the agent of the community rather than its master. "Responsibility" had another moral sense, as well. The ruler, while staying within the limits of his authority, carried out within those limits the duties of his office as vigorously and effectively as possible. A republican statesman was the trustee of the community. A sense of honor kept him in obedience to those who elected him. While observing the limits of delegated authority, he was expected to have the high moral and intellectual qualities required to discern the long-range interests of the community and to govern effectively.

The key to republicanism, then, is the precedence of the community over the government. America, at least republican America, is not merely an accidental collection of individuals dependent upon a particular government. The American community is the expression, at this moment in time, of that unique synthesis of people, culture, and land that occurred in the emergence of the nation. Communities have forebears and descendants. Their political acts are governed in the consciousness of these as well as of present necessities. Empires, on the other hand, are governed by the momentary necessities or even the whims of rulers. In an empire, by the calculus of the Founding Fathers, the rulers were the opposite of "responsible." They were corrupt and dangerous in two senses: They were usurpers of authority over (against) the rights of the people, that is, the community; and, they were incompetent in carrying out the high and necessary functions of government. One needs only to read over the indictment of George III in the Declaration of Independence to see how the two evils went together in the American mind.

The Founding Fathers, drawing on their understanding of English history, had a terminology for the contrary tendencies to which government was subjected. There was the "court party," which was devoted to the interests of the rulers, and the "country party," which sought to defend and preserve the community. The court party represented and favored the pressure toward the degeneracy of republicanism, that is, it represented an imperialist thrust. The country party's main duty was to guard against the cunning usurpations of the court. Allegiance to the "country" party rested upon an assumption that society took precedence over government, that government existed only to preserve and enhance society.

The "country" philosophy was also a philosophy of individual liberty. One of the many plausible guises under which evilly motivated rulers sought to undermine or overthrow the limitations put upon government by republicanism was that of protecting the individual from the community. But to the "country party" there was no contradiction between the liberty of the individual and the liberty of the community. Indeed, the liberty proclaimed by Revolutionary Americans encompassed both meanings. The separation out of individual liberty and the placing of it in conflict with the community by modern political philosophy has been the greatest asset imperialism has enjoyed—it has provided imperialism with its strongest motivating drive and its most powerful legal weapons. Government has aggrandized itself by posing as the defender of the individual against the community.

To the Founders the community was the context into which the individual was born or admitted, a context which provided him with a secure identity and the possibility of realizing his potential as a human being. Community implied a degree of homogeneity and stability, of givenness. Cultural activity was an expression of the personality of the community. Political activity, in a healthy and republican community, was the effort to enhance the well-being of the community in regard to its domestic peace and its freedom from the foreign enemy.

As understood by the Founders, individual liberty could only occur in an ordered community. While the group, in the final analysis, took precedence over the individual, the individual's existence, including his exercise of freedom and his possibilities for individual expression and achievement, was given a framework of relevance only by his membership in the community. One must be a member of the community, he must share in its culture and tradition by birth or active allegiance, before he could be a free and self-governing citizen. In practice in early America, citizenship was not bestowed upon the immigrant by the government, but by the community. Immigrants voted in some states before being granted federal naturalization. The government merely registered that the mutual adoption had taken place.

Individual liberty was thus a byproduct of membership in good standing of a free community, not a grant from government. Therefore, individual liberty was much more effectively guaranteed by limitation upon government than by grant of rights. To assume any other grounds for republican citizenship was to assume (and a great deal of what passes at present for democratic political philosophy does so assume) that man derived his worth from government, that he had no intrinsic value. This may indeed be true of imperial man. It is not true of republican man. Even man's relation to the Almighty, while transcending nations and cultures, has no means to express and perpetuate itself except through the personality of a particular community.

To put it another way, limited government is synonymous with republicanism. The limits have not to do with abstract mechanisms, checks and balances (which are merely incidental, though they make up almost entirely the modern pseudophilosophy of democratic government), or even with constitutions, which are not the substance of a republican society but simply the register of its existence. Republicanism consists essentially in the inviolability of the community, its superiority over the machinery of government. Individual liberty and the postulated equality of citizens before the law are not gifts of the government but products of the precedence of the community over the government, indicating the limited and secondary standing of the latter.

An empire, on the other hand, functions in indifference to both the individual and the community. It reverses the precedence of community and government. An empire may originate in the colonizing or military efforts of a particular people. Its institutions may reflect, palely, the institutions of the communities out of which it arose. Its founding people may remain on hand as a ruling caste in the empire, but in that case they will have become merely a class and not a people. Their identity will depend upon their political position in the empire, not their membership in a nourishing culture.

The republic passes over into empire when political activity is no longer directed toward enhancement of the well-being of a particular people, but has become a mechanism for managing them for the benefit of their rulers. That is to say, an empire's political behavior reflects management needs, reflects the interests of maintaining government itself, reflects the desires of those who happen to be in control of its machinery of administration, rather than the personality and will of the nation being governed. The government of an empire is abstract, manipulative, a government of, by, and for the government, not of, by, and for the people. Power flows downward rather than upward.

In an empire all institutions receive their legitimacy from the approval of government, rather than government being a means to nourish and protect institutions. In an empire the government is the basis of all things, in a republic the community. In an empire the genius of the people, as the American Founding Fathers called the particular native social fabric, no longer matters because an empire consists of many peoples, or, in effect, none. It consists of subjects, interchangeable persons, having no intrinsic value, to be manipulated in the interests of that abstraction, the empire. Subjects, for instance, whose neighborhoods or schools may be turned over to criminals should the rulers prefer to placate criminals rather than punish them. Subjects whose hallowed notions of family and morality may be put officially on a par with debased forms invented by diseased personalities. Or whose culture can be treated as inferior to some other that has been or is to be imported and officially recognized.

Or subjects whose lives may be expended in wars the relationship of which to the security and welfare of their community is tenuous. Thus imperialist foreign policy (like imperialistic domestic policy) is "irresponsible" in the republican sense. It reflects the vagaries of mind or the assumed self-interest of the imperial class. It has no point of reference, such as is axiomatic to a republican society—the well-being of the community. Republics go to war to defend their interests or presumed interests, including possibly their honor. Empires go to war because going to war is one of the things that "irresponsible" rulers do. Since imperial rulers are not responsible, they have power but not moral obligation, and represent themselves and not communities, they are capable of going to war for subjective self-gratification, making a remote land "safe for democracy," for instance. They are equally capable of ignominious retreat on the flimsy grounds of the evaporation of their fantasy. They choose illogically to ignore communism ninety miles away and fight it five thousand miles away—it is, after all, the duty of subjects to obey, not to question. The obedience of subjects to their rulers is easily distinguishable from the obedience of republican citizens to the laws and deliberate decisions made by their community.

The New Right, it seems to me, may best be understood as a largely spontaneous and as-yet-imperfectly-articulated defense of the American community (or rather communities, for there are several) against the inroads of imperialism. It has been forced out by a sense of alarm that the balance of power has shifted away from the community and toward an imperial ruling class, and a sense of fear that such a shift represents a malignant condition for a republican society. That is to say, viewed in light of the Founding Fathers and of the instinctive feeling of Americans about what it means to be American, the trends of recent decades forebode the end of the republic and anticipate the termination of a unique experiment in the self-governance of communities and the limitation of rulers.

The fact is that the balance of power has shifted against the people and in favor of the court; that government policy, both domestic and foreign, has for some time now been directed more and more by the interests and opinions of the class that dominates the centers of power, official and un-official, and its clients, and less and less by the well-being or beliefs of the people.

Most of the ills facing American society today can be viewed simply as the varied manifestations of the growth of what I have called imperialism. It is the onset of imperialism that accounts for the widespread sense of powerlessness and decline felt by Americans today, a malaise far deeper than that experienced in major crises of the past like the Civil War or the Great Depression. The trends of recent decades, unchecked and unreversed, foretell the transformation of republicanism into something else—the familiar, ancient forms of servitude, the end of liberty and dignity, except for the imperialist class—those lucky, ruthless, or cunning enough to belong to the court rather than the country.

That the form of republicanism remains intact, apparently, is of little significance. It is the substance which ought to be our concern. That members of the imperialist class, floating on a sea of luxury and irresponsibility such as was never known before in the world, do not see the degeneracy of the times, does not matter. The average American, rooted in the reality of work, responsibility, and survival, knows that he is not as well off, not as secure, not as proud or as easy as he once was.

It was the boast of the Founding Fathers and subsequent generations that America was the best country in the world for the common man—that was one of the meanings of republicanism. It may still be true, but how much longer? With the value of labor eaten away by inflation, neighborhoods threatened, education deteriorating, the minimal conditions of civility disappearing, the American, except for favored members of favored minorities, sees his hopes slipping away. Dimly, he apprehends a sinking from citizenship into peasantry, that he has become a subject rather than a citizen. His unease arises not only from a sense of deterioration but from the instinct that his rightful inheritance, as an American, is to be a proud and self-governing being.

The American body politic is now divided into a country party and a court party, republican and imperialist camps. Republicans are those who place their primary allegiance in the American community—its traditions, values, its very unique reality. They stand distinguished from those who are primarily motivated by the interests of the court and its clients. The latter dominate equally the Left and the Old Right and appear in various guises, as expediency dictates, but most often as adherents of the ideology of "liberalism."

What is today called the New Right is thus not a new but a very old phenomenon in American history and tradition. It is the American country party, provoked into militancy. The tendency, the preference, the despairs and hopes which the New Right signifies are deeply, fundamentally, originally, anciently American. They are not recognized as such, perhaps, because most of our history and political philosophy in recent decades has been imperialist, has been distorted so as to mask the will to power of the court party by an abstract and mechanistic discussion of a disembodied "democracy." The regime has ignored, as much as it could, the interests, even the survival of the living community of republican Americans. The New Right is purely and simply the revolt of the community against the threat to its dignity and self-determination posed by imperial rule. Its mission is to reorient American politics, domestic and foreign, around a clear and simple objective, the well-being of the American people.

The common man's instincts come far closer to the understandings of the Founders than do the apologists of received wisdom. Our course in recent decades conforms perfectly to the scenario familiar to the Fathers as the decay of republicanism by usurpation. Imperialism, remember, is not just bad policy, to be cured by repair of mechanism or a change of leaders. Imperialism is a condition, a state of decayed responsibility with implications for every part of society. Its ravages are evident everywhere in America today.

There is hardly anyone who has not been aware of the flow of power to Washington in the past few decades. More recently, almost everyone except paid apologists of the imperial class has become aware of the inefficiency, fraud, and waste that have accompanied that flow. Yet the discussion of this issue has been too trite and narrow. It is not a question of redistributing a given quantity of "power." Imperialism should be looked at within the framework of republican responsibility. The imperialist arrogance of Washington and its minions and the decay of will in the community go hand in hand. The social fabric has deteriorated as power has drained away from the community. The court has gathered power as it has shucked off responsibility. We are governed more, and less well.

Power has been shifted away from the voters and officers of the community, but responsibility has not gone with it. Washington is not "responsible" to those it rules, because the ruled cannot reach it, cannot exercise any effective authority over it. They are subjects, not citizens. Often no one knows who issued the directives that have impinged upon the community, and if they are known, they are out of reach. And Washington is not responsible in the sense of governing effectively either. None can be found to take the responsibility when the directives prove to be onerous. From representatives expressing the will of their people, the local fathers have become leaders in securing acquiescence in what nobody wants but nobody seems to know how to avoid, in what government does to us.

Even Congressmen no longer go to Washington to deliberate and achieve a consensus and decree the will of the people to the government. They have been transformed from delegates of the sovereign people into imperial lackeys. Their primary "responsibility," except possibly on election day, is to the bureaucracy. They maintain themselves by sitting atop and taking credit for the flow of government manna back to their communities. It is beyond the Congressman's power to be "responsible" in the republican sense because it is beyond his power to make the will of his community felt and beyond his power to prevent usurpations by the rulers except in small and incidental ways. Seeking to serve the people, he becomes frustrated or impotent; or else he becomes a willing and well-rewarded camp follower of the imperialists. Many thousands of bureaucrats and judges not "responsible," in the understanding of the Founding Fathers, to the public and even unknown to it, exercise power greater than Congressmen. They even, in many cases, enjoy pay and perquisites superior to those of the elected delegates, as complained of as the latter are. The Founding Fathers would have recognized this immediately as the rule, in all but name, of a "court" party.

But the decline of power and will in the community, the transfer of local authority and responsibility out, does not have a benefit in the increase of the individual liberty of the citizen vis-à-vis the community. Ordinary citizens have never been less secure in their incomes and persons, never had a harder struggle to maintain a sphere of decency for their families, never had less freedom to come and go without fear, never had less liberty and means to undertake enterprises independent of government authority. They are less free and happy, their aspirations in humane terms are lower than when affluence was much less in evidence.

Ordinary Americans, particularly in the largest and most liberal cities, are no longer proud members of self-governing communities. They are cowering nobodies, faceless interchangeable beings without a notion of being masters of their own fates. All this under an imperialist regime which seeks "quality" and "equality" with immense expenditures and police powers, yet is increasingly incapable of guaranteeing minimal conditions for civilized life, indeed often becomes the enemy of private efforts to maintain those conditions.

Another indicator of the state of decay which is imperialism is the shift of emphasis from production to consumption, from work to amusement, such as has taken place since the middle 1960's. It reflects an assumption of power by an irresponsible court party. "Aristocrats" concern themselves with what is due to them, not with the sordid details of providing it. All the emphasis is on distribution, none on production. The courts, the bureaucracy, and a careless Congress have erected so many lavish entitlements that society is threatened with bankruptcy on one side and disappointment of immense proportions on the other.

With typical imperialist behavior, the rulers have taken credit for the distribution and eschewed responsibility for the production. Distribution, no matter how irresponsible, is moral, production contemptible. Our rulers are inundated in a sea of money which they are ready to spend on themselves or for any purpose they see fit without any verifiable distinction between private greed and public need. It does not occur to an imperialist President that the public does not owe him a landing field on his ranch. It does not occur to an imperialist scholar that the government should not subsidize his viewpoint. The line between private appetite and public purpose has nearly ceased to exist.

It is not enough to blame bureaucracy. Bureaucracies have tendencies to self-aggrandizement that need to be watched, but they can perform useful and necessary public functions. The point is that our institutions are now managed in the spirit of and for the interests of the imperial class. The institutions exist primarily to perpetuate themselves and to provide sustenance for those who belong to them, not to fulfill clear and limited goals related to the well-being of the community. The community provides tribute, the rulers dispose.

The New Right, I believe, starts from a real if poorly articulated instinct that economic problems are at base problems of morale, that is, of morals. The well-integrated community produces its needs and a surplus. Only when the community becomes embattled, sees its production preyed upon by nonproducers and nonmembers, does economic morale begin to sag, with all the dire consequences—especially dire in a complex and a distribution-oriented economy. Of all the dire consequences of irresponsible distribution, inflation is the worst. Inflation is not a technical problem, it is a moral problem, a failure by rulers which takes the form of oppression of the prudent and productive. Communities with governments that take responsibility for their actions can control inflation.

Imperialism is not only a political phenomenon. The pervasive and progressive loss of function characteristic of our economy and of local and state government spills over into every area of life. The abandonment of responsibility to remote and abstract power is simultaneous with the decay of will and identity in nonpolitical institutions. Increasingly, all our institutions exist primarily to perpetuate themselves and provide employment rather than to perform the functions for which they were established. Do not deteriorating goods and services and corporate bailouts tell us that, even in business, responsibility decays? A society in which clergymen don't save souls, school children don't learn to read, reporters can't distinguish facts from feelings, tanks break down on their first run, jurists substitute whims for legal learning, has already gone a long way down the road to imperialism. We no longer judge by result and results no longer depend upon will and effort. In more and more areas of life success depends upon political manipulation, luck, and advantage. Cunning and bluster, the hallmarks of politics, become more important than accomplishment in more and more areas of life, as these are increasingly. politicized.

Republican societies reconcile individual ambition and social good by providing scope for the former and harnessing it to the benefit of the latter. One burns to make more money, another to compose a symphony, another to invent a new device or technique, another to fly farthest or fastest, all to do something well for the love of that thing or the distinction that doing well brings. Such achievements derive part of their meaning from being contributions to the common good by people who feel a sense of belonging to the community.

Thus a sound community automatically generates leadership. The very fact that it provides a meaningful framework for existence arouses ambitions and encourages talents. To lead the nation, to enhance its well-being, becomes the end of existence for the maturest and highest minds. To achieve honor and position within the community informs the efforts of the young. This is not merely political but affects every activity of life—business, professions, culture. Integrity is encouraged because it has an observable value in fundamental life relations with a given people, and is respected. Excellent performance is recognized, not just by a technical group or a government committee, but as a contribution to society. Thus the strongest individual ambitions and the strongest social instincts are reconciled. A free and flourishing society is possible. In the republican community, an approximate if not absolute relationship between reward and effort prevails. But in an empire success consists of access to the levers of political power, which accounts for a progressive decline in performance in all areas of life. Only in sports and to some extent show business does the desire for excellence still reign supreme—the circuses of the masses have to be good as the quality of bread declines.

One of the keys of republicanism, as understood by the Founders, was that rulers were temporary and delegated. They could be reduced regularly to the ranks of the people to take the consequences of the laws they had made. But in imperial America special privileges and immunities characterize the "court party" and its adherents. The erection of special privileges, in fact if not in name, is the sure sign of the rise to power of an imperialist class. Just as rulers cease to function responsibly, so do they aggrandize themselves. There is one law for the peasant, another for the lord. The imperialists decree busing for our children but not for theirs. They create inflation against which they are guarded by automatic raises while the rest of us survive as best we can. They decree permissiveness for criminals but expect protection for themselves. They subsidize schools of Hindus in California and ersatz Muslims in Detroit and suppress Christian schools set up by tenth-generation Americans in North Carolina. In the name of equality they destroy the safety and homogeneity of other people's neighborhoods, not their own.

The Founding Fathers realized that republican societies had a particular tone or atmosphere that differed from that of aristocratic or monarchical states. Republican citizens gave respect to leaders for their services. Imperial subjects, on the other hand, gave flattery to rulers because they were rulers. The immense sentimental adulation that surrounded the Kennedy family during the 1960's and 1970's is perhaps the most pointed evidence that can be produced for the pathological state of republicanism. The Kennedys demanded and received honor not for what they had done, but for what they *were*. A fawning press hid their indiscretions and sang their hosannas in a spirit that would have disgusted Washington or Jefferson, or even Franklin D. Roosevelt. A rather similar treatment was extended to Martin Luther King, and poor Mr. Nixon's troubles resulted largely from his pathetic efforts to secure similar status. Observing the special privileges and glamour surrounding some people, and sought by others, the Founding Fathers would have unhesitatingly diagnosed America as being in a "monarchical" frame of mind, hardly any longer possessing the spirit necessary for a republic.

The Founding Fathers realized that republics could not be proclaimed in a vacuum, but depended upon a republican social fabric. Lack of virtue in the people called forth corruption in the rulers. And corrupt rulers communicated their moral deformity to the entire social fabric. At the heart of the failure of republican responsibility is the substitution of alleged political virtue for private virtue, a failing that has had an irresistible appeal for a certain type of American since the pre-Civil War era and has occasionally burst forth into a predominant mode, as it did in the 1960's and 1970's.

The increasing deterioration of private virtues, the increasingly small number of people who can shoulder mature responsibilities, private or public, is evident in American society and in some of the more modern parts is epidemic. It relates directly to the style of the imperial class, typified by the Kennedys—the making of a ritualistic pronouncement as a substitute for the exercise of virtue and responsibility. By this style, once the proper incantation is said, one is entitled to reward. Government will now magically solve the problem. Day care centers will substitute for unloving mothers and unsustained marriages.

Rehabilitation programs will solve the problem of "citizens" who destroy their brains with drugs. More lenient laws and more generous handouts will cure the widespread disrespect for law. This is a profound and devastating kind of loss of responsibility.

The New Right is based on areas of American life when private virtue is still practiced or at least still recognized. Where the ability to speak the truth, to keep commitments, to exercise moral restraint, to labor productively, to take responsibility for work, family, and community, are taken for granted not only as values but as necessities. Ordinary decent citizens understand instinctively what the Founding Fathers recognized and articulated. Republics depend upon the virtue of the people. To put it another way, morality, a high moral tone, is the *sine qua non* of a republic. Self-government is for the self-governed. While some of the better parts of the Old Left and Old Right still maintain a vague sense of social responsibility and private decency, it is a flabby and attenuated sense, no longer relevant to the real condition of American society.

The New Right knows, for instance, that family is the indispensable basis of all civilized life. Whatever may be wrong with the American family at this moment in history, it is all we've got. Sound communities can only be built upon strong families. Alternative lifestyles do not constitute emancipation and progress, they constitute malignancy. New Rightists, perhaps, do not agree on every nuance of the abortion question. But they do agree that the cavalier attitude toward life, even unborn life, manifested by the liberal lifestyle, is retrogression, not progress. Much the same may be said about "gay rights" and the "alternative family." We have been shocked into reaction, not so much by the manifestations of sickness around us, as by the official sanctioning of it.

It is not a question of a government neutral toward lifestyles. It is a question of whose lifestyle will predominate, a question made by the imperialists with their relentless attacks on decent America. Nor is it a question of oppression or suppression of alternatives. It is a question of not permitting what is tolerable as a fringe of society from becoming the average. Our imperial governors, with characteristically cavalier disdain for consequences, have elevated the immorality that occurs at the fringes of any society and those lapses all flesh is heir to into programs and campaigns, into equality with—no, into *de facto* superiority to—those norms that not only enjoy divine sanction but without which society crumbles. Pluralism calls for tolerance, not disintegration.

At the bottom of the New Right movement lies a vague but deep sense that the worldview of the ruling imperial class in its social manifestations marks a pathological degradation of humanity. Its emphasis on supposed rationalism and openness have reached the point where they threaten the mysterious sanctities without which life loses meaning and becomes mere animal existence, a state in which tolerance becomes a perverse weapon and citizenship impossible. To put it another way, our leading class is decadent and must be replaced by fresher, stronger minds and spirits if we are to survive. It may be that abrogating the narrowness of small town morality was at some point a good thing. But liberation has not brought the Acropolis to Main Street, it has brought the Massage Parlor. The freedom sought by the imperialist is the wrong kind of freedom. It is not the freedom of self-governing republican citizens who prefer to be their own masters. It is the tired throwing off of responsibility, the decadent resignation of aspirations to higher humanity, that characterizes the subject. This point is grasped instantly by the ordinary citizen, but only with the greatest difficulty, if at all, by the liberal imperialist who sees what he has been taught to see, not what is there. It was this phenomenal blindness on the part of our rulers to the real consequences of their positions that to Alexander Solzhenitsyn was the most striking characteristic of American society.

It would be possible to draw out at much greater length the ramifications of our imperialist state, of how our malaise is related to usurpations of power that are easily comprehensible as the degeneracy of republicanism in the light of the wisdom of the Founders. But it is necessary here to anticipate the objections of liberals, including certain New Leftists who have eloquently diagnosed the pathology of American imperialism without realizing that they were a part of it. They will contend that government is not their primary value, that it is merely auxiliary to the democracy, equality, social progress, they wish to achieve.

The answer is that we must look at what they do, not at what they say. Modern liberalism has had only one empirically verifiable manifestation—the use of the government to manipulate and alter the community (which incidentally is often highly profitable, or at least gratifying, to those doing the altering). The manipulation may be deliberately punitive, as in the case of busing, or ostensibly benevolent as in the case of various kinds of "aid" that impinge upon the community. In either case it cannot be other than manipulation because it is done in accordance with some special vision entertained by the liberal of a better community, a vision outside of history and without specificity, a vision of a society endlessly open and malleable that never did and never can exist, a myth. If the liberal ever bore any relation to the real American community, he ceased to do so a long time ago.

Such a vision always entails the precedence of government over people, the means of manipulation over the community in being. The louder and more often the liberal talks about the people, the less specific he becomes—the further from the community of real people, the more abstract, the more imperialist. To him the people is everybody, that is, nobody. Whatever may be postulated about individual rights, in practice the individual ceases to have any significance except in the official hierarchy of manipulation. In the glossary of the Founding Fathers, the liberal is immediately identifiable as an "aristocrat," not a republican, a member of the "court" and not the "country."

I will also anticipate here the objections of libertarians, who will wish to brand the New Right, with its emphasis upon morality and patriotism, as just one more form of statism. Libertarianism, while encompassing some responsible criticism and high ideals, is an insufficient philosophy, though it is one that understandably flourishes among people who wish to be free of the burdens of a government that is becoming imperial rather than republican. The New Right differs from the Old Right and libertarianism essentially in understanding that economic problems are not technical problems but problems of morale, that is, essentially moral problems. The destruction of value by inflation and falling productivity and the loosening of bonds of contractual obligations are necessary and coterminous accompaniments of the loss of virtue in the community and in its rulers, not simply the direct result of too much government.

Free enterprise is a part of the genius of the American people, possibly a part of the genius of any dynamic and progressive people. The right to exchange goods and services, develop new enterprises, compete in the marketplace, is essential to material well-being, technological progress, and individual self-realization. There is no single social generalization applicable to the twentieth century world that is more easy to demonstrate than this.

Nevertheless, to the New Right, free enterprise is not an absolute. It is a means, not an end. New Rightists, including those who devote their lives productively to free enterprise, do not intend to establish a religion of the dollar bill. This clearly distinguishes them from certain elements of the Old Right and from libertarians. New Rightists have no intention of having their neighborhoods turned over to pornographers and dope peddlers, their natural resources controlled by foreign corporations, their national honor understood chiefly as a matter of dollars and cents, their labor cheapened and culture undermined by the removal of barriers to immigration, all in the name of the free market. They understand that such things as public morality, public responsibility, exist. Not only exist but are *sine qua nons* of a free society. Individual liberty flourishes not in a vacuum but is a possibility within a particular social context. Destroy that context by anarchy or oppression and individual liberty, as fundamental as it is to man's moral and material well-being, perishes along with every other humane value.

I wish to avoid the alleged besetting sin of the New Right, over-simplification. Thus, let us not exaggerate the ravages of imperialism. Its victories have not been pervasive. Much of the American community remains intact. But one must look beyond local and temporary setbacks and note the overall trend, which, previous to November 1980, had been steadily in favor of the imperialists. The 1980 elections, as yet, are only a check, not a defeat, for the imperialists. Their defeat remains to be consummated.

In further devoir to the dangers of over-simplification, it must be said, that there are two sides to every question. The increasing imperial arrogance of the governing class and its clients and the deterioration of will and identity in the community feed upon each other. The growth of imperialism is not simply the result of the machinations of evil men (though in a political regime that has produced several Supreme Court justices whom no prudent man would trust with the administration of his children's estate, evil machinations cannot be entirely discounted). Imperialism is a result of, as well as a cause of, the deterioration of community, though the last quarter century overt government action has greatly accelerated the deterioration of community by magnifying the unhealthiest elements of society and besieging the best.

There is a real question whether the American community is indeed viable any longer in other than an imperial form. Or, as the Founders would have put it, whether the people yet possess sufficient virtue to govern themselves. I believe we can give a cautious affirmative to the query. And I believe that the New Right represents that affirmation—an outpouring of positive belief in the people, an expression of the popular will that has risen above the routine of hog-trough politics—one might say, a resurfacing of the lost tradition of Jeffersonian democracy.

It is true that the multinational corporation, the industrial revolution, and what Joseph Wood Krutch called the "modern temper"—the dislocation of traditional morals, faith, relationships, and ways of life—have worked to undermine the viability of the republican community. The problems that afflict the American family today, for instance, can be blamed only in part on liberals and government. Such problems are not chiefly political problems and do not have chiefly political solutions. The greatest danger that faces the New Right is to avoid the trap of seeking a political solution to nonpolitical problems. To make the social issues primarily matters of political manipulation will be to play into the hands of imperialism. But here is a case, fortunately, where reform and liberty go together. We are once more happily in the place where the answer to many of our problems is not a grant of more power to the government but a limitation upon it, not politics but an end to politics.

New Right politics, then, do not or should not offer to solve such problems as the disintegration of family. What they can offer is the only hope for the political preconditions that will allow the family to save itself. To get the government off the backs of the people, as Mr. Reagan has so happily put it, to deter it from its abetting of social disintegration so that the healthy forces of survival and reconstruction natural to normal individuals and real communities can have scope for their work.

As the Founders recognized and often repeated, usurpers frequently seek to surround their activities with an aura of glamour and mystery, which lends them prestige and covers their shortcomings and greed. This phenomenon was explored with great insight by Jefferson and John Adams in their philosophical correspondence late in life. The clamor raised by the imperial class and its lackeys against "over-simplification" is a perfect example. The implication is that only they are wise enough to understand the complexities of the modern world, and that the common citizen, or even the well-informed one who does not share their particular view of life, had better keep his mouth shut. But republics can only achieve satisfactory decisions by open and honorable deliberation, something which the imperialists suppress by their control of the media and their penchant for branding all disagreement as stupid or evil.

The fact is, a little simplification such as is posed by the New Right is just what we need. We need to return to a simple republican form of government, a form which exists for one purpose—to enhance and defend the community. One of the reasons for our failures, social, economic, diplomatic, military, is that we have lacked a simple point of reference. The heads of our rulers, of the Left and the Old Right, have been full of idle ideologies and pretensions to imperial glory, of everything except the welfare of the American community.

All the great men of the world have been great because of their capacity for profound simplicity. And great issues are simple ones. Or at least, the first step in the solution of great problems is to grasp their simple essentials. The reason our problems seem complex is that they lack a point of reference. To the New Right, evils such as inflation, proliferation of crime, uncontrolled immigration, decay of civility and morality, and inertia in the face of foreign threats are not "complex problems" to be left in the keeping of shamans who worry them around but never solve them. They are the direct effects of "irresponsible" rule in the sense of George III. As such, they can be reversed.

What the New Right calls for is the reorientation of the government in accordance with American republicanism. The starting point of all policy should be the health of the American community in being, the enhancement of its domestic peace and harmony and its security from the foreign enemy. If the issues are viewed from a republican perspective, they *are* simple—what best will preserve and enhance the American people and their descendants. Such a formula will not solve all problems, of course, but it will provide the starting point for their solution. Republican America will be neither ashamed nor incapable of taking the steps that are necessary to secure its economic, moral, cultural, and physical well-being, and that of its posterity.

The republican restoration faces formidable opposition. Imperialism, in all the unbridled arrogance of its privilege and pretension, is deeply dug in in the leadership of both political parties, in the federal courts and bureaucracy, in the media and educational establishment, in the purlieus of inherited wealth. Still, there is much reason for optimism.

Our task is a largely negative and limited one, to curtail the imperial class and liberate the community's powers of creation and restoration. The Iranian crisis has renewed a widespread sense of patriotism in a way that could not have been foreseen. Mr. Reagan is the first President to come to office in more than a half century without the sanction of the court party, and he exhibits an almost providential ability to perceive simple truths and stick to them. Most important, perhaps, is that new generations have the capacity to see the world through different eyes.

All these things work in favor of the restoration of the republic, and suggest that the time is ripe for that periodic returning to our roots that Mr. Jefferson so earnestly recommended. What the future will resemble if we succeed in the renewal of the republic cannot be predicted, because for communities of self-confident, self-governing citizens, the future is open. If we fail, the future is certain to be shaped by the sad, sullen outlines of servitude.

(1982)

Thomas Jefferson, Conservative

A Review of *The Sage of Monticello*, by Dumas Malone, Volume Six of *Jefferson and His Time*, Boston: Little, Brown and Company, 1975, 551 pages.

In 1809 Thomas Jefferson yielded up the Presidency and crossed into Virginia. In the 17 active years remaining to him he never left it. The first volume of Malone's masterpiece, published in 1948, was *Jefferson the Virginian*. The sixth and last is *The Sage of Monticello*. Jefferson begins and ends with Virginia. Keep this fact in mind. It will save us from many errors and lead us as near to the truth as we can get in regard to this sometimes enigmatic Founding Father.

No great American, not even Lincoln, has been put to so many contradictory uses by later generations of enemies and apologists, and therefore none has undergone so much distortion. In fact, most of what has been asserted about Jefferson in the last hundred years—and even more of what has been implied or assumed about him—is so lacking in context and proportion as to be essentially false. What we commonly see is not Jefferson. It is a strange amalgam or composite in which the misconceptions of each succeeding generation have been combined and recombined until the original is no longer discernible.

Presuming we wish to know Jefferson rather than simply to manipulate his image for our own purposes, Malone is indispensable. *Jefferson and His Time* is a conspicuous example of an increasingly rare phenomenon, genuine scholarship. I mean that term as a compliment—to denote a work that avoids the extremes of pedantry and superficiality, that is exhaustive, thorough, honest, balanced, felicitous, reasonable and executed on a noble scale.

From Malone, and especially from the latest volume, we can, if we wish, begin to discern the real Jefferson. And that Jefferson is, in the broad outline of American history, identifiable in no other way than as a conservative. The real Jefferson is most visible in his last years. I do not mean by this that Jefferson was one of those proverbial persons who was liberal in youth and conservative in old age. There is no conflict between the young Jefferson and the old Jefferson except in the perceptions of image-manipulators. Jefferson was of a piece, his main themes were constant. But I do mean that the conservative Jefferson emerged most clearly in the last years, when he was not in office, when he was not bound by the necessary compromises of leading a party or speaking in the voice of community consensus rather than his own voice, when he was down home in his natural environment.

How did we get so far afield that it has taken half the lifetime of a great historian to recover the wherewithal of a proper understanding of Jefferson? First, New Englanders, embittered by the half-century setback which Jefferson and his friends administered after 1800 to their political style and goals, painted him as an effete snob, a visionary, a kind of squeamish Jacobin. If the New England Federalists and their descendants lacked political power, they made up for it in cultural power. Their loss at the polls was turned into a victory in the sophisticated battleground of historical writing. The understanding of Jefferson and his accomplishments that was handed down to posterity was created by Henry Adams. Adams, with brilliance, painstaking care and a cunningly contrived pseudo-objectivity, structured a perception of Jefferson and his times from which American historians—until Malone—had never really escaped. Jefferson, even when viewed sympathetically, was judged by New England standards. This meant that the essential outlines of his Virginian frame of reference were obliterated. Thus the mainsprings of his belief and action could not be detected accurately.

Jefferson's admirers have done him little better. It seemed that the Civil War and Federalist historians had repudiated and buried Jefferson forever. Then along came Vernon L. Parrington, the son of an English socialist (but raised in Kansas), who rediscovered Jefferson the agrarian liberal. But unfortunately what Parrington discovered was an imaginary combination of French philosophe and midwestern populist, not the planter of Albemarle County. Parrington, Claude Bowers and a host of other worthies soon turned Jefferson into the patron saint of Wilsonism, the New Deal and what currently passes for liberalism.

Thus, by a strange piling-up of ironies, the intellectual descendants of Jefferson's opponents converted him into one of them, a kind of urban, liberal, puritan dogmatist of egalitarianism. More recently, some of them, like Fawn Brodie, have discovered that the evidence does not fit this image, that Jefferson never was a certifiable modern liberal. They should have admitted that they had been wrong all along. Instead they chose to brand Jefferson as an aberration and a hypocrite for not being one of them, that is for not being what he never was and never wanted to be. Jefferson was an American republican, not a European social democrat. Jefferson was agrarian, not urban and industrial. Jefferson was a gentleman, which the class of admirers I am talking about here certainly is not.

All of these distorted notions of Jefferson have been possible only because of a lack of context, plausible because they have extrapolated one small portion of Jefferson and built an image on that foundation. This has been most conspicuous in the peculiar, dogmatic, ahistorical rendering of one phrase of the Declaration of Independence as a piece of egalitarian revelation. Indeed, without this one distortion of Jefferson (and of American history) the contemporary American left could hardly be seen to have any legitimate tradition at all. (Even more peculiarly, the same dogma is embraced as a main tenet by one school of "conservative" political scientists.)

There is one other important reason for misreading Jefferson that must be taken into account. Jefferson can be misunderstood in the same way that any great *writer* is subject to conflicting interpretations. And Jefferson is important as a writer, a thinker and a stylist. If he had never held public office, the immense body of his private correspondence would still be one of the most important

American cultural legacies of his period. In his correspondence he was imaginative, playful, speculative. He adapted himself somewhat to the person he was addressing. He liked to turn ideas around and examine them from all angles. Except in his most narrowly political activities he wrote as a philosopher, not as a tactician. Further, he was intellectually polite and magnanimous. Dogmatists found that Jefferson did not contradict them in person. When they later discovered that he disagreed, they called him a hypocrite. He was not; he was simply a polite listener, a gentleman. Thus Jefferson can be quoted against Jefferson. In order to see clearly the real Jefferson we have to know the context, we have to know the whole corpus of work, we have to know which were the constant themes and which the occasional ones. This Malone has made possible.

Who, then, was the real Jefferson? What were these constant themes? They are clear. None offer comfort to the contemporary left. First of all, Jefferson stood for freedom and enlightenment. That he is our best symbol for these virtuous goals is Malone's central theme. That does not mean, however, that his thought can be twisted to support something that very different men with very different goals postulate to be freedom and enlightenment. His concepts of freedom and enlightenment were always rooted in the given nature and the necessities of his Virginia community and always balanced harmoniously against competing claims. Read Jefferson on the need for every citizen to be a soldier, on the prudential limits that should have been observed in the French Revolution, on the inappropriateness of liberty for a people unprepared for it; read of Jefferson's approval of Governor Patrick Henry's summary execution of a Tory marauder.

Jefferson favored the liberty of the individual and the community, and he had in mind certain reforms that he felt would enhance them. However, Jefferson was nothing if not the enemy of programmatic, government-imposed reforms. His whole career proved this. But read his reaction to the nationalistic program of our first "progressive" President, John Quincy Adams:

> When all government, domestic and foreign, in little as in great things, shall be drawn to Washington as the centre of all power, it will render powerless the checks provided of one government on another, and will become as venal and oppressive as the government from which we have separated.

Jefferson is on record as fearing the harmful effects of slavery on the community. But he feared far more the harmful effects of *political* antislavery. Read him on the Missouri controversy and you will correct a thousand misrepresentations. Jefferson, it is true, wanted America to be an example to all mankind of successful free government. But when he said example that is just what he meant, example. He gives no comfort to those who want to impose democracy on others, but much comfort to those who want to defend American democracy from any and all enemies. Jefferson, it is true, mistrusted the clergy. In this respect he was typical of his generation. But Jefferson the citizen, as opposed to Jefferson the philosopher, lived within the church. Religion and piety troubled him not at all. What he feared was the sanctimonious, intermeddling, politicized Calvinist clergy—that is, what we would today call "liberal" churchmen.

Jefferson was the advocate of a free economy, but he was not doctrinaire about it. Like all his values, his belief in the free market was balanced against other claims. He believed in economic freedom within a stable society. Malone's chapter, "The Political Economy of a Country Gentleman," by simple adherence to the facts, corrects four generations of distortion. When viewed "in retrospect," he writes, Jefferson's "reaction to the economic problems of his day can better be described as conservative."

Jefferson championed public education, but it was not public education on the leveling Prussian-New England model that later became the American standard. The traditional classical curriculum was to be supplemented by more modern and practical subjects, but not jettisoned to make room for them. It was to be an education competitive, elitist, based on a belief in a natural aristocracy of talents and virtues. The rich would always take care of themselves. The purpose of public education was to make sure that the talented ones who appeared among the poor would not be lost. That is the exact opposite of what modern American public education aims at, for its goal is to reduce the educational level to the lowest common denominator—which, in effect, guarantees that the poor but promising youth does not learn enough to rise above his station or to compete with the privileged. "The natural aristocracy," wrote Jefferson, "I consider as the most precious gift of nature for the instruction, the trusts and government of society. . . . May we not even say that the government is best which provides most effectually for a pure selection of these natural aristoi into the offices of government?"

Dumas Malone has completed a great work—a work that is, like its subject, truthful, harmonious, balanced, fair, decorous, gentlemanly. What a rare thing for an American book in the 20th century, a book by a gentleman about a gentleman.

(1982)

Jefferson, New and Improved

I tremble for my country when I reflect that God is just.
— THOMAS JEFFERSON

A Review of *In Pursuit of Reason: The Life of Thomas Jefferson*, by Noble E. Cunningham, Jr., Baton Rouge and London: Louisiana State University Press, 1987, 414 pages.

With the exception of the driven and depressed Lincoln, no major figure in American history is, in the final analysis, more enigmatic than Jefferson. Without any exception, none is more complex. There is more to the enigma and complexity than a multitude of facets—political leader, botanist, architect, linguist, ethnographer, musician, man of letters, and much else. (If he had never held a public office. Jefferson's correspondence would still be one of the most valuable treasures of his era.) But behind these varied roles was a mind of a very high order. With deep and complicated reserves, yet covered by an impenetrable mask of everyday balance and harmony that was more than sufficient for the highest worldly success without beginning to exhaust its capacity or reveal its real nature. In many respects, the enigma of Jefferson, delightfully hinted at in Albert Jay Nock's early-20th-century biography, is similar to that of his contemporary, Goethe, and likewise will remain forever inaccessible to those of us who do not enjoy the mental and moral gifts of nature in such abundance.

But we do not really need to understand the whole personality to grasp the significance of Jefferson's career as a public man in the founding years of the American republic, and this new biography is concerned chiefly with the career of the public man. There was no mystery at all in what Jefferson stood for in the American political scene. This was clearly understood in his time and for a generation or two thereafter by both his friends and his enemies. But, while there is no mystery, there is a great deal of confusion, arising out of subsequent efforts to manipulate his image as an aegis for other causes of other days. Even had he not been so complex a puzzle as a man, his role in American history is so covered by ideological debris that reality can only be uncovered inch by inch. (Merrill D. Peterson's tour de force, *The Jefferson Image in the American Mind*, 1960, showed the many and contradictory uses to which he has been put.) In fact, the multivarious misunderstandings of Jefferson's political career tell us little about him. They tell us a great deal about the fragmentation, shallowness, and image-mongering that characterized American political and intellectual life after his time, a degeneration which he observed in his last years.

Jefferson had a chivalric and optimistic faith that the intelligence and patriotism of his fellow American freeholders (outside of Massachusetts and Connecticut) were such that they could be trusted to rule themselves. It followed that a free republican government was the proper form of government for Americans and that this government should interfere in their private affairs and pick their pockets as little as was consistent with public order and national independence. Unlike persons in the 19th century and since who seized upon and universalized a few words in the Declaration of Independence, he did not insist that liberty and republicanism were appropriate to every people, condition, and time. The element of messianic democratic universalism that came to characterize the American approach to the world was a product of a later time and was a devolved expression of that New England Puritanism which Jefferson despised, and which hated him.

To Jefferson and his friends, his victory and theirs in 1800 meant simply that they had established his view (which was not something he invented and promulgated from on high as a divine lawgiver, but something that arose naturally out of American conditions) as predominant. Yet by the time he died, in John Quincy Adams's would-be activist presidency, Jefferson well knew that his victory had been temporary.

The LSU Press has inaugurated a new series of Southern biographies, of which this is an early entry. The goal is a readable one-volume treatment, based upon accumulated scholarship and reflection, but aimed, apparently, at general readers. Given the alienation between historical scholarship and the reading public (if such a thing still exists), this is laudable. But it is hard to imagine a more difficult subject to take on in this way than Jefferson. There are many good specialized studies of particular aspects of Jefferson and room for many more, but it is no easy matter to boil him down to one smooth volume. The author sought to bypass all the accretions of confusion and to see Jefferson afresh, while admitting that he presents only his own view of a complicated subject. This is probably the proper strategy for the occasion, but perhaps unavoidably, it can succeed only at the cost of either distortion or blandness, in this case the latter. This is, in a way, a redundant book, though responsibly and gracefully written. Did I desire a readable and up-to-date one-volume life of Jefferson, I would hire the most skilled available editor to condense Dumas Malone's six volumes, which are as close to definitive as history can ever be. The book in hand fills a formal requirement, without adding anything either factual or interpretive to the world's body of knowledge.

Cunningham hoped to see Jefferson afresh and thus sought to reduce his life to a clear and manageable theme—his faith in reason in the affairs of man. Here I must part company with the author. While the observation is true, it is so general as to be nearly meaningless or, what is worse, lends itself to too many misrepresentations. Almost all the errors and confusions about Jefferson result from using his faith in man's reasonableness to provide an endorsement for any later movement which appealed to reason, no matter how different in spirit, in tacit assumptions, in social context, in intellectual fabric from Jefferson's own. Alexander Hamilton also believed in reason, but he drew rather different conclusions about its proper use. One would never gather from Cunningham's mild consensus history that the gentlemen's disagreement between the two reasoners was marked by violent sectional, ideological, and economic conflicts that reverberate to this day.

To put it another way, the theme of reason tells us little about the blood, sweat, and tears of Jefferson's politics—or those of his enemies. This is not only a political biography but also, alas, a superficial one. It is a verbal icon, a printed and bound version of the New Deal-era monument in Washington which could make Jefferson palatable to 20th-century Americans only by doctoring his quotation about slavery. This is not Malone's Jefferson, though it bears a resemblance to a fragment of that portrait. It is not Nock's or Parrington's or Bowers's or Peterson's or that of many others that could be named. It is George Bancroft's Jefferson. Bancroft was a clever New England scribbler of the 19th century who, unable to defeat Jefferson, took a narrow slice of him and created a putative whole that he found compatible. Exactly the same thing happened more recently when George Will and others converted Ronald Reagan, at one time a wild man from the West and potential threat to the Establishment, into just another Republican, tolerable if not beloved in Boston and Hartford.

After the violent twist of American society away from his dispensation in the later 19th century, Jefferson can be made to fit consensus history only by a good deal of selective emphasis. Cunningham thus follows the standard interpretation that Jefferson's allegiance to states' rights was merely a temporary expedient, adopted for the occasion, for the larger goal of the defense of civil liberties. But this is unhistorical. In his own time and several generations later, the Kentucky Resolutions of 1798, affirming state sovereignty, were the core of his political position. (Here we run into the mystification heaped up by the cleverly vengeful industry of several generations of Adamses, who convinced most later observers that Jefferson's presidency was a contradiction of his earlier position. It was not so seen by most at the time or for many decades following.)

The real Jefferson, by modern interpretation, put freedom ahead of states' rights. This is to indulge in a too-easy make-over of Jefferson to please ourselves and to miss the main point, which is that for Jefferson—and his followers—the two were synonymous and inextricable. It is self-evident in the historical record for those who have eyes to see, obvious to anyone who will read Jefferson's correspondence through from the 1790's to the 1820's or who will examine the context—the understanding of what his career meant to his supporters in his own time. And it is only thus that we can resolve what many 20th-century commentators have seen as a contradiction in Jefferson—the theoretical advocate of freedom who engaged on other occasions in what an ACLU devotee would regard as acts hostile to civil liberties. But there is no contradiction between the Jefferson who invoked state sovereignty against the federal sedition law and the Jefferson who approved Virginia's summary execution of a Tory marauder. The contradiction is in the eye of the beholder who attributes to Jefferson a set of assumptions which were not his own. From the point of view of state sovereignty, the two positions are perfectly consistent and democratic. In his role as a public man he trusted Virginia, and her sister and daughter states, to exercise power responsibly when necessary without permanent danger to liberty. (He had his doubts about greedy and self-righteous New Englanders and certain other Americans who were too impressed by Old World arrangements of authority or who had too many plots and plans for the use of public power.) Late in life, when he was no longer an active politician, Jefferson explicitly recommended the use of state interposition against unconstitutional internal improvements legislation—not a question of civil liberties and exactly what was forwarded a very few short years later by Calhoun against the tariff.

Nothing could be more wildly irrelevant to Jefferson's position—that liberty was best preserved by protecting the free American social fabric from the federal government, with such exercises of power as were unavoidable left to the wisdom of the people of the states—than that of the modern civil libertarian that freedom is something granted by the federal Bill of Rights after being wrested away from an untrustworthy state majority. In fact, Jefferson's view would still work: could we restore real federalism and limit the central government to war, diplomacy, and a few other necessary common functions, we could come as close as possible in an imperfect world to settling our major social problems. There is, in fact, no other possible solution for abortion, rampant crime, deteriorating education, and many other evils than a reassumption of power close to the people. It is true we would lose Massachusetts and a few other states of the Deep North, as Jefferson always did, but most of the states would govern themselves "reasonably," could they decide without interference. But this will never happen, not because of any defect in the Constitution but because of defects in the national character. It would not in the least have surprised Jefferson that a people who are no longer a nation of independent and public-spirited freeholders but a mass of consumers leavened by an occasional busybody reformer would have difficulty in governing themselves "by reason."

Here we must admit that Jefferson's was a creative and speculative intellect, which bruited a great many ideas in a great many forms to a great many people. Polite and imaginative and fond of discussion, he often adapted himself to his correspondent in a speculative vein, leaving the literal-minded with the impression that he agreed with them. But Jefferson always perfectly understood the difference between theoretical speculation and the real world of American freeholders, and as a public man he was eminently practical and consensus-oriented, as Alexander Hamilton discerned when he refused to countenance the efforts of his fellow Federalists to steal the election of 1800 for the charming scoundrel Burr. Jefferson was, as we said, a complex man. The failure to distinguish between the philosopher and the political leader has led some to regard him as inconsistent or hypocritical and others to take his theoretical projections as literal policy prescriptions. But there is really no problem if one takes care to understand the context of a quotation. Contrary to later assumptions, it was not Jefferson the philosophe who was revered and followed by his contemporaries and a majority of several succeeding generations but Jefferson the sane and balanced public man, not the author of "All Men Are Created Equal" but the republican gentleman who had averted Federalist usurpation. Cunningham presents not this latter Jefferson but rather that partial one who was pleasing to international philosophes and to the more belated and lukewarm of his supporters.

Jefferson's views on slavery, or rather the reaction to them by 20th-century intellectuals, or the 20th-century public for that matter, provide a fascinating case study in emotional avoidance of simple and obvious historical facts, in the great lengths that people will go to rationalize fantasies that they find comfortable. Cunningham's approach is again the conventional one, to emphasize Jefferson's antislavery sentiments, which, unfortunately, came to little. The whole story is less comforting to those who insist that figures of the past be like them. There is, indeed, a certain childish willfulness in the American mind that insists on chastising persons of other ages for not being like them, or else pretending that they were. Which is a certain way *not* to learn anything from history.

As to slavery, Jefferson was born into the higher ranks of a social system that long had been, was, and would long continue to be committed to it. He believed, as did many others, and often said, that on balance the situation was deleterious to the commonwealth and it ought to be done away with, *if* this were possible without damage to other values and interests. His speculations on the nature and relations of the races were deeper, but not much different in conclusions than those of his neighbors and most other Americans of his time.

He was, like his neighbors, committed to keeping the issue in the control of those whose concern it was. His famous letter (to John Holmes) during the Missouri controversy ("We have a wolf by the ears") has been repeatedly misrepresented by those who prefer ideological fantasy to accurate history. What is usually emphasized about the letter is that Jefferson was still committed to his antislavery sentiments, which is true but a misemphasis. In this letter, very clearly (and in many other statements at the same time), Jefferson was not pointing to the evils of slavery—he was pointing to the evils of antislavery, of free-soilism.

The letter is written to console a northerner in trouble with his constituents for favoring the compromise—that is, for favoring the admission of Missouri as a slave state. It is not slavery that Jefferson fears as "the death knell of the Union," it is antislavery, the notion that has been raised for the first time that Congress could tamper with the institutions of new states as a condition for admission. Looked at over the whole career and not sugar-coated and spiffed up to meet 20th-century standards, that is to say, viewed historically, Jefferson's views are easily understood and did not differ, except for being more detached in tone (as befitted an elder statesman), from those of most other Southerners of that time and later, including the leaders of the Confederacy. Those views were the exact opposite of, and hostile to, the Free-Soilers of the mid-19th century who claimed him as patron saint. Like all Southerners, Jefferson was unwilling to entertain outside interference.

That we have so nearly lost touch with Jefferson is nowhere better indicated than in his being claimed as the father of modern public education. Jefferson proposed for Virginia a system of public education, never fully implemented, designed not to supplant private education but to supplement it. His main concern beyond making rudimentary learning widely available was to rescue those gifted young men who appeared from time to time in the lower orders of society. He would provide them with the means and the opportunity, in a vigorously competitive and elitist setting, to progress into the aristocracy so that their talents would not be lost to themselves and to society. (The rich would, of course, see to their own success.) Nothing could be further from Jefferson's plan than the programmatic use of the schools as an arm of the state to rearrange society (though he did favor a necessary orthodoxy of political teaching in support of republicanism which our civil libertarians, committed to leftist revolution, will not allow).

Our public school system was built upon a Massachusetts-Prussian model that proceeded from the beginning with nearly opposite goals. Its purpose was to provide not leaders but a docile work force and conformist citizenry. Possibly this goal was even a good one given the conditions of the later 19th century, but it was not Jefferson's. Jefferson, defender of the aristocracy of talents against the aristocracy of privilege, would find anathema. I believe, a school system which expends vast resources in the hope of making marginal improvements in the minds of the dull-witted, while neglecting, demoralizing, and alienating the talented. (The main function of American public education is to make sure that the talented poor do not get a good education and are not able to rise and compete with the class that can afford private schooling, a class noted for its sterling verbal commitment to egalitarian public education.)

This brief sketch, I believe, captures something of the essential Jefferson. But, of course, history is many things and serves many purposes, and its fascination lies just in the fact that it is not and never can be definitive. Professor Cunningham has enjoyed a pleasant and prestigious appointment, by no means a sinecure, to provide a new account of Jefferson's life in relatively short compass. If one wants a reliable, factual, well-written overview of the life of Jefferson the public man, in some but not too great detail, then this book will serve the purpose. It is a pleasant but not very invigorating diversion for those who like their American history as untroubled as possible. And I have no doubt that a great many more readers will prefer Cunningham's filtertip cigarette to the pungent but authentic plug of old Virginia bright leaf that I have proffered above.

(1988)

Thomas Jefferson's Birthday

Thomas Jefferson's birthday went virtually unnoticed earlier this year, the 250th anniversary of his birth. Nothing is more indicative of how badly we Americans have squandered our moral capital and betrayed the substance of our history. We did have, of course, President Clinton's inaugural journey from Monticello, though it is hard to imagine anything further from the true spirit of Jeffersonian democracy than the motley crew of socialists, spoilsmen, image manipulators, and foreign agents who make up the present leadership of the Democratic Party (except perhaps the motley crew of stockjobbers, spoilsmen, image manipulators, and foreign agents who make up the leadership of the Republican Party).

Then there was the conference on "Jeffersonian Legacies," held at Mr. Jefferson's University and since issued as a book and a videotape for PBS, that was devoted to a motley lot of dubiously qualified Northeastern and California intellectuals preening about how much wiser and more enlightened they are about racial matters than Mr. Jefferson. In fact, Jefferson's discussion of the American racial dilemma in Query XIV of *Notes on the State of Virginia* says everything true that can be said about the subject, ethically and intellectually, as will be seen a hundred years from now, should there be any men and women left who are capable of Jefferson's range, clarity, honesty, and detachment.

Jefferson had the most capacious mind and, until his later years, the most optimistic temperament of any of the Founders. Had he never held a public office, his vast corpus of letters and writings would still be one of our most important legacies from that era. He was, on one side of his personality, a true intellectual, fond of ideas and speculation. The dull-witted and literal-minded have continually taken his statements out of context as dogmatic proposals to be enforced or opposed, failing to distinguish, as he did himself, between Jefferson the American public man and President and Jefferson the international man of letters.

Conservatives, in particular the heirs of his enemies the Federalists, have had a hard time with Jefferson, often finding in him the anticipation of all they hate. Which is just the reverse of the counterfeit coin peddled by the leftists of this century who once made him an unrecognizable idol (though they thankfully are no longer much inclined to do so). In other words, Jefferson has been erected again and again into a straw man to worship or to execrate. He is bigger than all of the trivial images that have been constructed. To rediscover him we must unravel layer after layer of misrepresentations piled up by successive generations of self-centered interpreters. (For instance, on the slavery question, liberal intellectuals made him one of them, and then attacked him for hypocrisy when they discovered that he wasn't. But this is silly. Jefferson was himself, easily discernible all along to any honest observer, and under no obligation to conform himself to the categories of trivial thinkers of later generations.)

Conservatives, misled by some of the more unscrupulous opponents of his own time, have had problems with Jefferson's religion. Undoubtedly he tended toward deism, as did most of the intelligent men of his time to some degree or other. But Jefferson was never an enemy of religion, despite the hysterical charges of New England preachers unhinged by the French Revolution and their personal loss of deference. Jefferson always conducted his family life within the Anglican communion, in contrast to John Adams, who is invariably described as an upholder of orthodoxy though he became a Unitarian (!) not out of youthful folly but of a mature decision.

Jefferson the public man was in fact the favorite candidate of the more tolerant Protestant denominations and religious minorities. What he opposed was what he called "priestcraft," by which he meant the clergy of New England hellbent on dominating the minds and actions of other men by force rather than free assent. The "priestcraft" has degenerated from Calvinist to transcendentalist and now to progressive-liberal, but the principle remains the same.

Likewise Jefferson's educational system has been praised and condemned as the progenitor of our modern public school establishment. But the debased system we have comes from Prussia by way of the New England reformers Horace Mann and John Dewey. Its rationale is egalitarian and regimented "progress." The goal of Jefferson's proposed educational system was excellence and the rescue of talent from obscurity for the good of the commonwealth. A resemblance is apparent only to the terminally shallow who mistake words for things.

The process of Jeffersonian obscurantism began early in the 19th century, when the village atheists of New England, from Emerson on down, who execrated Jefferson the public man, began to appropriate selective words of Jefferson the philosophe (like "all men are created equal") as ammunition in their own will to power ("priestcraft"). This was their common way of proceeding. For instance, at the same time they managed to turn the fox-hunting cavalier George Washington into a puritan prig congenial to themselves.

The process reached culmination in the 1850's, when a new party stole the name of Jefferson's party, "Republican," to cover a platform of business subsidy, abolitionist agitation, and puritanism—all things that Jefferson abhorred. It would never have occurred to him that his own personal philosophical position could be employed by very different men as an ideological juggernaut to coerce his fellow citizens by federal force. Jefferson the public man led and reflected a public consensus, not an ideological program. It was very clear to his own generation, and the subsequent generation or two in those parts of the country that followed him, what that consensus was.

Jefferson and his friends came to power (the "Revolution of 1800") in opposition to the economic and moral imperialism of Hamilton and his friends—a program of taxes, manipulation of the economy for the inevitable benefit of the few and the burden of the many, moral dragooning of the population, and involvement in foreign power politics. It was this threat that Jefferson and his friends put down, and kept down, for half a century—the happiest era of the Union.

Jefferson the philosophe is of great intellectual interest but of little political relevance to our very different, chastened age. It is Jefferson the public man we need to recover, as well as his program and his party: adherence to the limits of federal power in the Constitution; preservation of the rights of the states as the chief bulwark of our liberties (the "Principles of 1798," toasted by Jeffersonians for generations); low taxes; a simple and economical government that interferes as little as possible in the activities of the citizens; avoidance of "entangling alliances."

This was the platform of Jefferson the leader who postponed Hamiltonian calamities to the Republic and who was loved by the preponderance of the American people in his own time and long after. It is that Jefferson we need and who is our greatest asset against high-handed elites who oppress the people in the name of equality and popular rule. It is that Jefferson who said: "I am for a government rigorously frugal and simple." "Were we directed from Washington when to sow, and when to reap, we should soon want bread." "There is a natural aristocracy among men. The grounds of this are virtue and talent." "I am not among those who fear the people. They, and not the rich, are our dependence for continued freedom. And to preserve their independence, we must not let our rulers load us with perpetual debt. We must make our election between *economy and liberty*, or *profusion and servitude*."

Once Jeffersonian democrats were the most numerous of all American political types. During the second half of the 20th century they have scarcely been heard from. Yet, in my opinion, there are, out there in the hinterlands, millions of us waiting for a reassertion of the "Principles of 1798" and for another "Revolution of 1800." But, alas, we wait in vain for another Jefferson to lead.

(1993)

Why They Hate Jefferson

A Review of *The Long Affair: Thomas Jefferson and the French Revolution, 1785–1800*, by Conor Cruise O'Brien, Chicago: University of Chicago Press, 1996, 367 pages.

What a marathon of Jefferson-bashing we have had in the last few years. This book by the "global statesman" O'Brien follows several other critical biographies, all of which have been highlighted in the fashionable reviews. More than usually offensive to Jefferson admirers was a collection (*The View from Monticello*) by University of Virginia professors trashing their founder (not surprising since they are all carpetbaggers anyway); a slashing attack in *National Review*; and, worst of all, Ken Burns's latest television "documentary."

None of this literature tells us anything about Jefferson. There is no scholarship—that is, research and discovery—involved. We have here, rather, a case study in intellectual sociology: that is, an exhibit by fashionable intellectuals determining what is and is not acceptable to their version of the American regime. What they tell us is that Jefferson is out now.

Friends, you must have either Jefferson or Hamilton. All the fundamental conflicts in our history were adumbrated during the first decade of the General Government in the contest symbolized by these two men. Hamilton lost in the short run, but triumphed in the long run. He would find much that is agreeable in the present American regime—a plutocratic kritarchy which we persist, by long habit of self-deception, in calling a democracy. But Thomas Jefferson would not be at all happy with what has happened to this country; he might even suggest that the time had come for a little revolution. The host of petty intellectuals and pundits, elitists, and would-be elitists—tame scribblers of the American Empire—sense this, and so Jefferson must be dealt with appropriately. The Establishment is frightened by the rumblings they hear from the Great Beast (that is, we the American people). They are shocked to realize that Jefferson honestly did believe in the people; that he believed the soundest basis for government to be popular consent and a severely limited government.

Hamilton, on the other hand, believed in rule by "the [self-appointed] best" and in "energetic government" operating in the interest of private profit. For the better part of a century we had protective tariffs which burdened the great mass of the American people, agriculturalists, and consumers, while profiting large capital. Now that it is in the interest of large capital to ship American workers' jobs to the Third World, we have every petty pundit singing the praises of "free trade." Just what Alexander ordered.

Hamilton, it is true, was rather indifferent to the do-gooder side of the federal leviathan. Yet do-gooderism was axiomatic for the New Englanders who made up the largest base of his support: people whose instinct is immediately to translate every moral prompting into governmental coercion. This is why you and I now have to add the cost of airbags to our car, by federal decree, whether we want them or not.

O'Brien's brief against Jefferson is twofold. First, he favored the French Revolution, even its excesses, which show him to be an irresponsible bloody-minded parlor revolutionary. Second, Jefferson was not a racial egalitarian and is therefore an unacceptable symbol for modern America.

O'Brien, as a number of reviewers have pointed out, lacks the most funda-mental requirement of historianship—that is, the careful use of documents and understanding of context. He makes no distinction between Jefferson's friend-ship for the French people—his always cautious hopes that they might achieve popular government—and support for the Terror. On this subject (as on most oth-ers), there is much better treatment from Albert Jay Nock's old biography, *Jefferson*. As for Jefferson not being a racial egalitarian—well, neither were Lincoln, Teddy Roosevelt, and Woodrow Wilson or, for that matter, Harry Truman and Ike Eisenhower. So what?

What we have here is elitist hysteria, an old and familiar phenomenon. During the election of 1800, the president of Yale, Timothy Dwight, stumped New England trying, with the aid of most of the New England clerisy, to con-vince the people that Jefferson was a representative of the Illuminati. John Adams cowered in his fortified house in fear of The Mob, while Jefferson lived at ease among his 200 slaves. The Federalists persuaded themselves that the guil-lotines were about to be set up if that horrible decadent Southerner were elect-ed—ousting them from their power and prestige. Today, we have merely the lat-est version of the thing. Petty elitists, unsure of their unmerited positions and fearful of the people, conjure up a dark spectacle of terror. How unthinkable that we should have those yahoos out there calling the shots, instead of their betters.

The trouble is, Jefferson was always a liberal but never a Liberal. Liberals (for lack of a better term) for years perpetuated an elaborate hoax making Jefferson one of them—which he never was or could have been. Now that it is obvious that he really *wasn't*, an elaborate ex-communication—equally a hoax—from the American canon seems to them necessary. It would be comedic if it were not such a malicious perversion of the historical truth. The burden of O'Brien's teaching is that Jefferson does not belong in, and must be ejected from, the American civil religion. But does America have a civil religion? Ought we to have one? Who says so? And if we do, do we need some damned foreigner to tell us what is to be left in, and what out, of it? What Jefferson most fundamentally signifies is that we do not need secular priests governing our civic life; we need merely to trust in a limited, popular government while keeping a wary eye on the self-appointed clerisy.

The pundits are right. Jefferson does not offer aid and comfort to the present regime. And let us thank the Creator who endowed us with our inalienable rights for that. We still have in Jefferson a powerful symbol for liberty and the consent of the people that no number of pettifogging scribblers can suppress.

(1997)

American Counter-Revolution

A Review of *The American Counter Revolution: A Retreat From Liberty,* *1783–1800*, by Larry E. Tise, Mechanicsburg, Pennsylvania: Stackpole Books, 1999, 634 pages.

A good historian ought to make it clear where he is coming from rather than assume an impossible Olympian objectivity. Then, if he has handled his evidence honestly, he has fulfilled the demands of his craft—whether or not we agree with the interpretation he has placed upon his evidence. Ideally, interpretation should come separately from, and after, presentation of that evidence. Two historians, for instance, may agree that the New Deal was not really very radical a program. One of these may be pleased by this conclusion and the other regret it; both, however, in their honest description have done their job as historians. Their opinion *about* their finding, of course, is another question. (And as Sir Herbert Butterfield wisely warned long ago, historians' opinions can too easily become self-centered moral judgments, even preferences of taste masquerading as moral judgments.)

Larry Tise, by these criteria, is a good historian. He tells us up front (self-indulgently, alas, and at a little more length than necessary) what he is and where he is coming from: a liberal unhappy with what he considers the failed promise of the American Revolution. In the period he has under consideration, he believes that liberty (by which he means feminism and egalitarianism) was repudiated by its friends just as it was about to be realized in practice.

Tise provides us with a rich survey of evidence from America, Britain, Ireland, and France (including its colony of Santo Domingo) concerning shifts in public opinion during the French Revolution. Americans in this period, he believes, "marched from the worship of liberty to the worship of order." I would interpret what happened and why somewhat differently, but I agree that the phenomena he describes took place. And recognizing that what Tise considers a "reaction" did indeed occur among thinking Americans advances our understanding beyond the usual superficialities and is therefore welcome, despite the problem of mislabeling.

If only the author did not assume that the natural goal and *summum bonum* of history is a feminist, multicultural, egalitarian society, then he would have it right. When one believes, however, that multicultural egalitarianism is the appointed end of all human affairs, one must assume some fault, some perverse deviation to be ferreted out to explain why utopia was not realized at that time. Why *did* Americans give themselves over to evil—that is, succumb to anti-egalitarian opinions and a preference for order after the War of Independence?

This approach depends, however, on the tacit assumption that when the American revolutionaries proclaimed the cause of liberty and the rights of man, as they certainly did, they meant the same thing by them as did an end-of-the-millennium liberal, or at least a French Jacobin. The catch, of course, is that they didn't. The "reaction" of opinion and action toward order, including an insistence on patriarchy and homogeneity of citizenship, that followed the American Revolution was not a betrayal of anything—it was merely the normal and natural expression of Americans' inheritance and experience and the consolidation of their achievements. We need only reflect on what might have ensued had Americans followed the path Tise thinks they ought to have taken: an American Terror, Napoleon, or Santo Domingo? (There was a Napoleon—Alexander Hamilton—waiting in the wings. To think such horrors could not have happened belongs to the same order of thinking as to say that communism did not fail because "true communism" was never tried.)

Americans could have taken no other path than what they chose to take and still remain themselves. They were predominantly serious Christians, and liberals have never understood the problem Christians have with the French Revolution—which itself precluded Jacobinism. Their social fabric and mores were Puritan in New England, acquisitive bourgeois in the Middle States, and a volatile mixture of gentry and Border tribalism in the South. None of this lent itself to the kind of society prized by Professor Tise. Americans' conception of liberty arose from a solid legal and constitutional tradition and from real experience, not from speculation. It stipulated limited government of a kind not energized to pursue a feminist, multicultural utopia—a thing that it would never have occurred to them to pursue since the American people, unlike some Frenchmen, well understood that it had never existed in the history of the world, and never could exist. Americans, moreover, had a task before them—civilizing a continental wilderness—that only self-confident Anglo-Celtic males could have been expected to accomplish. It is ungrateful for a later generation, living at ease on their accomplishments, to find fault with them for not being as socially sensitive and noble as we supposedly are.

For Larry Tise, Thomas Jefferson is the greatest villain of all, "the most radical counter-revolutionary" of the period, who provided the emotional and intellectual stimulus for reaction (that is, a preference for self-governing order over egalitarianism). Tise is accurate in this judgment: I salute him for identifying the Jefferson whom I have been celebrating for over 30 years, though in the end he mislabels the great man.

Edmund Burke had it right, as usual. Asked how he could defend the Americans and the Irish while being so adamantly against the French revolutionaries, he explained that there is a difference between the desire for liberty "which arises from Penury and irritation, from scorned loyalty, and rejected Allegiance" and that "which is Speculative in Origin." The latter, of course, is Jacobinism, then and now.

But take heart, Mr. Historian of the Counter-Revolution! The Jacobinism that the founders of American liberty so wisely rejected is fastened tightly enough upon us now, though its goals of course can never be achieved, only projected into some future when evil reaction will have been overcome. That, really, is a part of its charm.   (1999)

The Virginian Roots of American Values

*"There is Jackson standing like a stone wall.
Rally behind the Virginians."*
— BARNARD ELLIOTT BEE

A Review of *Pursuits of Happiness: The Social Development of Early Modern British Colonies and the Formation of American Culture*, by Jack P. Greene, Chapel Hill and London: University of North Carolina Press, 1988, 284 pages.

We were British colonists for a long time. From the first permanent English colony on the mainland of North America (Jamestown, 1607) until the first guns of the American War of Independence (outside Boston, 1775) is 168 years. That is the same span of time that exists between now and the days of President Monroe. Although the heroic enterprise of founding a civilization in British North America was carried out by what was only a handful of people by modern standards—no more than would fit into a medium-sized metropolitan area today—understanding of that era is indispensable for any honest accounting of the American experience.

Yet outside the bounds of serious historical scholarship next to nothing is known and understood, and the public mind appears content with the kind of misleading and self-indulgent nostalgia that is enjoyed by the throngs that frequent Colonial Williamsburg. It would be more fitting, but out of step with the modern American temper, to ask ourselves how a few counties in Virginia, inhabited by a few hundred colonial freemen, could produce more statesmanship (that is, intelligence, ethics, patriotism, foresight) in the later 18th century than the entire Congress, federal judiciary, and executive branch today.

Fortunately, within the limited bounds of serious scholarship, colonial history is a vigorous, sophisticated, and relatively rigorous enterprise—more so than any other field of American history. There are several reasons for this. Colonial history presents a limited and finite, though large, body of historical records and literature. Unlike the diverse and proliferate 19th century, the field can still be mastered, almost, by a talented and energetic historian. There is not the maneuvering room for irresponsible generalization that larger fields encourage. Also, perhaps, the fact that American colonial history is a part of British history subjects it to the continuing discipline of English historians. They have their faults, but they do not generally go in for the kind of uncritical democratic romanticism that American historical writing has suffered from since George Bancroft began doing his thing in the early 19th century.

Jack P. Greene, one of the leading lights of current colonial and Revolutionary history, a scholar who has mastered the trick of being well-founded in the data and the literature without losing the trick of being able to draw out of them a meaningful synthesis, has in *Pursuits of Happiness* provided us with both a procreative interpretation and an accomplished socioeconomic portrait of the evolution and nature of colonial America.

The socioeconomic portrait, synthesizing a vast quantity of recent specialized literature, is of value in itself. Like all good colonial historians, Greene is aware that the mainland colonies were only part of the "settler societies" of the British in the New World. His colonial world includes not only the four regions of North America—the tobacco plantation society of the Chesapeake, New England, the Lower South, and the Middle Atlantic states—but also Ireland, the Atlantic colonies (Bermuda and the Bahamas), and the West Indies. Each had characteristics in common, each was distinct in itself, and each, as Greene is aware, could be further subdivided where useful. (Consider the difference between Massachusetts and Rhode Island, or between the two Carolinas.)

The thesis (really a two-parter) has to do with the course of development of these colonial areas and their relative centrality in the formation of American culture. The first part of the thesis tells us that the Chesapeake colonies, centered in Virginia, provided the norm for America; that is, the other areas converged toward them in both socioeconomic structure and social ethos. Among much other evidence that might be cited, it is clear that African slavery was not only accepted in law, custom, and public opinion throughout all parts of the colonial world, but in the period before the Revolution it was expanding to a significant degree, including the colonies northward of the Chesapeake.

The second part of the thesis, more interpretative than descriptive, postulates that though the American culture that developed from 1775 was a result of the "powerful convergence" of all four mainland regions, the norm and central model was Virginia. The New England model of society, the given of American historiography, was, in fact, on the decline in every sense, even in New England. Rather than an industrious and cohesive New England diffusing its civilizing values through the rest of the American hinterland, the predominant flow of values was the other way around. The Puritan model of Massachusetts-Connecticut was a backward-looking and closed system not really adaptable to American circumstances. Put another way, Americanization meant Virginianization, not Bostonization. The Virginia and not the Massachusetts conception of the good society provided the core of American values.

As Greene would have it, the liberty- and prosperity-seeking individualism that became the inspiration of the Revolution and the root of later American values grew and spread from the plantation society of the Chesapeake. (I am necessarily but not unfairly simplifying here.) After all, it was the planter son of a land-hungry Virginia pioneer who penned those words about "the pursuit of happiness."

It should not be assumed that the author is uncritically fond of the upper South social system that he finds at the center of the development of American culture. The Chesapeake colonies were, in his view, exploitive and excessively individualistic, although clearly, in the period before the War of Independence, the leading class was moving toward ever greater social responsibility.

The Southern colonies were certainly brutal in their early days, unavoidably so—but so were all the others. I would suggest that to see them as unrelievedly the abode of an atomistic and ruthless individualism is an exaggeration. Greene needs to look into the work of M.E. Bradford, in *A Better Guide than Reason* and elsewhere, in which Bradford demonstrates the growth of a Southern regime that worked along the lines of implied community understandings. The Southern colonies did have a sense of community. Unlike that of New England or modern urban society, however, it was much looser and more intangible—it manifested itself more in behavior than in institutions.

In that respect it had a flexibility that was indispensable and appropriate for the frontier. The American frontiersman, like American culture, had roots in Virginia, not Boston. Consider the rude but real chivalry of Southern frontiersmen like Colonel Boone and Colonel Crockett, or, as late as the early 20th century, the gentlemanly individualism of *The Virginian* in far-off Wyoming. On the other hand, while New England communal values did have, then and now, many constructive fruits—in some contexts they provided for a "gentler, kinder America"—they can be overrated. One should look into the conditions in the New England merchant and whaling fleets and the number of pious Massachusetts sea captains who engaged in the Africa-to-Brazil slave trade right up to the American Civil War.

If I must criticize a superb work in order to earn my supper as a reviewer, I would make two related points. Greene presents, for the first part of his thesis ("the process of early modern British colonial social development"), a dense and elaborately argued case, often bolstered by charts, graphs, and "models of development" taken from the social sciences. These devices make his case neither more nor less true, but they make it a good deal less clear and interesting. So distinguished a scholar does not need such apparatus, which on other occasions he has avoided.

In this approach he is engaging honorably in a style of argument that unfortunately marks much of the better American historical writing these days. It rests upon a laudable hesitancy to make too sweeping generalizations and a laudable desire to anchor interpretations in hard data and accepted models of description. But systematic and persuasive historical thought does not need the deceptive solidity of quantitative evidence so obtrusively presented. The wholesome fear of presumption and exaggeration dooms much of our good history to a limited audience.

My second criticism has to do with the conflation or confusion of two different orders of generalization in his two-part thesis. The first thesis postulates the normative character of Virginia for early modern British colonial social development, the second the normative character of Virginia in the formation of American culture. These are related and mutually supportive assertions, yet they are of two different kinds.

The first is a descriptive statement, for which the marshaling of socioeconomic evidence is necessary and appropriate. The second hypothesis is really in another realm of discourse. It is a value-laden, symbolic, and political assertion. In no way can proof of the first statement by descriptive evidence, no matter how convincing (and such evidence never goes undisputed for long), carry the day for the second statement. This would be to expect the sons of New England, who have for generations enjoyed the psychic, economic, and political advantages of prestige, to give up their privileged position without a fight, simply because they have been proved wrong.

Greene has, in fact, written only a prologue, only scratched the surface of the question. The really interesting part is how did we ever come to make the mistake of putting Massachusetts at the center of American culture to begin with. With due modesty, Greene offers only a brief and suggestive answer to this question. He knows it has something to do with the success of the New England-centered Bancroftian historical writing of the 19th century. And, he proposes, the anachronism of slavery forced the South steadily from the center of American experience. But this does not really explain how New England scribblers in the 19th century managed to preempt to themselves a central role in the founding of America that belonged to other and better men. It merely moves the questions back another notch.

My answer is that there have always been two ways of regarding the success of the American experience and values. One is to give thanks for the brains, hard work, courage, honor, and luck of our forefathers. This attitude teaches humility and respect for tradition. The second way is to view the success of America in boundlessly self-congratulatory and messianic terms, to believe quite literally that America has a divine mission above history and that law and tradition are to be trampled underfoot in the interest of ongoing democratic revelation.

The lasting success of George Bancroft was to make a compelling literary synthesis of three elements—the Puritan mission of the founding of New England as a City upon a Hill, democratic aspirations, and elitist messianism. These three elements are incongruous with each other and with the main line of American history, but they appeal irresistibly to a certain type of American character. This synthesis has been with us so long and appeals so powerfully to the elitist streak that lurks in the bosom of the most effusively professing democrats that we take it as natural. It is, in fact, highly unnatural in every sense.

As Greene shows, the Puritan mission was not central to the development of the American success story. Further, the relationship of New England to the growth of American democracy was (and remains) in the main negative. Historians have pointed out that Bancroftian history was chauvinist, racist (Bancroft was a believer in Teutonic supremacy and a Prussophile), uncritically Whiggish, and embodied a heretical conflation of American institutions with Divine Providence. But I mean more than this. I mean that history lied about the true source and nature of American democracy.

Bancroft assumed a pose as defender and interpreter of Jeffersonian and

Jacksonian democracy for which he was in no way suited. Once democracy had triumphed in spite of New England, he reinterpreted it to fit a New England model. (Please allow me to use "New England" here as a shorthand for a persistent streak of messianic elitism in American history that tends to center towards Boston. I know that New England includes Daniel Webster and Robert Frost as well as Emerson and Theodore Parker.)

I can make my point perhaps by taking note of the achievements of Bancroft's 20th-century disciple, Arthur M. Schlesinger, Jr. In what many regard as the classical interpretation of Jacksonian democracy, Schlesinger took a few highly untypical Northeastern intellectuals (untypical of their own region, which was Whiggishly conservative-progressive, and totally untypical of the great swelling of grass-roots Southern and Western sentiment that actually was Jacksonian democracy) and by literary power and ideological utility made them into the norm.

I do not mean to underestimate the symbolic power of democratic messianism. It runs a good deal broader and deeper than its publicists, in part because Bancroft managed to link it to the Union cause of the Civil War, although indeed the Union cause could be and was adequately sustained on other grounds. Consider that the Republican Party is now overwhelmingly Western and Southern conservative-populist, and that New England is a hopeless minority in American politics. But such is the power of symbolism that recently both parties adopted a New Englander as their presidential candidate.

Whatever this is, it is not my kind of democracy, not majority rule. The Virginia model—despite slavery—was not only more important and more viable and more truly the source of the better American values, it was also more democratic—it provided the possibility of consensual majority rule and a great deal of individual liberty of the right sort. The competing party did and still does regard democracy not as majority rule but as a code word for themselves—the vanguard of inspired carriers of democratic revelation, out to impose their sublime will on an unwilling people and a recalcitrant reality.

(1990)

Securing the Revolution

A Review of *Securing the Revolution: Ideology in American Politics, 1789–1815*, by Richard Buel, Jr., Ithaca: Cornell University Press, 1972, 391 pages.

The achievements of the battle-wise, book-wise men who made the American republic have a retrospective solidity that was not apparent to them. They knew that victory in the War of Independence had been contingent. They knew that American republicanism had emerged spontaneously from a social fabric fortuitously conducive to the reconciliation of liberty, order, and popular rule, and that such a unique balance was vulnerable both to prosperity and adversity, the life expectancy of republics not being great. Thus it is not surprising that the Fathers were concerned to design institutions which would prolong republicanism, that they disagreed over the designs, and that they regarded the founding less as an accomplishment than an experiment.

Hardly had the experiment begun, when the shock waves of the French explosion blew over them, underlining the fragility of the founding, both in the military insecurity of the American confederacy among clashing powers, and in the philosophical unease of the middle ground between the gut conservatism and armed doctrine of the Old World. It was at that moment the Fathers divided, Hamilton and Adams taking one road, Jefferson and Madison another. (These men should be regarded as reluctant symbols and spokesmen for divergent ideas and communities, not as instigators of movements. One thing "the first American party system" was not, was the product of personal ambition. In those days Americans eschewed the cult of the leader as death to republicanism.)

The great dividing of the 1790's has been commonly understood in one of two ways. One, popularized by literal-minded successors of Charles Beard, explains by economic class interests—debtors vs. creditors, farmers vs. merchants. The other is a chapter in a melodrama in which presidential Lone Rangers (Jefferson, Jackson, Lincoln, FDR, etc.) intermittently gallop in, to snatch democracy from the fatal embrace of reactionary forces. Mr. Buel has managed to rise above such "explanations." He has not written the ultimate book on the Hamilton-Jefferson cleavage, but he has discovered a wealth of instructive detail worthwhile to contemplate in its import. The book does not stand alone, but is best appreciated as a part of a remarkable recent flowering of good works on the early republic. It is the product of a still-developing school, more important products of which have been Bernard Bailyn's *Ideological Origins of the American Revolution* (1967) and Gordon Wood's *The Creation of the American Republic* (1969). While I can find much to argue with in these works, there is no question that they represent an advance to a higher and more inclusive synthesis than had been attained previously in understanding the early republic. Why this flowering has occurred while most eras of American history are being subjected to increasingly shallow vulgarization, to actual regression to old fanaticisms presented as "relevant" history, is not clear, but it is there.

The chief virtue of the new school, exemplified by the present work, is serious attention to ideas, as understood in their own time. The discovery that the ideas jingling in men's heads are as important as the change jingling in their pockets has been fruitful of subsidiary discoveries. For instance, a painstaking and detailed examination of the ideas of the Fathers has revealed a body of understandings and assumptions which has been dubbed "the ideology of republicanism," and not surprisingly this body of thought has been found not to contain mere intimations of Arthur Schlesinger. By paying attention to ideas, Buel has made the discovery that the early American government was deliberative, not majoritarian. He does not make that explicit, and one suspects that he has wrought more than he knows, but it is evident by the serious attention he pays to debates in Congress and other formal expressions of "public opinion." Unlike the fashionable determinist, he does not assume that such formulations are false consciousness, deceptive rationalizations of self-interest. Rather they are serious statements of belief, expressive of the speaker's being.

The point of this book, stated baldly and translated from the author's terminology into mine, is that the great Hamilton-Jefferson split was an honest difference of opinion over which of two possible relationships of the political elite to "public opinion" was most likely to shelter the fragile republic through its early grave dangers. To the Federalists, the elected leaders were the instructors and drivers of "public opinion," duty-bound to guide it into channels of wisdom, else all stability be lost. To the Jeffersonians, public opinion was to be trusted and reflected by the leaders; the threat to stability came from the reaction to the Federalist attempts to drive the people where they did not want to go. The first viewpoint was necessarily interventionist, the second laissez-faire. The author, understandably unable to liberate himself from modern democratic theory which conceives "public opinion" in terms of abstract, mechanical majorities of atomized individuals or pressure groups, has again wrought more than he knows. If we conceive public opinion rather as the instinctual consensus of a community, our understanding will be fuller. (Buel senses this when he tries to explain why the southern aristocracy was democratic while the northern bourgeois leadership was elitist—because the consensual relationship of the former to its community was sounder—yet the point eludes his grasp.) If this analysis contains truth, then it is not too difficult to detect a line of cleavage running through American history up to the present, between those who would drive and manipulate the community according to predetermined goals, and those who would lead and reflect the extant consensus. And if that extrapolation is true, there is still the formidable task of differentiating the two sides, since history never repeats itself with uncomplicated exactitude.

But there is a larger point, not made explicit by Buel, but apparent in the literature behind him. The cleavage did not represent in the 1790's a cleavage between pessimistic and optimistic views of human nature such as divided the

Europeans. The disagreement took place within an American consensus in which pessimistic and optimistic assumptions were inextricably (and perhaps confusedly) mingled, but in which the pessimistic strain was clearly predominant. The debate was over how best to thwart and ameliorate the corruption that, all the Fathers agreed, human nature made institutions inevitably heir to.

(1974)

Chapter Two

Jeffersonians

John Taylor

J ohn Taylor (1753–1824) of Caroline County, Virginia, who is always referred to as "John Taylor of Caroline," was one of the fathers of Southern politics.

More famous in his own time than later, his prestige was such that he was several times elected U.S. Senator from what was then the most powerful State in the Union without campaigning and against his wishes. He was a soldier in the Revolution who died regretting that the Revolution had ended in the construction of a federal government more dangerous than that of Great Britain to the colonies. He retired from a lucrative law practice to become not only a highly successful planter and agricultural reformer but the foremost political defender and philosopher that American agriculture has ever had. He was an eloquent libertarian advocate of economic, political, and religious freedom for the citizen, and an unbending defender of Southern slavery.

Taylor may even be said to have been a pioneer figure in Southern literature. His books and pamphlets are full not only of keen political and economic analysis, but are written in an amazing colloquial style—full of satire, hyperbole, and front-porch digressions—highly suggestive of the oral tradition evident in later Southern writers.

Taylor embodied many persistent and recurrent tendencies and themes of Southern politics. He represented both a conservative allegiance to local community and inherited ways and a radical-populist suspicion of capitalism, "progress," government, and routine logrolling politics. He was at the same time more radical and more conservative than his friend, admirer, and fellow Virginian planter Thomas Jefferson. Taylor was Jefferson's down-home side—exactly what Jefferson would have been had he been a little less cosmopolitan and a little less of a practical politician.

In many respects Taylor was a more authentic voice of Jeffersonianism than was Jefferson himself. Taylor's Old Republican defense of State rights, strict construction, and intelligent farming; his opposition to federal power, judicial oligarchy, paper money, stock jobbing, taxation, and expenditure, were reflexive, reluctant defenses of native soil and based upon the unyielding conviction that an unoppressed and predominant agricultural population was the only possible permanent basis for free government.

At the core of Taylor's thinking was a perennial idea in Western civilization: The world is divided between producers and parasites. The producers are decent folk who labor in the earth for their daily bread and produce everything of real economic and moral value in society. Such producers are numerous, unorganized, and unoffendingly honest. They are subject to endless depredations from those that Taylor referred to as "aristocrats." By "aristocrats" he meant not people of good birth but people, mostly Northerners, whose main business was manipulating the government for artificial advantages for themselves. Some of Taylor's keenest passages are devoted to exposing the gap between the plausible and beneficent reasons that are presented to justify "progressive" government actions, and the real motives and effects of such actions, which is the transfer of money and power from the producers to the parasites. To prevent this, Taylor would have said, is what democracy is all about. This view of the world, as much a folk attitude as a philosophical position, provides an explanatory key, perhaps, to much earlier and later Southern behavior.

(1985)

George Mason

A Review of *The Papers of George Mason 1725–1792*, 3 vols., edited by Robert A. Rutland, Chapel Hill: University of North Carolina Press, 1970, 1312 pages.

Apart from occasional half-hearted attempts to dragoon "The Father of the Bill of Rights" into the weird role of patron saint of the ACLU, none of the great lawgivers of the early Republic is so little known or revered in the twentieth century as Mason. The reasons for his eclipse are several. He eschewed office, particularly federal office. Already fifty when the Revolution began, he passed from the scene early, in 1792. His influence was greater in the wings than on center stage, so that much of his fame perished with his contemporaries. Worst of all, he was father to the lost cause of Antifederalism, a cause which stumbled in 1787 and which, after a deceptively successful holding action of three-quarters of a century, went down not only to total defeat but to obloquy in 1865.

There can be no question of his greatness. Although they fell out later, for many years the master of Mount Vernon turned to his Fairfax County neighbor at Gunston Hall the unguarded ear he lent few men. During the Revolution, Washington relied greatly on Mason's legislative vigor to maintain logistical efficiency on the diffuse Virginia homefront. Madison, who locked horns with him in the Federal Constitutional Convention and afterward in the battle over ratification in Virginia, called Mason the greatest debater he ever knew. John Randolph so loved the Virginia constitution of 1776, Mason's handiwork, that when the convention was called to revise it in 1829, Randolph attended the sessions wearing mourning and lamented that every man fancied himself a George Mason.

Jefferson said flatly that Mason was the wisest man of his generation. Well he might, for Jefferson, and Madison too, in the Virginia and Kentucky Resolves were merely trying too late to engraft onto the Constitution what Mason had warned them ten years before it fatally lacked: a mechanism giving the states as much power to counter the Federal Government as the three federal branches had to defend themselves from each other. Possibly also, Jefferson came to realize that "all men are created equal" was an unfortunate rewrite of Mason's far better-weighed phrase in the Virginia Declaration of Rights, "all men are born equally free and independent." Mason and the Antifederalists were not opposed in 1788 to knitting the Union together well, nor did they reject the achievement represented by the Constitution, to the writing of which Mason himself had contributed significantly. But they believed it needed some final perfection of design, the lack of which would leave it dangerously misshapen in the direction of centralism. Contrary to the general impression, the adoption of the Bill of Rights only partly overcame their objections. Foremost, they wanted to reserve to the states some degree of decisive power. The Tenth Amendment, a mere assertion with no means of enforcement by the states, ultimately proved worthless for this purpose.

A partial list of Mason's fears for the Constitution might cause conservatives to reflect whether or not he considered well: that the federal judiciary would swallow up the state judiciary; that the "marriage of the President and the Senate," particularly the power to make treaties which would have the force of the supreme law of land, would allow them to override the House and deprive the people of control of the most important internal matters; that the "necessary and proper" clause was a license for usurpation; that the President's advisers, not being constitutionally defined and limited, would some day scheme against the country and prevent inquiry into their own misconduct; that the unlimited power of taxation would become a destructive burden to the people; that the great powers of the Presidency must end eventually in what would be, in all but name, an elective monarchy more powerful than the British sovereign.

These handsome volumes, bringing together all the extant Mason papers, are designed for libraries and specialists rather than to be read cover to cover. It is doubtful that the volumes will succeed, at least for a while, in the editor's declared purpose of reviving interest in Mason and bringing recognition of his contributions. None of the fashionable intelligentsia is really interested in the Founders, particularly not in George Mason whose spotless toga clashes badly with a beard and beads. But if you are one of that small company of naysayers who believe there is value in the study of causes lost, who find refreshment from the poltroons and pygmies of our own era by visiting among the Fathers, who would gain in understanding of our present ills, then you might do well to look into the letters, laws, speeches and writing of this law-giver and stern patriot, the Solon and the Cato of Virginia.

(1970)

Nathaniel Macon

Nathaniel Macon (Dec. 17, 1758–June 29, 1837), "Old Republican states-man," the foremost public man of North Carolina in the early 19th century, was the sixth child of Gideon and Priscilla (Jones) Macon and was born at his father's plantation on Shocco Creek in what later became Warren County. The Macons were French Huguenots in origin, the Joneses English or Welsh. Both families had entered Virginia in the 17th century and were of the gentry when they moved to lands south of the Roanoke River in the 1730's. Macon's early life is known only in outline. Although he attended school under Charles Pettigrew and was enrolled in the College of New Jersey (Princeton) when the American War of Independence began, he was apparently, like Washington, largely self-taught. Certainly his reading was wide and his mind neither provincial nor narrow as has sometimes been suggested. His speeches indicate an astute knowledge of foreign lands and public finance, and in a not untypical letter Macon could casually men-tion David Hume, Gustavus Adolphus, and the Apocrypha.

Macon took the field with the New Jersey militia in 1776. When his college closed he returned home to Warren County to read law (which he never prac-ticed) and English history. The interruption in his military service was not unusu-al since the Revolutionary War was fought by fits and starts and gentlemen served at will. (A similar hiatus occurred in the service of James Monroe and John Marshall.) Macon reentered the army in 1780 in a company raised and com-manded by his brother. Characteristically, he refused a commission and the enlistment bounty. He was probably present with the American forces during the disastrous Camden campaign. In 1781, while a private soldier encamped on the Yadkin River, Macon received word of his election to the North Carolina Senate, which he reluctantly entered and to which he was reelected until 1786. He was immediately recognized as a leading member.

After the War of Independence, Macon served for a time in the House of Commons and was identified with Willie Jones and the predominant anti-Federalist sentiment in North Carolina. He declined to serve in the Continental Congress in 1786 and his brother, John, voted against the Federal Constitution in both North Carolina ratifying conventions. However, Macon accepted election to the federal House of Representatives and entered the Second Congress in 1791. He remained a member of the House for the next 24 years until he took a seat in the Senate, where he remained 13 years. He represented North Carolina in Congress from age 33 until his voluntary retirement at age 70.

In the House from 1791 to 1815, he was Speaker 1801–1807, candidate for Speaker in 1799 and 1809, and chairman of the Foreign Relations Committee 1809–1810. In the Senate from 1815 to 1828, he was chairman of the Foreign Relations Committee 1818–1826 and president pro tempore 1826–1828. In both houses he served on the main financial committees and chaired numerous select committees. During his congressional service he declined Cabinet appointments at least twice, and he served long periods as trustee of the university and militia officer and justice of the peace in Warren County. For the first third of the 19th century he was the dominant personality of the predominant Democratic-Republican Party and the most respected citizen of North Carolina both within and without the state.

It was Macon's pride that he never campaigned for an office or asked any man for a vote. His legislative and political skills were neither rhetorical nor managerial. His strength and influence lay in personal force, exemplary integrity, shrewdness, a contented (or static) public, and undeviating adherence to fundamental principles. These principles, forged in the Revolution, did not change in a political career of half a century. The principles included individual freedom, strict economy and accountability in government expenditures, frequent elections, limited discretion in officials, avoidance of debt and paper money, and republican simplicity in forms.

Macon was the purest possible example of one type of "republican" produced by the American Revolution. He was satisfied with a society of landowners who managed their own affairs and wanted neither benefits nor burdens from government. He wanted a government conducted with honesty, simplicity, and the maximum liberty for the individual, community, and state. He believed that North Carolina approached this ideal, and he fought a losing battle to hold the federal government to it. To Macon the success of a democracy depended not on the progressiveness and vision of leaders but upon the willing consent of the people. Opposing most appropriations and innovations, even when he stood nearly alone, he has been described as a "negative radical." True to the spirit of *esse quam videri*,[1] Macon practiced what he preached. He was in his seat faithfully when public business was being conducted, drew from the treasury only his actual travel expenses rather than the maximum allowance (as was the practice), and lived simply in Washington, often sharing a bed with a visiting constituent.

Ideological purity did not detract from Macon's political shrewdness (he advised Jefferson against the abortive Chase impeachment, for instance) or prevent him from being chivalric toward opponents in personal relations. Despite his firmness, Macon was often pragmatic in matters of political tactics and knew when to compromise and yield to his party on smaller issues. His judgment was always well-balanced, his dealings moderate. His speeches were businesslike and to the point, his first congressional speech reportedly being one sentence. With one pithy question in debate he burst many grand congressional bubbles. "Be not led astray by grand notions or magnificent opinions," Macon told a young follower. "Remember you belong to a meek state and just people, who want nothing but to enjoy the fruits of their labor honestly and to layout their profits in their own way." With this philosophy he dominated the state for decades. In only one brief period, 1801–1805, was he a dispenser of federal patronage, and then he refused to use it politically.

---

1. To be rather than to seem: the motto of North Carolina.

Macon's political career had three phases: Jeffersonian Republican leader, 1791–1807; "Tertium Quid," 1807 to about 1815; and elder statesman thereafter. When he entered the House in 1791, he was immediately identified with the group opposed to the emerging Federalists and took a leading role in the parliamentary battles of the 1790's in which the Jeffersonian coalition was forged. These services led to the Speakership, a post which, Macon said, he entered without seeking and left without regret. Losing the chair in a disagreement with the administration wing of the party, which he felt had compromised with Federalist principles and had used rather than eliminated the federal patronage, he was thereafter identified with the "Old Republican" group. He opposed taxes, the protective tariff, a navy, internal improvements (at federal expense), all expenditures not necessary to the honest fulfillment of the most essential functions of the government, a national bank, executive patronage and discretion, and any compromise with Northern antislavery agitation. The principles that John Taylor expounded and John Randolph dramatized, Macon personified. Remaining independent, never attending the party caucus and opposing both Madison's and Monroe's elections, he supported the incumbent administration when he could and never engaged in opposition for opposition's sake. He reluctantly voted for the Embargo. During the War of 1812 he was willing to raise and support troops but opposed a navy, national conscription, and executive discretion.

By the time he entered the Senate in 1815 Macon was already a venerable figure, a stature that increased as survivors of the Revolution and exponents of pure republican principles became rarer. Although he was evidently displeased with the increasingly dynamic politics of the postwar period and felt that true republican virtue was being lost, Macon undoubtedly had a not inconsiderable impact on the next generation as a prophet of both "Jacksonian democracy" and Southern separatism. Towns and counties across the South were named for him. He was widely discussed for the Vice Presidency in 1824 and received the electoral votes of Virginia for that office. In 1828 he was wooed unsuccessfully by John Quincy Adams as a running mate. He was lukewarm to Jackson but gave the Jacksonian coalition his support as a lesser evil from 1828, and served as a Van Buren elector in 1836. He evidently regarded the emergent Democatic Party as the nearest available approach to a coalition of Southern planters and Northern republicans against antislavery agitation and economic exploitation. Opposing nullification and considering secession the proper remedy, he also chastised Jackson for his responding proclamation, which he found to be as contrary "to what was the Constitution" as nullification. In 1835 Macon was unanimously elected presiding officer of the state constitutional convention, although in the end he opposed the revisions that were adopted, especially the change from annual to biennial elections.

Macon's private life was the source of his public principles. Indeed, his classical republicanism postulated that leaders should possess virtue independent of office and should reflect and defend their social fabric rather than attempt to mold it to their own design. His father died when he was five, leaving him land

and slaves that increased under his mother's management and his own. Above average in height, of impressive presence, dignified yet simple in manners, treating all classes with courtesy and attention, a pillar of his neighborhood, colloquial in private conversation, devoted to agriculture, horses, hunting, and an outdoor life, laboring in his own tobacco fields, sipping whiskey before meals and keeping fine wine only for guests, Macon was an exemplary patriarchal Southern planter. He never joined a church but attended services accompanied by his slaves and, not surprisingly, is said to have found the Baptist most to his taste. A lifelong resident of the most slave holding county of the state, he is said to have owned 2,000 acres and 70 slaves and to have divided his estate equally with his two daughters, Betsy and Seignora, on their marriages. His home, Buck Spring, about twelve miles northeast of Warrenton, was built in the most isolated portion of his holdings and was modest for so wealthy and eminent a statesman. The plantation has in recent years been the subject of a restoration project. Macon married Hannah Plummer on October 9, 1783. She died in 1790, leaving the two daughters and a son who died in 1792 at age six. Macon's son-in-law, Weldon N. Edwards, presided over the North Carolina secession convention in 1861.

Macon is said to have destroyed his own accumulated papers, probably out of the same "republican" distaste for pomp and idolatry that led him to oppose expenditures for a tomb for Washington and to forbid the erection of a monument over his own grave at Buck Spring. This fact has discouraged biographers, although, in fact, a large number of Macon letters survive in scattered depositories and publications. He has figured in many articles, addresses, and theses concerning him specifically or Jeffersonian and Jacksonian politics. William E. Dodd's *Life of Nathaniel Macon* (Raleigh, 1903) could be amplified and corrected in many details but remains a substantially accurate and usable work. Perhaps more valuable and practicable than a new biography would be a reliable and complete edition of Macon's speeches and letters, a project that probably could be encompassed in one volume.

Likenesses of Macon are rare. Neither the state nor the University of North Carolina owns a portrait. The massive American Library Association index to 19th century engravings does not even contain an entry for Macon. Perhaps the most readily available likeness is the unidentified portrait published in William Henry Smith's *Speakers of the House of Representatives* (Baltimore, 1928).

Macon was a Plutarchian figure who helped to mold the character of his era and his state. "Mr. Macon was one of those patriots who fill a vast space in the nation's eye," eulogized the Richmond *Enquirer*, chief organ of the Democratic Party, on his death. To Jefferson he was "the last of the Romans." John Randolph, in making his will, alluded to the Virginian he had named as his executor as "the wisest man I ever knew—except for Mr. Macon." Later generations preferred a different style of democracy and tended to agree with progress-minded John Quincy Adams, who found in Macon "a narrowness of mind which education cannot enlarge, and covered by an encrustation of prejudices which experience cannot remove." Hugh T. Lefler's history of North Carolina was typical of later evaluations in observing that North Carolina remained "the Rip Van Winkle" of the states until it "repudiated the spirit of Macon." Even a sympathetic writer, J.G. de Roulhac Hamilton, found him "not a constructive force," although a detailed reexamination of Macon's career might well reveal that he was more of a "progressive" on the state and local level than has been believed, that it was remote federal power in the hands of a hostile northern majority eager to tamper with the Southern social fabric and exploit the Southern economy that he wished to negate.

At any rate, Macon's republicanism was one of deliberate choice, not of inertia. As William E. Dodd commented with a sense of marvel, *"He actually believed in democracy,"* in allowing the people to govern themselves. He was of a generation, class, and region that "knew the difference between the demands of popular institutions and special interests" and which deliberately chose a limited government as the accurate reflection of its social fabric. Certainly it would seem that the "spirit of Macon" was long the spirit of North Carolina, a spirit which, however foreign to the modern temper, lies at the heart of the origins of American democracy. Perhaps no one ever served the state more unselfishly or better displayed her traditional modest virtues.

(1990)

Little Jimmy's Last Hurrah

A politician thinks of the next election;
a statesman, of the next generation.
— JAMES FREEMAN CLARKE

A Review of *The Last of the Fathers: James Madison and the Republican Legacy*, by Drew R. McCoy, Cambridge and New York: Cambridge University Press, 1989, 386 pages.

James Madison was not "The Father of the Constitution." I know you were probably taught that in school. I myself am guilty of having foisted that old truism of the history classroom off on countless sullen but gullible undergraduates. That comes of my believing what I was told, until firsthand investigation and reflection taught me better. What Madison is the father of is every trimming and time-serving politician who ever played the middle against both ends, obscured the real issues with verbiage, and bent the Constitution to fit his own abstract conceptions of government.

All of Madison's prominence was owed to three factors—an over-facile pen; his family connections and friendship with Jefferson; and his staying power (though he considered himself too frail to take part in the War of Independence in his 20's, he lived to be 85, being the last surviving member of the Philadelphia Convention and leaving the most extensive notes of the proceedings of that closed-door affair).

Far from being the prominent member of the Convention that he portrayed himself to be, having pushed himself in by means of his father's great holdings in one part of Virginia, he found his overly grandiose and overly abstract schemes swiftly shunted aside by more experienced and sensible men. (M.E. Bradford has given a good account of this in "The Great Convention as Comic Action.") His role in securing ratification in Virginia has often been exaggerated, as has the influence, at the time, of *The Federalist Papers*. (As if such men as General Washington and John Marshall needed the help of little Jimmy Madison in securing approval of the Constitution!)

His election as President rested not on any merit or popularity of his own, but simply on his friendship with Jefferson, by which he managed by a narrow margin to win precedence over Monroe, a far better man though not as artful a dodger. Madison left the Presidency having failed as an executive, as a party leader, and as a national symbol. His large reputation in history is mostly a creation of much later times—the New Deal era especially—when politicians have found his ambiguous and protean Constitution amenable to their purposes.

Madison was not in any sense a great thinker. In Jefferson's letters and writings we can find hundreds of quotable and striking thoughts; in all of Madison's vast scribblings, very little. Of all the Founding Fathers, he, because of his superficiality, lends himself the most readily to modernization and liberalization. That is why he is called "The Father of the Constitution."

Throughout his life, as is amply documented here though to a different import than I am placing on it, he did all in his power to prevent issues from being clarified and settled, which is the classic attitude of the politician as opposed to the statesman. First allied with Hamilton in the attempt to secure a strongly centralized government, he shifted to an alliance with Jefferson to the opposite end. In his later years, which are covered by this book, during the nullification crisis he secretly played both sides for all they were worth. First, he denied that the interposition of South Carolina against the tariff was the same thing as had been initiated (if not consummated) by Virginia and Kentucky in 1798–99, which was a falsehood. (In response Jefferson's son-in-law produced the original draft of the Kentucky Resolutions in Jefferson's hand, which was an even stronger assertion of state sovereignty than what was actually adopted.) Madison attacked nullification for going too far, and then he attacked its opponents for going too far the other way. This might be considered, as it is by Professor McCoy, to be a noble pursuit of "balance" among viewpoints. It might also be considered lying and cowardice.

There were in the early Republic only two honest positions to take. One was to side with Hamilton, Marshall, and Webster in the pursuit of a vigorous centralized government. The other choice was to follow Jefferson, John Taylor, and Calhoun in defending the agrarian republic. Congressional sovereignty versus state sovereignty; a commercial progressive society versus an agrarian one. (There was no question that the overwhelming majority of people preferred the Jeffersonian version at first, if not later.) Both these positions were forthright and patriotic, involving a sincere vision of the future of America.

Madison's response—exactly that of the vile cunning politician and the timid scholar in any situation—was to take both positions at once: divided sovereignty, whatever that is, and a "balance" of interests. He was followed in this by a host of cunning politicians, especially Martin Van Buren, the real architect of modern American democracy (and not his unwitting cover, Andrew Jackson). The practical result was to confuse the issues hopelessly, to prevent their clarification and peaceful solution, and to render the national discourse forever into a deceitful game that avoided real issues.

Since Madison's later career was spent on the Jeffersonian side, he did the most extensive damage to that side—by professing to uphold its principles while constantly cutting the ground from under them. His role in the slavery controversy was the same. He condemned slavery in principle, and also condemned its opposite, antislavery.

I should make it clear that I am conveying my view of Madison, not Professor McCoy's. He is a good deal more scholarly, sympathetic, and temperate in his evaluation than I am, though he is certainly aware of, and explores in detail and with insight, some of the ambiguities I have mentioned.

This book deals with Madison's later years (he left the White House in 1817 and lived until 1836) and with certain of his disciples of the next generation, whose careers and ideas are traced up to the Civil War and beyond. Thus the book is not about the early Republic, but is a study of antebellum America and particularly of the slavery issue, which Madison and his heirs failed totally to cope with. This middle period of American history is in many ways the most important and the least understood part of our past, and this book is an honest, original, and penetrating look at some aspects of it.

One of the most interesting unasked questions in American history is what happened to Virginia after its central and premier role in the Revolution and the early Republic. It retained for a long time its prestige, and any significant Virginia politician was *ipso facto* a national figure, but after Monroe it failed to make any creative or even important contribution to our political history. This was something that Calhoun often pointed out: If Virginia would only get its act together and take its proper place at the head of the Union, most problems could be solved. McCoy does not answer the question "why not" fully, but he asks it and contributes to its answer.

There are several reasons why most American historians have not asked the question. One is that they lack sufficient historical imagination for it to have occurred to them. A more important reason is that modern Americans are simply emotionally incapable of recognizing the fact that a preponderance of their great Founders and early leaders were, in their primary social identity, Southern slaveholders. Thus they are condemned always to puerile and superficial misunderstandings of their own history. For some reason it is easier to put this fact out of mind in dealing with the early period than with the antebellum period, although, in fact, slavery was quite as salient in American life in 1787, if not more so, as in 1860. McCoy is too good a historian to avoid the hard issues, however.

Madison spent his entire life as a slaveholder, and a major one, although like Jefferson and some others—though not all—of the Southern leaders of the early Republic, he was theoretically opposed to it. He was never able, and, McCoy suggests, not really willing, to do anything about it, which, obviously, was a great tragedy. Much of the book is concerned with three followers of Madison in the next generation who also failed to make much headway: Edward Coles, Nicholas P. Trist, and William Cabell Rives. Thus we have an intimate firsthand view of the Madisonian legacy in the immediate post-Madisonian period.

All three of these figures were Virginians of the planter class. Coles moved to Illinois, emancipated his slaves, and played an important part in averting the real possibility of slavery being introduced legally into Illinois. Thereafter he became increasingly bitter and marginalized. Having, he thought, attempted to implement the Madisonian desire for emancipation, he found Madison to be, in fact, restraining and rather lukewarm.

Nicholas P. Trist, another emigré Virginian, was an intellectual dilettante who spent most of his life in minor patronage positions in the federal government. He attempted, unsuccessfully, to apply "Madisonian" principles of balance to the seam-splitting, unruly America of the Jacksonian and antebellum eras, but only succeeded in being ineffectual and irrelevant.

The most important, but least interesting, of the three junior Madisonians was Rives, who was off and on Senator from Virginia as well as U.S. Minister to France, Madison's official biographer, and probably as famous a figure in his own time as Calhoun, Clay, or Webster. Rives played the perfect Madisonian role in national politics. He was definitely for state rights, but nullification was going too far. The South was definitely justified in rebutting outside interference with slavery, but it was not justified in actually defending slavery. When the question was national bank or no national bank, Rives supported a sort of seminational bank.

Having spent his entire career working, with considerable success, to disrupt Calhoun's efforts to clarify the issues to their fundamentals and unite the South, he ended—too late by his own standards—in the 1860's exactly where Calhoun had been decades before: as a member of the Confederate Congress. It was a career of total foolishness and failure.

What is most valuable in Professor McCoy's work is his exploration of all the gradations of opinion and reaction of Madison and his three disciples as they attempted to apply their version of the Founding principles to new times and new forces. These were not few and simple views and responses but many and complex ones, as McCoy makes clear in his sophisticated exposition, and they were concerned with such fundamental matters as executive versus legislative power, or state versus central authority; with traditional principles of political economy confronted by new conditions; and with the issue of slavery and the position of the black minority in American society.

The bottom line is an indication of failure. McCoy, like any good modern, sees this failure as a sign of moral weakness in Madison and in men like him who did not follow through on their professed antislavery views by becoming abolitionists and egalitarians. In a sense, this is an unhistorical reading of the period, because freeing the black people was simply not as important a priority to Madison as it now seems to us, nor was it ever conceivable for him to adopt the modern role of Olympian reformer or to forward emancipation without riding roughshod over all the principles of government that he held sacred.

But failure did occur in a way the author does not recognize. When a real leader appeared—Calhoun, who was also a statesman and political thinker of a high order—it was the Madisonian legacy of trimming and seeking an artificial "balance" that prevented the only solution that was possible in Madison's own conception of government: It was for the South to unite itself sufficiently to deal with the issues in its own time and in its own way according to federal and consensual principles within the Union. The failure to do so created, finally, a situation with no issue except conquest and the permanent destruction of the old federal Republic, which it had been Madison's fondest hope to preserve.

(1990)

St. George Tucker

St. George Tucker's "View of the Constitution of the United States" was the first extended, systematic commentary on the new constitution *after* it had been ratified by the people of the several states and amended by the Bill of Rights. Published by a distinguished patriot and jurist in 1803, it was for much of the first half of the nineteenth century an important handbook for American law students, lawyers, judges and statesmen.

Though nearly forgotten since, it remains an important piece of constitutional history and a key document of Jeffersonian republicanism. Two sufficient reasons may be given for the neglect of Tucker's work and related, supportive writings. First, his view of the federal government as a limited, delegated agent of the sovereign people of the several states, and not the judge of the extent of its own powers, was buried by the outcome of the Civil War, the ground having been well-prepared by Joseph Story and Daniel Webster for Abraham Lincoln. Secondly, Tucker's constitutional writings were appended as essays to a densely annotated edition of Sir William Blackstone's *Commentaries on the Laws of England* which he had prepared for the use of American law students, and therefore have been nearly inaccessible and unnoticed by scholars.

St. George Tucker was born in 1752 in the British colony of Bermuda. The Tuckers were a numerous and talented family, many of whom immigrated to the mainland colonies in North America to make their fortunes. St. George's brother, Thomas Tudor Tucker, made his way to South Carolina, represented that state in the first two Congresses, and was Treasurer of the United States from 1801 till 1828, on appointment of Thomas Jefferson.

St. George reached Virginia in 1771. For a year he studied law at the College of William and Mary as did Jefferson and Marshall, under George Wythe, soon to be a Signer of the Declaration of Independence and chief justice of Virginia. Talented, urbane, and sociable, he had no trouble making his way in the best society. In 1775, at the age of twenty-three, Tucker was admitted to the bar. In that same year he was present when Patrick Henry made his stirring appeal to liberty or death.

Shortly after, he took part in an expedition to Bermuda which gained possession of a large quantity of military stores that were of great use to Washington's army. Like all of the Tuckers, St. George married well, in 1778, to a wealthy widow, Frances (Bland) Randolph, and acquired large estates in Chesterfield County. He also acquired three step-sons, one of them the five-year-old John Randolph, later to be famous as "Randolph of Roanoke." Their relationship was often tense.

Tucker took an active part in the Revolutionary war. Having been elected colonel of the Chesterfield County militia, he led them to Greene's army and is said to have distinguished himself at the battle of Guilford Court House. During the Yorktown campaign, serving as a lieutenant colonel of horse and an aide to

Governor and General Thomas Nelson, he was wounded.

Tucker's letters to his wife during his military service, which were published in the *Magazine of American History*, July and September, 1881, are exhibits of marital felicity and valuable historical source for the last Southern campaign.

After the war his law practice flourished. He was appointed one of the committee to revise the laws of the commonwealth, and served with James Madison and Edmund Randolph as Virginia commissioners to the Annapolis Convention. Tucker's career as an expounder of the new constitutions of Virginia and of the United States began in 1790 when he succeeded Wythe as professor of law at William and Mary.

Contemplating the necessities of instruction, Tucker decided to use as a text Blackstone's famous commentaries on the English law. Blackstone (1723–1780) had for the first time brought the great chaotic mass of statutory and common law into a system that could be approached by students. Published in four volumes, 1765–1769, with later editions, his work supplanted the commentaries of Sir Edward Coke (1552–1634) on the fifteenth century treatises of Sir Thomas Littleton, as the premier legal text of the English-speaking world.

Blackstone was indispensable, but for Americans it was also problematic because suffused with the principles of a monarchical and aristocratic state which Americans had recently repudiated. Americans had exhibited to the world constitutions in which the people had exercised their sovereign authority to create governments that rested specifically on their consent at an identifiable moment of history, and not long growth of authority and precedent. Such governments were delegates rather than masters of the people, and were limited to those specific powers which the people had given them. And through regular elections or if necessary a drastic reassertion of sovereignty, the people could change their government and their governors.

It was necessary, then, to republicanize Blackstone. This Tucker accomplished by extensive notes to the body of the work and by writing several dozen essays, the longest of them "View of the Constitution of the United States" and "Of the Constitution of Virginia," which appeared as appendices in the various volumes of the work (expanding Blackstone's four volumes to five). This revised, Americanized Blackstone was published at Philadelphia in 1803 and was in wide use thereafter.

While its use cannot at this date be quantified, all authorities agree that it was influential. Later American editions of Blackstone followed Tucker's method and there is evidence of extensive use in Pennsylvania and South Carolina as well as Virginia. And doubtless it was taken westward by young Virginians who immigrated to every new state in the nineteenth century.

Besides his edition of Blackstone, Tucker published several and political pamphlets and articles under pseudonyms, as was customary at the time. These included "Reflections on the Policy and Necessity of Encouraging the Commerce of the Citizens of the United States," in *American Museum*, vol. 2 (September 1787), pp. 267–274; *Remarks on the Treaty of Amity . . . between*

Lord Grenville and Mr. Jay (Philadelphia: M. Carey, 1796); *Cautionary Hints to Congress, Respecting the Sale of Western Lands*, by "Columbus" (Philadelphia: M. Carey, 1796); *Letter to a Member of Congress, Respecting the Alien and Sedition Laws*, by "Columbus" (Richmond: 1799); *Reflections on the Cession of Louisiana to the United States*, by "Sylvester" (Washington: printed by Samuel Harrison Smith, 1803); and possibly others. The essays on the common law and on slavery had been printed as pamphlets before they were included by Tucker in his Blackstone.

St. George Tucker was also by avocation a writer of moderately good verse, both patriotic and humorous. These have been collected, with an interesting introduction, in William S. Prince, ed., *The Poems of St. George Tucker of Williamsburg, Virginia, 1752–1827* (New York: Vantage Press, 1977).

In 1803 Tucker became a judge of the highest court in Virginia. In 1813 he was appointed by Madison as the United States district judge for Virginia, an important post in which he had a distinguished career, resigning shortly before his death in 1827. As a jurist, Tucker never wavered from the principles he had set forth earlier as a professor of law.

Tucker established a virtual dynasty of legal and constitutional talent which carried on Jeffersonian principles through successive generations. A son, Henry St. George Tucker (1780–1848), served in the state legislature and the U.S. House of Representatives, was chief justice of Virginia, conducted a successful private law school at Winchester, declined appointment as Attorney General of the United States by President Jackson, became professor of law at the University of Virginia, and published books on natural law, constitutional law, and the laws of Virginia.

Another son, Nathaniel Beverley Tucker (1784–1851), was professor of law at William and Mary and published three novels and a number of works on political economy and public issues. He is a major figure in the intellectual history of the Old South.

In the next generation, St. George Tucker's grandsons were equally distinguished. John Randolph Tucker (1823–1897), son of Henry St. George, was attorney general of Virginia, professor of law at Washington and Lee, counsel in numerous major cases before the United States Supreme Court, served in the U.S. House of Representatives 1875–1887, and published, among other works, *The Constitution of the United States* (2 vols, 1899). Another son of Henry St. George was Nathaniel Beverley Tucker (1820–1890). He edited an antebellum Washington newspaper, was U.S. consul at Liverpool, and served the Confederate States as an economic agent abroad.

St. George Tucker's great-grandson Henry St. George Tucker (1853–1932), son of John Randolph Tucker, represented Virginia in the U.S. House of Representatives, 1876–1889 and 1922–1932, carrying on the states rights, populist, anti-big business tradition of the state and family. He was also professor of law at Washington and Lee, and published *Limitations on the Treaty-Making Power under the Constitution of the United States* and *Woman's Suffrage by*

Constitutional Amendment.

Given the massive changes in the extent and distribution of power since the Civil War, and the resulting adjustments in accepted constitutional understandings, Tucker's states rights, limited government principles are likely to seem strange to Americans today, unless it is remembered that they were the prevailing ideas of his time and for several generations after.

The Constitution that Tucker explicates is the Constitution that was ratified by the people of the several states. It is to be understood as explicated by the ratifiers, including their reservations, some of which were embodied in the first ten amendments, a further limitation on the delegated powers of the new general government. For the assumption that the meaning and authority of the Constitution is to be found in its ratifiers, and not in the learned discussions of the Framers at Philadelphia, who were after all only drafting a proposal for the people's consideration, Tucker has the support of Madison himself. (See Madison's letter to Thomas Ritchie, September 15, 1821.)

Tucker, then, does not stand in awe of the *Federalist Papers.* He recognizes them as special pleadings for the Constitution before ratification and amendment. He finds some things in them admirable, particularly the defence of an independent judiciary, but he quotes them most often in support of the limited nature of the new government. Though Tucker is well read in political philosophy, he does not need a long historical exposition of ideas to explain the Constitution. It is for him generally clear and specific—self-evident to those who ratified it. That does not mean that he cannot call upon Justinian, Grotius, Puffendorf, Vattel, Montesquieu, Locke, Rousseau, or other more nearly contemporary writers as needed.

Tucker is the exponent of Jeffersonian republicanism, or what has been called "South Atlantic republicanism," in contrast to the commercial republicanism of New England which has been taken to be the true form of American philosophy since the Civil War.

The political background is significant. The Constitution had been ratified by Virginia and New York reluctantly (and by North Carolina and Rhode Island not at all) with reservations and the understanding that amendments would be made. Twelve such amendments were proposed by the First Congress and ten of them swiftly ratified. This "Bill of Rights" was to reassert the limited nature of the new government's powers and their dependence solely upon the delegation of the people of the sovereign states.

Hardly had the government gotten underway than the largely Northern political faction gathered under Hamilton and Adams launched an initiative to stretch those powers as far as they would go, and make light of the limits. Much of this expansion represented a desire to use the government in mercantilist ways—a national bank, a funded national debt, a commercial treaty with Great Britain. All policies which profited the commercial classes of the North and were burdensome to the immense free-trade agricultural empire of the South.

Into this conflict burst the French Revolution. The great ideas of revolution and reaction that tore Europe apart did not go unnoticed in the New World, which had just had its own "revolution," whose leaders were well aware of the power of ideas. The relation of American neutral commerce to the belligerent powers was a vexing practical issue. The ideological heat from Europe intensified intra-American conflict.

Thus, the puritan clergy of New England denounced Jefferson as a Jacobin atheist who would set up the guillotine and undermine the moral foundations of society. The real conflict, perhaps, was cultural—the highly ordered, communal society of New England where most of life was to be regimented under leaders of proper principle—and the more easy-going laissez-faire life of the South. It is a curious fact that the bourgeois leaders of the North had visions of eminent uprisings of Jacobin mobs, and supported policies to stifle dissent, such as the Sedition and Alien Laws—while the aristocratic leaders of the South declared for the people and for policies of liberality. While Jefferson rested at ease among his two hundred slaves, John Adams barricaded himself in his Philadelphia mansion against the expected attack of the revolutionary mob. These differences in culture were expressed in political styles. John Adams rode to his inauguration in a coach with white horses, insisted on being addressed as "His Excellency," and demanded strictest social protocol. The genuine aristocrat Jefferson walked to his inaugural with the Virginia militia, established the order of pell-mell at leisurely White House functions, and sent his messages unostentatiously to Congress in writing rather than going in person.

If the Federalists called their opponents Jacobins, the Jeffersonians could reply that the Federalists were dangerously imbued with "monarchical" tendencies. They did not really trust the people, giving only lip service to republicanism, but wanted a government of large, even unlimited authority. Both Hamilton and Adams had expressed themselves to be devoted admirers of the British constitution, to which they attributed most of what was valuable in the American constitutions.

Tucker spends a good deal of effort drawing contrasts between the British and American constitutions, to the credit of the latter. Most of the admired British principles he considers to be imaginary rationalizations for quite different realities. This is his response to those who he felt over-stressed the British inheritance. What Americans had deliberately created was superior to what had merely evolved in a system that did not honor the sovereignty of the people.

In 1798 the Federalist Congress passed and Adams signed the Alien and Sedition acts. The Alien law allowed the president to deport any non-citizen he deemed undesirable. No judicial proceeding was involved. For Tucker and other Jeffersonians this was assumption by the federal legislature and executive of powers not delegated and, as well, a violation of the separation of powers since it gave the president authority that belonged properly to the judiciary.

Even worse was the Sedition law which provided for criminal prosecution in federal courts of persons deemed to have made publications that tended to bring the officers of the federal government into disrepute. Several conspicuous prosecutions were made. Tellingly, the Congress that passed the act designed it to expire on the date they would leave office—in case their opponents got control.

For Jeffersonians like Tucker the Sedition law was a violation of individual liberties, an assumption of power that had never been delegated to any part of the government (they had, after all, just ratified the Tenth Amendment), an invasion of state rights, and an obvious attempt to put down political opposition and criticism of those in power.

The Jeffersonian response was the series of reports and resolutions that came out of the legislatures of Kentucky and Virginia from 1798 to 1800, written by Jefferson and Madison. These reasserted that the federal government was of specific, limited, and delegated powers. It was the agent of the sovereign people of the states and not the proper judge of its own limits. When those limits were egregiously overstepped, it was the right and duty of the states to interpose their authority and render such usurpations null and void.

The conflict of federal versus state power remained theoretical and potential while the issues were settled by normal political process. Jefferson and his party triumphed in 1800 and remained in power for a quarter of a century (during which New England states asserted similar rights in protest of commercial and military policies). There was no showdown, but for Tucker and many others, for several generations, the "Principles of 1798" remained a primary text of constitutional discourse.

Tucker takes for granted the option of secession. If the Constitution draws its authority from the consent of the sovereign, the people of the several states, then the sovereign may withdraw that consent (not something to be done lightly, of course). The people's consent to the Constitution is not a one-time event, binding them ever after to be obedient to the government. Its withdrawal remains always an option against a government over-stepping its bounds, in the nature of the Constitution itself and in the right of revolution affirmed by the Declaration of Independence.

One of Tucker's principal concerns as a legal and political thinker is to affirm the standing of the judiciary as an independent and coequal power with the legislature and executive. This is an American accomplishment to be supported in state and federal governments both. For him the judiciary is the realm where individuals may seek relief from the oppressions of the government. Its power and independence are thus essential.

But by no means does this encroach upon the even more fundamental federal principle. It is the duty of the federal courts to restrain the other branches of the federal government, not to make policy and certainly not to invade the rights of the states. The jurisdiction of the federal courts is rightly limited to the delegated sphere of federal power and carries no imprimatur of supremacy over the state courts and their jurisdictions.

But Tucker sensed the potential for just such extensions of power, something which he and other Jeffersonian jurists were committed to resist. This is reflected in his serious attention to the question of the common law and its application to federal jurisprudence. To infuse the common law into federal jurisprudence would potentially give the federal courts power over every question in society. This was the path taken, successfully, by Justice Joseph Story in both teaching and decree, and which laid the groundwork for the judicial supremacy of the twentieth century. For Tucker there was a clear answer. The common law was infused into American law because each of the colonies had adopted such parts of it as were relevant or expedient. Each state was different in this respect and each the judge of its own business. But the federal judiciary was created by the people with specific, limited delegated powers. It was not among those powers to evolve or assume legal principles from some other source. The Constitution and the laws themselves were plain enough, and unlike the common law, rested upon the consent of the people.

The states rights idea is conventionally dismissed as a rationalized defence of minority interests, particularly in regard to slavery in the antebellum South. This makes Tucker's writing on slavery particularly interesting. In 1796 he published a pamphlet proposing a plan of gradual emancipation for Virginia, and included the same as an appendix to his Blackstone. His reasoning and proposals came to naught, but they show what it was still possible to consider and discuss in the South in Tucker's time. This was, of course, before the rise of militant abolitionism in the North, and the question was strictly one for Virginians to decide.

Tucker can be seen as prophetic in a number of ways. For instance, one of the chief defects or dangers he finds in the Constitution has to do with the president, and especially his powers in foreign affairs and the military. He would have preferred to have the House of Representatives as well as the President and Senate approve treaties. He understands that it will be potentially in the power of a president to bring on war by creating a situation in which the required declaration by Congress would be no more than an after-the-fact recognition.

Tucker remains a valuable expositor of early American republicanism, well worth the attention of any who wish to understand the origins of our system, both in regard to the Constitution and in regard to the larger idea of republican government which underlies it. Scattered through his disquisitions are many gems of quotable aphorism, as when he comments that a prosperous government and a prosperous people are not necessarily the same thing. Perhaps his thinking is most concisely distilled in this statement: "It is the due [external] restraint and not the moderation of rulers that constitutes a state of liberty; as the power to oppress, though never exercised, does a state of slavery."

(1999)

Burkean on the Bench

A Review of *Joseph Story and the American Constitution: A Study in Legal and Political Thought*, by James McClellan, Norman: University of Oklahoma Press, 1971, 413 pages.

When, in 1811, President Madison nominated Joseph Story for the "New England seat" on the Supreme Court, two better-known men had declined and a third had been rejected by the Senate. Story was a mere 32, but he had a well-deserved reputation for legal learning, and he had paid his political dues: In the Federalist stronghold of Essex County, Massachusetts, he had endured beatings and ostracism for outspoken adherence to Mr. Jefferson's party. Surprisingly, however, Story on the bench proved to be a Federalist of Federalists, the indefatigable ally of Marshall in the promotion of judicial power, federal supremacy and sanctity of contract.

Story sat until 1845, comforting Marshall's last quarter century and out-lasting him ten years. Marshall was as much Story's ally as Story Marshall's. As McClellan shows, Story outranked Marshall in intellect and was often his teacher. Nor was Story's influence circumscribed by the courtroom. Not only his decisions, but his voluminous writings, including the *Commentaries on the Constitution*, made him a Constitutional interpreter of unrivaled significance and a still-supreme authority in half a dozen specialized areas of law. Add to this a Promethean influence on legal education from his sixteen-year stint at Harvard (contemporaneous with his judicial career) and we have the greatest of all our justices.

With this study, audaciously ignoring the powerful taboos of legal positivism and liberal historiography, Professor McClellan has exhumed a forgotten statesman. More important, he has, in the process, peeled away generations of parasitic encrustations and taken a fresh look at the tree of American liberty. Story, the Burkean, was convinced that the roots of American government reached into the natural law of Christian Europe, for so healthy a growth could not possibly be nourished in the thin soil of "natural rights." The natural law flowed to us through the English common law, which it was ever Story's duty to support in American jurisprudence.

Within this framework of natural law through common law, Story created profound conservative constitutional doctrines of the religious foundation of government, church-state relations, property rights and the nature of the Union, which doctrines, save the last, give little comfort to the energumens of the recent Court. McClellan's investigation of Story on these doctrines, on natural law, common law and judicial review, confirms the suspicions that for long now we have been taught things about the origins and import of our fundamental law that are not so, that, indeed, the old oak was never intended by its planters to shelter the Wide-Open Society through which we are now suffering.

Alas, it was Story's doctrine of the organic Union, the nationalism proselytized by his friend Daniel Webster, that proved the undoing of all his other labors. As McClellan knows and as Acton pointed out long ago, the flaw of Federalism was the self-contradictory attempt to establish a conservative polity by innovatory and rationalistic contrivances, for instance, federal supremacy and judicial activism. The Federalists spied a threat to order from the masses and too loose government. They overlooked the potential mischief of a corrupt elite and too much government. In discarding the social contract notion of society, Story also threw out the compact idea of the Union, the last defense of the community. Thus the Federalists forged the very instruments of oligarchical federal power which have been the main weapons against the order, tradition and property they sought to secure.

Here I would enter an objection to McClellan's flogging of Jeffersonian democracy, which he, with most conservatives, finds the villain in American degeneracy. The trouble is that the Federalist skirts were not clean either. Despite some of the speculative opinions of their leader, the Jeffersonians, too, were spokesmen for tradition and order. The question was not between order and no order but between the rival orders of Virginia and New England. The Virginians warned that the Storyite philosophy would degenerate into "monarchy" (untrammeled executive authority), "aristocracy" (judicial or bureaucratic oligarchy forcing its will against the sense of the community), and "consolidation" (perilously centralized power).

Were they not right? It was the Jeffersonians who honored rooted and deliberative government, the Federalists a near-revolutionary activism. Worst of all, the conservative philosophy of Federalism was culturally intertwined with the millenarist progressivism of New England (as is foretold by Story's abolitionism and Unitarianism) and it was the latter that came to dominate and use the nationalistic instruments and morality forged by the former.

This objection, however, does not blunt the significance for our time of Story's commentary, McClellan's skilful exposition of which, appearing not long behind Kendall's and Carey's *Basic Symbols of the American Political Tradition*, gives heart to those who hope some day to wring from the judiciary a writ of replevin on the American inheritance of ordered liberty.

(1972)

The Jeffersonian Democrat Rediscovered

A Review of *A Plague on Both Your Houses*, by Robert W. Whitaker, New York: Robert B. Luce, 1976, 208 pages.

Hardly anyone has commented upon the seeming disappearance from American life of the Jeffersonian democrat. The Jeffersonian democrat was a hardy American breed, perhaps the only political type original to this continent. Outnumbering all other species between 1800 and 1861, he was a numerous beast long afterward and was spotted quite often even as late as the 1940's. Since then he seems to have disappeared, if not into extinction at least out of the official catalogs. The disappearance is not surprising—Jeffersonian democrats, since their first discovery in colonial America, have never enjoyed academic or media respectability.

Mr. Whitaker is a keen observer. He has spotted them in the interior where they are alive and well (although restless) and number in the millions. He calls them populists. ("Jeffersonian democrat" is the reviewer's gratuitous amendment of the author's terminology, for reasons that will become apparent.) Mr. Whitaker speaks not only as a man of science, demonstrating the existence of the phenomenon. He is also an angry and eloquent advocate in behalf of an endangered species with which he is proud to identify himself.

By the author's lights America has been dominated by three successive elites, each of which has played an important role in the nation's development but each of which, after a time in power, has grown arrogant and dysfunctional. First came the planter aristocracy that founded the Union and guided it through its early perils. Having outlived its usefulness it was overturned in the Civil War by a capitalist elite which bequeathed us our economic might. That was displaced by the third and current elite which may be dubbed the welfare-education establishment. Despite its own modest disclaimers, this establishment predominates: It consumes a huge proportion of the GNP, sets the nation's agenda, and enjoys the privilege of suppressing attacks on its own legitimacy. Each earlier elite in due course succumbed to a wave of protest from the masses and the provinces—an outsider's uprising that Mr. Whitaker calls populism. The burden of his chapter and verse is that our present masters have become oppressive and their hegemony is ripe for collapse.

While I could easily quarrel with some of the particulars of his historical scheme, I would not wish to detract from the power and eloquence of Mr. Whitaker's manifesto. He is, as one of my undergraduates once described Edmund Burke, "a leading revolt analyst"—and more. Nowhere have I read a more reasoned, penetrating, and enlightened philippic against the present establishment, or rather two establishments, for it is Janus-headed. "Both your houses" denominates the welfare-education complex and its lesser counterpart, the conservative establishment which (although rather incompetently) monopolizes "patriotism" and "free enterprise" as weapons of self-interest in the same way the welfare-education Liberals monopolize compassion, morality, and progress. (By a slight permutation in the imagination, the two houses which suffer Mr. Whitaker's well-deserved imprecation become the Democratic and Republican parties.)

Whitaker, then, cuts himself loose from all comfortable havens. He writes with the independence of mind of a man who has made his way unbeholden to either establishment and with the anger of one of the great multitude of outsiders who has felt first-hand the injustice and self-righteousness which it is their fate to bear. He is a real radical, not one of the pet radicals, useful and well-paid allies of the present regime, who are trotted out now and then by the media. Whitaker, to plagiarize another undergraduate essay on an earlier populist, Andrew Jackson, "has guts."

His indictment of the reigning elite is complete. It has not only become high-handed and counter-productive, it is indeed undermining our economy, our defenses against the foreign enemy, and our social peace. And it has become almost immune from public opinion and democratic process. For instance, it supplies public schools with busing and obscene textbooks "for no apparent reason," Mr. Whitaker writes tellingly, "except to demonstrate to parents that the establishment can attack their values and get away with it." The elite's methods and goals flout the democracy of which they claim to be the advanced spokesmen and protectors. The blood and sweat, not to mention the tears, of the millions is as nothing to them. Seldom has the case been better put. Our Liberalism *is* monolithic, inadaptable, terroristic, dishonest, and dysfunctional. It does bear a negative relationship to democracy, progress, freedom (including freedom of speech), and the common man. It is a vast imposition on the "producing majority"—to use a phrase of the late conservative theorist Frank S. Meyer, another Jeffersonian democrat whom Mr. Whitaker unconsciously resembles. The present establishment does exploit the working middle classes—economically, psychologically, and even, Whitaker suggests, genetically, by policies which favor the fecundity of minority groups against that of the majority.

In the American locus, Jeffersonian democracy has been the traditional faith of the producing majority; therefore, the term seems to me a better one than populist, an elastic appellation long ago robbed of denotative content by conservatives raising the alarum against imaginary bogeymen and Liberals attempting to co-opt an affiliation with "the people" to which they have no honest claim. Jeffersonian democracy divides the political world into "producers" and "aristocrats," the last a technical term not suggesting any of the virtues traditionally associated with aristocracies. Producers are those who do their biblical labor in the vineyards and add something to the total store of wealth of the community. A producer was synonymous with a good citizen and a true "republican" in the glossary of the Founding Fathers. An "aristocrat," in contradistinction, is one who lives by unearned privilege or clever maneuver, who profits by some artificial (that is, politically-decreed) special advantage at the expense of the producers.

A Jeffersonian democrat (or populist) is not a programmatic utopian or egalitarian at all. He is one who normally goes quietly about his business. He is, in fact, an American Tory, swearing no allegiance except to King (that is, Constitution) and Country. He is propelled into political action only by an acute sense of outrage when the "aristocrats" become too reckless and extortionate. In Jefferson's time those who turned the blood of the Revolution into gold by unnecessarily magnifying the national debt aroused this response. In Jackson's time it was the owners of the national bank who enjoyed a private, politically-granted monopoly of the credit mechanism. In Bryan's time it was, among others, railroads built by government subsidies and operated by rates rigged with government connivance. Whitaker's indictment of the welfare-education complex falls in the same tradition. And the "aristocrats," those who own the profitable orthodoxy, have always cloaked their privileges and benefits with arguments of morality and social beneficence, and branded those who enter objections as ignorant renegades unable to appreciate what all right-thinkers see is the only sensible and righteous scheme of things.

The distinction between producer and manipulator that underlies Jeffersonian democracy (though my formulation does Whitaker an injustice by slighting the sophistication of his analysis) has always seemed to me to be correct from the point of view of public ethics, although there is a danger that productive but intangible services to the commonweal will be misconstrued as parasitical. The distinction, indeed, is the whole point of what the Founding Fathers meant by a republican arrangement in which nobody had artificial privileges. And, as previously suggested, this is the distinctively and instinctively American stance. All alternative public ideologies are derivative of European conditions and theories and do not come naturally to the American, although unfortunately they seem to become more and more relevant as conditions alter in the Old World direction.

Later accretions to our national store of ideologies have tended to obscure what Jeffersonian democracy meant. It is the opposite of Marxism. It postulates: to each according to his merits. The common American is a conservative and a democrat because he is the traditional American and because he acts in self-defense, not from ideology. The common American (with the possible exception of one Puritan-derived minor version) is no enemy of religion, tradition, or private property. In fact, he may be the only numerous group left in the world who can be trusted with these inestimable treasures. (Incidentally, and contrary to a widespread but apparently ineradicable impression, Thomas Jefferson was a more religious man than his "conservative" enemies Hamilton and Adams, who gave lip service to orthodoxy but were at heart freethinkers. And that is not to mention the great orthodox mass of Jefferson's followers.) Jeffersonian democracy, despite the claims of its critics, has never carried democracy to excess, it has never defied the common man (although certain intellectuals clinging to its flanks may have). It has merely said that the common man, by definition, is more likely to be disinterested than any elite and that in the long run and in the larger things can be trusted to govern better than any privileged group. Its leaders have come out of the rural (usually Southern) gentry and they have more often been statesmen, as opposed to demagogues or caretakers, than the leaders of any alternative movements.

This last point is not irrelevant to the most recent presidential election and confirms Whitaker's description of the potential for revolt. Much of Mr. Carter's appeal to the electorate lay, it seems to me, in his populism. He seemed to touch faint, fond chords of memory far back in the national psyche, of a time predating the exactions of capital, labor, and bureaucracy, of a time when soft-spoken Southern statesmen administered the government as an exercise in dignity rather than as a trough overflowing with slops for the best-placed hogs. But the echo of the applause for his nomination had not died away before he revealed himself to be (unless he should yet fool us) the captive in substance, if not in style, of the establishment.

This would seem to militate against Whitaker's forecast of the imminent new day beyond the collapse of the present orthodoxy. No intelligent observer not in the pay of the establishment can fail to feel the force of his observations on its failures. The trouble is, most of us are in its pay, in some way or other. Our previous establishments had redeeming weaknesses. The planter elite was trained to ethical public service. The business elite, in the final analysis, had to submit to the discipline of the marketplace, and it did produce the goods. But neither had at its beck the resources of modern bureaucracy and mass media monopoly.

Yet Whitaker is right. Out there south and west of the Hudson, in the sprawling suburbs, towns, and farms, live the great millions of at least potential populists. They are the American nation. They do the work. It is they who will defend the republic, if it is to be defended, against the foreign enemy. It is their hopeful homes and unfulfilled ambitions that are the great reservoir of talents that are needed to reinvigorate the arts, sciences, and professions in each generation. They sustain the values that make communal existence possible. Right now, as Mr. Whitaker so eloquently specifies, they are beleaguered. Many a heroic parent among those millions is engaged in an embittering struggle to maintain decency, order, and productivity in the face of crime, drugs, obscenity, inflation, the insolence of thugs and officials. They have been betrayed, by and large, by their clergy and teachers. The businessmen and professionals to whom they look for leadership are sequestered in exclusive enclaves, buried in narrow specializations, or co-opted into a sterile conservatism or even into the establishment which threatens them. It could be that in those millions of modest homes, in the leaders they are producing or searching out, the future is being forged. So if you would know where America is coming from and where it is going, discard your comforting liberal or conservative incantations and pay attention to one honest, angry man who has been there.

(1976)

Up at the Forks of the Creek:
In Search of American Populism

In "Populism" we are confronted with a term that raises so many different connotations in different minds that we well may wonder if the term is usable at all. It is not quite as bad, in this respect, as democracy—a word so abused that no honest thinker employs it any more. Every regime in the world has been declared democratic, with the possible exception of the Vatican and the Sultanate of Muscat.

"Populism" implies "The People." Thus it is, in most quarters, a favorable sign or symbol, a sought-after asset in the public forum. Its fate is similar to that of "liberalism," a favorable term that has come in the 20th century to cover a very different set of phenomena than it did in the 19th, to the point that its use can be extremely misleading. A few years on the hustings can destroy any political label. Consider the straightforward old Anglo-Saxon term Whig. Even at its clearest point of meaning, Edmund Burke had to appeal from the Old Whigs to the New. And it meant something different in America than it did in England; and something different in 18th century America than it came to mean in 19th century America.

Populism has suffered similar abuse, and my paper will be in large part an extended essay in definition and precise description. I am a historian, not a political theorist, and I am an Americanist. I do not profess to know enough about Europe to know which movements are "populist." For instance, I do not have the slightest idea whether, in the Spanish Civil War, one side had "populist" tendencies and the other did not; or whether both or neither did. Just possibly my freedom from European assumptions and theoretical baggage will be an asset here in focusing on what American Populism is, or has been.

My impression of European history is that since the 17th century there has been a struggle between various interests and ideologies to control the central state, and that the central state has been a given. But as I understand American Populism, from its beginnings to the present moment, it is an expression of hostility to state power and those who exercise it or seek to exercise it. It is no surprise then that most Populists have looked to Thomas Jefferson, the great original American critic of consolidated power, as their patron saint, and that the history of true Populism is closely connected to the concept of the American Constitution as a restraint on power rather than a grant of power. Populists regard state power as always corrupt and corrupting, which is an inheritance, I believe of the English "Country ideology" or opposition value system which the Americans absorbed deeply in the colonial period and which underlay the American War of Independence.

Populism in the strictest historical sense refers to the People's Party which flourished in the later 19th century, in certain regions of the American Union.

Which brings us to another part of my definition of Populism. It has always been, in this country, a regional and not a class phenomenon. I take this idea, as well as my title "Up at the Fork of the Creek," from an early essay of the late M.E. Bradford.

The People's Party is often spoken of as a Midwestern phenomenon. Midwestern is actually a vague term. "Heartland" is a little better perhaps. But Populism was not a phenomenon of the "Heartland." It was a phenomenon of the far western fringes of the Heartland, and equally or more so of the rural South. (And also of the mining regions of the Far West, which gave it the peculiar counter-productive tangent of the Free Silver movement.) There were no Populists in Ohio and they were a minority in Iowa. In the Heartland one has to go west of the Mississippi to find a Populist and even all the way to the Missouri to find very many.

And in the South, contrary to what Left historians have assumed or claimed, we do not find Populists in the impoverished "poor white" regions. We find them chiefly in the upcountry plantation belt among the small planters and larger yeomen—the same regions, exactly, that had been most in favor of secession in 1861. The Georgia Populist leader Tom Watson was tutored in politics by the Confederate statesmen Robert Toombs and Alexander Stephens. I call to witness Leonidas Lafayette Polk of North Carolina, who was national president of the Farmers Alliance and was thought by many to be the frontrunner for the Populist presidential nomination in 1892, when he died suddenly. In earlier life Polk had been sergeant-major of the 26th North Carolina Regiment, Confederate States Army, famous for its two charges at Gettysburg. In both cases, he had the same enemy. (And it may be relevant to add that Senator Jesse Helms was born and raised in the county directly adjacent to the one from which Polk came.)

As Robert McMath has shown in his fine recent book, *American Populism: A Social History*, the People's Party flourished chiefly in market agricultural regions of grain, cotton, and tobacco, which were undergoing severe economic and social dislocation. And which were undergoing enough "modernization" to bring forth forms of organization that had not been seen among American agriculturalists before.

The greatest barrier to a proper understanding of American Populism lies in the confusion that has been spread, wittingly and unwittingly, by Liberal historians. Those who have professed to like Populism have been guilty of more distortion than those who dislike it. The Liberal establishment is always in search of respectable ancestors. This is why Arthur Schlesinger and Robert Remini have written their historical fantasies about Jacksonian democracy, portraying it as something that it clearly was not in order to make precedents for New Deal liberalism. Historical interpretation very often, of course, has to do with the manipulation of symbols for their influence on present concerns.

Those who dislike Jacksonian Democracy—or Populism—have actually pictured it more accurately, if critically, than those who have claimed to favor it. A New York intellectual like Richard Hofstadter, allowing for his value system, was more honest in picturing the Populists as rural bigots than others have been in treating them as forerunners of various Left movements of later times. Of course one man's rural bigot is another man's chosen of God.

The pre-Hofstadter generation of Liberal historians who wrote about Populism were Progressives and largely small-town Midwesterners, though not from the Populist regions. They saw Populism and the historical phenomenon of Progressivism, which followed closely on its heels, as part of the same liberalizing, reformist era of American history. This confusion still largely reigns. Were not both of these movements reactions to political corruption, poverty, and the oppressions of capital? Did not both seek to restore democracy to the people and correct the abuses of the "Gilded Age"? Did not Progressivism rise to the fore just as Populism was declining?

In order to understand the conflicts and tendencies in American society from that time to the present moment, I think we need to clearly grasp the differences between Populism and Progressivism.

Populism was weighted toward the South and West, a product of the culturally most conservative parts of American society. It was backward looking, even reactionary, like most normal societies throughout history. New forces had brought new conditions which seemed unsettling and unjust—according to old dispensations. Populism was, and is, a defensive attempt to correct these new forces.

Progressivism was weighted toward the North and East. It was a phenomenon of the most educated, modern parts of American society—a philosophy of the urban professional. Far from rejecting modernism, Progressives embraced it as an opportunity. Its evils could be brought under control by Progressives—by planning, expertise, organization. Such planning, of course, translated into wealth and power for the Progressives, what became the Liberal Establishment. The longterm result has been an endless series of expensive, unproductive social plans, like the "war on poverty." Expensive and unproductive, except to their managers. Morality has almost come to be defined as holding the proper attitude toward Progressive programs, and it is bad form to point out the interestedness of their proponents.

Populism is not an agenda, but a reluctant impulse of self-defense. Seldom have real Populist leaders sought to make themselves into a new elite. What they have sought to do is to protect their people from oppressive officials. This certainly characterizes the American Revolution, and the history of political assertion that preceded it. It characterizes the much-discussed phenomenon of the Christian Right currently. According to alarmed Liberals, bigoted fundamentalists are out to construct a police state and break down bedroom doors to impose their morality on more enlightened thinkers.

But, of course, what has actually happened, is that millions of decent sincere, often simple, Christians have been provoked into action by militant obscenity, blasphemy, and atheism (not to mention wholesale child murder) invading the public sphere and officially sanctioned by the ruling elite. They are quite right.

Separation of church and state in American tradition has not meant banishing of all Christian values to the closet. All that is really desired is to restore the status quo ante.

Where the People's Party put forward specific measures they were corrective—the direct election of Senators, cooperatives, free silver, regulation of railroads and banks in the interest of producers and consumers, income tax on great wealth—they were not forwarding a socialist society but reacting to abuses of state capitalism. The Republican party did not and never had favored an open economy. By free enterprise it meant private ownership with government support and subsidy. This is the only kind of free enterprise the Republican party has ever favored. And by charges of socialism levelled at the Populists, Republicans meant government acknowledgment of the complaints of agriculture and labor, which is the only kind of "socialism" the Republican Party has ever opposed.

To the extent Populism was ideological it rested not upon an agenda of the future but upon a vision of a past golden Jeffersonian age of widespread private property and limited government. It was simply old-fashioned American republicanism. Now it may be that this kind of thinking is merely nostalgic and sentimental and idealistic, as some of my socialist friends think and tell me. Sin we have always with us, and the price of liberty is eternal vigilance. But I do not think it is only nostalgic to believe that there was a time when America had a more honorable class of leaders and a higher sense of public ethics than we do now.

John Taylor of Caroline formulated the philosophy. It was not simply an idealization of agriculture, though that was part of it. And what is wrong with idealizing in favor of a healthier and more independent life for the mass of citizens? Taylor embodied the persistent and recurrent themes of American Populism as I define it. He represented both a conservative allegiance to local community and inherited ways and a radical-populist suspicion of capitalism (in the sense of abstract finance), "progress," government manipulations, and routine log-rolling.

In many ways Taylor was a more authentic and representative Jeffersonian than Jefferson himself. Taylor's opposition to federal power, judicial oligarchy, paper money, stock jobbing, taxation, and expenditure was based upon the belief—the essence of populism and the country ideology—that the world is divided between producers and parasites. The producers are decent folk, of whatever economic class, who labor for their daily bread and produce everything of real economic and moral value in society. They are subject, in the nature of the world, to endless depredations by people whose main occupation is manipulating the government for artificial advantages for themselves. The problem for the statesman was that these manipulators are eternal and come in many guises. They always appear plausible and public-spirited—whether it is Alexander Hamilton seeking national prosperity or the Great Society bureaucracy seeking an "end to poverty."

We have here the essence of populism. Taylor defines its instincts and its political program. It is still a deeply embedded folk attitude among the American people. In the simplest terms, Populism is the community defending itself against oppressive or inadequate agents of the state. "People" here is not a Marxist or even a particularly democratic term. It is a distinction between the body of the community and the wielders of state power and their beneficiaries.

In understanding the distinction between Populism and Progressivism, consider the difference between two third party presidential candidates of recent history. George Wallace came from the Black Belt of Alabama, laid the evils of American society personally at the doors of the establishment, and was supported by small town people, disaffected workers, and small businessmen. John Anderson came from the most rockribbed Republican and abolitionist district of Illinois and was supported by well educated upper middle class people who thought American problems were to be solved by turning over power to such clear-minded and honorably motivated persons as themselves. George Wallace is a Populist. John Anderson is a Progressive.

To bring it even closer to the present day—the campaign of 1992. Who was a Populist? Jerry Brown certainly enunciated certain populist themes. Yet, in the final analysis, it seems to me, he and his supporters are homeless progressives, who think if they get in power they can do better—that is, the social problems are solvable by the right sentiments and policies. Pat Buchanan also enunciated, even more clearly, certain Populist themes—which were successful as far as they went. But he suffered from a residual identification with the Republican party establishment which he was not willing to break—and thus fell short of thoroughgoing Populism.

And what of Ross Perot? Perot, I suggest, articulated various confused and undigested elements of both Populism and Progressivism—on the one hand, national direct referendum, on the other technology and management. Thus it was never clear whether he wanted to be a Populist or a Progressive. This mess perhaps explains why we all found Perot, in the end, somehow incomplete and unsatisfactory, even those of us who were disposed to be sympathetic.

The instincts of Populism are powerful enough in the American people still for there to have evolved on the part of the government-vested interests, the "court party" in terms of the country ideology, two distinct types of pseudo-populism to gull the people.

In the election of 1840, the Whig campaign managers of General William Henry Harrison put on a very "populistic" campaign, with torchlight parades, log cabins, coonskin hats, "Tippecanoe and Tyler, Too," and no platform. Was this populism? No, merely demagoguery. Here began the real vulgarization and degradation of the American political process which has proceeded apace ever since. Here, on the part of conservative politicians whose main objective, to recharter the national bank, was hardly mentioned in the election. Here, and not, contrary to most historians, in the election in 1828 of the aristocratic Andrew Jackson.

In the election of 1860, Abraham Lincoln, an ex-Whig and corporation lawyer fronting for manufacturing and banking interests, campaigned, insofar as his ambiguous and oracular statements can be made to cohere, against an imaginary "slave power" of the South that was conspiring to enslave the Northern working man. He also went under the slogan, "Vote Yourself a Farm," referring to the contemplated Homestead Act. Was this Populism? No, just demagoguery. Even the museum-specimen Progressive-conservative Herbert Hoover promised "A chicken in every pot and a car in every garage." And a presidential candidate named Bush, from a notorious investment banking family, was compelled to blather on insincerely about "no new taxes" and "family values."

The other common form of pseudo-populism practiced is that of modern bureaucratic Liberalism, which seems to address the concerns of the people but really uses them as an opportunity to push another agenda. The New Deal certainly drew much of its support from populist impulses. But it became the expression, under the great opportunist Franklin D. Roosevelt and his "Brain Trusters," of welfare state and managerial state elites.

Consider what happened to the crime bill in the last session of Congress. The people clearly think criminals are a problem and that they should be locked up faster, more often, more surely, and longer. In Clintonian pseudo-populism this was subtly transformed into "crime" (a disembodied abstraction), being a problem. Therefore we need to spend more money on playgrounds in the inner city to keep the boys from going astray.

None of this, of course, represents any real populism. Leaders who actually believe that us yahoos should get what we want offer a real threat to the Establishment. They have to be relegated to the fringe, blitzed by the media, and, in the case of Huey Long and George Wallace, shot.

American history was for a long time written from the New England viewpoint, and many tend to think of localism and self-government, populism, in terms of the New England town meeting. This, too, leads us astray. The parts of the Heartland settled by New Englanders were least likely to support the People's party, as I suggested earlier on in discussing its sources.

The New England town meeting did involve direct democracy, but within a very limited and closed society. It was not populist. It was always infused by a sense of religious communalism and collectivism and purposefulness in terms of social regimentation and improvement. In New England, only when you get beyond the core, up into the wilds of New Hampshire, do you begin to find real populism. At any rate, New England died, for all practical purposes, a long time ago, and offers no model for modern America.

In fact, its inheritance offers the greatest obstacle to Populism; that overwhelming impulse for respectability and conformity which Tocqueville saw as characteristic of Americans. He looked mostly at New England and New England influenced areas. Populism is not respectable. The Bryans, the Wallaces, the Huey Longs are not middle-class respectable. This is the largest single limitation on their success, the best weapon of the vested interests in putting down genuine populism. This is why innumerable beleaguered Midwestern farmers could not bring themselves to abandon the respectable Republican McKinley for the wild man Bryan in

1896. McKinley proved more "popular," if not more "populist," than Bryan.

One of the unnoticed aspects of the George Wallace campaigns was an attack on the immensely wealthy foundations. The suspicion of great wealth and unevenly distributed wealth is a normal and natural sentiment. It does not relate to socialism or to enmity to private property, but simply to the ancient conception that widely distributed property makes for the health and freedom of society.

The foundations, like Ford, Rockefeller, Carnegie, as Wallace pointed out, enabled great fortunes to escape taxes and use their wealth to inordinately influence public policy against the wishes of the people. From the point of view of democratic philosophy his position is unfaultable, and it will make a great platform plank for a future Populist leader, if one should appear. The Liberals, who picture themselves as radical critics of privilege, have always, always, gotten along comfortably with great wealth and made use of it. Great wealth is the initial stage of the concentration of power and an essential means for the manipulation of society by safe reforms—those reforms that enhance the state and its guardians. Thus the pseudo-Populist Clinton appointed a Wall Street operator as his chief economic adviser.

In America, as opposed to many countries in Europe, the question of minorities must always come up. Minorities are people and are a part of the polity. However, they are by definition, as minorities, not a part of the core people. It would be foolish to think that minorities could be enlisted on the side of populism. By their very status as vulnerable, minorities are the most pro-establishment part of the population. In the classic case of the African-Americans, they were first wards of the slaveholders; then of the Republican Party; and since the New Deal of the welfare state. As long as the status quo is reasonably good, and it has never been better for African-Americans in terms of benefits/burdens ratio, they are not likely to upset any apple carts. No group of Americans is more committed to the existing welfare state and more opposed to fundamental change.

American colonial society was the freest, most self-governing, and most minimally-governed society the modern world had seen, an inheritance that was continually reinforced by the frontier and that has remained a deep folk memory. There was never enough government force to rule against the community. Land and slaves could be acquired vastly more easily than in Europe, and skilled labor was vastly more independent and valuable.

Indeed, American colonial society was to a large extent made up of disinherited younger sons, displaced workers like the Scotch-Irish weavers, or in the case of the Washingtons a clergyman driven out of his parish by the Puritans—people unusually sensitive to abuses of power. Yet, though it had an always expanding edge, an escape valve of frontier opportunity, it was also a stable society. George Washington was the fifth generation of his family in America, as were many of his neighbors.

Indeed, the Revolution was brought on by American fear of official intent to end their de facto freedom from all government except the local: the arrival of troops, of taxes, of new courts to regulate trade, of a host of placemen fresh from

Britain to fill public offices that Americans had and could fill ably, and the fear of the imposition of an ecclesiastical hierarchy. It was these signs which motivated American communities to resist, ultimately to the point of war. What they were resisting, as the list of indictments in the Declaration makes clear, was too much and too unresponsive government.

I do not want to downplay the importance of ideology. The structure of ideas in people's heads, usually inherited except in diseased ages like our own when ideologies are taken up and put off like fashions, control their perception of events. The country ideology taught Americans to fear government, the court party, as potentially oppressive. This was populism, as I see it. The Americans were not a revolting proletariat seeking to reinvent society, but the people of a region of the British Empire seeking to defend themselves.

Not until the 19th century do we get thinkers who give us an abstract European view of the Declaration as a revolutionary program. This can only be done by filtering the Declaration, ahistorically, back and forth through the French Revolution and German transcendentalism. A philosophy which becomes as much a threat to the self-government and good sense of communities, as in the modern Liberal regime, as what was overthrown.

The populist instinct as I have defined it can be seen in the entire colonial period, more than a century and a half. There were, among the relative handful of Americans living on the edge of a wilderness, threatened by savages and hostile European powers, literally dozens of "rebellions" and "revolts," so called, during the time of colonial life. No colony escaped them. A few of these were palace revolutions, factional disputes, and slave uprisings, but most of them represent exactly what I have called Populism, uprisings of the community of certain regions against official abuses. Class warfare was never raised and the legitimacy of proprietary or royal rule was never disputed. Bad officials were simply removed or thwarted by popular action.

As one historian has written:

Eighteenth-century uprisings were in some important ways different from those of today. . . . not all eighteenth century mobs simply defied the law; some used extralegal means to implement official demands or to enforce laws not otherwise enforceable, others in effect extended the law in urgent situations beyond its technical limits. Since leading eighteenth-century Americans had known many occasions on which mobs took on the defense of the public welfare, which was, after all, the stated purpose of government, they were less likely to deny popular upheavals all legitimacy than are modern leaders. . . . they could still grant such incidents an established and necessary role in free societies. . . . These attitudes . . . shaped political events of the Revolutionary era. . . . [2]

---

2. Pauline Maier, "Popular Uprisings and Civil Authority in Eighteenth-Century America," reprinted in *Politics and Society in American History, 1607–1865*, 2 vols., ed. James Morton Smith (Englewood Cliffs, N.J.: Prentice-Hall, 1973), 1:102.

British officials complained constantly that Americans were "accustomed to live without law or gospel," and they sought to bring "chaos into form" and to reduce "anarchy into regular Government."[3] But Americans did not live without law. There was no anarchy—there was simply less obedience than English officials were accustomed to receive.

The colonial revolts used to be well-known and celebrated in American history. The fact that they are nearly forgotten tells us something perhaps about the heavy weight of authority in our own time. Bacon's Rebellion in Virginia; the revolution of 1689 in Maryland; successful resistance of Massachusetts Bay colony against attempts to revoke their charter, 1635–1638; Leisler's rebellion in New York, 1688; Culpeper's rebellion in North Carolina, 1677–1680; the ejection of the proprietary government from South Carolina in 1721, the colonist's reform of the proprietary regime in Georgia in the 1740's; the revolt of the frontier Paxton boys in Pennsylvania in 1763, which led a reluctant government to adopt new Indian policies and expand the franchise; the Regulator movements in the two Carolinas just before the Revolution.

There were many more. Left historians have strained hard to find proletarian revolt, but without success. All of these actions were populist as I have defined the term, defensive uprisings of regional communities against sins of ommission or commission on the part of officials. And all of them had a degree of success.

To characterize a few of the most important: Bacon's rebellion in Virginia in 1675 came after the royal governor had failed to call elections for 15 years and failed to authorize action against the Indians demanded by the settlers furthest west. Bacon organized his neighbors in the teeth of the governor's authority and put down the Indians. When the governor declared him an outlaw, he ejected the governor from the capital. The matter ended more or less when Bacon died suddenly and his forces dispersed. This was not a proletarian social revolution but a disciplining of official abuses by the people.[4]

Even more interesting, perhaps, is the end of proprietary rule in South Carolina. There was a serious Indian war in 1715, which the settlers themselves won without help from their Lords Proprietors. When the proprietors' agents pushed trade restrictions, the collection of quitrents, and attempted to control for themselves the lands that had been acquired in the Yemassee War, the militia simply gathered and threw out the proprietary agents, leaving the elected part of the government completely in place. The de facto regime was quietly recognized by the Crown.

If time allowed we might speak about Ethan Allen and the Green Mountain boys of Vermont who forced New York, New Hampshire, and the Congress to recognize them as a separate State; the "State of Franklin" in Tennessee, which though abortive, forced North Carolina and the Congress to confirm the land

---

3. Francis B. Simkins and Charles P. Roland, *A History of the South*, 4th edition (New York: Alfred A. Knopff, 2001), p. 49.
4. I recently learned that an ancestor of mine was one of Bacon's rebels.

policies it had advocated.

Our times are remote from these assertions of popular power, of course, but it seems to me we need to recognize them to understand the populist instincts of the American people. Such assertions of regional popular power against bad government continued into the new Union.

Consider the Whiskey Rebellion, the outcome of the machinations of that evil genius Alexander Hamilton. Among many other measures designed to profit the rich and organized at the expense of the ordinary and unorganized, Hamilton put through a distillery tax. The tax was not really needed. Its purpose was to lay the heavy hand of the government on the most undisciplined part of the people and make them like it. It bore very unevenly, contrary to the spirit if not the letter of the Constitution, on the westward regions where, because of transportation problems, it was convenient to turn much surplus agricultural produce into whiskey for easier shipment.

It was an enormity, a gratuitous act of power very much like busing in a later time. Nobody likes it except the ruling elite who do not participate in it. It exists simply to prove that they can do anything they want to us and we have to take it. The regions affected by the whiskey tax understood perfectly what was afoot— all classes. No one could be found to enforce and prosecute except outside appointees—something Americans not long before had conducted a successful war against.

But what is most interesting is the contrast between the official story that has dominated the accounts of establishment historians since the time, and what actually happened, which was, indeed, a populist triumph. According to the official account, a riotous revolt against just federal law broke out in the backwoods of Pennsylvania. President Washington sent out the army and dispersed the mobs and upheld the majesty of the government. According to John Marshall's biography of Washington and other Federalist accounts, the new Union was thus saved from anarchy and impotent government.

Here is what actually happened. The people in the affected areas simply refused to pay the tax. This was true everywhere from Pennsylvania to Georgia, not just in Pennsylvania, and their public officials backed them. In western Pennsylvania a few of the tax agents were roughed up slightly, had their horses' tails cropped or were doused with molasses, reminiscent of protests against British taxation.

There was no serious violence, but it gave Hamilton the opportunity to send armed marshals out to harass the people. The state of Pennsylvania called out the militia to defend itself from the federal gunslingers. There was an altercation in which two protesters and one federal marshal were killed. This was the pretext for Hamilton and Secretary of War Knox to send in troops—something vigorously opposed by the Virginians in the Cabinet, Jefferson and Edmund Randolph. The governor and the chief justice of Pennsylvania protested that the federal government was in violation of the Constitution, since such invasions could only be mounted at the call of the state, to suppress rebellion or repulse invasion. The state had not called and there was no rebellion and no invasion except by the federal government.

Hamilton mobilized the whole army, 13,000 men, and marched them into western Pennsylvania. They stayed a few weeks. Nothing happened. People waved politely from the fields as the soldiers marched by, the tax was paid quietly where the troops were, it still went uncollected everywhere else. The troops left and the tax ceased being paid. It was never paid again anywhere and when Jefferson and his friends got into office in 1801 it was not only repealed but refunded.

Meanwhile, Hamilton's official errand boys got warrants issued for "treason," against 150 citizens of western Pennsylvania, an extremely dubious constitutional proceeding. The grand jury dismissed two-thirds of the indictments immediately. Thirty-one people were brought to trial. The juries, against high-handed efforts by the federal judges to secure convictions, found not guilty in all but two cases. The two convictions were of a notorious drunk and a moron, men who obviously were not guilty of treasonable intent and who were later pardoned.

Thus ended perhaps the greatest populist triumph in American history, though it was subsequently reinterpreted to make the government oppressors look good. Whether this could happen now, given the federal establishment's near monopoly of heavy firepower, remains to be seen. There are some similarities, but a much more sinister scenario to the recent government massacre of women and children in Waco. Suppose the authorities of Texas had declined to go along with the federal invasion? Suppose the citizens to be suppressed had been more numerous or less odd? Would there have been a different outcome? In the court proceedings the judge was clearly partisan, as in the Whiskey Rebellion, yet the juries released many of the defendants. Will American populism have to take some such course in the future against entrenched and recalcitrant power that controls the courts, the communication media, and the police? Will the holders of power and privilege yield to persuasion and sentiment and political dialogue?

Populism, as I have defined it, is still deeply engrained in the American character, though it grows more diluted perhaps with each passing decade. It is always faced with John Taylor's dilemma, which means its successes will always be temporary and limited. If one bad agenda and establishment are defeated, there will always be others waiting plausibly in the wings to manipulate the state. This is an eternal dilemma of popular government. Such a dilemma is, of course, infinitely preferable to those presented by any other kind of government.

To be successful, populism does not need the established respectable leadership of a national political party. It needs wild men like Pat Buchanan who are ready to kick over the traces and call a spade a spade. It needs the support and assertion of at least some states, and some state authorities. The states are what we have got and the best instrument we have for checking federal power. It will take overwhelming populist sentiment, which is possible in the west and possible though less so, in the south, to begin to counter federal oppressions.

(Conference on "Populism and the New Politics," Cooper Union, New York City, December 2, 1994)

American Populism

A Review of *American Populism: A Social History, 1877–1898*, by Robert C. Mcmath, Jr., New York: Hill and Wang, 1993, 245 pages.

"Populist" is a term so fraught with distortion and so apt to raise misleading connotations that we probably should find another word to use. It is worse in this respect than even "Whig" or "liberal." Taken precisely, it refers to a political movement that swept some agricultural regions of the further Midwest and South in the late 19th century.

American historians have generally treated Populism in one of two ways: They have either confused it with the Progressivism that followed shortly on its heels, as a forerunner of the New Deal and modern liberalism; or, in a slightly more sophisticated and honest version, they have dismissed it as misguided rural bigotry irrelevant to the goals of enlightened urbanites.

The first interpretation is clearly wrong. It is true that there was some slight coincidence of political goals, in terms of federal legislation, arising from the Populists' search for specific remedies. But Populists were basically rural Jeffersonians who mistrusted the remote and concentrated power of the Eastern elites who were the most obviously observable cause of their own distresses. Most of the Progressives, at least in the East, were self-consciously modern. They believed in the rule of elite urban experts (themselves) to solve all social ills by the application of science and systematization (regimentation). They were hired hands of the ruling class despised by the Populists, and still are. No Progressive that I know of was an enthusiast for free silver, and Progressives from east of the Mississippi almost all joined the homefront clamor for the War to End All Wars. Populists did not, and in fact provided the greatest core of patriotic opposition.

The first school of historians wanted to find honorary ancestors for the 20th-century political movements they favored and over-emphasized the element of Populism that suggested a stronger central control of the economy. The latter school was a later generation of Ivy League liberals who wanted to distance themselves from the at-times messy and uncontrollable tendencies that were likely to develop if American yahoos from the boondocks were turned loose. Thus, they emphasized the bigoted and eccentric aspects of the Populists that were more likely to lead to Joe McCarthy than to George McGovern.

Most certainly the Populists were ethnocentric, and some of them were eccentric as well. But there is not the least evidence that the Populists were any more ethnocentric or eccentric than any other Americans of their time, including the conservatives and the Progressives. As American historians have tended over and over to do, these writers built their interpretations of our multivarious and magnificent past on small fragments of movements rather than the whole. (They have done this with the Revolution, Jacksonian democracy, Reconstruction, and much else.) That is, they always emphasize the bits of evidence that support whatever interpretation the Northeastern intelligentsia finds fashionable at any particular moment and ignore the substantial evidence that conflicts. Thus, Arthur Schlesinger uses a few Boston intellectuals to interpret Jacksonian democracy, and Populist historians have used a few crazy Kansans to characterize a much larger and different movement.

We now have for the first time a careful, accurate, full, and well-synthesized survey of Populism in the work of McMath, an economic historian. McMath understands the social and religious fabric, the mores, and the inheritance of political ideas out of which Populism arose. He understands the ecology and economy of the grain, cotton, tobacco, and mining regions where the movement flourished.

He gives a clear and succinct account of the origins of Populism, its impulses, its social fabric, its political history (nationally, regionally, and state-by-state), and its relation to other phenomena such as the cooperative, labor, and free-silver movements. More importantly, he understands the basic political inheritance, which was not socialist or Progressive but which rested on pious allegiance to Jeffersonian democracy and the defense of the liberties of the common decent people who labored in the earth and produced real goods, as opposed to the slick operators who did not delve and spin but grew rich on the government. (The bank and railroad corporations that the Populists attacked were, after all, not paragons of private enterprise but rather privileged collaborators of the political elite.) The author also understands that these instincts are as much or more "conservative" than "liberal," although he clearly prefers the latter.

No, Populists were not the kind of people who wanted to confiscate your income, unless you were particularly rich and arrogant. They were not the kind of people who would make you wear your seat belt and forbid you to light up a stogie, for your own good, or send your children across town to achieve some abstract balance of school population and the Marines halfway round the world to save democracy in some place where they don't know democracy from cornflakes. We ought to give the glory of fathering (or rather mothering) those great accomplishments to the Progressives. A Populist, on the other hand, is someone who thinks those bastards in Washington have too much power. He votes for George Wallace, Ross Perot, or Pat Buchanan, not for George McGovern, George Bush, or Bill Clinton.

Ponder this wonderful reactionary and timely passage from Ignatius Donnelly's oration at a Populist National Convention:

> We meet in the midst of a nation brought to the verge of moral, political, and material ruin. Corruption dominates the ballot box, the legislatures, the Congress, and touches even the ermine of the bench. . . . The newspapers are subsidized or muzzled; public opinion silenced; business prostrated, our homes covered with mortgages, labor impoverished, and the land concentrated in the hands of capitalists . . . the fruits of the

toil of millions are boldly stolen to build up colossal fortunes, unprecedented in the history of the world, while their possessors despise the republic and endanger liberty. . . . We charge that the controlling influences dominating the old political parties have allowed the existing dreadful conditions to develop without serious effort to restrain or prevent them. They have agreed together to ignore in the coming campaign every issue. . . . In this crisis of human affairs the intelligent working people and producers of the United States have come together in the name of justice, order and society, to defend liberty, prosperity and justice.

(1994)

George Wallace

A Review of *George Wallace: American Populist*, by Stephan Lesher,
Reading, Massachusetts: Addison-Wesley, 1994, 587 pages.

In a healthy society people live with a wide time frame. They know and
make use of the experience of their forebears. They build houses and plant trees
that will be enjoyed by their descendants. Among the many things which our
Founding Fathers took for granted but which we have lost was a social fabric in
which people knew the character, at least the public character, of their leaders in
depth. Public esteem was a reward of real, remembered services to the commonwealth, not of media celebrity or promises of payoffs.

Thus, in a healthy society, people would know that George Bush, running for
the Senate in Texas in 1964, claimed to oppose the Civil Rights Act of that year,
although this stance belied his constant support for "civil rights" bills both before
and after. People would have understood that Bush was in the habit of lying on
the hustings to obtain office, and no one over the age of 13 would have believed
him in 1988 when he promised not to raise taxes and to bear down on thugs. Had
we anything but the shortest memory, we would have known that he would likely do the opposite—raise taxes and persecute policemen for violating the "rights"
of thugs.

Of course, it was not in the interest of either his opponents or the media to
point out the lie, because as mutual members of the ruling class they were even
more committed than Bush was to raising taxes and coddling criminals. Indeed,
they attacked Bush not for making false promises to the American people but for
dividing the common front of the Establishment by even discussing forbidden
policy alternatives. The people had little choice but to take the lesser evil.
Routinely, we accept the most preposterous claims by public figures because the
frame of reference of our public discourse is so short.

The other side of the unconsciousness of history is the neglect of posterity:
American public discourse, which suffers from terminal infantilism, is carried on
as if posterity did not exist. It does not matter if we pile up an unpayable debt
(which our descendants will have every moral right and practical incentive to
repudiate), nor do we even consider whether it will really be a good thing if those
descendants have to live in a society dominated by Mexicans and Chinese.

These reflections are prompted by the first full-scale biography of George
Wallace, as well as by a recognition of how completely Wallace has dropped
from public consciousness. The biography is a good one, not sympathetic but
balanced and knowledgeable. Lesher is a liberal—but also an experienced and
honest reporter who has covered Wallace closely for much of the past 35 years.
He has not relied solely on his own observations, however, but has done solid historical research as well, making his book as thorough a biography as we are like-

ly to have. Not the least of its virtues is a documented, blow-by-blow account of the civil rights upheavals of the 1960's, a subject that so far has been recounted only as mythology and that badly needs detached historical examination. The author has a feel for Wallace's Scotch-Irish forebears, Reconstruction, and the beleaguered rural life of the South in the late 19th and early 20th centuries. He is therefore in a position to appreciate the roots of American populism and George Wallace himself as its representative.

Lesher makes large and, I believe, well-founded claims for Wallace's importance. "Wallace is the most influential loser in modern American politics. . . . Every President from Nixon to Clinton based his successful campaign on some key elements from the Wallace political canon. . . . From 1968 to 1992 no person was elected President without clearly embracing and articulating (though not necessarily implementing) the Wallace issues." Accepting this argument requires an effective memory of the tepidness of Republican discourse prior to the feisty little governor of Alabama's dashing foray into the northern primaries in 1964. In that day, no Republican would touch the "populist" issues of crime, busing, welfare, "family values"—since doing so was regarded as treasonous consorting with the enemy. (Wallace's other issues, including the over-concentration of wealth and the excessive power of foreign capital, are just beginning to be addressed.)

Prior to Wallace's dramatic appearance, so far as the national public discourse was concerned, the racial problems of the United States were confined to the South. The public understanding was limited to a view of noble Democratic and Republican statesmen passing legislation intended to force the South into rising to the impeccable standard of social justice enjoyed by the rest of the country. Wallace's campaigns, along with the Watts riots, revealed that hypocrisy. It was the Wallace Democrats who made Ronald Reagan President and who sent George Bush back to Texas. Lest we forget the importance of George Wallace at the apex of his career (and students entering college now were born after he was shot and after the McGovern campaign), it is necessary to recall some figures from the Democratic primaries in 1972: Michigan—Wallace 51 percent, McGovern 27 percent, Humphrey 16 percent; Maryland—Wallace 39 percent, Humphrey 27 percent, McGovern 22 percent.

Wallace's impact is not surprising. It takes a heroic and intelligent outsider to change the public discourse and bring focus to real issues, always. Ruling-class politicians say only what it is already known to be safe to say. Such is "the genius of American politics." The interest of Establishment politicians is never in the truth, never in effective policy; it is, first, in maintaining their own power, and, second, in looking after the undiscussed interests of those who keep the brown bags full of cash.

Not only liberals but also Republican conservatives conducted one of the nastiest campaigns in American history against Wallace. He was, for instance, the victim of Nixon's dirty tricks as much as or more than McGovern. I well remember how *National Review* pulled out all the stops to prevent defection from

Republicans to Wallace. Wallace was a conservative only on social issues, wrote that perspicative journal; he was a populist and socialist on economic issues! After all, his state actually spent money on welfare and sought federal dollars! As if there were a single Republican governor, congressman, or presidential contender who did not do exactly the same. And all in defense of the Nixon regime of price controls and affirmative action.

From this juncture, looking over the evidence of that day, it is clear that what the left and right establishments feared was not George Wallace, socialism, or racism. What they feared was the American people. As Wallace put it in 1972: "When the government tries to force masses of people against their will to conform to certain guidelines involving their children, their taxes, their labor unions, their property, it would have been a phenomenon if they had not given vent to their antagonism and anger at this drive to make everyone conform to what the pseudo-intellectual thought the average citizen should conform to." Or, as he said on another occasion: "When politicians succumb to anarchists in the street, then they haven't got what it takes to lead us out of the morass." What he said then is still true, and no one has said it any better since.

This is populism. It is a threat to the subsidies, tariffs, and contracts that Big Business defines as "free enterprise" (the only kind of free enterprise the Republican Party has ever defended). It claims that farmers and labor want a fair shake, a level field, so it is "socialism" (the only kind of socialism the Republican Party has ever opposed). Populism is also a threat to the most hallowed of all American values: respectability. America, which is nothing if it is not a land of "pseudo-intellectuals," is governed by fashion. No issue in America is ever considered on its truth or falsehood, only on whether the "right people" find it acceptable or unacceptable. Our Founding Fathers understood that patriotism and justice would often be limited by self-interest, ambition, stupidity, and demagoguery. They could not imagine a situation in which millions were so lacking in ordinary firmness of character that they would be unable even to consider a question of truth and justice. No one wants to say something that is not in fashion. Wallace's astounding and colorful candor had to be put down.

His was a candor that has not since been equaled, though Pat Buchanan perhaps came close—and received a similar response. I still remember with pleasure how Wallace refused to be defined and confined by the media but insisted on and succeeded in making his own points. My favorite of many is the occasion on which an arrogant Republican fouled the Senate chamber with the accusation that Wallace was mentally disturbed, basing it upon the small veteran's disability pension that Wallace received. Said Wallace: "I receive 10 percent disability for a nervous condition caused by being shot at by Japanese airplanes and anti-aircraft guns in combat missions during World War II. To what does Senator Morse attribute his condition?"

What American has paid a higher price than Wallace for his public courage? Two decades of invalidism and pain. Lesher recounts fully Wallace's recantation of white supremacy, his deliberate efforts at reconciliation with the black people of his state and of the country at large. As he rightly observes: "It was supreme-ly ironic that as Wallace and the South moved closer to the goal of racial recon-ciliation, much of America was turning in the other direction." But Lesher, I fear, does not really know the true explanation for this irony. It is not that the South, for the first time in its four centuries of history, has been converted to the abstract ideology of equality. It is, rather, that the South, unlike modern America, is still predominantly a Christian society.

(1994)

Faulkner's Declaration of Independence

When William Faulkner addressed the Delta Council, an organization of farmers, at Cleveland, Mississippi in 1952, he spoke about the Declaration of Independence. The noble American postulate of the right to life, liberty, and the pursuit of happiness, Faulkner observed, seemed to have devolved into little more than a shorthand for material security. His insight was confirmed a few years later when Vice-President Nixon confessed to being unable to counter Khrushchev's argument that capitalism appealed only to man's baser nature while communism was a spiritual philosophy.

Americans once knew, said Faulkner, what the right to life, liberty, and the pursuit of happiness meant, because most men had been without it. Historically, that right was identified with strenuous efforts, not with material abundance. The men who made the hard and often fatal ocean voyages to found new colonies, who challenged the world's greatest power for their independence, who repeatedly penetrated the wilderness, were not seeking comfort. To pursue happiness did not mean an easy sinking into an anonymous hedonistic mass; it meant taking an active responsibility. "Which was exactly what we did, in those old days."

Our Founding Fathers did not glory chiefly in the fact that we were a prosperous people (though they did find that a source of satisfaction) but in the fact that we were a virtuous people. And "virtue" did not mean a mere puritanical avoidance of minor vices or that commercially circumspect behavior designed "to win friends and influence people." Virtue had a stern Roman connotation. It was a striving for republican ethics and personal honor. Men were not virtuous because they enjoyed the boon of self-government. Rather, they enjoyed the boon of self-government because they were virtuous enough to earn and to keep it.

Americans "did not mean," said Faulkner, "just to chase happiness, but to work for it." And by happiness they meant "not just pleasure, idleness, but peace, dignity, independence and self-respect; that man's inalienable right was, the peace and freedom in which, by his own efforts and sweat, he could gain dignity and independence, owing nothing to any man." Faulkner's words must be seen primarily in light of the biblical injunction about the necessity to labor for our daily bread, an assumption that implies a transcendent dimension in labor. Faulkner also knew that "inalienable right" was a term used in a political context. Man's happiness was not pursued atomistically, but within a civil community. The pursuit of happiness could not properly be read to mean putting consumption before labor or pleasure before obligation. Nor could it validate the distortions of sophists who, beginning in the 19th century, took the dependent clause about equality as the main point, as a jeremiad. Equality was merely the condition appertaining to the individual struggle for freedom and dignity, not a program to be implemented or a guarantee of results.

Faulkner was attempting to reemphasize the sacramental aspect of man's work and liberty, to free them from the materialist and utilitarian aura they had taken on. Man must live by bread, but he does not live by bread alone. The sane man, as Faulkner more than once illustrated in his fiction by contrary example, does not work to pile up riches. He works for the welfare of those of his blood and name—including the generations to come—and for his own dignity as a member of the community. His work and the liberty that makes it possible are not to be seen chiefly as a utilitarian search for maximum profit. Neither democracy nor economic productivity are satisfactory without the spiritual striving that Faulkner was pointing to. He knew, of course, that man would usually fall short of spiritual goals oftener than he would attain them.

Though he was probably not conscious of it, Faulkner was following a theme common in 19th-century Southern political literature. American democracy depended not so much upon its pragmatic methodology of the greatest good for the greatest number as upon its chivalric inheritance of striving for a code of conduct worthy of republicanism. The consent of the governed, Calhoun repeatedly warned in his fruitless attempts to clarify the concept of majority rule, was not a mere counting up of heads with the pie to be divided among the party with the largest numbers. It was a condition of intangible spiritual assent to the higher purposes of a commonwealth, an assent which required restraint and magnanimity on all sides.

Faulkner called upon his audience to remember not just the pragmatic and productive side of their liberty and labor but the chivalric and spiritual side. It is the linking of honor, courage, and loyalty to the earning of our daily bread that gives us whatever dignity we achieve. It is this that tells the plowman that he is not merely scratching in the earth but making it fruitful according to divine injunction; that tells the entrepreneur that he is not just making a quick buck but creating something useful; that tells the writer he is not only satisfying his vanity but communicating something of value to his fellow man.

Faulkner was not optimistic. "We knew it once, had it once. . . . Only, something happened to us." The farmers who could not comprehend accepting a payment from the government *not* to grow cotton were anachronistic, even in the 1930's, even in Mississippi. We no longer "believed in liberty and freedom and independence, as the old fathers in the old strong, dangerous times had meant it."

The materialist view of democracy has gained more ground since Faulkner spoke. Many would even argue today that America is actually *premised* upon rejection of the sacramental view, as if the Founding Fathers' unwillingness to state a preference among Christian denominations was equivalent to a rejection of Christianity. As a society, we act as if we believe that the health of the commonwealth consists of things that can be counted—the GNP, the growth rate, the unemployment rate. But the social organism, like the human, can give off good vital signs and still be despairing unto death. Does economic growth always mean a better life for our citizens? Possibly, but so far as one can tell from public discussion it is an independent and eternal value. We are even told that it is our unavoidable fate to admit millions of foreigners to take their places as factors of production and consumption. It is not worth asking, apparently, whether this "growth" will be of actual benefit to our citizens. Beyond that, if, in the process of economic growth, our culture turns into something other than what we want, then that is seen as merely an unfortunate byproduct.

Our national defense is a question only of material means—more money, a better defense; less money, a poorer defense. It does not seem relevant to ask what we are defending and whether we have the guts to do it: It is all a question of means. The soldier willing to die for his country is identical to the mercenary; the leader of dash and courage is interchangeable with the military bureaucrat— after all, they receive the same training and are paid the same salaries. A society that has a spiritual certainty that its existence is worth defending regards the question of means as merely subsidiary, instrumental. A society that, on the other hand, believes it can purchase its defense with money alone is already so far out of touch with reality that its survival is in doubt. So is the society that believes its defense to be a question simply of efficiency in the use of material means. Such a society is suffering from the materialist delusion that it can ignore the terrible contingency of human fate and the need to strive for courage and wisdom.

The same delusion suggests that by relieving a man's material wants you make him virtuous. It might, indeed, in some cases help, but the formula is misleading. If, in so doing, you succeed also in convincing him—and others—that they need no longer strive for virtue, then you have undermined the possibility of a commonwealth in which either prosperity or virtue can flourish. Further, such utilitarian assumptions are bound to work against the individual liberty that the Declaration and Faulkner referred to; they are bound to lead to collectivism.

Faulkner quoted a maxim of an Irish statesman which said that God granted man liberty only on the condition of eternal vigilance, "which condition, if he break it, servitude is the consequence of his crime and the punishment of his guilt." A child I know wrote the President that in order to save fuel he should make everyone ride horses. From the materialist perspective that pervades our society the youngster was completely logical and public-spirited. His innocent ignorance of the coercion that would be required to implement his suggestion was no different from the ignorance that marks most of our social policy. A well-known scientist recently declared that "we" have the technology to solve the problem of world-wide hunger and that therefore "we must" do so. He assumes, alas, that it is merely a question of means. If his hope is only that the demonstration of available means will enlighten mankind and allow it to save itself from hunger, then I applaud him, though I think he is mistaken. For how will he deal with communism and its planned hunger, or with those societies for which the solution to hunger is to receive perpetual aid from others? But if he means by his assertion that some collective American "we" should undertake to solve the world's problem, then I regard him as a social enemy. I can see what such a materialist fantasy will mean to an American working-man who is not hungry but who is strained to pay for his family's medical needs, for the gas he needs to get to a place to earn a living, and for a neighborhood where his children will be safe—

his last neighborhood having been ruined by the same people who propose that it is his duty to save the world from hunger.

I do not wish to draw from all this, and I do not think Faulkner intended to draw from it, primarily the conclusion that the free market is preferable to the collectivist state, although that is true. The free marketplace is a pillar of prosperity and a prop to republican liberty. However, I think Faulkner meant that we have our priorities reversed. We are putting the instrument before the spirit. The market does not guarantee virtue. It does not guarantee anything except perhaps a chance to make the most of what nature and our parents gave us. To the contrary, our virtue, won over and over again in daily struggle, is a necessary precondition for the free market. To ignore this is not merely a mistake; it poses a peril that, in our confusion of values, we will lose both our liberty *and* our daily bread. Yet to ignore it is exactly what America does—at least at the level of public discussion and decision, while many of us, mercifully, still continue to observe moral reality as we plow our humble furrows.

(1983)

Chapter Three

The Lost Constitution

What the Founders Didn't Count On

> *I assert that the people of the United States . . . have
> sufficient patriotism and intelligence to sit in judgment on
> every question which has arisen or which will arise no matter
> how long our government will endure.*
>
> — WILLIAM JENNINGS BRYAN

As citizens it is fitting that we engage in acts of civic piety while celebrating the bicentennial of the federal Constitution. That celebration acknowledges that in some sense the Constitution is a success. Given the long record of the crimes, follies, and misfortunes of mankind and the perishability of free and popular governments, it is a success in which we can take great satisfaction. But as a historian and even as a conscientious citizen, I cannot put aside a disquieting question: Which Constitution am I being asked to celebrate?

Even if we do not subscribe to an "evolutionary" rendering of the Constitution (as opposed to "original intent"), we are forced to recognize that the Constitution has a history. Besides many lesser scars, it carries on its face the great and bloody gash of Civil War and Reconstruction, an unparalleled social upheaval which was in its essence a question of constitutional interpretation. Even if, carried away by the moment and the warm glow of patriotism (not something to be despised), we can put aside the complications of history, still, we are confronted with a Constitution that means different things to different people— things that are sometimes mutually exclusive.

The Framers and several subsequent generations of Americans were fond of days of public prayer and thanksgiving. (Even that majority who, contrary to what some would tell you, were not Puritans.) Such would provide a proper way to observe the bicentennial of the Constitution. We could reflect on our legacy, and rather than wallow in self-congratulation, could perhaps consider how we could better be worthy of it. But alas, our brilliant legal minds have recently discovered that the Constitution has "evolved" so as now to prohibit public religious observances.

It is curious that the more our rabid secularists exclude genuine religion from public life, the more permeated with pseudo-religious emotion public life becomes. The people who want to exclude prayer from public schools are the very same people who whip up and profit from a misplaced religious emotion for the late Kennedy brothers and the late Dr. King. This is to turn the Founding Fathers on their heads, for they would neither have excluded religion from public life nor deified common human beings. And would have considered either tendency anti-republican.

With our best option excluded, how then should we approach this bicentennial? I think I have a good idea of how we shouldn't celebrate it, presuming we want to be true to the spirit of the Founders. How we will celebrate, officially, will, alas, be a lot closer to showbiz than to public prayer and thanksgiving.

Opposing the Bork nomination, someone recently wrote to the "Letters" column of *Time* (August 3, pp. 8–9): "His reliance on original intent precludes the notion that the Founding Fathers originally intended us to evolve as a people into something better than we were. The nation, and indeed the President's legacy, would be better served by a Justice who views the Constitution as a living part of the present rather than a relic from the past."

This passage encapsulates a vast region of mischief and misunderstanding, which includes both the proponents and the opponents of "original intent." A few obviously political points can be made: Would we be a better people by having more abortions? by executing fewer murderers? by having fewer prayers in fewer places? by oppressing more people with reverse discrimination? But it is more interesting that the letter-writer does not reject "original intent." Indeed, logically, no one can. Rather he has supplanted the "original intent" of the written Constitution with an "original intent" of the Founding Fathers for us to "evolve as a people into something better than we were." Those realistic republicans, the Framers, skeptical of human nature and anxious to construct a power that was both effective and limited, content with compromise, have been converted into a priestly caste who bequeathed to us a secret mission of evolving into better beings.

This appeal to the higher law is legally, logically, and historically an absurdity. It traces back not to the Founding but to transcendentalism, which was a 19th-century vulgarization, by a small but influential group of Americans, of German philosophy. Carlyle took Emerson around the London slums again and again, but he could never make him believe in the reality of the Devil. This letter-writer could be taken around history again and again but could never be convinced that the Framers did not share his aspirations. They were sensibly hopeful men and principled republicans, which is not the same as devotees of national "evolution."

This confusion of the Constitution with some sort of subjective higher law, one way or another, is nearly pervasive among both the "liberals" and the "conservatives," though it takes different forms at different times. Though a good deal more clever and circumstantial about it, the faculty of the Harvard Law School (and thus the Supreme Court for the last 40 years) present essentially the same view of the Constitution. They have read into it an intent, or at least a natural tendency, to evolve into meanings that extend the ideological program of social democracy. The Constitution evolves, but only in the direction *they* say. Although evolution is presumably by definition open-ended, it cannot evolve in directions they do not approve of, even if such an evolution is compatible with its letter and history. The Supreme Court is supposed to read the election returns, but only if the returns turn out their way. Once the Court has discovered something in the Constitution, no one else is allowed to discover something that contradicts it—a curiously limited and controlled form of evolution. Thus there is a federal right to prevent the states from *prohibiting* abortions, but there can be no federal right to prevent the states from allowing them. In fact, both propositions are nonsense because in the real "original intent" of the Constitution (even with the 14th Amendment added) abortion is not a matter in which there is any federal power, nor any judicial power except in the most limited sense.

The simple truth is that the Constitution of our forefathers is not very compatible with the commercial progressivism by-way-of-federal-power of the "conservatives" and not compatible at all with the programmatic egalitarianism by-way-of-federal-power of the "liberals." Since these have become the foremost American values (at least in effective political terms), the Constitution has had to give. The question is not between "original intent" and interpretation, it is who will interpret; not whether the Constitution will give, but how much and in what direction.

So incompatible is the Constitution with programmatic egalitarianism that we have had to invent a secret history of abolitionism on the part of the Framers (which has been alluded to in every bicentennial statement I have seen, with greater zeal by "conservatives" than by "liberals"). On the flimsiest evidence, against both the letter and the substantive history of the instrument, we have postulated that the Framers intended to do away with slavery but could not quite manage it immediately. It is true that some, not all, had vaguely antislavery sentiments which in general had a lower priority than the interests of the Maine codfish industry, but no one believed—neither the Framers nor the public—that they possessed the power to abolish slavery. (It is one thing to be pleased that the 13th and 14th Amendments did away with slavery three generations after the Founding; it is another to attribute false motives and anachronistic powers to the Founders.) Judging from the number of times this false history is alluded to, our self-esteem seems to be bound up with it. Perhaps we have a secret, unacknowledged fear to admit the Founders were really not entirely like us, because we would then have to throw them out completely.

Anyone who has honestly and closely studied the Founding years and the period that followed knows how large state rights loomed in the understanding of the Constitution in those days. Although there was some disagreement, some ambivalence, and even a few cases of disingenuousness among the Founders about the locus of sovereignty, there can be no doubt that most of the Founders and the subsequent two or three generations of statesmen accepted as natural and right the broadest possible idea of state rights. To most of the Founding generation, the Bill of Rights meant primarily a binding of the federal government by the states. To most people of the time, the victory of Jefferson and his friends in 1800 signified primarily the defeat of a too assertive federal power. Throughout the first half of the 19th century, the absolute central principle of the Jeffersonian Party and of the Democratic Party which came along later was state rights—the belief that the states were the truest representatives of the people's will and the best guardians of the people's liberty. And this belief was matched by democratic sentiment—the more faith one had in the people the more allegiance one gave to state rights. As recently as 1932 the Democratic Party went on record against the dangers of an overextended federal government.

It is not likely that state rights will be affirmed during our current bicentennial, even in a historical context. What would the Founders, or indeed anyone before 1932, have made of a situation in which the states have all but disappeared except as administrative units and electoral counters of the federal machinery? And all in the name of freedom and the rights of the individual? Today the federal government, and usually the unelected parts of it, determines the qualifications of the voters and the apportionment of the legislatures of the states. It determines the curriculum and student assignments of their public schools, the rules of proceedings in their criminal courts, the speed limits on their highways, and the number of parking spaces for the handicapped in their public and private buildings. We observe the strange spectacle of legislatures *required* to pass laws according to specifications drawn up by federal judges and federal bureaucrats, which, of course, is not lawmaking at all. The states may have larger budgets and do more things than ever before, but their constitutional authority has never been lower.

In the perspective of American history or of the Founders, this is an absolutely amazing development, a revolution consummated mostly since 1960, which has had less impact on the public consciousness than the Super Bowl or Michael Jackson. (Because, I think, the predominant strain in the national character has become utilitarian—it cares only for ends and does not care how they are accomplished—the idea of principles simply doesn't exist. This may be good or bad, but it is utterly incompatible with the Constitution.)

The appeal to federally guaranteed individual rights as the chief (evolutionary) feature of the Constitution is essentially antidemocratic. It takes the Constitution away from the people, whose Constitution it is, and gives it into the keeping of an elite class that considers itself the master of mysteries that no majority, either state or federal, can tamper with. It is not the dead hand of the past ("a relic from the past") that the advocates of an evolutionary Constitution fear. What they fear is the restraining hand of consensus, that is, of democracy.

An evolutionary Constitution implies a path of evolution, either inevitable or actively pursued. But who is to discern the path? The Supreme Court of the later 19th century thought the path was illuminated by Herbert Spencer; more recently egalitarian social democracy has been the beacon. In either case we have a guardian class of savants privileged to lead the way. The status of such men rests not on talents or public services but on claims to special revelation. In other words, they are not republican delegates of the people but priestly oracles—what the Founders would have immediately seen to be clever usurpers, and to us hardly distinguishable from the vanguard of the proletariat.

It is true that majorities can be wrong and that minorities have indefeasible rights enshrined within the spirit of the Constitution. But make no mistake, our elitist interpreters and molders of the Constitution are not talking about the rights of minorities to be defended and to defend themselves. They are talking about the rights of a minority, themselves, to rule, to be the sovereign, the ultimate authority. And this is not a theory, but a fact.

It is a curious truth that those who claim rationality, the liberals, with their permanent revolution and reliance on the supposedly objective spirit and findings of social science, always resort to the most irrational view of the Constitution—on the one hand to a mystical and disembodied appeal beyond the letter, and on the other to the most petty and deceitful manipulations of the plain sense. One of the most obvious results of this is to remove the Constitution from the people and have it perform as a cover for elitism.

But in fact, the Constitution, properly considered, does not give any rights at all. The most essential point of a written constitution is that it is a limitation of government. The people establish institutions and give up to them certain powers, and no more. The government is not presumed to give the people their rights; and indeed the Bill of Rights is cast in a negative form: "The Congress shall make no law . . ." That is, our rights are not a grant from the federal government, and the chief duty of the federal government is to refrain from interfering with them and leave to our real communities their day-to-day definition and application. By this analysis, all that the 14th Amendment "intended" was to make the freed men citizens.

There is a certain liberal spirit, genuinely American and legitimately derived from Jefferson, which says that the earth belongs to the living generation, which must be free to make its own arrangements. But our current evolutionists represent the exact opposite of this spirit—they represent not a forthright amendment by popular consent (which can be completely compatible with the spirit of traditions and institutions) but an essentially rigid and disguised manipulation of the existing Constitution.

I have said that the appeal over the Constitution to the higher law is pervasive. For example, I have before me a *Reader's Digest* (Sept. 1987) containing the reflections of the ex-Chief Justice Burger on how our Constitution should be viewed and celebrated. It is impossible to imagine anything more "mainstream." I set aside the silliness of the title, "The Birth of a True Nation." (Was the United States an "untrue" nation before the Constitution?) I quote the blurb, which is not the language of Burger but is a not-unfair representation of his sentiments expressed on this and other occasions: "Two centuries ago in Philadelphia, one of the most extraordinary events in all human history occurred, and America— and the world—were thereby transformed."

The framing of the Constitution was a remarkable event, but I will have to reflect a little on the invention of the wheel and the appearance of Jesus before conceding "one of the most extraordinary events in all human history." Further, the Constitution was not a unique event but a part of a series of events which ought to be understood not as "a miracle at Philadelphia" (to quote the title of a popular work—one does not know whether the pseudo-religion or the pseudo-history is more odious), but rather as a realistic human achievement. Every clause of the *Digest*'s statement is, in fact, either a falsehood or a gross exaggeration.

America was not transformed *by* the Constitution, except in a limited sense that a new governmental machinery was launched at the highest level. It remained the same society, essentially, as it had the year before. The Constitution did not create republicanism, which had already been created by the people of the States as the first step in the Revolution. It did not create the idea of the written constitution, which also had already been done by the states, which is why John Adams wrote his *A Defence of the Constitutions of the United States*.

But we have here not only America transformed but also the *world*! Now it is true that the Founders sometimes appealed to Mankind. However, they did not deal in emotions, ideologies, and fantasies, but principles. They had a modest hope that by the successful operation of republican principles they might provide an example and inspiration for other peoples. Nothing could have been further from them than the spirit of making the world "safe for democracy." If someone had blathered "global democracy"—the official rhetoric of the chosen intellectuals of the Reagan administration—to General Washington, he would have reached for his sword. "Global democracy," in specific historical terms, goes back to the 1930's, when it was created as a mélange of Wilsonism and Soviet popular front propaganda. Given the propensity of American governments for dropping high explosives on the "enemies of democracy," such propaganda can do nothing in the 1980's but make every intelligent foreigner feel uneasy and render prudent discussion of the national interest nearly impossible. In the past 50 years, a great achievement in the founding of government for Americans becomes a cover for the dreams of "conservative" politicians and intellectuals for world transformation.

I am less offended by the factual license of the ex-Chief Justice's blurb than I am by its spirit. The *tone* is all wrong, for a bicentennial statement. It smacks of a spoiled child congratulating himself on Daddy's riches. The Framers, I believe, would not want to be worshiped as workers of a .miracle. What they would want is the "decent respect" of sensible men for the hard-won achievements of their fathers.

To treat the accomplishment of the Philadelphia Convention as though it were a manifestation of divine intervention in history is to avoid understanding to what degree it was an accomplishment of the American people as they then existed and of the American leadership class at large, and of the historical opportunity that then existed. The Framers were giants because they were representatives of the American political fabric of the time. The Constitution was not a miracle or even a piece of good luck. It was an achievement that grew out of the experiences and virtues of Americans of that day.

After all, some of the best men were not even in Philadelphia. There were leaders in the ratification conventions on both sides equal in abilities to the Framers, and most states could have fielded several delegations of equal stature. Virginia sent Washington, Wythe, Mason (who refused to sign) and Madison (then an unknown factor). It did not send Jefferson, Marshall, Monroe, Patrick Henry, any of the Lees, or numerous others entitled to rank as Founders if not Framers. Indeed, Virginia could have found several dozen men equal or superior to McClung or Blair or Edmund Randolph.

The glorification of the Framers as demigods is a form of mystification that naturally lends itself to elitist rule. If the Constitution is a miracle, then it has to be treated as a holy object and handled only by the priests, not by the common run of humanity. To treat the Philadelphia Convention as a gathering of demigods is worse than foolish and undemocratic; so far it prevents any real appreciation of their achievement.

The members of the Convention, the Framers, were an able lot; some were great. Yet, in the final analysis, they were not omnipotent or omniscient but merely the delegates of the states. Some very able men who were selected by the states refused to go, either because they had more pressing business or were suspicious of the proceedings. Others were quite desultory in attendance, and several of the best men there refused to sign the finished product.

Nor did the Framers establish or proclaim a new Constitution, something they had no authority to do. What they did was draw up a convincing and appealing proposal—convincing and appealing because it tended to meet the occasion and to anticipate the future—a proposal that, after a considerable amount of explanation and qualification and amendments promised, was approved eventually by an effective majority of the people in each of the states—that is, by the people of the United States as already defined by existing political communities. Those who ratified the Constitution are its real Founders (as opposed to its Framers). It is wrong, therefore, to cite the debates in Philadelphia as definitive of "original intent," as useful and illuminating as they may be in a subsidiary sense. It is the powers that ratified it that determine, in the final analysis, what the "intention" of the Constitution is. Fortunately, to declare this is merely to declare the validity of democracy and of federalism.

How far we fall short of their achievement. In truth, in the Framers' Constitution, one of the things they took for granted (that we have lost) was an adequate supply of intelligence and honor. Reflect on that magical period in the history of self-government during the last decade when we had Gerald Ford for President, Nelson Rockefeller for Vice President, Warren Burger for Chief

Justice, and Tip O'Neill for Speaker. At the time of the Framers the justices of the peace of any small county in Virginia or the selectmen of any town in Connecticut could have mustered more intelligence (I leave aside less measurable virtues) than the whole of the government today.

By intelligence I mean learning, wisdom, foresight, digested experience, detachment, ethics. Not shrewdness in self-promotion, conceit, visionary schemes, and vague good intentions. The Founding Fathers did not anticipate the ravages of the two-party system and its ability to deter the best from public life and foist vocal mediocrities on the public, The Constitution presupposed an inexhaustible supply of able and honorable and *independent* public men (whose ambitions needed to be watched). Almost all of our leaders are now the creatures of political parties (what percentage of the people believe the Democrats and Republicans are part of the Constitution?), which means that ipso facto they are more adept at winning offices than at filling them, at manipulation and self-promotion than at statesmanship.

The replacement of the independent gentleman by the professional politician beginning in the 19th century, a reflection of changes in society and of the capacity of clever men to manipulate even wisely constructed institutions to their advantage, provided as serious a distortion of the Constitution as did the concomitant rise of lawyers. It would astound our politicians today to learn that at the time of the Founders and even long after, people held public office for the honor and that in most cases, rather than filling their own snouts at the public trough (except for a few securities speculators), they actually made a sacrifice of their private interests to serve in public office. The Constitution presupposed an aristocratic rather than a bourgeois class of office holders and aspirants, members of Congress, and Presidential Electors, who would always be capable of independent judgment. That is, the operation of the Constitution rested in part on something that has ceased to exist. The essence of republican government was that the will of the people prevailed but that it was formulated by able and independent delegates. When we say the will of the people, we have to avoid the mystical and high-flying references to something strongly akin to the General Will, which we all know is not the will of the people but the will of the vanguard of the proletariat on behalf of the people—what the people would want if they were as smart as their masters. This too easily merges over into "all mankind," so that everyone in the world becomes by extension an American citizen—something which if taken literally constitutes a grave threat both to the United States and mankind. The will of the people under the Constitution can only mean the deliberate sense of the political communities, that is the states, that make up the United States, expressed through the republican mechanisms that are established. This suggests that judicial review must be relegated to a subsidiary role.

Original intent, properly speaking, is a legal and not a constitutional idea. The original intent of a piece of legislation may be juridically determined by reference to its legislative history (though given the trickery and evasiveness of recent Congresses this is not as simple as it might be). However, "original intent" of the Constitution is not similarly determinable because the intent was given to the Constitution by the people who ratified it. An appeal to the Philadelphia convention, known chiefly through the partial notes of Madison, is not strictly analogous to an appeal to legislative history. The Constitution can be interpreted finally only historically, not juridically. It is also important to note that the "original intent" of a particular provision of the Constitution and the "original intent" of the Constitution in the large sense are different questions.

I have often heard members of Congress and other public officers answer a constitutional question with the quip that they are not constitutional lawyers. Nonsense! Members of Congress, the President, and more importantly, the people and officials of the states have just as much standing in interpreting the Constitution as any panel of lawyers or law professors, whether or not the latter have yet been appointed to the federal bench. The Founders never intended that the high *political* questions of constitutional interpretation would be at the mercy of lawyers' tricks.

The Federalist justices of the early 19th century—Marshall, Story, etc.— were legalists and devotees of the British common law. In one of the most misguided feats in American history, they infused judicial review into the constitutional fabric, believing they were providing a check to unruly popular passions and lending stability to the institutions of self-government. But while they did inject a type of stability that was useful in the progressive commercial sense, the law had a pragmatic and centralizing tendency that carried the emphasis away from the historical rights of the states and from the consent of the people. It is not difficult to understand why Jefferson feared the judiciary as the greatest of all enemies of republican government.

There is a piece of erroneous folklore, again dating to 19th century distortions of the Founding, that the Constitution is in the special keeping of lawyers. In fact relatively few of the Framers were practicing lawyers. Primarily they occupied their time as owners of plantations or other large estates or as merchants (that is, not counter-jumpers but traders on a large scale). They were also clergymen and educators, among other represented professions. It is true that a good many were trained in law. Law was considered a useful study which enhanced one's ability to manage one's own interests and participate in public life because it was a storehouse of English traditions of order and liberty. However, it was not considered, except by a few of the Framers who were not the most trustworthy, that a decent man would devote his primary attention to the daily practice of law.

The Founders recognized no aristocracies except those of talent, service, and social weight. They would regard the Constitution today as the tool of an aristocracy of federal judges, drawn from a class of lawyers and law professors whose study is not of noble traditions of liberty and order but of the defense of large vested interests, whether of big business or the established left-wing causes of the New Class. It would be difficult to imagine any group, taken as a group, more dissimilar to the great landowners and republican gentlemen of the

Founding than the choice legal scholars of late-20th-century America. The former were representatives of their communities and the bearers of wisdom and vision, the latter are the representatives of vested interests and of arcane manipulations.

We have here more than the elitist tendencies of 20th-century liberalism or "guardian democracy." We are going to have to go back a lot further than the Warren Court or the New Deal to remedy the ill. An evolutionary captivity of the Constitution was inevitable once the Constitution was given over largely into the hands of lawyers and treated primarily as a legal document, the understanding of which was to rest on the reasonings of judges.

This was a major mistake that the Framers, for the most part, did not expect. The Constitution was not intended to be, except in a subsidiary sense, a legal document. It was not expected that it would be interpreted by lawyers (people who argue cases for pay) much less by law professors (people who teach others how to argue for pay). The Constitution is a political document. Lawyers and judges are qualified to deal with legal matters. Study of the law per se, or pursuance of legal procedures per se, will never yield an accurate or lasting interpretation of the Constitution in the large sense. Justice O'Connor recently observed that every Supreme Court decision becomes, at the hands of clever lawyers, raw material for a hundred new cases.

This would be no great problem if we were merely dealing with *legal* questions brought on by the complications of modern society. But through the 14th Amendment and the usurpations of all three branches of the federal government, every conceivable legal question has also been made into a *constitutional* question. And even if this process yields a workable rendering of particular clauses of the Constitution, it should not be allowed cumulatively to determine the meaning of the Constitution itself.

We know that the Constitution has changed and continues to do so. If we look into what Constitution deserves our respect, we find two current views. One view, put forth by recent Supreme Courts and their defenders, says that the Constitution is an evolutionary document whose great virtue lies in its adaptability. According to this, it follows that it is the right or even the duty of the Supreme Court from time to time to bring the Constitution "up to date" with "modern" sensibilities.

We can hardly deny that the Constitution has changed and evolved. It has a history. However, from the observation that the Constitution must be viewed historically, it does not necessarily follow that the Supreme Court should be the arbiter of that change. In fact, this would not have been accepted by the main body of Founders.

The other view of the Constitution current today is that we are bound by its "intent" unless we want to amend it in the proper way. The Founders, at least that majority who were not over-involved in a specific agenda, would not have demurred from this proposition. But is it not obviously true that *the intent of the Constitution is a historical question*? That is to say, questions of "original intent" are most properly answered, not by legal reasoning and legal tradition, nor by abstract speculation on democratic philosophy or individual "rights," but by reference to the historical record.

In emphasizing the historical record there are two things I am not saying. I am not suggesting, in the manner of Charles Beard, that there is some secret dirty story to be ferreted out by historians. Nor am I saying that only professional historians can be allowed to put the Constitution in context, for any intelligent person may make a valid historical observation.

If we do not rely on the stream of legal interpretation to discern the intent of the Constitution nor on the specialist knowledge of historians nor on philosophical speculation (however relevant any of these may be in a subordinate sense), what do we rely on? We rely on history, and history, if it is not a specialist's but a people's history, is exactly what we mean by tradition—a widely shared understanding handed down from generation to generation.

A people's history may well embody some mythological elements (like the Founders' abolitionism) and some evolutionary developments (like reinterpretation of some basic points in the Civil War) because popular traditions are never precisely accurate in the specialist's sense. But after all, the Constitution rests upon the consent of the people. And it is therefore, in the final analysis, the people who have a right to determine its intent. If we argue that this is a perilous or unworkable doctrine, then we are merely declaring that democracy and federalism are unacceptable.

Of course, if we accept this proposition, our problems are only beginning (I can hear the cries of "simplistic!"), for we are still faced with the task of translating the people's understanding, which is a tacit thing, into the established mechanisms of government. This would seem to require the services of a statesman who, in Andrew Lytle's definition, has the mission of clarifying for a given people their alternatives. Since we have no statesmen, then perhaps the best we can do is get the best judges we can find and trust them. This, indeed, has been the position of most of those who have thought of themselves as conservatives through this century, though it cannot be considered a resoundingly successful strategy to say the least.

The defenders of "original intent" argue with ability and earnestness and morality and sense. But the Constitution they defend is not the federal republican instrument ratified in 1787–1788. It is the one invented and refounded in the middle of the 19th century by democratic nationalists to accompany and foster the development of a commercial republic, a Constitution under which lawyers formed an aristocracy, an impulse which Tocqueville observed at work in its early stages. As the world goes, that Constitution, compared to the one invented by the Supreme Court in the middle of the 20th century, will serve us just fine if (a big "if") we can get it back.

I am inclined to think that the Framers, men of another age, would be profoundly uncomfortable with the state of our society today. But, being creative realists, and observing the ill fit between the Constitution and our society and the misuses to which the Constitution has been put, they might well conclude that we ought to follow their example and make a new Constitution, more in keeping with our aspirations, even though they would doubt that we had the wisdom and virtue to build as well as they.

(1987)

The Achievement of M.E. Bradford

A Review of *A Better Guide Than Reason: Studies in the American Revolution*, by M.E. Bradford, La Salle, Illinois: Sherwood Sugden, 1979, 220 pages.

The world's largest, most ancient, and most exemplary republic observed its bicentennial not long ago. One would expect such an occasion to be a time of rededication and renewal, of restoration and recovery. Instead, we had a value-free official celebration that was expensive, dull, and that touched only a small minority of citizens. At least the New Leftists of the People's Bicentennial, unlike the middle class bureaucrats of the official observance, took the American Revolution seriously. Still, they failed to persuade most of us that the redheaded Southern planters, hardbitten New England fishermen, and cold-eyed backcountry riflemen who fought it should be understood chiefly as predecessors of Mao and Fidel.

All the wealth, talent, and global power of the American mass media did not succeed, as far as I know, in producing one memorable show that portrayed the American founding meaningfully to the American people. We were allowed to read about Jefferson's sex life and the rascal Aaron Burr and to view the imaginary adventures of African villagers snatched to bondage in America. But apparently the deeds of George Washington, Patrick Henry, Sam Adams, or Francis Marion, the events of Lexington, Saratoga, Valley Forge, or Kings Mountain, do not provide any stuff which the masters of the media find marketable.

All in all, one suspects that those Americans who came closer to partaking of the spirit of the Revolution were that small number who dressed up in uniforms and fired off muzzle-loading muskets. At least their intent was to commemorate an inheritance that was genuinely, if sometimes dimly felt, rather than to celebrate in an orgy of self-congratulation something appreciated perversely or not at all.

The lack of energy, conviction, and meaning in the bicentennial provides the best evidence, though other proofs are all around us, of how alienated the American people have become from their roots. In fact, we are on the verge of ceasing to have any identity at all *as a people*, of ceasing to acknowledge any kinship that transcends allegiance to a shared standard of living.

If you agree with the foregoing analysis, then you will also agree with Jeffrey Hart, Professor of English at Dartmouth University and an editor of *National Review*, who writes in the Introduction to *A Better Guide Than Reason* that some of the essays in this book "are among the most important of our time." For Bradford, in a stunning feat of intellectual courage and originality, has done nothing less than to provide us with the necessary means to rediscover our founding, the original basis of our commonwealth.

Under Bradford's direction, we can grasp for ourselves the identity of the American people at the founding of the Republic, free and clear of the obfuscations and misrepresentations piled up by succeeding generations of partisans. He has made it possible for us to see clearly for the first time in more than a century the nature and import of that process by which the scattered English inhabitants of North America articulated themselves into a republican realm. He tells us in a full-blooded and circumstantial account what our forefathers were like, what they believed and why, what they meant and *what they did not mean* in the great documents to which they pledged their lives, fortunes, and honor.

A providentially peculiar combination of training and heritage laid the groundwork for this achievement. Bradford, Professor of English and American Studies at the University of Dallas, is by vocation a student of literature and by heritage a Southern Agrarian. For him, as for our Founding Fathers, politics, history, and literature are not separate, mutually exclusive, and merely technical activities. History and literature are moral and aesthetic studies, the ends of which are the cultivation of good men. And since the quality of men is defined, collectively, by the quality of their citizenship, politics and literature are by nature a seamless fabric. It is part of Bradford's feat that he has miraculously restored the fabric.

As a student of literature, and particularly the highly political English literature of the century prior to the American war, he reads the great documents of the American founding with a lost apprehension of the connotations of the language in which they were written. As a Southerner, he reads these same documents with an inherited appreciation of how the American communities that produced them actually worked. For as Bradford points out, Southern things are the most American of American things.

Bradford's eleven essays have a three-fold thrust. One group aims at recovering the American Revolution that was understood by the men who made it. Characterized in the English tradition out of which it came, this Revolution was "Old Whig" or "Country Whig." It looked backward rather than forward; it was preservative of customary values and arrangements; it happened in reaction to innovations of the British government and was not a manifestation of a radicalized impulse for remaking the world by a utopian calculus. Many would agree with Bradford that the American Revolution was a conservative event, but no other writer has matched his portrayal of why and how that was so.

Among this first group are essays on three Founding Fathers whose neglect in recent years has been, Bradford suggests, deliberate. A full understanding of these men and of how representative they were would undermine many partial and peculiar interpretations that have been put forward of the meaning of the Revolution. The three are Patrick Henry of Virginia, John Dickinson of Pennsylvania who, though unknown today was perhaps the most revered American of his time except for Washington, and William Henry Drayton of South Carolina.

Among the essays designed to recover the import of the Revolution we can place also the initial one which takes up our forefathers' identification with the history of republican Rome. The Roman Republic, after which Americans modelled their own, was one in which citizenship consisted of shared manners and mores, access to a common law, and a strenuous sense of patriotism—not a republic of undiscriminating access to rights and privileges.

Bradford's second group of essays have to do with the derailment of the Old Whig tradition in the 19th century. He finds in the implemented political thought of Abraham Lincoln "a rhetoric for continuing revolution." Lincoln's selective reading of the Declaration of Independence, with an unduly emphasized and distorted interpretation of the concept of equality, injected into the American body politic a messianic style and disintegrative ferment that still bedevil us. Paradoxically, Lincoln's inheritance remains a crippling and self-contradictory impediment in the train of many of those Americans who style themselves conservatives.

Two essays provide the background for Lincoln's derailment of American tradition. One is a devoir to Russell Kirk, the other a comparison of Benjamin Franklin's autobiography with Thomas Jefferson's only book, *Notes on the State of Virginia*. The American tradition was bipolar. Counterposed to the predominant Old Whiggery of the South and Middle States was the Puritan inheritance of New England which implanted deeply in the American fabric a latent proclivity for destructive rebellion as opposed to the restorative effort of the original War of Independence.

In laying out the fundamental differences between Jefferson and Franklin, often thought to be on the same wing of the Revolution, liberals and cosmopolitans together, Bradford is at his most subtle and skillful. They were very different kinds of cosmopolitans and liberals. Jefferson, whatever his private opinions, was as a public man first and always a Virginian, navigating with reference to the fixed star of Virginia law and custom. Franklin prefigured the modern American—a rootless solipsist, literally a self-made man, gliding and manipulating his pleasant and benevolent way through a world that lacked any stable identity.

Bradford's third point relates his understanding of the American Revolution to the populist tradition. He identifies himself clearly with those Americans who live actually or in spirit "up at the forks of the creek"—those who feel government primarily as an unfriendly outside force aimed at manipulating the settled and revered things—from Bacon's Rebellion of the 1670's to the anti-busing campaigns of the 1970's. He affirms the ancientry and legitimacy of this way of thinking and suggests that it still lies endemic though unrecognized in the American body politic.

American scholars, as a rule, value intense analysis of small questions and effect a scientific neutrality. Small questions often lead to sterility and neutrality sometimes leads to unconscious enslavement to some current fashion. Bradford's breadth of learning in history, literature, and political thought is grandly anomalous. He writes with old-fashioned eloquence, informed by the love of a living community of people.

The best revolutions are restorative—what Jefferson had in mind when he advocated a little one now and then. Not revolution that uproots the healthy trunk but that which cuts away the excrescences and overgrowths so that the trunk may breathe. In that sense no one who reads and digests *A Better Guide* can fail to be revolutionized. We had thought that the great Southern political tradition—that of Patrick Henry and Jefferson, John Taylor and John Randolph, Calhoun and Davis, the 19th century agrarians and the 20th century Agrarians—was dead. Not so; it is alive and well and those worthy spokesmen of the South have found a worthy successor in M.E. Bradford.

(1982)

The Liberty and Responsibility of the Press

Mass communication is an economic as well as all intellectual activity. As a consequence, in few areas of human endeavor does the mutual dependence of economic and political liberty stand out so plainly. Despite the peculiarly political dimension of mass communication, in every historic society the processes of mass communication have been organized in patterns closely parallel to the organization of other economic activities, and the degree of liberty of the press has depended upon the degree of economic liberty.

In the classic European monarchy the privileges of the press were limited and licensed in the same way that the "rights" to other economic activities were distributed to the favored few. In the United States of the first half of the nineteenth century, where the prevailing form of business organization was the competitive local proprietorship, newspapers multiplied, launched by printers with a proverbial shirt-tail of type. When the mass-market, national corporation appeared, the newspaper chain with its more or less standardized product and urban mass audience followed closely behind.

In a socialistic state, like Great Britain today, the communication system is a mixture of government monopoly and private enterprise. In Communist Russia all instruments of communication, from the orbiting satellite to the wall poster, are government monopolies. It can easily be seen that the optimal conditions for freedom of the press are as much economic as political, i.e., while the government has a special interest in the press as a political activity, this relationship usually manifests itself in a manner very similar to the relationship of the government to other economic activities. Where the means of communication are privately owned, where that ownership is widely dispersed, and where there are the strictest legal or philosophical limits to government intervention in economic life, there will be the maximum freedom of the press.

The view of freedom of the press prevailing now in that part of the academy which devotes itself to the special study of mass communications, ignores the relationship of economic and intellectual freedom, except in cases where, by special pleading, an economic argument can be made for government intervention as promoting freedom. Not surprisingly, the philosophy of the press which prevails in American academic departments of Mass Communications and Journalism closely parallels the collectivist, social-democratic philosophy of government and economics which prevails in other departments of the universities. Because of the undoubted preeminence of freedom of the press among the political freedoms, an analysis of the social-democratic view of mass communications is especially valuable in illuminating the contradictions and philosophical weaknesses of the social-democratic polity when contrasted with the constitutional republic.

The definitive statement of the prevailing Liberal analysis of the nature and conditions of freedom of the press is contained in the work, *Four Theories of the*

Press, by Fredrick S. Siebert, Wilbur Schramm, and Theodore Peterson (Univ. of Illinois Press, Urbana, Ill.: 1956). This work, building upon the 1947 report of the Commission on Freedom of the Press chaired by Robert Maynard Hutchins, contains the theoretical premises of the regnant academic view and is widely used as a text by professors of journalism.[1]

The authors undertake to construct four theoretical models of communication systems, suggesting that every historic system has approximated one of the models or some mixture of them. The models described are the Authoritarian, the Libertarian, the Soviet Communist, and the Social Responsibility, the last being the one that in the prevailing view either does or should exist in the United States. The Social Responsibility model has had great influence. Indeed, the recent establishment of a government television network and the recent entry of the federal government into the "textbook development" field were giant steps toward its realization and direct results of its influence.

In Siebert's description of the Authoritarian and Libertarian press theories, there is little to quibble with as far as they go. The Authoritarian system is found in the classic monarchy in which the government limits access to instruments of mass communication and prevents or punishes the publishing of facts or opinions which the rulers do not desire to see published. Truth is prescriptive. There is no demand for a free press to embellish or obscure it. In the Libertarian system, which prevailed in the United States in the nineteenth century, government is absent from mass communication entirely, apart from occasional publication of its proceedings. Any group (or individual) with the means may broadcast whatever information or opinions it chooses, limited only by the possibility of prosecution for libel, sedition, or obscenity—narrowly construed and containing long hallowed exceptions. Truth is to be arrived at by free competition in the marketplace of ideas. Taken as broad theoretical models rather than precise historical descriptions and allowing for an under-emphasis of the economic as opposed to the legal basis of Libertarianism, Siebert's analyses are sound and useful.

Schramm, in his description of the Soviet Communist model communication system has made a valuable contribution to the understanding of intellectual freedom. The Soviet system is not authoritarian, it is totalitarian. It aims not only at negative suppression of ideas uncongenial to the rulers but at positive, systematic, and pervasive use of mass communication to enforce acceptance of "facts" and opinions approved by the rulers and acts pursuant to those facts and opinions. Truth is defined as what is useful to the state.

One would think that the Libertarian theory, providing for nearly pure freedom of the press and coinciding with the openness and dispersal of power in American political institutions, would attract the allegiance of scholars professing to be "liberal." Such is not the case. The theory which draws the loyalty of

---

1. The view summarized in *Four Theories* is elaborated in Commission on Freedom of the Press, *A Free and Responsible Press* (Chicago: University of Chicago Press, 1947); and in William Ernest Hocking (a member of the Commission), *Freedom of the Press: A Framework of Principle* (Chicago: University of Chicago Press, 1947).

the majority is something described as Social Responsibility, and discussed at length in *Four Theories* by Theodore Peterson, who crystallizes and summarizes a prior body of academic theorizing. Social Responsibility is offered as a superior substitute for a libertarian arrangement of the press, allegedly allowing room for both freedom and government control. It fails in the same way that collective "participatory democracy" fails as a substitute for constitutional republicanism, i.e., government control becomes the reality and freedom is freedom only in the Orwellian sense.

The Social Responsibility system of the press, according to its definers, is an outgrowth of the Libertarian system in twentieth-century democratic states. Its *raison d'être* is that "the power and near monopoly position of the media impose on them an obligation to be socially responsible, to see that all sides are fairly represented and that the public has enough information to decide; and that if the media do not take on themselves such responsibility, it may be necessary for some other agency of the public to enforce it." To further the cause of "social responsibility" the government "may enact legislation to forbid flagrant abuses of the press . . . or it may enter the field of communication to supplement existing media," according to the theory.[2]

The goal of this paper is to dispute the claim that a Social Responsibility system of the press, as defined, exists or can exist in any sense parallel to the Libertarian, Authoritarian, and Soviet Communist systems. Further, I wish to suggest that Social Responsibility, in theory and practice, is not a refinement of Libertarianism as claimed, but is simply another name for a system not very different from the Authoritarian.

Peterson constructs the Social Responsibility theory upon a large initial ambiguity, for he is never clear as to whether he believes the Social Responsibility system does exist or merely ought to exist. The student is expected to accept that it is at the same time the *status quo* and a goal to be strived for. While Authoritarian, Libertarian, and Soviet Communist press systems have existed in institutionalized forms which have acted directly on the day-to-day operation of mass communication instruments and have carried the force of law, Social Responsibility, in its negative aspects, has as yet no institutionalized forms.

Peterson offers, as proof that the Social Responsibility system is already operative, the evidence that scholars have defined it and certain publishers have testified that, yes, they indeed do feel constrained to conduct their enterprises in accordance with proper social responsibility. Yet, evidently, no concrete means for "correction of abuses" in the press, extant or potential, are described. One suspects that the author leaves the nature of the means purposefully vague because their exact forms would be shocking and unlovely. Under the Authoritarian and Soviet systems, deviations from "social responsibility" are called to account by the police power. Libertarian systems leave deviations to be

---

2. *Four Theories*, pp. 5, 95.

corrected by the self-righting process of competition among ideas. (Whether this arrangement works is not the issue here.) The Social Responsibility theory, offered as a model for the nation, is not a coherent theory because it provides us with no definable means for recognizing abuses of the press and no honest clue to the procedures that are to be used to punish them.

Suppose that contemporary publishers were acting in a manner which more closely resembled an agreed upon definition of socially responsible conduct than did publishers at an earlier point in history. This would mean, in terms of institutions, only that individuals were acting in a different manner within a Libertarian system, not that a new system had appeared. Of course, no consensus on socially responsible press conduct can ever be achieved by publishers or even by critics of the press.

Social Responsibility, so far as it exists, then, is really formed by two disparate phenomena: increasing self-regulation by the press and increasing government participation in mass communications. The first, contrary to Peterson's contentions, constitutes no sharp departure from the individual choice which has characterized the Libertarian press tradition in America. The second, also exactly contrary to Peterson, is a radical and dangerous departure from the Liberation tradition. In other words, Social Responsibility, to the extent that it relies on self-regulation by the publishers, does not exist; it is simply Libertarianism. To the extent that it relies on government control it is merely a disguise for Authoritarianism.

The supporters of the Social Responsibility theory are motivated to construct a new press system by the belief that the Libertarian system has failed. They observe that technology has narrowed the base of control of mass media by making participation more expensive, thereby restricting admittance to the free marketplace of ideas, and that psychology has called into question the rationality of men, thereby undermining the self-righting process by which truth was to emerge in the Libertarian competition. There is weight in their observations, and persons not Liberal, substituting the fallen nature of man for economic concentration and the irrational psyche, might agree that the Libertarian system is philosophically inadequate.

However, the Liberal theorists of Social Responsibility do not admit that they are repudiating the Libertarian ideal. Instead they claim that they are improving and saving it. The claim reveals that they have neither a real understanding nor an appreciation of the positive values of freedom. The Social Responsibility advocates assume that Libertarian organization was justifiable because of its ability to achieve truth through the free competition of ideas. Since, in their opinion, the competition no longer works properly, liberty is no longer justifiable.

To say that the free marketplace of ideas does not work toward truth, that men are not necessarily capable of distinguishing truth, is to postulate a truth which is perceived by some men (in this case Peterson and other critics of the Libertarian press) and not by others. This is to distort completely the rationale of

Libertarianism, the whole point of which is that truth cannot be pre-defined by one part of mankind for another. To the Liberals, the Libertarian system is working properly only if their "truth" triumphs. The individual's right to perceive and judge for himself is of no value unless the results are "acceptable" to them.

A conservative, whose truth, in ultimate matters, is prescribed in the Christian tradition, may without immodesty discount the truth-producing capacity of the free marketplace of ideas (although he may still heartily approve of it as a prudent political arrangement). But when a group of secular theorists postulate their own temporal judgments as the truth to be enforced upon others, then they have taken the first step common to all the intolerant and oppressive movements of history.

Recognizing, no doubt, the essentially elitist and authoritarian tendency of the Social Responsibility theory, the academic advocates cloak its tangible aspects in ambiguity.

"Government remains the residual legatee of responsibility for an adequate press performance," Peterson asserts. Further:

> To the extent that the press recognizes its responsibilities and makes them the basis of operational policies, the libertarian system will satisfy the needs of society. To the extent that the press does not assume its responsibilities, some other agency must see that the essential functions of mass communication are carried out.[3]

What is called for is an agency or agencies, invested with the power of the state, to act as a check on the press. But upon what basis are we to decide whether the press has performed "adequately" and satisfied "the needs of society?" For Social Responsibility to work there must be some group in society with power to establish a standard against which violations may be judged. The Social Responsibility theorists, however, refuse to define their standards or the legal and institutional means by which they will be enforced. The closest they will come is to suggest that "a rather considerable fraction of articulate Americans" are demanding "certain standards of performance from the press."[4]

It is proposed to bind publishers to "responsibility in exchange for their freedom."[5] Who does the binding? To whose concept of responsibility? By what right and what process, and upon whose authority, is the freedom of the publisher made conditional? The answer is not stated but we can assume that it will be upon the authority of the elite of "scholars" and "critics" who Peterson presents as authorities on the failings of the press. Where does the "considerable fraction of articulate Americans" arrive at its standards? What are their credentials for overseeing the conscience of the publisher and tampering with the flow of information to the citizens?

---

3. *Ibid.*, p. 74.
4. *Ibid.*, p. 77.
5. *Ibid.*, p. 76.

We are never informed precisely but we can catch the drift when we observe that Peterson proceeds to catalog the past sins of the press without experiencing the slightest urge to define the standard of judgment which he is using. Presumably the faults he notes will be corrected when the punitive phase of Social Responsibility is instituted. The standards which the "scholars" and "critics" employ, although vaguely defined, are so absolute in their minds that it is not even necessary to offer a philosophical defense for them. Note that nowhere do they suggest that the "right" standards be arrived at by democratic process (i.e., by the people or the legislators) which is usually considered the logical methodology of a democratic society. The standards, to the "critics," are given.

Below, in italics, are some of the faults of the press discovered by Peterson and used to justify government intervention in communications, followed by my criticism of his claims:[6]

"The press has resisted social change." Who is to say when it is responsible to abet change and when it is responsible to resist change? Was it responsible to resist the reforms advocated by Franklin D. Roosevelt in New York in 1930? Was it responsible to resist similar reforms advocated by Huey P. Long in Louisiana at the same time? To whom is it irresponsible to resist change? Do we dare entrust the regulation of communications to men who lack the intellectual power to perceive the flaw in the unqualified endorsement of the proposition that to resist change is wrong? The idea of forbidding newspapers to resist social change brings directly to mind the Marcusian New Left formula of tolerance of all movements to the Left and violent suppression of the Right.

"The press has wielded its enormous power for its own ends." So what? So does every other institution in society. Businessmen wield power for economic gain. Clergymen wield power for spiritual ends which they value (or at any rate they once did). Professors wield power for ideas which they believe to be true. Politicians and bureaucrats wield power for their own ends—usually power itself. Will those who enforce Social Responsibility be more exempt than the publishers from temptation to wield power for their own ends? Will diversity in the marketplace of ideas be increased by substituting for the now-too-uniform standards of thousands of publishers, editors, and broadcasters the even more uniform standards of an unidentified class of "critics" backed by the police power of the state?

"Radio and television have depended too heavily on conservative commentators and have avoided genuine, healthful controversy." Of course, the first half of the sentence, as an empirical observation, is patently preposterous. Who can draw up a list of more than a handful of commentators on the air waves who could reasonably be described as conservative? Can conservative commentators not be controversial? For "healthful controversy" read advocacy of leftwing nostrums. Indeed, the press has engaged in so much controversy of the latter sort, at the expense of straightforward reporting, that a majority of middle class

---

6. Found in *Ibid.*, pp. 78, 79, 88, 93.

Americans surveyed said they entertained doubts about the truthfulness of report-ing, while thirty percent are convinced that the press is completely untrustwor-thy.[7] What the academic advocates of press "responsibility" want to encourage in their government-dominated "supplementary" mass media is more of the same "interpretive reporting" that has already ruined the press.

"The press is controlled by one socio-economic class, loosely the 'business class'." There is no differentiated "business class" in the United States with inter-ests clearly in conflict with the interests of any other classes. Is the range of view-points between the *Chicago Tribune* and the *Washington Post* not indicative that something other than economic interests dictates the contents of newspapers? How are "business" interests to be separated from publishing which is necessar-ily a business? By exchanging them for government interests? Indeed, then the press will be as "responsible" as it is in the Soviet Union, where, according to the constitution, the state is obliged to supply the means of printing to anyone who asks for it.

"The press has developed a curious sort of objectivity—a spurious objectiv-ity which results in half-truths, incompleteness, incomprehensibility . . . the media have not bothered to evaluate for the reader the trustworthiness of con-flicting sources, nor have they supplied the perspective essential to a complete understanding of a given situation." This criticism of the press is precisely true, but unfortunately a truth arrived at for all the wrong reasons. Every person in the United States who is capable of relatively objective observation is aware that practically all the national and international news distributed to the American people is full of half-truths and characterized by a spurious objectivity—because events are always filtered through the Procrustean mentality of the New York journalistic community (or its provincial imitators), a group whose ideological and occasionally even reportorial zeal is great but whose intellectual prowess is superficial and integrity invisible.

Objectivity, i.e., stating two sides of a question with detachment and without partisanship, observing events as they arise without distorting them by *a priori* ideological assumptions, and refraining from creating artificial and self-fulfilling news (the greatest sin of the American press), is possible. It is sometimes achieved by the best British journalism when reporting a remote foreign ques-tion, but seldom is found in the United States except occasionally in local media. "Interpretive reporting" has reached such a pitch in the American media, partic-ularly national television, that it has become almost impossible for even the most industrious citizen to consistently perceive the true dimensions of any public questions. However, what the Liberal critics of the press want is not more detach-ment and objectivity but still more "interpretation" (their own). Improvement will surely not be secured by making the government the controller of commu-nications and thus the creator of its own interpretations.

"The government can encourage new ventures in the communications indus-

---

7. "The Troubled American," *Newsweek*, Oct. 6, 1969.

try. It can adopt new legal remedies to rectify chronic, patent abuses of press freedom. And it can enter the communications field to supplement the privately-owned media." Who decides what new ventures are worth encouraging? Where do the funds come from out of a budget overburdened with social services?

Ventures such as the government has made into communications have had the effect of further restricting admittance to or distorting the workings of the free marketplace of ideas, not of lubricating them. Why, for instance, should there be only three national television networks? Why should social engineering agencies of the government have millions of public dollars to publicize themselves and to squelch the helpless private critics of their controversial activities"? Why should, government education bureaucrats tamper with the contents of history texts to promote the viewpoint of certain groups, as they have recently done in regard to Negro history?

As long as it is conceded that broadcasting franchises are to be granted by government, why are measures not taken to secure the widest dispersal of ownership (i.e., greater competition) of media in each locality? In two of the three largest cities of my native state the television franchises were granted to companies which already owned the two (Liberal) newspapers. In another city, only by accident was the franchise given to an independent company which presents an opposing viewpoint to the two (Liberal) local newspapers, and that company has been continually harrassed by the Federal Communications Commission.

Government itself is the greatest enemy of the free flow of ideas, just as is government, unregulated, the greatest enemy of political freedom. But the Liberal theorists of the press have made the same discovery that their colleagues in political science made some years ago: that freedom *from* government (the kind of freedom the United States was founded to secure) is only a "negative" and puny kind of freedom, compared to the *positive* "freedom" we can have when the government becomes big enough to insure our comfort and equality.

Measures other than government censorship of the existing media or ownership of its own, offer far better promise of increasing the circulation of more diversified ideas. Some hopeful trends are already indicated in the natural course of events—the proliferation of suburban newspapers, the flourishing of magazines of opinion, the rise of local editorializing in radio and television, evidences of skepticism in the mass audience. Technological breakthrough promises eventually to break the monopoly of large capital over daily newspaper production by elimination of some of the more costly procedures.

When ownership of the means of communication is found to be concentrated into too few private hands, the social democrat's response characteristically is to concentrate it even further into the hands of one owner—the government, purportedly as a means of preserving the liberty which is endangered by oligarchy. Actually, of course, because he foresees that he will be the master of the media that are so concentrated. Men who really cherish liberty will seek means of dividing control into a greater number of private hands.

"The media have failed in their function of fairly representing the con-

stituent elements of society." Again, unfortunately, a truth arrived at for the wrong reasons. By this criticism the Social Responsibility theorists mean that they feel that the press has given too much attention to the Establishment and not enough to radicals and minority groups. But, of course, the real problem with the present media is that they have distorted the fair representation of the constituent groups of society by giving *too much* attention to minority groups and radicals. It is almost impossible, for example, to read in any national media a fair representation of the viewpoint on any question of conservative and moderate Southern white citizens (who make up nearly a quarter of the population of the United States), but I have already received far more "information" than I can use about the wisdom and nobility of the numerically insignificant minority of Americans who supported Sen. Eugene McCarthy during the last presidential election. The public television network has so far provided only a greater distortion in the same direction.

By advocating that the government guarantee fair representation of all sides of a question in media presentation, the Social Responsibility theorists do not mean that the unrepresented majority of moderate and conservative citizens be heard from (they do not recognize the existence of any legitimate criticism of government from that direction) but that an even greater airing be given to the views of ever more leftist minorities. And by advocating that more coverage be given to minority groups they do not mean that fair, detached coverage be given, but that favorable coverage be given, whether it is justified in a particular instance or not.

In other words, the intellectuals who desire to control the press ostensibly to provide a more meaningful dialogue, actually suffer from the same mentality that characterizes those who presently control the press. Melioristic fervor is so predominant and old-fashioned processes of logical thought so attenuated that they are scarcely able to perceive the true requirements of fairness and detachment, i.e. the ability to honestly state and represent a viewpoint with which one does not agree and the self-restraint necessary to refrain from using one's position as a reporter or commentator to unfairly prejudice a case.

The Social Responsibility theory, already semi-official policy, in essence proposes that supervision of the mass media be given to an academic elite which will have instruments of government force at its beck, and whose standards of judgment will be supplied by the ideology of contemporary Liberalism, rather than genuine scholarly detachment. In addition, this elite will be provided by the taxpayers with its own communications media which it may use in attempting to impose its views upon the taxpayer or his children. (How long before an indifferent or skeptical public would elicit a demand from the elite for compulsory viewing? For it is every man's duty to apprise himself of the "true facts" of all public questions.)

This system, when carried completely into effect, would replace the present system of control of mass communications by a business-professional group with diverse private authority, accountable to the state only through the imposition of a few traditional and general restrictions designed to protect individual rights or bar overt subversion. Private ownership would be allowed to survive as long as it satisfied the elite critics of the press. Otherwise, legal processes (the unspecified punitive side of Social Responsibility) will be set up to bring the privately-controlled media to heel. As long as private ownership remains and outside standards are not forced upon the publisher, Social Responsibility will not have become a genuine system. The affirmation of some publishers that Libertarianism has already been transformed into Social Responsibility are judicious, or more probably, naive verbal concessions to the prevailing collectivist ethos which seeks to obscure all individual power and responsibility.

In the nineteenth century there were a multitude of competing newspapers in America, most of them unabashedly partisan and biased, but the public political debate, if fallen somewhat from the elevation of the founding fathers, was far more mature and fruitful than today. By keeping its bias in mind, one could read such a newspaper and glean from it the basic facts one needed to make up one's own mind.

This competitive multitude gave way to a few great competitive urban dailies, the ownership of which was concentrated in a few hands. Such papers had their faults—sensationalism and the creation of artificial news—but at their best they created a class of professional editors and reporters who were what editors and reporters should be: zealous investigators and reporters of facts for the sake of facts, mistrusting all men and owing ideological allegiance to none. It was possible to follow such a newspaper and have an excellent idea of what was going on in the world. Though they were sometimes biased it was an honest and spirited partisanship.

The television networks today, and the great urban papers, piously proclaim their "responsibility" and fairness, yet their bias is blatant and far more pernicious than the earlier varieties because it is disguised and hypocritical. As a result the political dialogue of the nation has become unbelievably puerile and detached from reality. There is scarcely a politician who can afford to state frankly and simply what he believes. If he is a Liberal he must utter whatever pious melioristic platitude is in fashion. If he is a Conservative, he must be evasive and pretend not to be offended by biased reporting, lest the "commentators," with piously pained expressions and sanctimoniously pained tones, soon "interpret" and misrepresent him into a national hate object.

Proponents of an open press are quite right to fear that economic concentration endangers the optimum functioning of freedom of the press. Indeed, the major trend of American society at this point in history is for economic, social, and political concentrations of many kinds to call into question the future of all freedoms. Although private economic concentration is restricting that free flow of information required for the proper functioning of a republican society, the twentieth century teaches no more obvious lesson than the dangers of seeking relief by concentrating ever more power into the hands of men who already wield the coercive apparatus of the state; and nowhere is the lesson taught by totalitarianism more salient than in the area of mass communications.

Concentration of economic control in the mass media may be dissipated by the vicissitudes of time, technology, and the marketplace. Undue uniformity of ideas may be combatted by debate and altered by changing circumstances and interests which transform men's lights, but from political oligarchies which control not only the powers of the state but the means of information, there is seldom any appeal except the sword.

(1970)

Real Majority Rule

Democracy, Churchill is supposed to have said, is a very unsatisfactory form of government—only it's better than any other kind that has been tried. If man cannot be trusted to govern himself, Jefferson wrote, how can he be trusted to govern others, which was a definitive reply to the elitism of Hamilton (and of Hamilton's successors). C.S. Lewis defended democracy in the same way as Jefferson, from a Christian perspective.

These sentiments reflect conclusions based upon common sense and common decency. All things considered, it is better for the community to choose those who exercise power; and once chosen, it is better for the rulers to exercise power in accordance with the sense of community than against it. But, given this sensible agreement upon proceeding, there is no need to indulge in the too common American proclivity of sanctifying the democratic process. Majority rule is a good thing, but the voice of the people is not necessarily or even usually the voice of God.

More seriously, majority rule is not as clear a concept as may at first appear, and there are many problems in its definition and application. Like making war, love, or money, and all other important human activities, making a majority, the real thing, is an art, not a simple utilitarian matter of counting papers in a box.

Of course, politicians have been busy distorting and discrediting majority rule ever since it was invented, and the meaning of "democracy" has been hopelessly compromised by bad usage in this century. Nearly every state in the world is now a "democracy," except for our masters, the Kuwaitis. Justice William Brennan believed it was "democracy" when he issued orders defined by himself, to be obeyed by all, even though they went against not only the will of the majority but against law, tradition, history, and reason as well. Far better to stick with the old American concept of republicanism, which means simply a government resting on the consent of the people.

But what do we mean by "people"? What do we mean by "majority"? Americans appear to concentrate lately much more on the choosing of our rulers—the counting of ballots—and much less on whether, once chosen, they rule in accord with the sense of the community. But what was heinous about the totalitarian dictatorships of this century was not so much the way their leaders were chosen as the unrestrained powers they exercised in office.

In fact, in our federal government, even when decisions are not made by judges and bureaucrats (as they often are), they are made by coalitions of interests, not by the sense of the majority of the people in any way our Founders would recognize. Deliberation was essential to the Founders—debate that, if it did not lead to complete agreement, educated all sides and promoted understanding and concession and a higher consensus. The intended design of the Constitution was to check and refine majorities—not to defeat them but to insure that they were real and solid and not mere temporary expressions of passions or selfish interests. And every controlling majority in the Constitution was federally weighted to give recognition to the smaller states.

This was a rather different thing, and a better rendering of majority rule than the counting of heads queued up by party whips and lobbyists. Our Congress is not a deliberative or even a legislative body—it is only a continually shifting bipartisan collection of successful pork-barrelers. True debate and deliberation disappeared long ago, when the government became chiefly a matter of dispensing favors to some at the expense of others.

Problems in determining and implementing the sense of the majority increase progressively with the number of decisions the government makes. It is doubtful if there is any majority sense of the people in regard to most of the vast legislation, expenditure, and regulation that now comes out of Washington, nor even any public opinion at all. The more things that are decided by the central state, and the fewer by society, the less majority rule there can be.

Setting the problem of the ongoing consent of the governed aside, even the process of electing our rulers seldom corresponds to glowing civics text descriptions of the will of the people in action. In the presidential election of 1992, there was no decision by a majority. The Establishment, including its media wing, has assiduously ignored this and acted as though it did not happen. The primary fact of the election was that it showed both ruling parties to be national minorities. Mr. Clinton won with 43 percent of the vote, with half the eligible voters not participating at all. A putatively popular incumbent President received even less.

Yet the Establishment acts as though a continuing mandate exists for the present two parties. But the next election could be even more devastating to the hope of majority rule, which is one reason the media scramble to suppress and defame all serious challengers to the status quo. Should there be a three- or four-way race in this year's election, it is conceivable that a President could be elected by a 35 percent plurality if it were well placed in California and a few other large states.

The problem is not with the Electoral College—that it is indirect and gives added weight to the smaller states and is therefore undemocratic. These aspects are completely in keeping with the design of the Constitution. The problem is the gimmicks which politicians have rigged into the practice by law and custom. Why, when we have popular vote, should all the electoral votes of a state go to a candidate who won by 51 percent (or by 35 percent in a three-way field)? Not because this is a better form of democracy, but because it makes it easier for politicians to win elections. (It also gives more power to party members in states that are less loyal to the party than in those that are loyal.) This is *not* in keeping with the spirit of the Constitution.

How many Americans think that the Democrats and Republicans are in the Constitution? In fact, the Constitution pervasively and deliberately seeks to minimize the power of political parties. The presidential electors were supposed to be outstanding citizens who gathered in their state capitals to deliberate and make a choice—not the obscure party hacks they are now. The electors could be chosen in any way the state determined—by the legislature or by the state's (not federal) franchise, and in the latter case either by a general ticket or by districts.

Such was the practice in the beginning. Nor did political party conventions, that is, conclaves of professional politicians and would-be professional politicians, determine who the candidates were to be. But now the party conventions, themselves rigged with all sorts of tricks to distort majority rule, along with the media, decide the candidates.

Under the Constitution, if there was no majority in the Electoral College, then the election would be decided by the House of Representatives among the top contenders—with each state having one vote. It was a sensible way to evolve a majority, a firmer and more federal consensus. It was not expected that all the members of the House would be party hacks. In the beginning they were not.

Our present party system did not begin to take hold until the 1830's, and then chiefly in states like New York, Pennsylvania, and Ohio where both state and federal patronage were sizable, and organizations could be built and maintained on spoils. Representation elsewhere, in Massachusetts and South Carolina, for instance, continued to be based upon principle rather than organization. In the early days of the government, a federal representative could know and be known by nearly every substantial citizen in his district. Moreover, he had to meet the people face to face and debate his potential opponents. He was the representative of his people, who knew his character, and not the creature of party.

There remained many relatively independent members of Congress right down to the War Between the States. In fact, elections, the counting of heads, were relatively unimportant. Once the two or three candidates had debated around the district, it was pretty clear who was the choice, and the others often withdrew before the count. Serving in Congress was not a money-making proposition or a long-term career.

It was also true that many congressional districts, and this was also true of state legislative districts, through continuity over time, had developed characters of their own, even if they did not always strictly reflect "one man, one vote." Artificial creations like congressional districts and counties acquired identities for those who lived there, so that being the representative of "the Old Ninth" carried with it a strong if intangible identification with a particular known history, geography, and collection of communities.

The Supreme Court's "one man, one vote" decisions have destroyed all of this. Even though state constitutions, presumably the voice of the people, chose to distribute legislative power in part by considerations other than numbers, in the interest of better representation, the voice of the people meant nothing compared to the Justices' notions of equality. So today we have legislative districts devised by computer that divide not only counties but neighborhoods, which snake up and down 100-foot corridors of superhighways, and change every few years. These changes have hardly been remarked upon, but they have hopelessly distorted the relationship between representatives and their constituents and compromised the will of the majority.

Moreover, who are the people forming the majority? When I last went to
renew my driving license, in a peaceful suburb in conservative South Carolina,
the motor vehicle employees were busy (under federal mandate) registering to
vote a considerable number of Asians and Hispanics—whether citizens or not,
who knows?

It was not thus at the founding of the American Republic. George
Washington and John Adams received the suffrages of their fellow citizens in
much different fashion. Most elections were indirect except those for the representative bodies; these, not the executive and judicial, had most of the power, and
the number of decisions made by the public sector at any level was small. Voting
was viva voce. The justices of the peace spread a table under the trees by the
courthouse and the citizen came and declared his choice in front of the whole
public (before or after to be feted with rum and barbecue by the candidates'
friends). It was a manly act of citizenship, allied to serving in the militia or on a
jury. It was limited to those who had achieved responsible ownership of productive private property.

Of course, since human nature was present in those days, there was demagoguery and clandestine manipulation, but some eras and societies are more honorable than others. When the election, which often took several days, was over,
there was a general public knowledge of the sense of the community. The utilitarian counting of heads with which we are now so obsessed was an afterthought.

Can we really say today that our counting of papers in a box, or of holes in
a computer card, produces majority rule in any but a superficial sense? Do we
really think, when such vast amounts of power, wealth, and vanity are at stake,
that politicians, who control the machinery and the ground rules of the elections,
always, or even usually, behave honestly?[8]

My enlightenment came in 1968 when I volunteered as a poll watcher for the
Wallace campaign in a liberal college town in the South. I discovered, as did the
Republican watcher, that the Democratic precinct manager, an old time leftist of
local notoriety, was giving two ballots to the black voters, and instructing them
on how to fill them out. When confronted, she avowed unashamedly that she was
making amends for their previous disfranchisement, which was only fair. We
reported this to the Republican county committee, and were ready to swear affi-
davits. We were told later that the FBI was notified. Nothing further was ever
heard. Nixon carried the state by a plurality over Wallace. It was not in the interest of Republican politicians to upset the system. I had my youthful eyes opened
to the difference between politics and democracy.

Does anyone really believe that John F. Kennedy defeated Nixon fair and
square in 1960? In an incredibly close election divided by less than one percentage point and with evidence of fraud in several key states? Nixon made the
"statesmanlike" decision not to protest and upset the apple cart. A real democratic statesman would have insisted that the true will of the people be deter-

8. This was written four years before the presidential election debacle of 2000.

mined, whatever the consequences to the convenient party games. The consequences for American society were immense—the deification of Kennedy by the media, his martyrdom, and the implementation of social revolution by Johnson on the emotions produced by that martyrdom. Yet in what sense can Kennedy's election be said to represent the unqualified will of the people?

It is absurd to congratulate ourselves on our right to go to the polls and choose between Tweedledee and Tweedledum when in fact our government, though it is never mentioned in polite circles, is in many aspects a plutocracy. We plain folk are over-shadowed by accumulations of wealth that make the difference in property between George Washington and a tenant farmer insignificant. Decisions are made more often than anyone likes to admit by the wielders of great capital. It is a measure of real power when one can exercise it without even being noticed. How often behind some foreign policy decision we find lurking the interests of the Rockefellers and other big money manipulators. One does not have to be a conspiratorialist to see the distortion of majority rule this represents.

How else to explain a buffoon like Nelson Rockefeller becoming governor of a powerful state, Vice President (by appointment), and a perennial presidential candidate without any trace of intellectual or moral qualification? Somewhere Carroll Quigley, President Clinton's mentor and an admiring historian of our Establishment, records an anecdote of Averell Harriman, the multimillionaire Democratic mover and shaker. When he first heard of Jimmy Carter, Harriman, who was temporarily out of the loop, remarked in a moment of senescent candor: "He can't be President. I don't even know him." As Orwell remarked long ago, some animals are more equal than others.

History begins about 1960 for our media and politicians. They know no more of the spirit and little more of the letter of early American history and government than I do of the Han dynasty. The complications that may well arise in the 1996 presidential election, if there is no majority, could become a virtue. They could invoke further deliberation and compromise and the addressing of neglected issues. They won't, because we will see the media and the two parties coalescing to put down challenges to their hegemony.

The 1824 election saw a crisis that may have meaning for ours soon to come. With the Virginia dynasty at an end, there were now four presidential candidates, and the Electoral College had registered no majority. The politicians' machinations then kicked into gear—Henry Clay on behalf of John Quincy Adams, Martin Van Buren and various other sleazy operators for General Jackson, and many others.

In the House, 13 states were needed to elect a President. Twelve, after much wheeling and dealing, were for Adams, including some which had favored Jackson, who had the largest plurality, in the canvass. The New York delegation, thanks to Van Buren, was equally divided, with one undecided. The undecided was Stephen Van Rensselaer, a wealthy fool of the Nelson Rockefeller type who, like Van Buren, had originally supported Crawford, now out of the running.

Besieged by Adams and Jackson advocates, the old man prayed while the count was being taken. When he opened his eyes it was revealed to him that Adams should be President—and so he was. There followed one of the most beleaguered and divisive administrations in American history, which led to the rapid formation of competing political parties—parties competing less on principles than on personalities, spoils, and organization. Thus was set the basic text of American political discourse, the gift of Van Buren to the democratic process: the politician who seeks the middle, is all things to all men, pretends that divisive issues do not exist, and gives a plausible but noncommittal answer to every question.

The Lincoln crisis gives us another historical lesson. Though a clear winner in 1860 in the Electoral College, Lincoln had slightly less than 40 percent of the popular vote, more narrowly concentrated than in any election before or since. Clearly a majority of the American people never favored his hardline policies, which led to war and social revolution. We ought to give some thought to exactly what is meant by government of, by, and for the people.

In fact, glancing back over American history, very few of the largest and most decisive acts have been taken by means of real majority rule. How often has the peace candidate inaugurated war shortly after his election, prior to rather than as a consequence of majority consensus? And no Southerner can forget Reconstruction, with the qualified barred from the polling places, the unqualified marshaled to vote, dishonest officials routinely certifying fraudulent election returns, and the presence of military intimidation. Indeed, it is clear that Samuel J. Tilden was elected President in 1876 and not Rutherford B. Hayes, who was sworn in nonetheless.

In 1824, 1844, 1848, 1856, 1860, 1876, 1880, 1884, 1888, 1892, 1912, 1916, 1948, 1960, 1968, and 1992, Presidents were elected without a majority, and in 1836, 1852, 1976, and 1980, the majority was less than one percent. After a number of these narrow elections, there followed great and irrevocable decisions. We need to find ways of determining firmer and truer majorities and mandates—of taking the real sense of the people rather than abiding by the deceitful choices offered by party and media hacks.

One need is to derail the present party system and force a more honest deliberation of public issues. Possibly the American people are already moving in that direction. Even more important is the need to devolve decision-making back to places where the will of the people can really be known and effected.

(1996)

The Electoral College, 2000

To anyone who has spent some time with the Framers and ratifiers of the U.S. Constitution, most current talk about that document seems not about the Constitution at all but about some fanciful construct of wishful thinking, accumulated misunderstandings, and successful usurpations. This is certainly so in regard to the recent discussions of the Electoral College.

True, the Electoral College was, as is now complained of, in part designed to take the selection of president a remove or two from the people. The reason for this was not to thwart the people's will but to induce deliberation and mature consideration of the public good and the virtues of candidates by persons who were in a position to have some solid knowledge of the matter. This design, of course, has been rendered null by the machinations of political parties. Electors are now anonymous party hacks whose names often do not even appear on the ballot and who would not know what you are talking about if you mentioned deliberation and judgment.

But an even more important consideration in the design of the Electoral College was the representation of the states. There was no possibility of a mass vote, since each state set its own qualifications for the franchise and chose the electors in its own manner—by the legislature or by districts in the beginning. States no longer set their franchise: The federal government now requires us to allow 18-year-olds to vote and to register aliens when they show up at the drivers' license bureau.

Nevertheless, the Electoral College, at least potentially, represents the states. The smaller states were given more weight, by a design (and necessity at the time) that permeates the real Constitution. If the Electoral College yielded no majority, the House of Representatives was to make the choice, *with each state having one vote*. In fact, the Framers expected this to happen quite often.

The functioning of the Electoral College was perverted in the 19th century by political party organizations. The people could (and can today) vote only for candidates selected by party conventions, which are neither democratic nor recognized by the Constitution. (A lot of Americans probably think the two parties are part of the Constitution.) This is, in fact, a much more serious denial of majority rule than the weight given to small states in the college. So is the winner-take-all system, another invention of the party hacks.

There is nothing in the Constitution that requires all the votes of a state to go to one candidate. According to present practice, a candidate may win California with a 35-percent vote in a three-way race and receive all of California's electoral votes, thereby disenfranchising two thirds of the voters. The only reason for this is that it is convenient for political parties.

If we really wanted to live up to the majority rule and preserve the virtues of the Electoral College, we would take the high constitutional function away from parties and choose electors by districts and as independents—men and women known for character and reason and an understanding of the people they represent. (Of course, they would have to be real districts, not ones designed by federal judges to maximize the success of favored groups.)

They would assemble in their state capitals and vote after deliberation and without reference to party organization or to polls and predictions and media declarations of winners on the basis of one percent of the votes. This would be closer to real majority rule and the real Constitution, and the results might be quite interesting.

(2000)

By Whose Consent?

A Review of *The Morality of Consent*, by Alexander M. Bickel, New Haven and London: Yale University Press, 1975, 156 pages.

The dust jacket flaps of *The Morality of Consent* contain some rather unspecific blurbs and a biographical sketch of the author. One suspects that the writer of that copy, like the reviewer, despaired of summarizing in brief compass the purport of this difficult work, which is, frankly, unfinished to a degree not suggested by most of the critical notices that have appeared. According to an unsigned foreword, Alexander M. Bickel, legal scholar and public philosopher, "had left the manuscript for this book" at his death in 1974. However, the reader soon realizes that what the author left were lectures (on democratic process, the nature of citizenship, aspects of civil disobedience, and moral authority), the metamorphosis of which into a book unfortunately had been terminated short of a fully articulated statement. Therefore, the temptation cannot entirely be resisted to grapple with the more important work adumbrated here rather than the slight though piquant volume actually in hand.

The title suggests a treatise on the rights of minorities or on the conditions of willing acquiescence in a democratic government. Both these topics recur in the lecture-essays, but it is not precisely accurate to postulate them as a main theme. A better title would have been "The Computing Principle." This principle, which Bickel professed to draw from Edmund Burke, is the home base for every foray. Although it is never fully defined, it may be described fairly, perhaps, as a maxim of pragmatism and caution, a warning to take into account circumstances and consequences in the governing of men. Bickel skillfully posed the desirability of this principle, as a mode of proceedings, over against a single-minded moralistic pursuit of ends.

The Morality of Consent has been described in some quarters as a conservative statement. It is a work diffused, though unevenly and ambivalently, with self-consciously Burkean insights, a work that boldly confronts some fashionable fallacies of the day, a work frankly antimajoritarian and anti-contractarian. Yet it is mistakenly called conservative because it rests upon a misapplication of the Burkean calculus. One may agree with Burke that "political reason is a computing principle" without agreeing that Bickel has computed with the right denominations. For Burke the "circumstances" that were to be taken into account in political action were substantive. He had in mind the orders, estates, personae, lands, locales, faith, customs, attitudes, habits, mores, forms, and ceremonies that made up the fabric of Europe. Burke's point of departure was a spirit of awe and respect, of presumption in favor of the society-in-being as a product of history. But where Burke approached extant circumstances with awe and allegiance, Bickel approached with a prudential respect but with, at bottom, a disembodied and provisional commitment. When Bickel urges us to take into account "circumstances," the "circumstances" are essentially momentary things that will in due course be adjusted to a preconceived doctrinaire program. To put it another way, Burke was concerned to adapt change to the what-is; Bickel was concerned to adjust the what-is as smoothly as possible to change. Even while he tells us that "we cannot survive a politics of moral attack" he approves the motives and consequences of most of the moral attacks that have occurred in recent decades, although he is prepared to quibble (and it is only a quibble) about the means and pace.

It is not too much to say, in fact, that Bickel accepted as legitimate and natural a scenario of American history as a process in which circumstances are made to adjust, by successive waves of moral attacks, to a progressivist agenda. Bickel was, then, in the final analysis, one of the schemers decried by Burke, albeit as moderate and decent as possible for such a one to be. Rather than the manifesto of a conservative judicial philosophy that it presumes to be, *The Morality of Consent* reduces to a circular letter to fellow schemers warning them to proceed a little less heedlessly than they have been doing in recent years, especially in their reliance upon the judicial oligarchy to achieve their ends. Pay attention to the consent of the governed, not as worthy of respect in itself, but because you are likely to run into trouble if you don't.

Despite many wise observations that would persuade us to a contrary conclusion, Bickel was at bottom devoted not to substance, but to processes. He was an advocate, perhaps one of the last able advocates, of the Open Society—that society defined only by procedure, where everything is always subject to question. This is true, *even though* the burden of these essays is to warn against pursuing the theory of the Open Society too literally and thoroughly. To Bickel the Whig tradition as it came to America consisted entirely of the legal stratagems and structures that evolved to defend a certain type of community, not the substance of that community itself. But this is to miss the point of Burke (a point shared pervasively in the "republicanism" of the American Founding Fathers)— liberty (to have the kind of society that Englishmen had come to feel natural) depends on the social fabric—on disposition, character, and virtue—and not on some body of rules. For example, free speech in its meaningful aspects arises from a particular tradition of manners ("the rights of Englishmen") not from the First Amendment ("the rights of Man") which provides it a mere negative protection. Bickel is antimajoritarian not because minorities are worthy of respect as a part of Creation but because majorities can potentially interfere with those processes held to be the highest morality, for he tells us that "the highest morality is almost always the morality of process." There is a sense, even a Burkean sense, in which that is true: in Anglo-American history the defense of hallowed individual rights *is* interconnected with procedural checks on magistrates, but the true sense is not the one explicated here.

Though egalitarian, the Open Society is elitist because it always assumes in practice that inevitable progress is something that a reluctant or indifferent mass is persuaded to consent to by an enlightened minority which retains a veto over an intransigent majority. In other words, the consent of some is more important than the consent of others. How else can one reconcile Bickel's criticism of unlimited claims to civil disobedience and advocacy of consent and constitutionalism with his seeming praise for "the achievement, however qualified, of the antiwar movement in toppling a sitting president, in the midst of war, in 1968, before a single national vote had been cast." The failure of a handful of radicals to achieve their private moral vision of foreign policy, then, would cause a Bickellian more discomfort than the anguish of ten thousand parents at Louisville oppressed by a "law" to which no representative body has or could give assent. When it comes to consent, the former are more equal than the latter. That is at bottom a peculiar philosophy of democratic processes and consent.

The end effect of the elevation of procedure to the highest value is to make government, which is the receptacle of all procedures, precedent and superior to society. Society becomes that malleable and unfixed entity which wise men in control of government do things to. This is exactly to reverse the Burkean-Whig order, expressed by Calhoun, a better student of Burke and a better philosopher of the ethics of consent, who postulated that society precedes government, which exists to preserve and enhance it.

In sum, this statement barely scratches the surface of the problem of consent as it is raised in our time, which is that we have passed by forfeit from a republic resting on the consent of its constituent parts to what the Founding Fathers would have called an "aristocracy," meaning an oligarchy. It will take better arguments than these to counter the oligarchs and restore deliberative government, however encouraging it may be that a voice of caution—more than that, a voice of conscience—has been raised within the ranks of the oligarchical party.

(1976)

Lani Guinier

Not since Pat Buchanan ran for President has the media hysteria reached the level brought on by the (aborted) nomination of Professor Lani Guinier to head the civil rights division of the Justice Department. "Ms. Guinier Buys Into Calhounism" screams the headline attached to an anti-Guinier diatribe by neoconservative columnist Paul Gigot. "Quota Queen" shouts a finger-pointing *Wall Street Journal* op-ed by neocon Clint Bolick. And Abe Rosenthal, per usual, cries wolf: "She stands for racial polarization."

When the air-raid sirens go off all at once, we can reasonably assume that there is something more going on than doth meet the eye. Note the use of "Quota Queen," a racist slur that has overtones of "Welfare Queen." And the absolute ultimate indictment: Guinier, says Mr. Gigot, agrees with John C. Calhoun and not Martin Luther King!

There are probably very good reasons for questioning Ms. Guinier's fitness to serve in sensitive areas of the Justice Department. What is interesting about this furor is that she was not done in by conservatives but by those who claim to be dedicated to democratism. So far as one can disentangle any hard information from the hysterical rhetoric and the usual neoconservative tissue of historical, philosophical, and constitutional ignorance, vulgarity, and mendacity, the objections to Ms. Guinier seem to revolve around two of her beliefs: that the black minority and the white majority in America do not have entirely compatible interests, and that there should therefore be some institutionalized weight given to the votes of black people even when they conflict with majority rule.

That is to say, she has questioned the allegedly sacred and traditional American principle of equality and thus touched the raw nerve of democratic socialist mythology. Regarding her first position, Ms. Guinier has simply told the truth—always a dangerous course in American politics. If the quotidian fact, known to every school child in America, that different people have different situations and different interests is publicly acknowledged, what happens to the neocon dream of a society of utterly interchangeable goods? People might discuss real issues rather than chimerical goals and might actually reach a settlement.

As to her second point, nothing could be more American than to question unrestricted majority rule. Our Founding Fathers believed in a government resting ultimately upon the consent of the people (as opposed to the divine right of a monarch or the inherited privileges of an aristocracy, and, of course, by "people" they meant the responsible members of society, not every respirating creature with two legs). They were republicans, not democrats—social, global, or any other kind. They believed majority rule should be limited and chastened even as it, generally and in the long run, prevailed.

After all, they gave us a Constitution with a bicameral legislature; a "popular" House elected within property and other qualifications; a states' rights

Senate; bills that must be read thrice before passage; an indirectly elected President with a veto power; and an independent judiciary. And all this merely to alleviate majority rule in a government that was itself extremely limited in its functions and jurisdiction.

In the spirit of the Founders, John C. Calhoun saw that the restrictions on majority rule were not, in every respect working as they had been intended. Contrary to Madison's expectation that various interests in a large country would check each other, different interests had concentrated in different regions, making a "numerical majority" that exploited a minority. Some few small additions were therefore needed in the accepted devices by which the majority was to be restrained.

Further, Calhoun illuminated the moral principle behind such restrictions, which he summed up as the "concurrent majority." The "mere numerical majority" was not itself an ethical or an adequately democratic idea. What was needed was a higher consensus, a larger majority reaching a decision after deliberation and compromise—a process that could only be invoked by investing the minority with certain institutionalized powers of self-defense. Far from being a rejection of majority rule, the resulting consensus was democratically and morally preferable to the dictate of a 51 percent majority, which might itself be merely a temporary and expedient coalition of self-seekers. Not everyone thinks as poorly of Calhoun's idea as does Mr. Gigot. A blue-ribbon commission in Britain, which recently delivered the most extensive and hopeful report ever made on the problems of Northern Ireland, makes Calhoun the centerpiece of its proposals.

Ms. Guinier's particular ideas and the interests that have occasioned them may be good or bad, but there is certainly nothing in the least un-American or undemocratic in a philosophical consideration of the imperfections of majority rule, or of the possibility of different constitutional arrangements. The only thing that is really threatened by such discussion is the "democratic" orthodoxies of those who wish to keep all public debate in channels approved by themselves.

One obvious result of this is to make public discourse vapid and dishonest. Ms. Guinier seems, in fact, to have been willing to write about real and hard issues forthrightly, however provocative some of her solutions might be. And her defenders are quite right that the critics have vulgarized and caricatured her serious intellectual positions. The critics have blurred the valid distinction between a theoretical discussion and a public position and made it impossible for anyone who has ever said anything worthwhile, anything serious enough to be misunderstood by fools, to serve in office.

But surely honest and reasonable people should make a distinction between an intellectual position and conduct in public office. Such a distinction, for instance, was very clear in the case of Jefferson—for Jefferson the President and American political leader was not the same man as the *philosophe* who speculated in private letters to his friends. The Establishment, of course, wants to guarantee that anyone who has ever held any intellectual positions, has ever argued or speculated in a way that they have not approved, is excluded from public office. All officeholders, in their ideal world, would be as brilliant as Dan Quayle or as principled as Judge Souter (and would never include an M.E. Bradford or a Robert Bork).

There is an even deeper dishonesty here—because, in fact, there are extant at this moment in American society institutionalized special privileges for blacks that violate majority rule (as well as traditional principles of law), since a clear majority, for instance, disapproves of affirmative action and busing. Race-norming in employment, double prosecution of offenses against blacks, reparations rather than punishment for riots, and much else is already institutionalized in our society, Ms. Guinier's critics are not really opposed to this special privilege (though they may worry a bit about quotas cutting into their own turf). What they are opposed to is talking about it honestly in public.

From their viewpoint, they are quite right. Confirmation hearings for Ms. Guinier might well have developed into the first honest and open public discussion of affirmative action in American history—the undoubted result of which would have been vast outrage and the possible unraveling of the civil rights establishment. Open and honest deliberation among all the relevant opinions was essential to Calhoun's concurrent majority. Real majority rule is the last thing Ms. Guinier's critics want, even less than she does.

Finally, where Ms. Guinier parts from Calhoun and where she goes wrong is not where she doubts majority rule as sufficient for the protection of a minority. This is an honored American tradition. What *is* wrong with her position is the moral stance of the parties. All Calhoun wanted was to protect one part of society from another part—to prevent the federal government from exploiting the economy of the minority South for the benefit of the majority North. It was merely a self-protection and an elaboration of the accepted concept of limited government. But what Ms. Guinier poses, of course, is something quite different: not a right of defense, but a permanent, untouchable privilege under an imperial state—for a guaranteed income levy on the majority. Here lies the real problem and the real abandonment of democracy.

(1993)

10th Amendment Madness

Hearing Senator Dole babble about the Tenth Amendment is a sad reminder—as if more evidence were needed—of the terminal ignorance and insincerity of our rulers. But one cannot expect a politician who has been a (very successful) functionary of the imperial state all his life to understand that the delegation of powers by the people has to do with something other than how the (shrinking) pie will be divided up. The Tenth Amendment does not have anything to do with who will pay for "motor voter" bills or "free" school lunches or any other of the "benefits" that our rulers provide us for the inestimable privilege of serving them. It has to do with the basic function of the Constitution: that is, the limitation of government.

Let us peruse this forgotten relic closely:

The powers not delegated to the United States by the Constitution, nor prohibited by it to the States, are reserved to the States respectively, or to the people.

The amendment is the capstone of those amendments adopted in concluding the process of ratification of the original Constitution. It follows a long list of "shall nots" directed at the federal government and in particular the Congress. More than that, if we are to believe Madison and nearly every other Founder, it provides the fundamental key to construing the Constitution—the Constitution as ratified by the people of the States (old and new)—not the opinions of the Philadelphia projectors nor the extra-constitutional imaginings of Publius so beloved of shallow political philosophers. The Constitution as validated by the consent of the people of the States is defined by the Tenth Amendment. The federal government, in all its branches, has those powers delegated in the instrument. All other powers are *reserved.*

But the great tragedy of American history is that the Tenth Amendment is not self-enforcing (else there would have been no need for the previous nine amendments). The Attorney General of South Carolina is suing in the federal courts on Tenth Amendment grounds against the unfunded mandate of the "motor voter" bill. This is all to the well and good as it contributes to educate the public and a favorable court decision will be helpful. Nonetheless, to ask the federal courts to validate the Tenth Amendment is to give away the game before the first whistle. The people of the states have not delegated to federal judges the right to decide what their rights are. This is a power they have reserved to themselves.

The Tenth Amendment is not to be left up to the federal government to interpret for itself. The essence of our Constitution is that Power must not be allowed to define its own limits. It must be checked by other Power. It is up to the States themselves to make the Tenth Amendment good, to enforce it by every means at their disposal. The name of this country is, after all, the United States, a confederation, and not the American Empire.

(1995)

Unconstitutional

*Can the liberties of a nation be thought secure, when we have
removed their only firm basis, a conviction in the minds of the
people that these liberties are the gift of God?*
— THOMAS JEFFERSON

    Books Reviewed: *American Political Theology: Historical Perspective and
Theoretical Analysis*, edited by Charles W. Dunn, New York: Praeger, 1984, 195
pages; and *The Moral Foundations of the American Republic*, third edition, edited by Robert H. Horwitz, Charlottesville: University Press of Virginia, 1986, 347
pages.

Not long ago *Time* magazine celebrated America with a special issue.
Among the ornaments of this production was an essay by an ersatz
"Tocqueville," purporting to provide an account of what that wise observer would
say today, were he to update his ruminations on democracy in America. The new-
fangled Tocqueville observed that the old Tocqueville had been wrong in his prediction that America would be characterized by an ever-increasing "tyranny of
the majority." To the contrary, apparently on the evidence of vast numbers "doing
their own thing," he could find no American majority at all.

But, of course, hordes of the otherwise indistinguishable, individualizing
themselves by adherence to varying fads, do not disprove Tocqueville. Rather,
they fit in exactly with what he expected. In the same issue of *Time* was an
extended paean to what the editors consider one of our most salient national characteristics, a pervasive and inescapable popular culture (which, they did not say,
trivializes and debases our land and much of the rest of the world as well). And
Time itself, with its compulsive weekly emissions, straitjacketing the proliferating mystery and variety of life into a pat formula, precisely calculated to gull the
rootless half-educated into believing they are being made party to some insider's
insight into reality, is as good evidence as anyone could want for the sad truth of
the wise Frenchman's prognostication of a ubiquitous conformity of mind.

As we begin to contemplate the approaching bicentennial of the United
States Constitution, Tocqueville seems more and more apposite. He was, of
course, concerned not so much with the American Constitution as with the
American constitution. It is among the virtues of the two books at hand that they
recognize implicitly that the two phenomena, though distinct, are ineluctably
interrelated. They share the further virtue of explicit acknowledgment that neither the upper- nor the lower-case phenomenon can properly be discussed without reference to a moral dimension.

In *American Political Theology*, Charles W. Dunn has admirably fulfilled his modest and useful intention to provide in textbook fashion a dispassionate exposition "of how, why, and when" politics and religion intersect. This is no small feat in treating a subject so vast, undefined, and fraught with intense conflict, and the work can be of considerable usefulness to teachers at any level who need a clear historical and theoretical analysis of the intersection as it has presented itself in the experience of our country.

Four sections present periods of theological-political tension in American history by means of exposition of background and an evenhanded selection of excerpts from primary documents. The four periods are the Founding, the Civil War, the Social Gospel and New Deal, and the present-day confrontation of "humanism" and Christianity. Two additional chapters, "The Theological Dimensions of Presidential Leadership" and "A Theory of American Political Theology," are less successful, though they do serve to clarify the conflict of liberal and conservative theologies and the interpenetration of theological with economic, political, and social concerns. Dunn's work constitutes what an old-fashioned scholar would call "a real advance in science"—that is, it leaves the analytical state of the subject in an improved condition.

This analytical success is partly due to the shaping and delimiting provided by the concept of theology. Theology, morality, and ethics are of course not the same thing. They are analytically distinct considered in their political aspect, not to mention their personal application. In public discussion we often tend to conflate these concepts under a too imprecise rubric of "moral" considerations. I committed this conflation in my third paragraph above. If there is any fault to be found with *The Moral Foundations of the American Republic*, an excellent book of essays by 14 contributors, it is that the different senses of "moral" tend to be run together and to be treated as if all were synonyms for "democracy."

Given the secularist and amoral terms of contemporary debate and the present moral condition of the Republic, a collection which focuses on the centrality of moral foundations is a great contribution and a good sign. The contributors are mostly political scientists, with a few historians thrown in. They include liberals of a thoughtful sort (Richard Hofstadter, Wilson Carey McWilliams, Robert A. Dahl) and moderate conservatives (Walter Berns, James Ceaser, and others, nearly all followers, apparently, of the late Leo Strauss). The essays are, for the most part, intellectually and ethically muscular and will well repay reading by anyone who is already fairly well-grounded in the Founding. As appears from the learned and graceful introductory essay by Will Morrisey, the contributors play against each other, advancing toward the truth in dialectical fashion: means vs. ends; public vs. private; principles vs. self-interest; equality vs. liberty; limited vs. pure democracy; character vs. intellect. All the right questions are defined by Morrisey without an ungentlemanly insistence on specific answers. Should any reader be so enterprising as to secure a large grant to organize a symposium for the bicentennial, I recommend Morrisey's essay as an ideal outline for discussion.

The conservative contributors to this collection, while worthily exploring worthy subjects and usually besting their liberal opponents, seem regrettably lim-ited by the conventions of Straussian political science. In assessing the American Constitution, one of these conventions is the formula: Morality = Equality = Democracy. The equation is not true, either as a general proposition or as a description of the American tradition. The Founders were moral men, and they may have been, in some sense, egalitarians. But their moral sense, which rested upon revelation and tradition, was quite distinct from their egalitarianism, which was historical and circumstantial. To postulate the chief *moral* foundation of democracy in terms of *equality* is quite literally to flout all the wisdom of the ages and to universalize a particular modern tendency that was in fact foreign to the Founders. It is to make morality dependent upon democracy rather than the other way around. Even worse, it is to meet the liberal on his own treacherous ground and therefore restrict ourselves to a limited and hopeless battle for the recovery of the Constitution, for it is precisely the impulse to make morality and egalitarianism equivalent that lies at the root of all serious deformations of the Constitution.

The grounds of my misgivings about *The Moral Foundations of the American Republic* can best be seen, perhaps, by comparing it with another, neg-lected work of a few years ago. *The Theology of Christian Resistance: A Symposium* (edited by Gary North; Geneva Divinity School Press, 1983), took up the same questions of the moral foundations of the constitutional republic. The scholars who contributed to that symposium, however, wrote from *inside* of a lived and felt constitutional and theological tradition, a tradition described by Dunn neutrally but with historical substance. *The Moral Foundations of the American Republic*, however, remains within the bounds of the abstractions of 20th-century democratist political theory and nowhere seriously questions the secular Liberal Establishment.

(1986)

In the Beginning

A Review of *Novus Ordo Seclorum: The Intellectual Origins of the Constitution*, by Forrest McDonald, Lawrence: University Press of Kansas, 1985, 359 pages.

If it is true that the Constitution of the United States is to be construed by its *intent* rather than by mysterious and highly malleable forces of "evolution," then recovery of the intellectual context out of which it arose is of the highest priority. However, the discovery of intent is primarily a question of *historical* understanding rather than a matter of the sort of legal sophistries used by 19th-century nationalists who rationalized what was established as a Federal republic into a consolidated commercial democracy. Nor is intent a matter of the speculative inquiries into various abstract symbols such as "democracy," "equality," "liberty," engaged in by all 20th-century liberals and most 20th-century conservatives.

For these reasons, the vigorous, convention-busting work of Forrest McDonald, a historian steeped, as a historian should be, in the primary documents of the Founding era, is a contribution to constitutional government that can not easily be overestimated. Nothing finer, perhaps, has been written in brief and lucid compass than McDonald's four chapters on the intellectual context of the Founders, both as to the implicit and often unelaborated assumptions which all held in common and as to the points of difference among them.

"The Rights of Englishmen" sets forth the legal heritage of the American colonists with a specificity that corrects innumerable liberal and libertarian misreadings. "Systems of Political Theory" illuminates the American fix on the European and English heritage of political thought, reducing some of the usually emphasized thinkers to their proper lesser role and highlighting others that were important but have been less noticed. "Systems of Political Economy" does the same for economics, which was an emerging category of systematic thought just at the time of the Founding. "The Lessons of Experience, 1776–1787" reviews what had been learned from the Revolution and the making of the state constitutions. All this is expounded with a deep though uncluttered and practical learning that is reminiscent of the Founding generation itself. The chapters which discuss the personnel and proceedings of the Philadelphia Convention, ground which McDonald has covered extensively elsewhere, are less successful, though they do serve the purpose of making a connection between the Convention and the ideas described in earlier chapters.

There is one quite serious lack in the work. There ought to have been a chapter dealing with the debates of the state conventions which ratified the Constitution. For the Constitution, as it came from Philadelphia, was nothing more than a draft, a committee report. It gathered its validity entirely, and therefore in the final analysis its *intent*, from its adoption by the people of the states.

That ratification embodied a significant further elucidation and amendment of the terms by which it was to be understood. But McDonald is a conservative of the Federalist persuasion whose hero is Alexander Hamilton. From that standpoint, as from the standpoint of 19th-century nationalists and 20th-century liberals, it is unseemly to dwell upon the fact that it was ratification by the states and not drafting by the Convention which gave the Constitution its validity.

Therefore, investigation of the intent of the Constitution conventionally concentrates on the discussions in Philadelphia. To pursue the meaning of the Constitution further would throw us all the way back to that ancient, once supreme but long discredited idea of states' rights.

McDonald is our best historian of the Founding era. No one has sounded that era more deeply and fruitfully, and it is a kind of counsel of perfection to ask for more. Yet, if he could be persuaded to study the polemics of the 19th century, between the states' rights school of Calhoun, Stephens, John Taylor, Dabney, Bledsoe, and numerous others, and the consolidators—such as Story, Curtis, Bancroft, and Sumner—then he would gain insight into how the very context of the Founding was subtly warped by the latter in ways that have affected the historical vision of all later commentators, including, perhaps, even McDonald himself.

(1987)

From Union to Empire

I am convinced 'twas Calhoun who divined
How the great western star's last race would run.
— ALLEN TATE, Fragments of a Meditation

My subject is our lost and stolen heritage of states' rights; my goal is to point out a few home truths that were clear to our Founders and forefathers but that we have lost. Just a few years ago, we had a bicentennial celebration of the Constitution. As far as I am aware, republicanism and federalism, the two most salient features of the Constitution, were never mentioned. Instead, we had a glorification of multiculturalism.

Federalism implies states' rights, and states' rights imply a right of secession. The cause of states' rights is the cause of liberty; they rise or fall together. If we had been able to maintain the real union of sovereign states founded by our forefathers, then there would not be, could not be, the imperial central state that we suffer under today. The loss of states' rights is mirrored by the rise of the American empire, where a vast proportion of the citizens' wealth is engrossed by bureaucracy; where our personal and local affairs are ever more minutely and inflexibly managed by a remote power; where our resources are squandered meddling in the affairs of distant peoples.

That happy old Union was a friendly contract—the states managing their own affairs, joining together in matters of defense, and enjoying free trade among themselves, and indeed, enjoying free trade with the world, because the Constitution, as is sometimes forgotten, required all taxes to be uniform throughout the Union and absolutely forbade taxation of the exports of any state. The federal government was empowered to lay a modest customs duty to raise revenue for its limited tasks, but otherwise had no power to restrict or assist enterprises.

That is what the States United meant to our Founders—a happy Union of mutual consent and support. It did not mean a government that dictated the arrangement of every parking lot in every public and private building in every town, and the kind of grass that a citizen must plant around his boat dock. It did not mean the incineration of women and children who might have aroused the ire of a rogue federal police force, unknown to the Constitution and armed as for a foreign enemy. It did not mean that billions would be spent (as in Kuwait) restoring an oriental despot to his throne; or that a hero would be made out of the successful general who killed more women, children, soldiers trying to surrender, and his own men than he did armed enemies. Had George Washington been confronted with these things, he would have reached for his sword.

The founding fathers knew that republican societies were fragile—that they tended to degenerate into empires if extended beyond a small state, though they

hoped the federal principle would block this tendency in America. Their definition of self-government was the superiority of the community to its rulers. In a
reversal of the age-old pattern of mankind, the rulers (a necessary evil) became
delegates of the community temporarily assigned to take care of some part of the
public business. In an empire, like the one from which they had seceded, the
community existed for the support and gratification of the rulers. A republican
America was to be governed in the interest of the communities that made it up;
its rulers were 'responsible.' An empire, to the contrary, was governed by the
needs, ideas, interests, even whims, of the rulers. A republic passes over into
empire when political activity is no longer directed toward the well-being of the
people (mostly by leaving them alone), but becomes a mechanism for managing
people for the benefit of their rulers. That is to say, an empire's government
reflects management needs, and reflects the desires and will of those who control the machinery, rather than the interests and will of those being governed.
Who can doubt that we are now an empire? The American people no longer think
of the government as theirs, but as a hostile, manipulative, unjust, and unresponsive distant ruler.

A republic goes to war to defend itself and its vital interests, including possibly its honour. Empires go to war because going to war is one of the things irresponsible rulers do. The point of reference for a republic is its own well-being.
An empire has no point of reference except expansion of its authority. Its foreign
policy will be abstract, and will reflect on the vagaries of mind of the rulers, who
might, for instance, proclaim that it is their subjects' duty to establish a New
World Order, whatever the cost to their own blood and treasure. Who can doubt
that the once-proud republican Union of the states is now an empire?

An empire contains not free citizens, but subjects, interchangeable persons
having no intrinsic value except as taxpayers and cannon fodder. So, if the governors of an empire should feel that it is easier for them to placate criminals than
to punish them, they will turn over the neighbourhoods and schools of their subjects to criminals, and even punish officers of the law for acting too zealously
against the criminal class, thus violating the first rule of good government, which
is the preservation of order. A people's culture may be changed by imperial edict
to reflect a trumped-up multiculturalism (a sure sign of an empire), or their religion persecuted. And, of course, violating one of the essential rules of republicanism, that the laws be equal to all, the imperialists exempt themselves from the
commands they lay down for the rest of us. The republican right of self-government and the right of self-determination both necessarily incorporate the right of
secession—that a people may withdraw from an imperial power to defend its liberty, property, culture, and faith.

We know the problems. Where should we look for solutions? Changing the
personnel of the White House, the Congress, and the Supreme Court has been of
little avail. Thomas Jefferson gives us the answer: our most ancient and best tradition, states' rights. In his first inaugural address, Jefferson remarked that in
most ways Americans were very happily situated, and then asked:

What more is necessary to make us a happy and prosperous people? Still one thing more, fellow citizens—a wise and frugal government, which shall restrain men from injuring one another, which shall leave them otherwise free to regulate their own pursuits . . . and shall not take from the mouth of labour the bread that it has earned. This is the sum of good government.[9]

But how to preserve this form of government? What should we do, or not do? Jefferson answered: preserve elections (not the party system), maintain equal justice under the law, rely on the militia, avoid debt, maintain the freedoms of speech, religion, and trial by jury, and avoid entangling alliances. And most important: 'the support of the state governments in all their rights, as the most competent administrations for our domestic concerns and the surest bulwarks against anti-republican tendencies.'[10]

There is a large sophistical literature which tells us that states' rights was for Jefferson just a temporary expedient for other goals. This is false. For his own generation and several following, it was understood that the state sovereignty of the Kentucky resolutions was Jefferson's primary platform as an American leader.

John C. Calhoun, speaking in exactly the same tradition a generation later, said:

The question is in truth between the people and the supreme court. We contend, that the great conservative principle of our system is in the people of the States, as parties to the Constitutional compact, and our opponents that it is in the supreme court. . . . Without a full practical recognition of the rights and sovereignty of the States, our union and liberty must perish. State rights would be found . . . in all cases of difficulty and danger [to be] the only conservative principle in the system, the only one that could interpose an effectual check to the danger.[11]

By conservative principle he means not a political position of right as opposed to left—he means that which conserves and preserves the Constitution as it was intended. Contrast that with our present position. Forrest McDonald, our greatest living Constitutional scholar, writes:

Political scientists and historians are in agreement that federalism is the greatest contribution of the Founding Fathers to the science of government. It is also the only feature of the Constitution that has been successfully exported, that can be employed to protect liberty elsewhere in the world. Yet what we invented, and others imitate, no

---

9. *The Life and Selected Writings of Thomas Jefferson*, Adrienne Koch and William Peden, eds. (New York: Modern Library, 1944), pp. 323–24.
10. *Ibid.*
11. *The Essential Calhoun*, Clyde N. Wilson, ed. (New Brunswick, N.J.: Transaction, 1992), pp. 299–302.

longer exists on its native shores.[12]

Why are states' rights the last best bulwark of our liberties? It is a question of the sovereignty of the people—in which we all profess to believe. Every political community has a sovereign, an ultimate authority. The sovereign may delegate functions (as the states did to the federal government) though it may not alienate authority. It may not always rule from day to day, but it is that place in the society that has the last word when all else is said and done.

All agree that in America the people are sovereign—we are republicans, not monarchists or aristocrats. But what people? The term is not self-defining, any more than is the term liberty. What do we mean by the people? How do we know when the people have spoken? A simple electoral majority, which can shift the next day, is insufficient in bottom-line questions of sovereignty. By people, do we mean that if a million Chinese wade ashore in California and out vote everybody else, then they are sovereign? I think not.

In American terms, the government of the people can only mean the people of the states as living, historical, corporate, indestructible, political communities. The whole of the Constitution rests upon its acceptance by the people acting through their states. The whole of the government reflects this by the representation of the states in every legitimate proceeding. There is no place in the Constitution as originally understood where a mere numerical majority in some branch of the federal government can do as it pleases. The sovereign power resides, ultimately, in the people of the states. Even today, three-fourths of the states can amend the Constitution—that is, they can abolish the Supreme Court or the income tax, or even dissolve the Union. In no other way can we say the sovereign people have spoken their final word. States' rights is the American government, however much in abeyance its practice may have become.

The alternative to state sovereignty, as Calhoun pointed out, is to give the final say-so to the black-robed deities of the Court, who go into their closets, commune with the gods, and tell us what *our* Constitution means and what orders we must obey, no matter how absurd their interpretation may be. But this is to abandon the sovereignty of the people, that is, to abandon democracy or republicanism and to abandon constitutional government for oligarchy—and for an oligarchy based upon mystification rather than reason. James Madison, thought to be the Constitution's father, tells us that the meaning of the Constitution is to be sought 'not in the opinions or intentions of the body which planned and proposed it, but in those of the state conventions where it received all the authority which it possesses.'[13] *All the authority which it possesses!*

The sovereignty of the people, in which we all believe, can mean nothing except, purely and simply, the people of each state acting in their sovereign con-

---

12. Forrest McDonald, 'Federalism in America,' in *Requiem: Variations on Eighteenth Century Themes*, Forrest McDonald, ed. (Lawrence: University Press of Kansas, 1989).
13. James Madison, *Writings of James Madison*, Gaillard Hunt, ed. (New York: G.P. Putnam's Sons, 1900–1910), vol. 9, p. 372.

stitution-making capacity—as they did in the American Revolution when they threw off their king and assumed their own sovereignty, making their own constitutions. This was a revolution in the sense of a transfer of the locus of sovereignty, not in the sense of social upheaval. The people of each state ratified the Constitution as freely consenting sovereigns, agreeing to make an instrument, limited and precise, for some of their common business.

The case of South Carolina is illustrative but not unusual. The people of South Carolina were sovereign and independent before the Declaration of Independence. Through their own governor, legislature, courts, and armed forces they were exercising every sovereign power—taxation, war, treaty-making, and the execution of felons. The week before the Declaration of Independence, Colonel Moultrie and the South Carolina forces, from their palmetto log fort on Sullivan's Island, repulsed and defeated a British fleet that threatened to suppress their sovereign self-government.

The question is not altered by the fact that the Union has been expanded to fifty states. The Founding Fathers wisely made the Union expansible. The Congress may *admit* new states (or not), but the federal government does not *create* new states. States create themselves. The federal government may administer the territory, the land, before statehood, but only the sovereign people can adopt a constitution and incorporate themselves into a political society. Only by a sovereign act of free consent can a state ratify the U.S. Constitution—if we believe in government of the people. This is as true of the new states as the old, of Montana as of South Carolina—if we believe the people are sovereign.

Americans are natural republicans, not monarchists or aristocrats. That is, we believe government rests upon consent of the governed—this is the key phrase of the Declaration of Independence. Government is legitimate in just so far as it rests upon consent, that is, the people accede to the government. The opposite of accede is secede—the withdrawal of consent. The right to self-government rests on the right to withdraw consent from an oppressive government. That is the only really effective restriction on power, in the final analysis.

The American Revolution was not seen by our Fathers as a one-time event after which we were bound forever by the government. Of course, they did not wish to encourage so decisive a proceeding as secession for 'light and transient causes,' but it remained, in the final analysis, an option. Jefferson referred specifically to the 'secession' of the colonies from Britain, and he was willing to entertain the idea that in the future there might be two or more confederacies among the Americans (just as there had been many states and confederacies among the freedom-loving Greeks). The point was to preserve the right of self-government. What was sacred was not the Union but the consent of the governed, to which the Union might or might not be of assistance. Jefferson and the other Founders were patriots, not nationalists.

Anyone who has studied, with any degree of depth and honesty, the founding years and the period which followed understands that the idea of states' rights was considered obvious by our forefathers, however wildly irrelevant it may seem today. Centralisers were always on the defensive, and always compelled to conceal their intent. The United States were universally spoken of in the plural. It was clearly understood that the Bill of Rights meant the states binding the federal government to stay out of certain areas. ('Congress shall make no law. . . .') To most people at the time, and for several generations thereafter, the electoral victory of Jefferson and his friends in 1800 meant primarily the putting to rest of a too-assertive idea of national power. General Hamilton was sent home and his schemes of centralisation were put to rest, and so it remained until the War Between the States. But even that, though it fatally compromised the idea of states' rights, did not destroy it.

The states' rights interpretation of the Constitution was not, as its enemies have alleged, a mere theoretical rationalisation made up for the defense of slavery. It is, rather, a living heritage of great power, absolutely central to the understanding of the American liberty. It was the fundamental issue of the most bloody war in which Americans have been involved. Lost and stolen as the idea may be, American history cannot be understood without it.

Alexis de Tocqueville, the French historian thought by many to be the most profound foreign observer of America, wrote this in the 1830's:

The Union was formed by the voluntary agreement of the states; and these, in uniting together, have not forfeited their nationality, nor have they been reduced to the condition of one and the same people. If one of the states chose to withdraw its name from the contract, it would be difficult to disprove its right to do so.[14]

Tocqueville was merely expressing what everyone already knew.

Lord Acton, the great British historian who devoted his life to the study of liberty and to what was conducive to and inimical to the establishment and preservation of liberty, wrote shortly after the war that the defeat at Appomattox was a greater setback for genuine liberty than Waterloo had been a victory. Waterloo ended an empire; Appomattox established one. Acton wrote also:

The theory which gave to the people of the states the same right of last resort against Washington as against Great Britain possessed an independent force of its own, northern statesmen of great authority maintained it, its treatment by Calhoun and Stephens forms as essential a constituent in the progress of democratic thinking as Rousseau or Jefferson.[15]

Here is a very simple proposition that our forefathers understood—that indeed governed everything they did. The only way to preserve civil liberty is to

14. Alexis de Tocqueville, *Democracy in America* (New York: Vintage Books, 1990), vol. 1, pp. 387–88.
15. *Selected Writings of Lord Acton*, J. Rufus Fears, ed. (Indianapolis: Liberty Press, 1985), vol. 1, pp. 170–71, 363.

check government power. The only way to check power is to disperse and divide it. Some of the Founders hoped that a federal system would allow growth without centralisation (or 'consolidation' as they called it). This, the main check, has failed. It was also hoped that the division of legislative, executive, and judicial power in the general government would help. Let us be clear—these checks and balances do not work. They ceased to work a long time ago. The Supreme Court does not check the Congress, or the President—it checks us. There is no serious conflict of power among the federal branches. The acts of all of them are directed toward checking the people of the states.

The federal government will never check itself—that is the *raison d'être* of federalism. It must be checked by the states. And this ultimately is of no avail unless it is backed by the right of secession. Curiously, recognition of the right of secession often obviates its use, because where it is a real possibility, power is motivated, has incentive, to check itself and be responsible.

Federalism is one of the least understood, both theoretically and practically, of all political forms. The habit of not even thinking about it, as in the Constitution bicentennial, provides a great obstacle, which there are signs today of a tendency to overcome. We must beware of phony forms of top-down federalism that will be invented by cornered politicians. Federalism is not when the central government graciously allows the states to do this or that; that is just another form of administration. True federalism is when the people of the states set limits to the central government.

States' rights has fallen into disuse not because it is unsound in history, in constitutional law, or in democratic theory . It remains highly persuasive on all these grounds to any honest mind. It has fallen into disuse because it presented the most powerful obstacle to the consolidation of irresponsible power—that consolidation which our forefathers decried as the greatest single threat to liberty. For that reason, states' rights had to be covered under a blanket of lies and usurpations by those who thought they could rule us better than we can rule ourselves. At the most critical time, the War Between the States, states' rights was suppressed by force, and the American idea of consent of the governed was replaced by the European idea of obedience. But force can only settle questions of power, not of right.

States' rights are historically sound, constitutionally sound, ethically sound, and sound from the point of view of democracy. Where they fall short is simply in the realm of political will and agenda—the practical effort to implement them. That can change.

The people of the states have a *right* to protect themselves against an out-of-bounds federal government, and to determine when the proper bounds have been passed—or to interpose their sovereignty, as Jefferson said, as Madison said, as Calhoun said. Proclaiming a right, of course, does not make it prevail. For a long time now, a century at least, the course of history has been moving in the direction of consolidation, the gathering of concentrated power in one central, irresponsible, imperial government.

But there is hope. We now see, all over the Western world, a ferment of people against consolidation, in favour of regionalism, devolution, secession, break-up of unnatural states, and the return to historic identities in preference to universal bureaucracies. You know the signs in the break-up of the Soviet Union and Czechoslovakia, and you can see the signs in the secessionist movements in Britain, Italy, Canada, and many other countries.

There is reason to believe that the consolidation phase of history may be coming to an end. We may be ready for a new flowering of freedom for families and communities. We know that the great periods of Western history have been not those of powerful states but of multiple and dispersed sovereignty—flourishing liberty for small communities. We know that such freedom equals creativity in wealth, art, intellect, and every other good thing. All over the Western world, once again people are thinking of liberty—the most characteristic and unique of Western values—and are doubting the central state that has been worshipped since the French Revolution.

I know there are many moral and social problems that are not solved by political arrangements, and that the level of statesmanship in the states is not much higher, if at all, than in the federal government. But if we are to speak of curbing the central power, the states are what we have got. They exist. They are historical, political, cultural realities, the indestructible bottom line of the American system.

It would be a shame if, in this world-historical time of devolution, Americans did not look back to an ancient and honourable tradition that lies readily at hand. To check power, to return the American empire to republicanism, we do not need to resort to the drastic right of revolution nor to the destructive goal of anarchic individualism. We have in the states ready-made instruments. All that is lacking is the will. Our goal should be the restoration of the real American Union of sovereign states in place of the upstart empire under which we live.

This essay was delivered as a paper at the Ludwig von Mises Institute conference on Secession in April 1995, and was published under the title "Secession: The Last, Best Bulwark of Our Liberties" in David Gordon, ed., Secession, State and Liberty (Transaction, 1998).

Chapter Four

Empire

Global Democracy and American Tradition

If we are to achieve the kind of world we all hope to see—
with peace, freedom,and economic progress—democracy has
to continue to expand. Democracy is a vital,
even revolutionary force.
— SECRETARY OF STATE GEORGE SHULTZ,
Congressional testimony in favor of establishment of
a National Endowment for Democracy, 1983

The terms liberty, equality, right and justice, used in
a political sense, are merely terms of convention, and of
comparative excellence, there being no such thing,
in practice, as either of these qualities being carried out
purely, according to the abstract notions of theories.
— JAMES FENIMORE COOPER, *The American Democrat*, 1838

When we leave our door and go out among our fellows, we carry with us a certain self-image of what we are or ought to be. This image may or may not correspond to our real character or to the way others perceive us. The same is true of nations when they go among their fellows. Of course, relations between nations are chiefly relations between governments, and given the vast apparatus of the modern state, whether in the free or the unfree world, this is bound to become a complicated encounter—as if we went onto the street accompanied by a bodyguard and a publicity agent.

For Americans, how we rationalize our relations with other nations has always involved a certain amount of abstractness. While we were long secure behind our oceans, there was more choice than necessity in the face we presented to the world, compared to less favored peoples. Unlike most European states, we had no frontiers bristling with fortifications and barriers of language or religion and competing dynasties or forms of government. And we were not, to the same degree, compelled to go abroad in search of markets, raw materials, and colonies for surplus or discontented populations.

Having made several preliminary forays into an active role in the world, Americans found themselves at the end of World War II, unwittingly and somewhat unwillingly, cast in the role of an imperial people with worldwide powers and responsibilities. There are examples in history of other peoples who achieved this status without deliberate design. What was unique about the American situation was the ease and suddenness with which world dominance was acquired. For the average American World War II was an experience of economic gain, not sacrifice. By world standards, casualties were minor. In contrast, Roman territory was devastated several times before Cato's imperative was achieved. And the graves of British soldiers, seamen, merchants, missionaries, and officials, who expended their lives over two centuries or more in building an Empire, circle the hot zones of the globe.

We are concerned here with the history and present condition of the image which Americans have of their role among the nations, with the implicit assumptions which are a starting place for their actions. We are not concerned directly with the facts and events of the world, a subject on which there are vast libraries of contending data and theory. In the next block we may meet a mugger, a con man, a panhandler, or a street-corner evangelist. These will not make any fundamental alteration in our self-image. However, how we handle ourselves in these encounters will be determined by our character and our idea of how we *ought* to behave.

The twentieth century has been marked by cataclysmic events. It has also been marked by a continuing struggle of articulate Americans to understand and to define satisfactorily their role in the world. We need only remember the intensity of the debate over the League of Nations after World War I, the strife between isolationists and inter-nationalists before World War II, or the heat of the struggle between policies of containment and liberation during the long course of the Cold War.

Yet, since World War II, the predominant rationale of American involvement with other peoples, the character we have aspired to, has been some version of that given by Secretary Shultz in the passage quoted at the head of this essay. It is the goal of America in the world to expand the self-evident benefits of democracy. Sometimes this has been presented as a military mission, as in Korea and Vietnam. At other times it has been seen as a process of peaceful involvement through such ventures as the Peace Corps, Alliance for Progress, the Fulbright program, or the Reagan administration's "Project Democracy," for which Shultz was seeking support.

The only principled opposition to this view has been the postwar conservative movement, a movement that gathered strength steadily in the 1960's and 1970's, and, so it was thought, achieved power and validity during the Reagan reign of the 1980's. (Many leftward movements objected to particular aspects of American intervention in the world, but not to the vision of a democratic mission.) It was a truism that the postwar conservative movement rested upon alle-giance to tradition, to the free market, and most of all to a principled anticom-munism. One of the tenets of this anticommunism was that the Cold War was a life-and-death struggle between Western civilization and a godless totalitarian-ism. The history of the Cold War seemed to prove that the mild democratic plat-itudes and benevolent social-worker approach of the liberals were inadequate to the occasion and certain to lead to defeat. Something of the spirit of conservative anticommunism was summed up in the title of a book by James Burnham, *Containment or Liberation?*, and by Russell Kirk's remark that peoples did not fight and die for a standard of living.

How did a conservative President, who was thought to have been the heir and spokesman for Cold War hardliners, come to rest the foreign policy motives of his administration upon a philosophical base of "revolutionary" global democracy? Is the idea of a democratic mission a workable concept for guiding American actions in the world? To what extent is the self-image of America as the active exporter of democracy in keeping with the best of American traditions?

I wish to provide speculative explorations of these three questions as a con-tribution to the ongoing effort of Americans to visualize adequately their role and goal in the world. The last question is explored in this essay. A succeeding essay, "Global Democracy and Conservatism," will take up the first two. The historical scheme presented is suggestive of a possible line of interpretation. To "prove" it, in a strict scholarly sense, would take several lifetimes of research.

Preserving Domestic Happiness: The Founders' Vision

The tradition of debate on the American role in the world began at least as early as the end of the Revolution. In the Philadelphia Convention, during a dis-cussion of the treaty making powers of the Senate, Charles Pinckney of South Carolina remarked:

Our true situation appears to me to be this—a new extensive Country, containing with-in itself the materials for forming a Government capable of extending to its citizens all the blessings of civil and religious liberty—capable of making them happy at home. This is the great end of Republican Establishments. We mistake the object of our Government, if we hope or wish that it is to make us respectable abroad. Conquest or superiority among other powers is not or ought not ever to be the object of republican systems. If they are sufficiently active and energetic to rescue us from contempt and preserve our domestic happiness and security, it is all we can expect from them—it is more than almost any other Government ensures to its citizens.[1]

Alexander Hamilton, who fancied himself a realist of power, but who was out of step with most of his fellow members and adopted countrymen, replied

---

1. Gaillard Hunt and James B. Scott, eds., *The Debates in the Federal Convention of 1787* (New York: Oxford, 1920), 159–60, (Madison's notes).

that Pinckney's distinction between domestic tranquility and prestige abroad "was an ideal distinction. No Government could give us tranquility and happiness at home, which did not possess sufficient stability and strength to make us respectable abroad."[2] Hamilton was really more concerned here with getting in a plug for "energetic government" than in defining a stance for foreign policy, but he took the opportunity to suggest the need for greater realism in regard to the world and activism in national defense than Pinckney had called for.

Both advocates and critics of later "idealistic" American intervention in world affairs have seen a precedent or portent in Pinckney's attitude toward later events which they approved of or deplored. Pinckney did, obviously, endorse a species of "American exceptionalism." But his view of the world can by no means be called utopian. He wanted the United States to be strong and secure from "contempt," and did not have a high opinion of what governments in general could aspire to, even "republican systems."

American commentators, especially conservatives, have often resorted to a theory that the debates of the early republic on foreign policy were carried on between Jeffersonian "idealists" (such as Pinckney, who was an incipient Jeffersonian Republican) and Hamiltonian "realists."[3] Somewhat under the domination of Henry Adams, whose spell has never been broken by American students of this period, we have thought that the Jeffersonians expressed a failed and misguided softness, and the Hamiltonians a hard-headed toughness in dealing with the dangers of the world. By this calculation, anticommunist conservatives and advocates of strong national defense should look to the Federalists as their forebears and to Jefferson and his friends as having spawned the over-trusting liberalism of a later day.

However, statements of American exceptionalism and "idealism" can be found in abundance among *all* the Founders, Federalists as well as Republicans. If anything, the Federalists were not only more activist but a good deal more missionary and utopian in their view of the American role than were the Jeffersonians. For instance, Hamilton himself had remarked on an earlier occasion that the cause of America was "the cause of virtue and mankind."[4] And John Adams had described the settlement of America "as the opening of a grand scheme and design in Providence for the illumination of the ignorant, and the emancipation of the slavish part of mankind over the earth."[5]

The view expressed by Pinckney may or may not have been "realistic," but it offers a good deal more comfort to an isolationist than to a global-democratic and missionary image of the American place in the world. Even so, there is very

---

2. *Ibid.*
3. This was one of the arguments developed in two otherwise excellent and stimulating articles by James E. Dornan in the *Intercollegiate Review*, "The Founding Fathers, Conservativism, and American Foreign Policy," vol. 7, nos. 1–2, Fall 1970, pp. 31–43, and "The Search for Purpose in American Foreign Policy," vol. 7, no. 3, Winter 1970–71, pp. 97–110.
4. Quoted with source in Dornan's first article cited above, p. 39.
5. Quoted with source in *ibid.*, p. 38.

little precedent for any notion of active democratic expansionism on either side of the division between the Founders. There is a vast qualitative difference between envisioning America as an example to the world and feeling a mission to implement and enforce that example across the sea.

These early statesmen all had a quite natural belief in the superiority and value of their own hard-won republican institutions. They hoped these would set a precedent for mankind, suffering under the weight of arbitrary governments. This did not suggest (as all of American history up to at least the late nineteenth century proves) a proselytizing mission for the quotidian American republic. And while the rhetoric was often high-flying, it was mostly conscious self-assertion in response to the official wisdom of the Old World, which professed to scorn the viability and durability of republican institutions. *Nothing* in American actions for the next century indicated a belief that those institutions were intrinsically applicable to every people, place, and time, much less that there was a duty to impose them.

Such an attitude did reflect a belief in American exceptionalism, which from the point of view of jaded and cynical thinkers of the Old World (except for German metaphysicians) represented a delusionary claim to immunity from the realities of sin and sorrow. But such exceptionalism was, at that time, historically based and laced with realism and practicality. Exceptionalism rested on an apprehension that the English-speaking New World was free of certain built-in defects of the Old—rival nationalisms, hardened class interests, scarce resources. American society had enjoyed widespread ownership of property, vast unoccupied lands, the unmixed heritage of the best parts of British law and liberty, a fortuitous experience of colonial self-government, a successful war of independence, and a nearly unprecedented opportunity of constitution-making.

When Jefferson quoted with approval the wish of Silas Deane, who had preceded him as a representative in Europe, for "an ocean of fire between us and the Old World,"[6] he dreamed not of utopia but of the preservation of a real historical opportunity. He realized that what Americans had achieved rested upon fortuitous circumstances and was not necessarily repeatable. The New World could serve as an inspiration and example for the better spirits of the Old, but had no mission to impose its pattern beyond North America. The "policy" side of this belief was expressed in Washington's farewell address and Jefferson's first inaugural, in the warnings against entangling alliances which were taken to heart by generation after generation of Americans.

This general view was shared by all sensible Federalists and Republicans, despite the abortive forays of Hamilton into power politics. By its very nature republicanism called for non-intervention, not proselytization. Rather than free institutions being a license to reform the world, they were, on the contrary, a command for the maximum non-involvement. By republican theory, the involve-

---

6. To Elbridge Gerry, May 13, 1797, in Adrienne Koch and William Peden, eds., *The Life and Selected Writings of Thomas Jefferson* (New York: Modern Library, 1944), p. 543.

ments of free governments in the world were likely to be fewer and more honorable than those of other states, not because of any particular virtue on the part of Americans, but because such governments were restrained by the necessity that their wars and treaties be undertaken by open deliberation and supported by the sense of the community. This was still an important idea some decades later when James Fenimore Cooper, a conservative and Democrat, commented that "democracies pay more respect to abstract justice, in the management of their foreign concerns, than either aristocracies or monarchies."[7] This was a purely descriptive statement, not a moralistic assertion, and would not have been disputed by Cooper's contemporary conservative, Tocqueville.

Those of the Founders who hoped to preserve America immune from the ills of the Old World were realistic enough to know that their desires would be imperfectly realized. Said Jefferson in 1785:

The justest dispositions possible in ourselves, will not secure us against it [war]. It would be necessary that all other nations were also just. Justice, indeed, on our part, will save us from those wars which would have been produced by a contrary disposition. But how can we prevent those produced by the wrongs of other nations?[8]

"We must make the interest of every nation stand surety for their justice, and their own loss to follow injury to us, as effect follows its cause," he wrote some years later.[9]

We were, after all, still a relatively weak power with hostile colonies on our borders and a partly mercantile economy that was vulnerable to European tumults. Yet republican non-involvement remained a sound *point of departure* for conceiving the American role in the world. It might be argued that that role long reflected a healthy synthesis of Pinckney's optimism and isolationism and Hamilton's realism and concern for national prestige. Possibly this still constitutes the basic, instinctual view of most of the American people, if not of their leaders.

Non-Interventionist Realism: The Nineteenth Century

We cannot really find the principles of Reaganite global democratic revolution in Washington or Jefferson or anywhere else before this century. We will have to look for more exotic sources and a different and curious family tree. Nothing in the mainstream course of American history in the nineteenth century provides any precedent for a missionary role in the world, although certain lesser intellectual currents were portentous.

The advance westward, including the War of 1812 and the Mexican War

---

7. Cooper, *The American Democrat* (Baltimore: Penguin Books, 1969), p. 123.
8. To John Jay, August 23, 1785, in Koch and Peden, p. 378. In *The Federalist* Nos. 3 and 4, Jay pursued Jefferson's distinction between unjust and just wars, affirming that the Union would be efficacious in avoiding the former.
9. To Edward Rutledge, June 24, 1797, Koch and Peden, 544.

and territorial acquisitions, were by no stretch of the imagination foreign interventionism or the pursuit of global democracy. The movement of an exuberant agricultural people into nearly empty and undeveloped lands on their own frontiers is different in kind from ventures overseas for profit, ideology, glory, or power. "Manifest Destiny" meant the conquest of new spaces for Americans and their democratic institutions, not the imposition of these institutions on other peoples.

An optimistic, non-interventionist realism is clearly seen in the attitude of Americans toward the Latin American revolutions of the early nineteenth century, as symbolized by the Monroe Doctrine. Americans, in general, were delighted that other peoples of the New World sought to throw off the oppressive system of the Old World and copy their republican institutions. But Americans also had realistic doubts, strengthened by the passage of time, about the possibility of success among other peoples. Except for a few volunteer military adventurers, there was no thought of American involvement. Americans were in fact quite content to acquiesce in the *de facto* maintenance of Latin American independence by British maritime power. They continued to observe a realistic detachment in their dealings with these countries, insisting on strict enforcement of the rights of American citizens. They looked upon Latin American republics, in other words, with friendly but skeptical detachment.

Anyone who will read the primary documents of Americans' experiences in and reflections on Latin America in the nineteenth century will see that they were pleased whenever evidences were shown of successful republican self-government, but understood that democratic ideals were not fully applicable to the situation. They did not think that democratic process in itself was intrinsically the magic cure for all the ills of those societies. They realized, in fact, that authoritarian features, uncongenial to American taste, were often the lesser evil in those circumstances. Nor did they feel, unlike their twentieth century successors, any need to undermine the more reactionary features of life, such as the army, Church, or great landowners, or assume foolishly that an American-style democracy would appear if they could be overthrown.[10]

Of course, this non-interventionism can be partly attributed to an awareness of America's relative weakness, that would not allow too much intermeddling in the world. But nowhere can we find any evidence that the future achievement of unassailable American strength, which all anticipated, would be a grant of power to alter the world. It would merely make more secure the republican example.

The French Revolution and the wars of Napoleon required realism from American statesmen, as Hamilton had anticipated. While we were relatively secure beyond the Atlantic, some involvement was inevitable because of the colonial powers still on our borders and because a substantial portion of the

---

10. For purposes unrelated to this essay, I have read hundreds of dispatches from American ministers and consuls in Latin America in the mid-nineteenth century, including Democrats and Whigs, Northerners and Southerners. I have above summarized a nearly unanimous attitude.

American economy—that of New England—was mercantile—which inevitably brought national interests and honor into conflict with Europe.

Undoubtedly, also, the French Revolution had an impact, positive and negative, on American thought. Some Americans, notably in New England, recoiled in horror and professed to see the dangers of the same in America. Other Americans delighted in the possibility of republican principles gaining a lodgement in the heart of Europe. Relations with Britain and France, ideological, diplomatic, and economic, were a source of sharp controversy in the later eighteenth and early nineteenth centuries. Yet these were basically domestic disputes. Almost no responsible native American sympathized with the Revolution after its excesses became apparent. While competing parties labelled each other as Jacobins and monarchists, in the final analysis Americans realized that both the reactionaries and the revolutionaries of Europe were operating in a different context. This conclusion, that American republicanism was as distinct from the revolutionary movements of Europe as it was from the monarchical establishments, was a standard convention of American discourse in regard to Europe throughout the nineteenth century.

Jefferson, often thought to be the most optimistically universalist of American democrats among the early statesmen, always took a hopeful but cautious attitude toward French developments, at which he was present as an observer during the early stages. He advocated sensible reforms appropriate to the European situation, not revolution, and was quick to apprehend that no American or European interest would be served by radicalism.[11]

The Federalist election propaganda which imagined Jefferson, who was living peacefully among his books, farms, and 200 slaves, as plotting to guillotine the clergy, was a product of hysteria which had much to do with religious and economic dislocations in domestic New England society and nothing to do with Jefferson's beliefs or actions. Jefferson wanted the New World to be an example to the Old, not vice versa. European revolutionaries no more provided a guide for America than did European reactionaries. He knew that the long-range cause of liberty was not served by the form which the Revolution took. "I was a sincere well-wisher to the success of the French Revolution, and still wish it may end in the establishment of a free and well-ordered republic," he wrote at the time he was being pilloried in the northern press as a Jacobin, "but I have not been insensible under the atrocious depredations they have committed on our commerce. The first object of my heart is my own country."[12]

Shortly before his ascension to the Presidency he remarked on the rise of Napoleon: "On what grounds a revolution has been made, we are not informed, and are still more at a loss to divine what will be its issue; whether we are to have

---

11. It is necessary to read over all of Jefferson's correspondence with American and French friends as he followed the course of events. A small but good selection appears in Koch and Peden's collection, pp. 414–556 passim.
12. To Elbridge Gerry, January 26, 1799, in Koch and Peden, p. 546.

over again the history of Robespierre, of Caesar, or the new phenomenon of an usurpation of the government for the purpose of making it free."[13]

Much the same can be said for the general American reaction to the European revolutions of 1848. There was satisfaction that our example was being honored and sympathy with national independence movements, but no felt mission to promote the event and a certain amount of skepticism as to the possibilities of success. Americans understood that movements of social revolution were different in kind from their own revolution in favor of republican institutions. If for no other reason than the strength of the establishments that they had to overcome, European revolutionaries were bound to run to excesses of radicalism or militarism rather than follow the American example of a stable government of the people.

Yet seeds were planted for a later day. An influx of German refugees with universalist ideas swelled the ranks of the new Republican party in the 1850's. In New England, the reaction to the French Revolution had a course similar to that of Germany—an adoption and transformation of the revolutionary impulse into a native form. One could see in John Adams something of the Puritan idealism that many have found to be a historical source of the peculiar abstractness and self-righteousness which they have found in American foreign policy. But when Transcendentalism had been added to the secularized remnants of this "City upon a Hill" ideology that had figured in the founding of Massachusetts, the ground was being cleared to erect a new temple of universalized aggressive Americanism.

For Emerson, the American was not simply something to be celebrated as an example in which we could take national pride—he was a model for the future of the world. The world was to be seized—by a new type who was a universal model for the future (and at the same time remarkably Bostonian). By filtering American "exceptionalism" and the Declaration of Independence back and forth through Transcendentalism, a subtle but lasting transformation was made in concepts of the American role in the world. This was projected not only forward, but backward in American history, so that later historians thought they saw precedents in the American Revolution for a global democratic revolution in the twentieth. From Emerson's new man it was but a short step to Whitman and the conversion of democracy from the stern and manly republican principles of the Founders into an amorphous, universalistic egalitarianism.

These tendencies gained their first high-level political expression in John Quincy Adams, who wrote, in an official document: "The general history of mankind, for the last three thousand years, demonstrates beyond all contradiction the progressive improvement in the condition of man, by means of the establishment of the principles of International Law, tending to social benevolence and humanity." He also predicted a future world free of colonialism, "unfair" trade

---

13. To Dr. William Bache, February 2, 1800, *ibid.*, p. 556.

restrictions, and monarchy.[14] But Adams was not a typical American figure of his time, nor did these mystical aspirations interfere with his hard-headed nationalistic diplomacy.

Certain tendencies were thus evident to the discerning, but these remained, politically and in public morale, a lesser key throughout the nineteenth century. The American democracy of the nineteenth century was a rooted optimism about American conditions and the American common man, essentially isolationist and telluric, if not, indeed, xenophobic. There is nothing in the substantial history of the (largely Southern and Western) movements of Jeffersonian and Jacksonian democracy—their leaders, their rank and file, their policies, their social impulses—to provide a precedent for participation in a universal global democratic revolution. The same can be said for Lincoln, whose domestic revolution brought absolutely no change in the American role in the world. As Tocqueville remarked of the American democracy: "The foreign policy of the United States . . . consists more in abstaining than in acting."[15]

The Rise of Internationalism

One does not have to be a foolish economic determinist—a believer in the supremacy of abstract economic laws, whether the free market or Marxism—to note the impact of economic factors on the relationships of nations. Two developments took Americans, or rather a portion of their leadership class, out of their traditional benevolent isolationism at the end of the nineteenth century. First, a growing awareness of a substantial though still somewhat marginal economic interest in Latin America, Asia, and the islands of the Pacific—trade and investment which brought contact with native peoples and potential rivalry with European powers. This was not an over-riding necessity for America, as it was for Britain, which depended upon overseas markets and raw materials. Nor did imperialism ever become a widespread popular program of national self-assertion as it did among the German and French publics.

But by the end of the nineteenth century there were signs among the leadership class of an internationalist philosophy. This had two sides, whose unrecognized incompatibility has confused American foreign policy and the American self-image ever since, right down to late twentieth century Reaganism and its critics. On the one hand was a kind of realistic assessment, anticipated by Hamilton and typified in part by Theodore Roosevelt, that we were, whether we will or not, a power in the earth, and as such we had no choice but to take a vigorous and well-thought-out role. One could see this, possibly, as no more than traditional prudent national interest extended to new circumstances.

The other face, analytically distinguishable though often mingled in the same minds, was a proselytizing version of American exceptionalism. It drew not

---

14. George Lipsky, *John Quincy Adams: His Theory and Ideas* (New York: Crowell, 1950), p. 279; W.C. Ford, ed., *Writings of John Quincy Adams* (New York: Macmillan, 1913–17), vol. 6, p. 396.
15. Alexis de Tocqueville, *Democracy in America* (New York: Anchor Books, 1969), p. 228.

from traditional impulses and understandings but from new ones—Progressivism and the degenerate form of Protestantism known as the Social Gospel. It sought a militant American role in reforming the world—in exactly the same spirit as the reformation of American slums, corrupt city governments and renegade corporations. It was an enthusiastic adoption, with an American twist, of the late imperialistic philosophy of the "white man's burden."

These combined tendencies were to have their culmination in Wilson's program to make the world safe for democracy, a formula from which Americans, or at least American intellectuals, have never escaped, and which provides our basic way of looking at the world, right down to the Reaganite obsession with the export of "vital," "revolutionary" democracy.

This new imperialism had in its origins a basically Anglo-Saxon cast. Not all imperialists were sympathetic to the new immigration, but in fact, the vast immigration of new peoples into the United States in the late nineteenth and early twentieth centuries and imperialism reinforced each other by making America seem more international than ever before. The idea of the "melting pot," which appeared at this time, was the domestic face of the international mission.

Even so, the new American imperialism was in neither respect really universalistic or egalitarian. It involved bringing the law to the natives, who were not, or at least not yet, ready for Americanization—it was paternal, not brotherly, just as the melting pot was really more conformist than pluralistic. In regard to European powers one could still see something of the old detachment and suspicion. Henry Cabot Lodge, though an early imperialist, would have agreed with Cooper's comment a half century earlier: "An opinion is seldom given in Europe of anything American, unless from impure motives."[16] But there was also a considerable movement toward coalescence with the other Western democracies, particularly Britain.

It would be too easy, though a great temptation to conservatives, to make a distinction between "realistic" internationalists like Roosevelt and "utopian" ones like Wilson. But, as in earlier periods, the two aspects were inextricably confused everywhere. Roosevelt viewed World War I a good deal more enthusiastically and in some respects more blindly than did Wilson. It is misleading to blame on a particular political party or figure tendencies that are in fact widespread and deeply reflective of our national character as it has evolved.

Opposition to the new internationalism of the turn of the century took two forms. One, which has been less emphasized, but which has continued to run inarticulate and unrecognized through the American consciousness, was reflected by Bryan. It was traditional and Jeffersonian: exceptionalism with non-entanglement. It continued to believe in a benevolent but largely non-exportable American democracy. It felt that to imitate European powers in foreign ventures would lead to imitating them in domestic oppressions as well. Traces of this can be found, along with other elements, among the America Firsters of the 1930's,

---

16. Cooper, *American Democrat*, p. 209.

in figures as diverse as Charles A. Beard and Charles A. Lindbergh. Such a feeling was neither utopian nor pacifist, but it was non-interventionist. Possibly this strain of native belief and tendency has been more important than has generally been recognized. We have tended to characterize American opinion that was hesitant in such situations as the Korean and Vietnamese wars in terms provided by liberal historians, as rooted in the other, leftist form of opposition that was developing to American imperialism in the early twentieth century rather than in traditional non-interventionism.

Less important before the Thirties but portentous for the future was the socialist critique of imperialism, which was curiously both isolationist and internationalist. It believed in the desirability, often the inevitability, of "world democratic revolution." Its view of the world drew from European socialism, not traditional republicanism. It opposed American internationalism because it was contaminated by big business and Christianity—it was insufficiently universalist and utopian.

As always, the actual political situation was more ambiguous than this analysis suggests. Most people do not see all the time all of the implications of their positions, and all parties and movements resort at times to convenient vagueness in order to broaden their appeal. Further, unexpected historical events tend to override formulations of foreign policy and upset ideal patterns of conflict—events like TR's sending of the fleet to the Philippines in anticipation of a war with Spain over Cuba, like nationalist unrest in the Balkan portion of the Austrian empire in 1914, like Hitler's invasion of Russia, or the overthrow of the Iranian emperor by militant Muslims.

After World War I, Americans, in the traditional phrase, "retreated into isolationism." That is, they exhibited a certain regret that they had defied all the teachings of the fathers and abandoned their splendid isolation for entangling alliances. Yet a transformation had been made in the American self-image, the Rubicon had been crossed.

America then settled into a kind of grudging and limited activity in the world. Republican administrations in the Twenties busied themselves with international economic and naval agreements, and intervened in Latin America when necessary—all very Anglo-Saxon and Protestant enterprises and moderate and realistic versions of Wilson's failed fantasies. It was not so much a repudiation as a dilution of Wilsonism. Such internationalism was not universalist, however. The Third World, except for Latin America, China, and Japan, hardly entered into American consciousness. The European empires were the *de facto* keepers of world order. And Europe had been able to contain the new and frightening element of Bolshevism. Unlike the Kaiser, this posed no immediate threat to Western life.

Project World Democracy: The Post-War Era

From the fall of the League of Nations to the rise of fascism in American consciousness there were no serious conflicts over foreign policy, but there was also little real consensus or clarity in regard to the American role in the world. Roosevelt accomplished recognition of the Soviet Union in 1933 with only muted criticism. The old self-image having been abandoned in 1917, and the new Wilsonian one having been found to be disillusioning, nothing had yet replaced it. Americans were without a concept of their place in the world, and, except for the diehard Wilsonians, hardly felt the lack.

When war was renewed in Europe, Americans divided into three groups. The isolationists, centered in the Midwest and fuelled somewhat by Anglophobia and anti-New Deal discontents, could see no reason for American involvement in the troubles of the Old World and could discern no difference between fascist and communist totalitarianism.

Another large segment of opinion was not eager for involvement but watched with increasing uneasiness the threats posed by aggressive and indecent regimes to the Pacific, to Western Europe, and to a tolerable world. They came slowly to face the necessity that rearmament was in order and that some involvement might be inevitable.

The third segment of opinion, developed on the Left during the 1930's and brought to full fruition during and after the war by massive official and unofficial propaganda, assumed the global democratic mission of America. (Remember, we are concerned less with events and real conditions than with how Americans were molded to conceive of their role in the world.)

The prewar period saw the first appearance in America of the Popular Front. Large segments of the Left, of various hues of red and pink, promoted an internationalist philosophy disembodied from the American national interest and the traditional guiding principles. We were the arsenal of democracy, which was threatened with extinction by aggressive fascist regimes (though apparently not by Stalinism). Already well-established in the 1930's, this philosophy had no principled opposition, and very little intelligent criticism, after the German attack on Russia, which silenced its critics to the Left, and Pearl Harbor, which ended isolationism.

In the view of the global democrats, an alliance with Soviet Russia was not a distasteful necessity—it was a glorious opportunity to be enthusiastically embraced, a mingling of the two major constituents of the future world order. Anyone who looks through the official statements, the news media, and the film entertainment of the time cannot escape this impression. Global democrats largely controlled the interpretation of the war from the news media and Washington bureaus, all of which teemed with plans for the postwar construction of world democracy. The fighting and dying in the air, the seas, and the lands was a sideshow being carried on by expendables. Indeed, for Eleanor Roosevelt, American fighting men should not return as heroes but should be quarantined for fear they had developed fascist tendencies while serving their country.

While Wilson had visualized a postwar order of nations, bound by legal agreements and deliberative institutions, global democracy was something new for Americans. It looked to a merging of peoples and an international order in which power would be as real but as amorphous and "democratic" as in the Soviet Union. The "right-wing extremism" which began to rise in the early 1950's, and was so decried by the intellectual class, rested to a considerable extent upon the inarticulate fear of many Americans that there were plans afoot to deprive them of their traditional self-government in favor of an anonymous world government. There is little doubt among scholars that FDR felt that a new world order would be constructed by himself and Stalin, with Churchill, representing the old order, curtailed as much as possible.

This line was less a mobilization of morale for the war, though it took on that aspect occasionally, than it was a plan for the post-war world. The war became a step in the global democratic revolution. The defeat of the fascist powers was only the first goal in an ongoing transformation of the world. While many or most Americans thought in terms of defeating their enemies, reestablishing a degree of order and decency in the world, and going back to peaceful pursuits, by this view the end of the war would be but a beginning.

For the first time America had become not an end but a means, expendable material for construction of a new world order (although the new order often curiously resembled America writ large). Lip service was given to American values and ideals, but these were portrayed as nearly interchangeable with the Soviet variety. Curiously, not only were the defeated powers to be reconstructed, but also the victorious powers! While the guns still roared, the reform of the Western Allies was already projected—as a war goal—welfare state expansion in Britain, civil rights in the U.S. For the first time this was put not upon grounds of domestic justice but grounds of world opinion—the necessity to conform to an egalitarian world order. All of this was determined and proclaimed by the New Deal elite as *war goals*. Victorious American society must alter itself to please world opinion. The European empires would be liberated and form themselves into democratic constituents of the new world. The men who were fighting the war and the people who sustained them were expendable not only for the defense of their country but for the vision of their internationalist elite, which had pre-empted the meaning of the victory. Nor were they consulted. World peace was to be imposed by the elite through the regimentation of wartime.

Without the intensity of psychological stress and the pervasiveness of regimentation brought on by the war, so radical a break with American traditions could never have played in Peoria. As it was, this program would have gotten nowhere if it had not met a certain receptivity, if it could not have been given a plausible coincidence with the more modest and sensible goals of the masses of citizens and made to seem a fulfillment of traditional democratic ideals. But there was a rather tenuous connection between these schemes and the real aspirations and needs of the peoples of the world. The firm, serious role that Americans would be called upon to play when the fantasy of Soviet cooperation collapsed was nowhere anticipated, with the result of vast confusion, suspicion, and resentment when the Cold War impinged upon the victory and peace.

Those who grew up in the Fifties can remember the unqualified and uncritical promotion of the United Nations in the schools and media in those days. The dying of Americans in the snows of Korea to stem Communist barbarism was portrayed as a United Nations police action, as if it were some disembodied exercise of world brotherhood. The pro-UN propaganda reached every hamlet in America with an intensity that was not even matched by the world wars. Its disappearance in recent years is an unexpected phenomenon which has hardly been noticed. The glorification of the United Nations continued until it became evident that the UN was intransigently anti-Zionist, which the American public could not accept: (The American public did not realize and the American intelligentsia did not care that the UN was almost as intransigently anti-Western.) Having failed of the vision, the UN was increasingly abandoned for unilateral American initiatives for the world democratic revolution, of which the Reagan "Project Democracy" is only the latest of quite a long line.

The application of the global democratic vision to relations with the Communist World was a disaster mitigated only by belated realistic actions of the early Cold War, which still stand as models of American generosity and good sense. But the American elite were reluctant to abandon their global democratic ideology, which no longer fit the circumstances.

In terms of intellectual rationalizations, there were two significant responses to the Cold War. One was the evolution of an American conservative anticommunism which insisted on strong military *and* moral mobilization against a threat to civilization and religion. Its criticisms of American policy during the 1960's and 1970's mainly concentrated on the need to view the world realistically as an arena of conflict rather than as a ground for the building of democratic utopia. Democratic societies, desirable as a long-term goal insofar as they were feasible, were not the measure of the emergency.

The second response was Cold War liberalism, summed up, as has so often been the case, most cogently and persuasively by Arthur Schlesinger, Jr., in *The Vital Center*. The gist of this philosophy was to steer a course between the hateful extremes of communism and anticommunism, both of which were threats to the evolution of the world toward universal democratic norms. This view has clearly remained supreme in good times and bad. It has dominated public expression and controlled both parties, and even the conservative wing of the Republicans when in power, both in regard to the Soviet world and the Third World.

The application of the concept of world democratic revolution to the Third World was also a disaster, which American policy makers and opinion molders have clung to till this day. The American stumbling in Indochina and Central America stemmed directly from the concept of a democratic mission, which caused continual misconceptions of the needs and possibilities of the societies being defended and crippling disillusionment when the concept proved fantastic and inapplicable.

Possibly the American people at large did not share fully in either the philosophy of conservative anticommunism or that of Cold War liberalism. Perhaps they shouldered the burdens of World War II and the Cold War in a reluctant and defensive effort to restrain aggressive and indecent dictatorships, not to reduce the world to the American model or any other model. Perhaps all they wanted was a government, in the words of Charles Pinckney, "sufficiently active and energetic to rescue us from contempt and preserve our domestic happiness and security. . . ." For this they did not need any philosophy. All they needed was a normal and traditional faith in their country and its institutions.

(1988)

Global Democracy and Conservatism

*We are told, "We should not protect those who do not have
full democracy." This is the most remarkable argument of the
lot. This is the Leitmotif I hear in your newspapers and in the
speeches of some of your political leaders. Who in the world,
ever, on the front line of defense against totalitarianism, has
been able to sustain full democracy?*
— ALEKSANDR SOLZHENITSYN, AFL-CIO address, 1975

In "Global Democracy and American Tradition" (published in the
Intercollegiate Review, Fall 1988), I began an unfriendly exploration of the concept of "Global Democracy," which I suggested has constituted the philosophical
rationale of President Reagan's foreign policy, as put forth by the President and
his chief spokesmen and lieutenants. My primary purpose is not to analyze the
Communist world or the Third World nor to pass judgment on the success or failure of any particular foreign policy actions of the United States. Rather, my interest is in evaluating the idea that Americans have of themselves as players on the
world stage.

In the final analysis, our concept of the role we ought to play in relationship
to other nations will often have a decisive impact on our actions, or inaction. And
our self-image will remain a constant influence even if changes take place in the
outer world—for instance, the weakening of autocracy in the Soviet Union that
many believe to be occurring—that justify radical shifts in our actions. I am not
a foreign policy expert but a citizen anxious that our relations with the world conform to the high principles of republican honor that were bequeathed by our
Founders.

To frame a discussion of the Global Democracy concept I will pose three
rhetorical questions. (1) To what extent is the self-image of America as an active
exporter of democracy in keeping with the best of American traditions? (2) How
did a conservative President, who was thought to have been the heir and
spokesman for Cold War hardliners, come to rest the foreign policy motives of
his administration upon a philosophical basis of "revolutionary" global democracy? (3) Is the idea of a democratic mission a workable concept for guiding
American actions in the world? I will first summarize the answer given in
"Global Democracy and American Tradition" to (1) and then suggest an
exploratory answer to question (2). A future essay will perhaps take up the third
question.

*(1) To what extent is the self-image of America as an active exporter of
democracy in keeping with the best of American traditions?*

Not very much. The exuberant desire to spread "Global Democracy" bears
about the same relationship to the traditions of republican self-government as a

modern commercialized Christmas does to the story of Bethlehem.

If we trace historically how Americans have understood their identity among the other nations of the earth, we find a long tradition, going back to the Founding Fathers, of belief in American "exceptionalism." However, this exceptionalism was not missionary. A recognition of the fortuitous purchase of Americans on the benefits of self-government did not until well into this century imply in any sense a belief in "democracy" as an exportable universal to be actively proselytized as desirable for every society in the world. The avoidance of entangling alliances, enjoined by Washington and Jefferson, was the keystone of American policy.

In the mainstream tradition America's successes were not seen as the product of peculiar virtue or particular techniques but of special historical circumstances. Rather than giving a license for the imposition of American forms on other peoples, the successes were a limitation on action—because most of the world could not reduplicate the luck of America and because republicanism itself was seen in part as a freedom from burdens on the people, including burdens of foreign adventurism. The consequence of this American self-image was a realistic and healthy reluctance to become too deeply involved in the world. Americans were content to defend themselves and to demonstrate, not impose, democracy. America, in the description of the conservative thinker Wilmoore Kendall (as paraphrased by Gregory Wolfe), was properly to be seen "not as a savior nation but a mission to make self-government possible."[17]

(2) How did a conservative President, who was thought to have been the heir and spokesman for Cold War hardliners, come to rest the foreign policy motives of his administration upon a philosophical basis of "revolutionary" global democracy?

The consolidation during the World War II era (the formative years, intellectually, of Ronald Reagan and his spokesmen) of an internationalist utopianism, which shouldered an American mission to implement democracy around the globe, was a peculiar historical development, deserving more analysis than it has received. While drawing on an earlier Wilsonian tradition, this phenomenon was largely the public face of the antifascist popular front of the 1930's and a rationalization of the Russian alliance during World War II. Where Wilsonism was legalistic and, at least in intent, preservative, global democracy was romantic and revolutionary.

Since World War II, for the first time, there has been an official philosophy that regarded America and her democratic institutions less as an end in themselves than as a means for the transformation of the world by the globalization of the American example. Since this has been for some decades a constant and unexamined premise of the American establishment and its intellectuals, under Democratic administrations and Republican, and has been deployed to rationalize every American action in the postwar world, it is not too surprising to find

---

17. Kendall, *The Conservative Affirmation in America* (Chicago: Gateway Editions, 1985), p. xi.

Ronald Reagan an adherent of this philosophy.

It is a little surprising, however, when considered in the light of the postwar conservative philosophy which provided the only viable intellectual criticism of global democracy, and of which Ronald Reagan was thought by many to be an adherent. When an anti-establishment politician rises into power it is quite conventional and expected for him to make a pragmatic accommodation with the prevailing consensus. But it does present a puzzle when he casts completely aside what were assumed to be convictions, exuberantly embraces a contradictory rhetoric, and gives that rhetoric a systematization and official imprimatur that it did not enjoy before.

Prior to and even after World War II conservatism was isolationist. By about 1960, the Democratic party began moving away from armed interventionism toward a softer and more pacific version of global democracy, while the Republican establishment, under Nixon and Ford, moved into the trenches abandoned by the Democrats and espoused a slightly more militant version of the American role. (This transition was not complete even by 1960, when many thought Kennedy to be a tougher cold warrior than Nixon.)

At the same time, the post war conservative movement, out of power, mounted an attack on the premises of global democracy itself. Conservatives thought in terms not of the spread of American style democracy but in terms of the preservation of Western civilization from the evils of Soviet and Chinese imperialism, whether these evils were expressed in military attack or internal subversion. They saw themselves as defending the essentials of a traditional Western order against a godless, outlaw philosophy that brought lies, murder, and social death in its wake.

Conservatism of the 1950's and 1960's was defined by the cold eloquence of James Burnham and the early *National Review* and the candidacy of Senator Goldwater during the early days of the Vietnam buildup. Adherents of this view were energized by the loss of China and Cuba, the rape of Hungary, the American abandonment of allies at the time of the Suez Canal seizure, the Bay of Pigs, the premature liberation of the Congo and the resulting debacle in which the U.S. officially supported the forces of disorder, the ungrateful anti-Americanism of the United Nations and the liberated European colonies, and the tragedy of the Vietnam effort which was both caused by and then emasculated by confused global-democratic objectives which led to such self-defeating absurdities as the Kennedy-engineered murder of Diem. Conservatives were encouraged by the saving of the Philippines and Greece, anticommunist coups in Guatemala and Indonesia, and the overthrow of Allende.

The lesson learned from these events was the need not only for a powerful America (a proposition which met relatively little opposition in the abstract) but for the clear formulation of a moral esprit in defense of a Western-oriented world order. The world had to be viewed as an arena of potentially calamitous conflict between Western civilization and its enemies, not as a field for advanced social work. The sacrifices required by duty could not be sustained merely by preference for democratic techniques and a high standard of living. They required commitment to the intrinsic value of Western civilization.

James Burnham summed up the conservative critique of the liberal era of foreign policy: "Looking back over the record, however, it seems to be the case that what statisticians would call 'the long-term secular trend' of United States foreign policy has been, since the very earliest years of the Cold War, toward ever-increasing softness."[18] The remarks of Solzhenitsyn quoted at the head of this essay convey another aspect of the critique of liberal anti-communism guided by global democracy, as did his further remarks on the same occasion:

Something incomprehensible to the ordinary human mind has taken place. We over there, the powerless, average Soviet people, couldn't understand, year after year and decade after decade, what was happening. How were we to explain this? England, France, the United States, were victorious in World War II. Victorious states always dictate peace; they receive firm conditions; they create the sort of situation which accords with their philosophy, their concept of liberty, their concept of national interest. Instead of this, beginning in Yalta, your statesmen of the West, for some inexplicable reason, have signed one capitulation after another. During these thirty years, more was surrendered to totalitarianism than any defeated country has ever surrendered after any war in history.[19]

While the movement of the Third World toward prosperity and self-government was hoped for by conservatives, no unrealistic expectations were entertained for this and it was subordinate to the prior and larger question of the preservation of the West. Democracy in the abstract was not the measure of success in this struggle. Allies and effective regimes were not to be abandoned or undermined because they failed to meet some abstract test of democratic processes. The most essential difference between the conservative movement and liberal anticommunism had to do with the question of democracy in the Third World.

For the liberals in the final analysis, the spread of democracy and not the containment or rollback of Communism was the goal. And this rested on the belief that democracy itself—viewed in terms of the idealized civilities and living standards of Bridgeport, Connecticut, or Columbus, Ohio—reflecting the social origins of most of the American intelligentsia and officialdom—was *per se* the chief bar to the spread of Communism. Conservatives did not believe that democracy in itself was necessarily a bar to totalitarian subversion, and perhaps not attainable at all in the conditions of the Third World. An effective, even if ugly regime free from totalitarian control might well be preferable both practically and morally to the confusions of an abstractly proclaimed and temporary

---

18. Burnham, *Suicide of the West: An Essay in the Meaning and Destiny of Liberalism* (New York: John Day, 1964), p. 266.
19. AFL-CIO Address, Washington, June 30, 1975.

democracy. The conservative view rested, in the minds of its proponents, on solid evidence and a realist appreciation of the human condition.

In other words, democratic values and processes were not in themselves sufficient to defeat a force of the ideological and armed might of Communism, especially in the conditions of the Third World. Liberals, with their tradition of no enemies to the left, were not adequate to the occasion. Liberals, or many of them, wished to contain Communism without unsettling anyone too badly, and in the meantime to spread the blessings of social democracy around the globe via American largesse to the deprived, who only needed the hope of an American standard of living to make them into fine world citizens.

The conservatives had a tougher and more traditional view of the proper American goal in the world. They were far more tolerant of what was encompassed in the Western order and were willing to include regimes that varied from the American norm if they were effective and not totalitarian. They wanted the Third World to be free of Communist takeover, but did not have any strong imperatives for its evolution after that. The belief that an authoritarian regime, which might evolve into a more humane form, was preferable to a totalitarian one, was already clearly developed in conservative thinking, even though its most publicized spokesmen, who were Liberals or former Liberals, did not appear until the Reagan era.

Thus, during the Vietnam War, the Liberals concerned themselves with incidents of misbehavior on the part of Americans or their allies, as if in the midst of civil war and invasion, in an Asiatic land riven by class, ethnic, religious, and ideological struggle, civility and democratic process ought to be perfected, equal to what had been theoretically achieved in Boston and Detroit, else the game was not worth the effort. The conservatives concerned themselves with vanquishing the enemy as a precondition for the settlement of all other questions.

Put another way, the doves seemed to believe that the most effective barrier to Communism would be the achievement of a democratic situation. The hawks believed that the most effective barrier was military victory and a viable government suitable to the emergency. It is not difficult to see how these views reflect competing self-images of America and its role in the world—views as different as the roles of a social worker and a policeman.

Of course, in the hurly-burly of the struggle of political parties and the incessant intervention of the all-powerful news media, who recreated the world anew each day according to their own agenda, these differences were never clearly formulated. Nor did any politician, in office, adhere unequivocally to either view. The overwhelming instinct of American politicians is to obscure fundamental conflicts, not face them. Given both the fundamental divisions over the philosophical grounding of anticommunist action and the refusal to face these divisions frankly, Americans still have not achieved any clear idea of what it is they should have learned from the experience of the Vietnam expedition. The commonest explanation is that it was a failure of hawkish strategy, when in fact that was never even tried and the debacle can best be seen as a failure of global-democratic motivations.

While conservatism sometimes degenerated into a ruthless over-simplification (the luxury of those out of power) like Senator Goldwater's remark about lobbing one into the men's room of the Kremlin, it in fact rested upon a world view that was a large improvement in sophistication and complexity and seriousness over the pious simplicities of New Deal global democraticism. It was not egalitarian, but it was not at its best parochial either. It took a long view of world history and was free of the American messianism that was reflected in the speeches of FDR, Kennedy, Johnson, Nixon, and later Ronald Reagan. It was conservative in resting upon a deep piety toward the world as it was, rather than an enthusiasm for a blueprint of a world that was supposed to be. And while it was interventionist, it adhered to the best of earlier American traditions in that its interventionism was motivated by a desire to defend America rather than to impose an American pattern as the solution for all the world's ills.

During his period out of office, President Reagan and those who supported him, at least until establishment Republicans began to join his bandwagon about 1979, were assumed to adhere to the conservative view. To what extent have conservative expectations been realized? My contention is that they have not been realized at all. Rather, there has been a betrayal of the hard-won conservative position just at the time when it seemed to have won widespread popular support.

It is not my intention to quarrel with specific acts of the Reagan foreign policy. Indeed, there has been a military buildup and a certain stiffening of the American bargaining posture which, luckily assisted by unprecedented changes within the Soviet Empire, has been a limited success. (Though what effect, if any, this will have on the solution of such a problem as the Sandinistas, where global-democratic rhetoric has crippled American policy, remains to be seen). Rather, I am concerned with the philosophical base of American action. In the President's official rhetoric, the defense of Western civilization as the ground of American policy has been abandoned in favor of an image of America as a missionary power bent on universalizing the techniques of egalitarian democracy. That is to say, conservatism, essentially defensive, has been replaced by the discredited, simplistic philosophy of the President's erstwhile opponents.

Perhaps the most concrete evidence for my contention about the grounds of Reaganist foreign policy can be found in the establishment of "Project Democracy." (Though there is much other evidence, including the statements of nearly all of the late Republican presidential contenders, and especially those who most obviously aspired to the mantle of "conservatism.")

The idea of an Endowment for Democracy was launched by the President in a speech to the British Parliament in 1982. He saw the role of this new agency as to "foster the infrastructure of democracy—the system of a free press, unions, political parties, universities—which allows a people to choose their own way, to develop their own culture, to reconcile their own differences through peaceful means."[20] Secretary Schultz elaborated this program in a presentation to

---

20. "Project Democracy," in *State Department Bulletin*, vol. 83 (April 1983), p. 47.

Congress the next year:

If we are to achieve the kind of world we all hope to see—with peace, freedom, and economic progress—democracy has to continue to expand. Democracy is a vital, even revolutionary force.[21]

The Secretary went on to outline the details. "Project Democracy" would support conferences, meetings, dissemination of books and journals, and special programs in universities, all of which would "strengthen the basic institutions of democratic society—unions, parties, media, universities, business, legal/judicial systems, religious and community action groups. . . ."[22] It did not get any more specific than this, except for mention of a $65 million annual budget for a program deemed "critical to our national security."

Many aspects of these formulations are curious. First, we see the ineluctable tendency of the modern state, even under a laissez-faire, budget-cutting administration, to convert every idea and inspiration into a bureaucracy, another instrument in the consolidation of its power. (In a sense there is nothing in Project Democracy, except for the emphasis on its "revolutionary" intent, that constitutes anything more than a bureaucratic restructuring of activities that the American government has funded for decades.)

More telling is the preoccupation with democracy as consisting of a cluster of techniques and social organizations, revealing a strange ignorance both of the substantive history of liberty and of the fact that such techniques exist and are employed in every society, whether democratic, monarchical, fascist, authoritarian, or communist. While intrinsically political, they are not specifically "democratic." Also puzzling is the relative neglect of the expected Reaganite emphasis on free trade and free economy in favor of "techniques of democracy" and the preference for "infrastructure" as the ground for friendship between nations rather than traditional cultural affinities.

I submit that here is a phenomenon deserving of major attention by future historians. How are we to explain this capitulation? The explanation, I suggest, will be many-faceted. Part of it will lie in the character and career of the President himself and his own early nurturing in evangelistic Lincolnian rhetoric and the pieties of New Deal Democracy. (Might Reagan have been a different President if his own war experiences had been genuine trials rather than celluloid celebrations of American virtue?)

Another variety of explanation will lie in the power of establishments. If global democracy is incompatible with the philosophy of the postwar conservative movement, there is nothing in it that cannot conveniently be embraced by the Republican establishment. Reagan came to power on a conservative and populist reaction. But for personnel and policy he relied on neither conservatives nor pop-

---

21. *Ibid.*, p. 47.
22. *Ibid.*, p. 48.

ulists. For personnel he relied on retreaded administrators from the dubious days of Nixon and Ford. For policy, or at least for rhetoric, he relied on neo-conservatives, former Humphrey Democrats who had changed their ground but not their goals. It is these, probably, who have provided the particular formulations, the missionary duty of democratic transformation of the world, the preference for "techniques," the egalitarian emphasis.

In the most tangible terms, the refurbishing of global democracy in place of postwar conservative philosophy has saved the patronage and the face of both the Republican establishment and that part of the liberal intelligentsia who were nimble enough to see the writing on the wall, even though both had been putatively defeated at the polls. The Republican establishment has been able to preserve what it has always prized most, its "moderation," its sense of superiority to conservatives and populists, and its continuity with the accomplishments of preceding Democratic statesmen. The neo-conservatives have saved the official authority of their Liberal orthodoxy. They have also saved a system which calls for their own particular talents as adepts in public policy as an instrumental science.

There is no need to bemoan a conspiracy here. The co-opting of anti-establishment movements by the entrenched is an old, old story. The predecessor whom Ronald Reagan most resembles is Andrew Jackson—who came to power as an outsider and by tremendous popularity made himself the establishment, in the process incorporating most of his old enemies, abandoning his original purposes, and alienating all of his early supporters. The only difference is that Jackson's popularity rested upon real services to the Republic.

Secretary Schultz admitted that the efforts of Project Democracy would be limited in regard to the Soviet Union and Eastern Europe,[23] leaving the implication that the spread of "revolutionary" democracy was intended primarily for the Third World or our allies. Presumably it is our duty to promote world democratic revolution—a duty that would exist even if there were no international Communist threat to be countered. It would be hard to imagine a more complete capitulation of postwar conservatism to postwar liberalism. Not only in this formulation is democracy *per se* the most effective barrier against offensive regimes, but America is to be understood as enjoying a mission to evangelize the "vital, even revolutionary" force of democracy to the four corners of the globe. We have here merely an updating of the "peace through persuasion" and "progress through technique" philosophy of liberalism, which Reagan was thought to have conclusively vanquished at the polls, not only as it applies to foreign policy but to such questions as poverty and crime as well.

It is not a question of whether these programs are good or bad. Clearly, their effect, if any, depends upon implementation, and what has already happened is enough to confirm the worst fears of conservatives. (See *International Papers* for

---

23. *Ibid.*, p. 49.

April and August 1988.) If, as Secretary Schultz said, the benefits of global democracy will have little impact on the Soviet world, where will they take effect? Without any alteration in its theory, the National Endowment for Democracy could at some future time become a convenient arm for the implementation of the foreign policy of the Reverend Mr. Jesse Jackson or some similar figure. What began as a defensive move to counteract Communist penetration could easily be converted into a rationale for the aggressive destabilization of friendly or neutral regimes when their failure to conform to some administration's idea of democracy is deemed "critical to our national security"—El Salvador, Chile, South Africa, some hapless Arab state, or even Israel.

If this seems far-fetched, recall that not too many years ago an American president, filled with enthusiasm for the consummation of democracy by means of money, technology, and moralistic rhetoric, required American citizens to go 8,000 miles from home to battle Communists in the rice paddies and barren hills of the former French colonial empire, while ignoring the entrenched Communists in Cuba, which every sane American statesman from the first moment of the birth of the Union has understood to be of vital concern to American interests. Such are the fruits of an enthusiasm for "global democracy."

The words of Solzhenitsyn are again appropos. In regard to evidence of an increasing American weakness since World War II in facing threats, he remarked that "decline in courage is ironically emphasized by occasional explosions of anger and inflexibility on the part of the same bureaucrats when dealing with weak governments and weak countries, not supported by anyone. . . ."[24]

Conservatism, with its realist appreciation of the intractability of the human condition and its defensive orientation might possibly have provided an avenue away from such eventualities. Whatever the merits of the global democracy theory, it seems to be an abandonment, by a conservative administration, of conservative wisdom in favor of the old concept of America as the "savior nation." As has been convincingly said, postwar conservatism rested upon the triple pillars of free market, tradition, and anticommunism. Global democracy has no necessary correlation with any of these things.

(1989)

---

24. Harvard Address, reprinted in *Imprimis*, vol. 1, no. 7 (August 1978).

The Future of American Nationalism

One of the most interesting of many superb memoirs of the American Civil War left by participants on both sides is that of the erudite Confederate General Dick Taylor, called *Destruction and Reconstruction*. During the closing days of the war, Taylor found himself in command of the last remnants of organized Confederate troops in the Gulf States. After the surrender of the armies of Lee and Johnston and the capture of his brother-in-law President Davis, Taylor saw nothing for it but to open surrender negotiations with the nearest federal commander.

Hungry and shabby, he went to meet General Canby under a flag of truce, and was received by that splendidly accoutred Union officer with quiet courtesy and respect. Conquered and conqueror sat down to a welcome breakfast. In his usual dry and understated way, Taylor remembered what happened next:

> There was, as ever, a skeleton at the feast, in the person of a general officer who had recently left Germany to become a citizen and soldier of the United States. This person, with the strong accent and idioms of the Fatherland, comforted me by assurances that we of the South would speedily recognize our ignorance and errors, especially about slavery and the rights of the States, and rejoice in the results of the war. In vain Canby and Palmer tried to suppress him. . . . I apologized meekly for my ignorance, on the ground that my ancestors had come from England to Virginia in 1608, and, in the short intervening period of two hundred and fifty-odd years, had found no time to transmit to me correct ideas of the duties of American citizenship. Moreover, my grandfather, commanding the 9th Virginia regiment in our Revolutionary army, had assisted in the defeat and capture of the Hessian mercenaries at Trenton, and I lamented that he had not, by association with these worthies, enlightened his understanding. My friend smiled blandly, and assured me of his willingness to instruct me.

Taylor was too much the gentleman to mention, that the person to be instructed by the newcomer on the principles of Americanism was the son of a President of the United States.

This small incident speaks volumes about the history and nature of American nationalism. (Nationalism I will herein consider to be a people's idea of themselves, their more or less conscious and public identity, which reflects their history and values. This is the implicit basis for their internal cohesion and their mobilized interaction with other nations. The experiences attendant upon interaction, friendly or unfriendly, with other peoples will play back and become a formative influence upon the sense of identity itself.)

One of the central features of American nationalism is that it has not only constantly evolved, but has undergone sea-changes at least three times, though Americans are hardly aware of it, one indication of which is that very few could today sympathize with Taylor's viewpoint. When President Ronald Reagan celebrated America as a "City upon a Hill," a beacon to all mankind, he paid tribute to what he believes is a long-continued tradition of American prosperity, egalitarianism, and good works, without recognizing that the modern America that he celebrates is something quite foreign and in many respects inimical to what the Puritan settlers of Massachusetts Bay in the seventeenth century had in mind when they expressed their aspirations to become a "City upon a Hill." This is perhaps as it should be, since nationalism is a mythology, a form of consciousness, the success of which is measured not by its historical accuracy but by its power to bind a given community into a common sense of interest and identity.

Yet if our goal is understanding the nature of American nationalism, and its relationship to the nationalisms of other parts of the world, it is necessary to take a historical view as well as describe the current consciousness. One thing is clear, American nationalism has always had about it, in its articulated aspects, and compared to the nationalisms of Europe, something of the nature of a doctrine, a set of beliefs, as opposed to the allegiances of blood, dynasty, language, history, religion, and territory that form the core of European senses of national identity. Which is not necessarily to say that American nationalism has always lacked an ethnic and religious core or always been understood in terms of a universal to be applied to all mankind.

The thirteen British colonies of North America that united to fight a successful war of independence and to found a constitutional federal union were quite diverse in their histories, economies, interests, and culture. What they shared in common was a British Protestant origin, a strong sense of the value of those inherited parts of British constitutional liberty and self-government that were most useful and pertinent to them, and the experience of the Revolution and constitution-making itself.

A sense of American nationalism was not absent from the War of Independence, but it was relatively muted, especially in comparison to the nationalist outbreaks in Europe which began a few decades later. (Dick Taylor's German interlocutor was more than likely an offspring of the Revolutions of 1848.) And while Americans sometimes appealed to the opinion of mankind and thought of themselves as an example to peoples everywhere oppressed by arbitrary governments, they were not really universalists or egalitarians. Their attitude was more that of a younger son declaring his equality with his older brothers than of a revolutionary eager to impart "democracy"—a bad word to them— throughout the universe.

Neither their geographical situation—their isolation from the Old World and the prospect of a nearly empty continent to be settled—nor their inclination, suggested to them any mission to expand democratic revolution to the world. They were, indeed, highly content with their own principles, prospects, and nature. It did not occur to them that they were Citizens of the World. Their British Protestant culture was nearly unremarked upon, not because it was rejected but because it was so taken for granted.

What held the American states together in a loose political unity was not

nationalism but a constitutional settlement embodying federal republican principles. One of the implicit aspects of this settlement was that it was to preserve an
already existent identity. (Americans still swear allegiance to the Constitution,
not to the nation or to any explicit set of political dogmas.) This historical truth
is little understood today. In fact official American belief regards the Declaration
of Independence as the beginning of an endless process of active movement
toward an ever more egalitarian and universalist society. This is because of the
intervention between us and the Founding Fathers of that sea-change in the thinking of men that is summed up in the term "the French Revolution."

While Americans before the Civil War were often quite truculent in assert-
ing their rights and honor over against other countries, and in upholding the superiority of their republican, constitutional liberties to arbitrary governments elsewhere, they were not nationalists in the sense that was later to be understood.
There were in antebellum America no loyalty oaths or pledges of allegiance to
the flag or the nation. Freeborn American citizens would have considered such to
be an insult to their patriotism as well as an invasion of the rights of their states.

It is true that during the early nineteenth century rhetorical emphasis was
increasingly laid on an idea of nationalism. New Englanders, who had always
had the most organized sense of community and mission among Americans,
strove, with a good deal of success, to promote New England ideals of the future
of America, as those ideals had been transformed by the devolution of Puritanism
into a progress-oriented economic system and by Transcendentalism, a German
stepchild of the French Revolution.

Americans of other sorts were no less patriotic, and in fact were far more
typical, but the New Englanders were the more articulate. The outcome of the
Civil War completed a process by which the New England community, in an idealized form, became the prototype of Americanism, both at home and abroad.
(For example, the first American dictionary, produced by Noah Webster of
Connecticut, was not an American dictionary at all, but a New England dictionary, establishing spellings and pronunciations that were not at all typically
American but which were proselytized as standards by subsequent generations of
schoolmarms.)

Until the Civil War nationalism was a sentiment with many different acceptable connotations. It was not an instrumental concept except occasionally as an
assertion against foreign interference. It involved no particular imperatives or
organized missions, except as regarded the empty lands on the borders of the
Union which might become future states. And even so, the westward movement
was largely a matter of individual initiative, not national self-assertion.

It was in the crucible of the Civil War that the first American nationalism in
the strict sense was formed. The Civil War has faded in memory and significance
to generations of Americans who have seen two World Wars, a worldwide
empire, and vast social changes. Yet the Civil War—in terms of the mobilization
and casualties, and in terms of the consequences—is still the largest event in our
history.

The central issue in the Civil War, to which all other questions including slavery and centralization were subordinate, was the movement of American society into modernization. Modernization, among other things, implies economic, political, and cultural centralization and nationalism. To modernization the divergent development of the American South provided a formidable obstacle. The South was vast, politically skilled, increasingly unified as the antebellum period wore on, and firmly opposed to both economic nationalism (in the form of protective tariffs, federal subsidy for the transportation infrastructure, free public lands, and a central banking system) and to cultural nationalism in its New England variety. Furthermore, it had the weight of prestige and tradition on its side in its appeal to the traditional limited constitutional settlement, a tradition which at least latently counted on the allegiance of many Americans outside the South who were dubious about the effects of modernization.

It was during the Civil War, with the appeals to the Union as a mystic indissoluble bond, to unlimited exercise of power by the agents of a putative national majority, to loyalty oaths and the archetypal image of Uncle Sam, that American nationalism came into being. The outcome settled certain issues seemingly, forever. The formerly plural United States was now a nation-state with a centralized economic policy under the aegis of a federal government restrained by no constitutional checks that were not internal to itself. Further, the course of the war had if not universalized the concept of American citizenship, immensely broadened it. Contrary to widespread belief, immigration of new peoples into the United States had been a minor phenomenon in the early days of the Republic. (George Washington was already the fifth generation of his family in America.) Not until the 1840's did it become substantial. Among the major components of the new nationalism were the Irish and German immigrants, who indeed made the Northern victory in the Civil War possible.

Less important at the time and not originally intended as a consequence, but of immense importance to the future, was the emancipation and then enfranchisement of the Afro-American population, the first as a military measure and the second as a political necessity for the ruling party. Before the war no respectable Northern politician had dared suggest much more than a restriction of slavery in the territories, with a hint of a future gradual elimination of the institution, though without any concrete suggestion as to how this would be done or what would be the status of the freedmen.

Yet in the nationalist mythology that was formed in the struggle for the Union, next in importance to the Union itself and in time more important, was the moral imperative of equality and universalization of citizenship enshrined in the Fourteenth Amendment. The success of the new mythology was indicated by the fact that while it is possible to criticize almost anything else in American history—the Constitution, George Washington, Franklin D. Roosevelt—it is nearly impossible to criticize, even on limited historical grounds, the righteousness of the movement for emancipation and equality for the freedmen. With the crusade for equality American nationalism had achieved not only its political and economic goals but had fashioned a moral imperative in compelling form.

But what emerged was a strange form of universalized democracy. Government of, by, and for the people had come to mean all people in a new and uniquely American way. This universal principle, however, was embodied in a quotidian context of an American society that was still overwhelmingly British Protestant not only in its composition but in its values and aspirations. In fact, the very aspiration for equal liberty and opportunity was itself a form of idealism that rested upon a peculiarly Anglo-Saxon heritage.

In the half century between the Civil War and World War I, American nationalism was subjected to immense stresses. Regionalism did not disappear. The South, in some respects, remained obdurate, and the new states of the Plains and Rocky Mountains sometimes erupted in quite radical forms of populist revolt. More important were the stresses associated with the creation of a modern industrial nation-state, which tended to wipe away and recreate classes, localities, occupations and ways of life. These stresses have been suffered by every modernizing society and in themselves are capable of great disruption. But in America, simultaneously with these vast social changes came another unprecedented dislocation: an immense immigration of new peoples from the east and south of Europe, altering the ethnic and religious composition of the population to an extent that no other modern society had ever undergone.

History is always seeking new forms of equilibrium. Out of this social crucible came, uneasily and unevenly, a new form of American nationalism, which eventually established its hegemony. The settlement that emerged was part and parcel of the Progressive era. Progressivism was not simply the clearcut reform movement of the history textbooks—it was a sea-change in consciousness, the completion of a stage of mental modernization with vast and sometimes ambivalent and contradictory implications with which we are still living and which historians have barely begun to describe adequately.

The Progressive settlement that emerged, symbolized in different ways by such politicians as Theodore Roosevelt and Woodrow Wilson and such writers as Herbert Croly and Walter Lippmann, had two aspects. Externally, it implied the emergence of the United States as a world power of the first class, along with Britain, France, and Germany. There might be disagreement about the exact implications of this and the policies to be pursued, but it was soon clear that traditional American isolation would give way to a determination to act aggressively on the world stage. In this situation, which had behind it the seeming force of inevitability, a spokesman for the older America like William Jennings Bryan could only appear as a hopeless archaism.

One of the more obviously observable internal results of the triumph of nationalist Progressivism was a change in the nature of American leadership. The old gentry, which had evolved leaders from the locality, had been supplanted by a national, even international, class of politicians, publicists, experts, intellectuals, and financiers who acted in many respects together, had, broadly speaking, common goals, and who considered themselves to be the natural masters of the nation. To a considerable extent the new nationalism was not a product of the grassroots but an ideology of the masters.

Another internal aspect of the new nationalism was "the Melting Pot." The Melting Pot was the American answer to the immense changes brought by the New Immigration. It had many aspects and could change its character depending upon which angle it was viewed from. It was amorphous enough to provide comfort both to the old stock American uneasy at the changes sweeping over his country and the immigrant uneasy at his place in the New World.

To the immigrant the Melting Pot offered opportunity and assimilation: Americanization, which would bring with it prosperity and full participation in democracy. To the old American it offered the prospect of melting down an alien mass into a form that was compatible with what he valued. It was a little unclear whether the immigrant would become in time an Anglo-American or whether all would become together something new. In the very vagueness was its strength.

There was about it something of the aspect of the old American imposing his culture on the newcomer as a condition of acceptance; this was to be accomplished chiefly in the time-tested ways in which New Englanders had always proposed to tame wild Southerners and Westerners—through the public school, disciplined labor, economic progress, moral exhortation, and appeals to an idealism of American uniqueness. There was also about it an aspect of the immigrant himself contributing to a newly emergent culture. These ambiguities were not and never have been resolved. The power of the Melting Pot ideal is not in its logic but in its art, its ability to command common consent from diverse groups.

There were a number of concrete results of the process. Catholics and Jews, from being small tolerated minorities, became equal partners in the American religious commitment with Protestants. The British Protestants went from an overwhelming to a bare majority. Inherited differences in values, however, would inevitably complicate many areas of American life and politics—the form and function of city governments, the role of the public schools, the relationship of church and state, and perhaps most importantly, the national stance toward other nations, many of which were traditional homes or traditional enemies of large groups of voters. The debacle of Prohibition was one example of the ensuing mess. The politics of ethnic coalition was another.

Both the old American and the new American, just to the extent that they valued their own culture and religious forms, were bound to feel a certain uneasiness with the compromise which bound them together. Yet America provided a generally high standard of living and economic opportunity, vast elbow room, and a freedom from the pressure for conformity that results from external threat. The nationalism that emerged from the Melting Pot was a resounding success of which Americans were justly celebratory. It provided at its best a graceful surmounting of problems such as no large society had ever faced and in the larger things showed a remarkable tolerance and cohesion. World War I revealed some, but not insurmountable tensions. World War II consolidated the success of Americanization. A regiment of Japanese-American volunteers piled up an impressive combat record and the Allied forces in Europe were led to victory by a German-American, Eisenhower. Americans were massively united, first in their reluctance to enter the war and then in determination to win it.

Moreover, World War II, in the expansion of federal power and the mobilization of egalitarian sentiment against fascism, laid the basis for another major movement—the extension of *de facto* equality to the black Americans who had emerged from slavery some generations before. (It is wrong to say, in the often-used phrase, that the Civil Rights revolution was a completion of the long-deferred commitment to equality, because there never really had been any such commitment before except in a very rhetorical, limited, and expedient sense.)

During and after World War II American society for the third time made a perilous leap into the cauldron of history, boiling down its existing consensus in the optimistic prospect of molding itself into a newer and more daring form. The Civil Rights revolution and a revolutionary alteration of the immigration laws were simultaneously undertaken in the 1960's. It was as if the Melting Pot, having proven itself able to boil down all of Europe, was now to test its capacity to do the same for the whole world. So natural and inevitable a next step in the progress of the success of American democracy did this seem, that it was hardly noticed. The almost complete triumph of the Melting Pot ideal is indicated by the fact that Americans, with no noticeable demurrer, celebrated the centenary of the Statue of Liberty not as a memorial to liberty but as a memorial to ethnic diversity.

The attempt to create a third form of American nationalism also had an external as well as an internal aspect. From an actor on the world stage America perforce became the leader of the world. Its prosperity, its security, its freedom from major internal stress, its tolerance, its confidence that the present is always better than the past and the future will always be better than the present, provided the model for the world, at least in the minds of its leaders.

For the first time the American leadership class, the politicians and intellectuals who were the inheritors of the Progressive era's belief in elite and expert rule, in technique, optimism, and progress, began to regard American success not as an end but as a means. The successful mobilization against totalitarianism of the right, which they believed, perhaps mistakenly, to be a demon from the past rather than a portent of the future, proved to them the need and possibility for worldwide democracy on the American model—democracy conceived in terms of the American standard of living and middle class civilities and technological expertise.

From the war onward the ideal of global democracy under American leadership and example provided the rationale of American interaction with the world. Its instruments were the United Nations and other international organizations, which were invested with the same mystic devotion that the concept of "Union" had once enjoyed; massive economic aid to bring the rest of the world up to American standards; and, less certainly, a determination to provide military security. This international mission was to be carried out at the same time as revolution at home—the Great Society, the Civil Rights revolution, and the opening of the borders were to perfect the American example at home so that there could not be left in the world any doubters in the sincerity and success of American equality and democracy.

In some respects, if not all, global democracy, which has continued to the present time as the chief justification of American foreign policy under both Democratic and Republican, liberal and conservative administrations, is an elite ideology rather than a movement of the grassroots. Until the attack on Pearl Harbor, for instance, despite massive interventionist propaganda and a complete commitment to an antifascist crusade on the part of the leadership, Americans at large were overwhelmingly resistant to involvement in external quarrels. Following the war, burdens of the Cold War were shouldered, but often quite reluctantly.

The global democracy ideology left many Americans ill-prepared for the resistant reality of the real world. Americans, generally, could not understand how other peoples might regard what Americans considered as self-evidently generous assistance to be unwanted dictation, as, in fact, imperialism. Few Americans and no American leaders were able to conceive that the benefits of technology and the dollar applied to undeveloped society did not always lead to unalloyed progress, as witness the disintegration of the viable tribal societies of black Africa without their replacement by anything stable or satisfactory. The U.N. proved a disappointment to most of its devotees.

The great triumph over fascism was succeeded by the Iron Curtain, then by the draw in Korea, and then by the debacle of a high-minded effort to defend democracy in the former French colonies in Indochina. While American democracy might provide an appealing contrast to Soviet imperialism, it provided little guidance in dealing with militant fundamentalism in the vast Islamic world. The Afghans who resisted Communism did not aspire to democracy but aspired, in a predemocratic way, to the preservation of their religion and way of life. And what was to happen to the idealism of global democracy when it was found that those foreigners one was called upon to defend from Communism were not democrats but merely practitioners of an older and nearly as ugly if not quite as thoroughgoing a form of oppression as that against which they were fighting? Thus global democracy provided no basis for an anticommunist policy in Central America.

Despite these setbacks and confusions, global democracy has maintained a remarkable hold upon the imagination of the American leadership class. The real question is whether an insistence on applying the measure of democracy—conceived in a rather abstract and implicitly American way—really provides an adequate basis for relationships with other peoples. One does not have to believe in a cynical foreign policy to be wary of a rather rootless and insubstantial form of idealism. This is as true after as before the dissolution of communism. Nor is it clear that the American public as a whole, as opposed to the leadership class, is really committed to a mission to defend and implement American style democracy. The felt necessity of the leadership to idealize every step as surrounded with an immaculate democracy has prevented any constructive American role in situations, such as Latin America, where democracy may be chimerical under any circumstances.

Global democracy may prove more dangerous to allies and neutrals than to enemies. Amazingly, the same American liberals who believe that America should not police the world when it is a question of an aggressor leftist regime, find no problem in subverting governments of the right. Even though, presumably, such intervention is only morally justified by self-defence and regimes of the right, however distasteful, pose no threat to America. Thus, an ideology put forth by Reaganites as a defence against totalitarianism can just as easily, and without any change in assumptions, be used to undermine some friendly regime that some future Democratic administration finds inadequate by its own standards of democracy. Global democracy already has a substantial record of abandonment of American allies.

Internally, American society is now engaged in an experiment to test the limits at which a coherent nationalism can be maintained in a democratic system by a shared doctrine of equality and prosperity, without any binding cultural, ethnic, religious, or ethical cohesion. The strategy of the leadership toward this problem is one of optimism. Refuse to recognize the problem and it will go away. Assume that it is already solved and it will be. Optimism, positive thinking, is one of the most characteristic of American traits and attitudes.

The history of America has been such as to provide a realistic basis for optimism. A good deal of morale has been restored during the Reagan years (though it remains to be seen how genuine and deep this restoration will prove under possible future stresses). There have always been naysayers and prophets of doom in the past and America has always ignored them and proved them wrong. There is no question that American society has already tested and transcended the limits of all previous experience in creating national unity out of diversity. Optimism, the expectation of the best, is in itself one of the causes of success, Americans deeply believe, while pessimism is sure to find what it expects.

Yet the essence of statesmanship is to see and prepare for the dangers of the future. It is perhaps not too pessimistic to observe that the final answer is not yet in on the most recent and ongoing experiment in testing the limits of national cohesion. Vast segments of American society have been and are being Hispanicized and Asianized. No one knows what the long-range consequences of this will be. To some extent it works against not only traditional Western culture and religion, but also against liberal tendencies, such as separation of church and state and feminism. Many of the new immigrants bring value systems not wholly compatible with the traditional and prospective functioning of American society.

Many observers, including the New Immigrants themselves, question the ideal of the Melting Pot. Some regard it as an intolerable oppression to give up Spanish for English or abandon their traditional male supremacy for more egalitarian American standards. Egalitarianism among groups does not necessarily translate into liberty among individuals. And what is good for particular groups is increasingly substituted for what is good for society as a whole, far beyond the degree to which the ideal of democracy as a consensual compromise between various groups would allow. Striving for Americanization has been replaced by striving for status in a hierarchy of victimization.

A pessimist would point to the increasing attenuation of the values and institutions that used to provide unity in diversity. The decimated public schools no longer provide a common standard of culture and values, or even a common standard of educational achievement. Americans used to be unified by the Constitution—viewed largely as a negative restraint on government. But the Constitution now means whatever the most powerful and adept political forces want it to mean, and is viewed primarily as an instrument to serve the interests of minorities of all kinds.

Amidst a general decline of morals and the traditional family, it is difficult to find any ethical standards that firmly bind most of the population, and society increasingly resorts to bureaucracy and legal hair-splitting to enforce behaviors that once were enforced by social pressure. No one knows how deeply the resentments of older Americans now run against the establishment policies of affirmative action, (the old ideal of equal opportunity having been swiftly supplanted by one of special privilege), unlimited immigration, intolerable toleration of crime, and official hostility to Christianity. It is possible that these resentments are much deeper and more lasting than the insouciant leadership, choosing to ignore the problems except in election rhetoric, will admit. They may even be intensifying in a young population that no longer has the experience of real national unity.

Even so, by a curious paradox, it is the unprivileged groups who remain the most committed to an unquestioning American nationalism—that is, a real love of country that transcends the question of "What's in it for me." Middle Americans, Southerners, the ethnic groups less officially recognized and privileged have responded most readily to the Reaganite formulation of American nationalism in terms of pride and opportunity.

A shared culture has in the past provided a basis for unity among peoples otherwise diverse. But the most enduring and valuable forms of culture, at least in their formative stages, are a product of homogeniety and stability. Americanization has tended to attenuate both high culture and folk culture. What has been gained in inclusiveness has been lost in focus. As Tocqueville and other early observers pointed out, the thrust of American democracy was toward standardization—a standardization which might be at a quite comfortable level but which tended to pull down the higher manifestations of culture.

Americans build splendid palaces in which to display the music and art created in other ages on other continents. It is a culture derivative and poured in from the top, not evolved from the grassroots, and therefore has a limited power to bind deeply. Without Southern and Jewish writers, both imperfectly Americanized, there would hardly be any American literature of world class in the later 20th century. The two most original forms of American folk culture, Southern black music (the various forms of jazz), and Southern white music ("country music") are being attenuated by standardization at the same time that they are admired around the world as both admirable and uniquely American.

To many the loss of some cultural coherence may be a small price to pay for a tolerant diversity, high standard of living, and democratic spirit, but culture is not only valuable in itself but makes up an essential binding ingredient that can hold a people together even under reverses and oppression. (The resurgence of Poland provides perhaps the most telling example today.) It may even be that, in the long run, a coherent culture is an economic necessity.

Even those societies of the past that were basically commercial had some religious unity or civic ethic to hold them together. Recent efforts, sometimes heroic and ingenious, of various American politicians and thinkers to provide a civic ethic or even a civic religion of shared values may indicate a recognition of the problem, however dim, but they do not indicate that it has yet been convincingly solved.

Like every other nation, America is more or less bound together by its sense of oneness in contrast to other peoples. However, even that sense seems to become increasingly decimated as the society grows both more diverse and more international. What remains to bind Americans together are the middle class virtues, increasingly under attack, and the high standard of living and standardization of consumer goods. If that is so, there may be a real danger of confusing prosperity and patriotism. All nations from time to time encounter situations in which it is necessary to put aside self-interest and differences and sacrifice for a higher common good. The sense of American nationalism that has developed during the Reagan years may be similar to the philosophies of certain Protestant sects who guarantee their followers that prosperity will ensue from a proper religious orientation. When the prosperity fails to materialize, or something happens to remind that this world is, after all, a vale of tears, the faithful may become cynics.

(1990)

Making War

Movies Reviewed: *Wake Island* (1942), directed by John Farrow, black & white, 88 minutes; *Go Tell the Spartans* (1978), directed by Ted Post, color, 114 minutes; and *Saigon: Year of the Cat* (1983), directed by Stephen Frears, color, 106 minutes.

Americans learn their wars primarily through the movies. Who, except for the few who were actually there, can imagine World War II without thinking of John Wayne? The popular medium gives us a way to digest what would otherwise be too terrible to contemplate, to absorb it into the national psyche.

Generally speaking, British World War II movies are much better than American. The British leave out the silly common-man comic relief touches, ethnic group representation, and excessive firefights that Americans want and concentrate on the experience and character of men at war. An exception, and possibly the best American film to come out of the war, is *Wake Island*. *Wake Island* tells the story of a few hundred American Marines and construction workers who were caught on the barren Pacific atoll of Wake after Pearl Harbor. Without any hope of relief, they fight skillfully and to the last against overwhelming Japanese sea, land, and air forces.

The combat is well rendered, but the emphasis is on the characters—the Marine commander (Brian Donlevy) who has left a motherless young daughter in Hawaii; common Marines like the inevitable William Bendix and a very young Robert Preston; the engineers and construction men who decline a chance to escape; a handful of pilots (including Macdonald Carey) who sacrifice themselves against impossible odds.

It is a propaganda film, and a very good one. It shows Americans coming together to sacrifice their lives for their country. For their country: because it is, under the circumstances, the right thing to do. There is not a word about saving the world for democracy, nor a single glowing tribute to Eleanor Roosevelt's wonderful plans for postwar reconstruction; not even much about Mother, Apple Pie, and The Girl I Left Behind. Instead there is something approaching the high mode of Western epic—courageously facing unavoidable fate.

The Marine leader mentions (attention, Ruth Bader Ginsburg!) that he is a graduate of the Virginia Military Institute—to which the leader of the construction crew (Walter Abel) replies that he is a Notre Dame man himself. Imagine that. Racist, sexist VMI! Reactionary Notre Dame! Both in a film designed to arouse American patriotism. Someone must have known how to appeal to Americans at a deeper level than the average studio executive in Hollywood could aim at, even then—much less today. The most memorable scene in the film is the nighttime burial of casualties, with crosses prominently displayed and the reading of prayers. There are no atheists in the foxholes, one Marine comments.

Really. *Wake Island* will remind you of what our country once was and probably will never be again.

I doubt if we will ever see a good film about the Gulf War, because the whole thing was too silly to make good drama. There have been several unsuccessful attempts at the Grenada invasion, including Clint Eastwood's worst film, *Heartbreak Ridge*, which was almost as embarrassing as John Wayne's *The Green Berets*. And we certainly have not come to grips with that strange episode in American history known as the Vietnam War.

The Hollywood treatment so far certainly won't do. The accepted wisdom is that the Oliver Stone and Francis Ford Coppola productions, *Platoon* and *Apocalypse Now!*, told the story for us. But in retrospect, these films appear hysterical creations of the alienated. They tell us little about war and nothing about the American experience. The makers of these films hate quotidian America, and their hatred both predates and postdates the war. Michael Cimino's *The Deer Hunter* is a partial exception, since the characters bear some resemblance to actual Americans.

Two films, largely overlooked, do come to grips with the Vietnam War in a way that can reconcile us to the past and teach us a few lessons for the future. *Go Tell the Spartans* and *Saigon: Year of the Cat* frame the war perfectly. The first tells of the beginning of the American involvement; the second, of the end. Both portray the tragedy of the time with insight and without hysteria.

Go Tell the Spartans casts Burt Lancaster as a tough regular army officer in the early days of American "advisors." The title of the film is found carved over the gate of a French cemetery near an outpost that Lancaster and his motley crew are left to defend. The Americans should learn something from this, but they don't. Moral ambiguities abound. What if the nice young girl is really, as the South Vietnamese liaison says, a Vietcong who will slit your throat at the first opportunity? The arrogance and ignorance of the brass come through—the Great Society bureaucracy abroad. We can hardly have a better picture of the idiocy of the McNamara war machine: An electronic map supposedly shows, by colored lights, where the enemy activity is most intense. We come away knowing that, at the beginning, the end was already ordained.

Saigon: Year of the Cat was panned by reviewers. I think I know why: Its portrayal of the American establishment, especially the Saigon ambassador (well played by E.G. Marshall), is too close to the truth of intellectual and moral failure. Frederic Forrest is a CIA operative who is unable to convince his superiors that "Vietnamization" has failed and that North Vietnam is on the verge of a final push. Judi Dench is an English bank manager who provides a point of view of sane detachment from which to witness the unfolding collapse. The last American departure is portrayed vividly, as is something almost never mentioned in America: the shameful abandonment of allies to their enemies.

These two works of cinematic art, if pondered, might provide us a way of thinking about that strange interlude that may help us restrain our messianic leaders on some other bloody occasion.

(2000)

The Lincoln War Crimes Trial:
A History Lesson

In the previous chapter we discussed the early stages of the North American War of Secession of 1861-63 as the minority Lincoln government attempted to suppress the legal secession of the Southern United States by military invasion. In this chapter we will discuss the conclusion of the war and some of its consequences.

In the spring of 1863 General R.E. Lee's Confederate army crossed the Potomac for the second time in the hope of relieving devastated areas of the Confederacy and bringing the war to a successful conclusion.

For several weeks he maneuvered freely in Pennsylvania without encountering United States forces, which were under strict orders to protect the Lincoln government in Washington. The Confederates observed the rules of civilized warfare, despite the systematic atrocities that had been visited upon civilians in the South by the Lincoln forces. Pennsylvanians worked peacefully in their fields as the ragged but confident Confederates marched by.

About the first of July, Lee found the U.S. forces entrenched at Gettysburg, a town in Southern Pennsylvania. Though having superior numbers, "Honest Abe's" armies were unable to initiate any forward movement. ("Honest Abe" was a name given to Lincoln by his early associates and later political enemies, for the same reason that the biggest boy in a class is called "Tiny.") Union morale was low. While there were many good men in the ranks who had volunteered to fight for the preservation of the American Union, there were also many unwilling conscripts and large numbers of foreigners who had been lured into the army by bounties and who were ignorant of the issues of the war and of American principles of liberty and self-government.

Among the better U.S. soldiers there was much discontent over the recent illegal "Emancipation Proclamation," which in their view had changed the nature of the war, and over the dismissal of the popular General McClellan. Historians have often noted that generally speaking, the best generals and soldiers in the "Union" armies were not supporters of the Republican party or the Lincoln administration. Republicans and especially abolitionists tended to avoid military service in the war they had initiated.

After several days of probing attacks by Lee, the decisive breakthrough came on July 3, the eve of a day revered by lovers of liberty and self-government throughout the world. Pickett's fresh division and Pettigrew's seasoned veterans broke through the center of the Union line, its weakest point in terms of terrain. Military historians have noted the striking similarity between this attack and the French breaking of the Austrian center at the Battle of Solferino just four years before.

There were heavy casualties on both sides, but the ever vigilant General

Longstreet exploited the breakthrough and rolled up one wing of the Union army. The other wing began retreating toward Washington to defend the government there. The noted Confederate cavalryman Stuart arrived at last and began to dog the retreat, which was made miserable by torrential rains and blistering heat.

Some U.S. troops fought bravely, especially General Hancock, a Pennsylvanian, later President of the U.S., and Col. Joshua Chamberlain of Maine, later U.S. ambassador to the Confederate States. But when the Democratic governors of New York and Illinois ordered their regiments to suspend fighting and return home, the remaining "Union" forces retreated to the inner defenses of the capital, ironically named for a great Virginian who was a relative of General Lee.

On Independence Day following the battle, former President Franklin Pierce addressed a cheering crowd at the capitol in Concord, New Hampshire. Pierce had never wavered in his support for the Constitution despite threats from the Lincoln government. The tide has turned, Pierce told the audience, and the Constitution and liberty of the Fathers would soon be restored in peace. (It should be pointed out that relatively new telegraph lines made communication almost instantaneous by 1863.)

Lincoln had always been careful to stay away from fighting, visiting his forces only in quiet periods, in contrast to President Davis who was often on the battlefield. Immediately upon receiving the news of Gettysburg, Lincoln wired General Grant, an undistinguished officer who had been trying unsuccessfully for months, with a large force, to capture the small Confederate garrison at Vicksburg on the Mississippi River. Grant was ordered to retreat at once into Tennessee and bring his army by rail to the defense of Washington. For reasons which have long been disputed by historians, Grant refused to carry out this order.

Grant was replaced by General Rosecrans, who attempted to carry out Lincoln's orders. He found, unfortunately, Confederate General Forrest had got in his rear and destroyed his immense supply bases along the Tennessee River. His hands were further tied by an uprising across central and western Kentucky. Rosecrans finally came to rest near Columbus, Ohio, where he could subsist his army.

Taking advantage of Rosecrans's withdrawal, Confederate General Dick Taylor, son of a former President of the U.S., moved down the Mississippi to liberate New Orleans. The "Union" commanders there, General "Beast" Butler and Admiral Porter, who were unsavory characters even by the standards of the Lincoln party, absconded from New Orleans with $2 million in cotton for their personal profit. They were later heard of in South America, where Butler tried unsuccessfully to make himself President of Uruguay. President Davis was able to declare that now, after two years of forcible obstruction, "the Mississippi flows unvexed to the sea."

The rejoicing of the people of New Orleans, white and black, at freedom from military occupation was riotous. It was truly *laissez le bon temps rouler.*

More importantly, ships began to make their way through the dissolving (and illegal) naval blockade and enter New Orleans and other Southern ports, bringing much needed munitions and medicines. Among the ships were a number from the Northern States looking for cotton and ready to pay gold rather than the rapidly depreciating U.S. greenbacks. A number of Lincoln's strongest New England supporters were involved in this trade, which was illegal to them by Lincoln's order.

A small force left behind in Mississippi by Rosecrans was captured by Forrest. The commander of this force was one General Sherman. Among papers found with Sherman were plans from the Lincoln government for a war of terrorism to be waged systematically against women and children in the South. These included detailed instructions, with illustrations for the soldiers. Houses were to be pillaged and then burned, along with all farm buildings and tools and standing crops. Livestock was to be killed or carried away and food confiscated or destroyed.

Particular emphasis was laid on destructions of family heirlooms—pictures of dead loved ones, Bibles, wedding dresses, and pianos. There were also directions as to how to persuade, or coerce if persuasion failed, black servants into divulging the whereabouts of hidden valuables.

The revelation of these papers shocked the world and played a significant part in the later war crimes trial of Lincoln. Sherman had issued additional orders, urging his soldiers to "make the damned traitorous rebel women and children howl." At his trial later, Sherman defended himself. His actions had been called for, he said, because Americans had too much freedom and needed to be brought under obedience to government like Europeans. The trial of the *United States vs. Sherman* resulted in a famous precedent-setting verdict of not guilty by reason of insanity.

Meanwhile, Lee waited outside Washington without attacking and the Confederate government renewed the offer made in 1861 and never answered, to negotiate all issues with the U.S. in good faith, on principles of justice and equity. Many of the remaining Union soldiers slipped quietly away, consoling themselves with a popular song in the New York music halls, which went "I ain't gonna fight for Ole Abe no more, no more!"

There then occurred one of those extraordinary unexpected historical events which brought about a dramatic shift in the situation. Lincoln attempted to escape Washington in disguise. He was taken prisoner by Colonel Mosby, a Confederate partisan who operated freely in northern Virginia. Very shortly after, Mosby's men intercepted a band of assassins intent on killing Lincoln. It was soon revealed that Booth, a double agent, had been hired by the "Union" Secretary of War Edwin M. Stanton and certain Radical Republican leaders in Congress, to remove "Honest Abe" and make way for a military dictatorship under a reliable Republican.

Subsequently indicted by the U.S. for his part in the attempted assassination, Stanton hanged himself in his prison cell, shouting "Now I belong to the ages!"

Vice President Hannibal Hamlin fled to Boston and then to Canada where he issued a statement that he bore no responsibility for the illegal acts and aggressions committed by the administration.

Relieved of military pressure, Maryland, Kentucky, and Missouri convened conventions of the people in free elections, seceded from the Union, and asked to join the Confederate States. With some opposition they were admitted to the Confederate Union. Meanwhile, California and Oregon declared their independence and formed a new Confederacy of the Pacific. The CSA was the first to recognize this new union.

Needless to say, the successful establishment of independence by the seceding States had far-reaching consequences, not only for North America, but throughout the world. The great American principle that governments rest upon the consent of the governed had been conspicuously vindicated.

With the capture of Lincoln, the flight of Hamlin, and the discrediting of the would be assassins in Congress, the North was without a head. An unprecedented agreement among governors, later vindicated by constitutional amendment, advanced the 1864 elections to the fall of 1863. Vallandigham of Ohio and Seymour of New York, both strong opponents of Lincoln's usurpations, were elected President and Vice-President with a Democratic Congress. Outside of New England and industrial centers dominated by pro-tariff forces, the Republican party fell away in strength, though the pompous Senator from Massachusetts, Charles Sumner, and the fanatical Stevens of Pennsylvania led a bitter minority in Congress.

Immediately upon his inauguration, President Vallandigham accepted the Confederate offer of negotiation. In a moving address to the country he expressed his wish that the real Union, the one established by the Fathers for all Americans, could be reunited. But he feared the scars of war had made this impossible. All could take comfort in the fact that there were now two great free confederacies favoring the world with examples of liberty and self-government.

The Confederate States waived demands for reparations. The resulting treaty of peace and friendship had two main provisions. As to territory, the Confederacy was recognized as ruler of the Indian territories and the southern portion of New Mexico (later Arizona) and Union-seized western Virginia was returned to the Old Dominion.

The other important provision provided for a lasting cancellation of all tariff barriers between the two Unions. This establishment of the principle of free trade over the continent (it had been preceded by the repeal of the British Corn Laws) must be given credit for the flourishing prosperity of the two confederacies that followed, as well as their immunity from the imperial wars that have wracked Europe and Asia. It is noteworthy that the Republican tariff industrialists, who fought free trade tooth and nail, found that their profits were not lost, as they had feared, but increased.

President Vallandigham and the Democratic Congress of the U.S. returned to Jeffersonian principles not only on the tariff but across the board. The debacle of the Lincoln administration and its corruption had provided all the evidence needed of the abuses and danger of centralized government. War contracting had showed up tremendous graft for political favorites. Expenditures were curtailed, corruption prosecuted (it was said at one point that every other Lincoln appointee was in jail or under indictment), and the national banking fraud dismantled. The corrupt and brutal Indian policy of Lincoln was terminated in favor of a return to the moderate Jeffersonian policy. To this is attributed the subsequent relative freedom of the U.S. from Indian wars.

There remained one vexing problem. What to do with Lincoln, in comfortable confinement in Richmond, receiving every courtesy from his captors. Doubtless the failed President's disappointment and sorrow were deepened when his son Robert, who had spent the war at Harvard, denounced Lincoln as a fraud and a failure and attempted to launch his own political career, and Mrs. Lincoln had to be confined to a mental asylum. (The indictment of Mrs. Lincoln for unauthorized expenditures from the White House accounts was quietly dropped.)

The fate of Lincoln became the subject of international interest. Count Bismarck of Prussia and the Czar of Russia called an international conference in support of Lincoln, which justified his actions on the grounds that legitimate governments must have the power to suppress rebellious subjects and provinces. Britain, France and many of the smaller states of Europe countered with a declaration upholding the American doctrine that governments rest on the consent of the governed.

An idea that gained attention at the time was put forward by the Rev. Mr. Joseph Wilson, a Presbyterian minister in Augusta, Georgia. The peace-loving nations should establish a world government to punish aggressions such as those Lincoln had committed. After all, such offenses were against all humanity and not just the invaded peoples. The press soon reported that the idea had really come from the Rev. Wilson's twelve-year old son, Woodrow. (Woodrow, who became a college president, was later noted for his fruitless lectures in favor of world government.)

Who did have jurisdiction over the numerous crimes? True, Lincoln had made unscrupulous war upon the Southern people in an attempt to suppress their freedom. But he had also, in so doing, violated the Constitution of the United States and caused great suffering to the citizens of the U.S. After mature consideration, Lincoln was turned over to the authorities of the U.S. to be prosecuted in their courts. Ironically, the Confederate Vice-President Alexander Stephens, an old friend of Lincoln, volunteered for his defense team.

The list of indictments was long:

- Violation of the Constitution and his oath of office by invading and waging war against states that had legally and democratically withdrawn their consent from his government, inaugurating one of the cruelest wars in recent history.
- Raising troops without the approval of Congress and expending funds

without appropriation.

- Suspending the writ of habeas corpus and interfering with the press without due process, imprisoning thousands of citizens without charge or trial, and closing courts by military force where no hostilities were occurring.
- Corrupting the currency by manipulations and paper swindles unheard of in previous U.S. history.
- Fraud and corruption by appointees and contractors with his knowledge and connivance.
- Continuing the war by raising ever larger bodies of troops by conscription and hiring of foreign mercenaries and refusing to negotiate in good faith for an end to hostilities.
- Confiscation of millions of dollars of property by his agents in the South, especially cotton, without legal proceedings.
- Waging war against women and children and civilian property as a matter of policy (rather than as unavoidably incident to combat). (General Sherman and others were called to testify as to their operations and the source of their orders.)

Two questions widely discussed at the time could not be formulated into systematic charges against Lincoln. One was the huge number of deaths among the black population in the South as a result of forcible dislocation by "Union" forces. No accurate count was ever achieved, but the numbers ran into several hundred thousand persons who had died of disease, or starvation, and exposure on the roads or in army camps.

The second unpursued charge had to do with the deliberate starvation and murder of Confederate prisoners. When Lincoln was captured, the guards fled the camps where these prisoners had been confined. Many Northern citizens were willing to testify to the terrible conditions in the camps—exposure and starvation where food and medicine were readily available. One of the strongest impulses for the restoration of good feelings between the former compatriots of the North and South was the Christian aid and comfort given by many Northerners for the relief of these prisoners.

These atrocities could not be directly charged to Lincoln, though they were pursued against a number of lesser officers. Lincoln was charged with contributing to numerous deaths by being the first civilized authority to declare medicine a contraband of war and refusing the Confederate offer to allow Northern doctors to attend the Union prisoners in their hands.

The trial, long and complex, was held in the new U.S. capital, Chicago. Eminent lawyers were engaged on both sides. A number of Radical Republican politicians, hoping to revive political careers, were eager to take the stand against their former president.

The impression that most observers had of Lincoln at the trial was that of a wily corporation lawyer and astute political animal and of a powerful but somewhat warped personality. His employment of specious arguments and false dilemmas, semantic maneuvers, and homely and sometimes bawdy anecdotes to divert attention from the prosecution's points became increasingly transparent as the weeks of the trial wore on.

The high point of the trial came when Lincoln, on the stand, avowed that though he now regretted much that had happened, everything had been according to God's inscrutable will and he had acted only so that government of the people, by the people, and for the people should not perish from the earth. The courtroom erupted in guffaws, whistles, and howls of derision that went on for an hour.

Found guilty, the former leader's sentence was suspended on condition that he never enter the territory of the United States again. His subsequent wanderings became the subject of a famous story and play, "The Man Without a Country," and were most notable for his collaboration with Karl Marx, whom he met in the British Museum Library, in the early Communist movement that was to have so great an impact on European history.

About the time the war crimes trial ended, General Lee was inaugurated as the second President of the Confederate States. Speaking by the statue of Washington on the capitol grounds at Richmond, he described the first recommendation he would send to Congress. The Southern people had been deeply moved by the loyalty and shared suffering of most of their black servant population during the war. It was time to fulfil the hopes of the Southern Founders of American liberty. He called for a plan that would provide freedom at the age of maturity, along with land or training in a skilled trade, for all slaves born after a date to be set. The plan had already been approved by the clergy of all denominations in the Confederate States and by many other leading citizens. (It is to Lee's farseeing wisdom that peaceful relations between white and black in the CSA have not been disrupted by the strife that has characterized other countries of the New world.)

In closing, Lee advised the people of the free Confederacy to put aside all malice and resentment, look forward to the future, and give thanks to the Almighty for his infinite mercy in vindicating to the world the great American principle that governments rest on the consent of the governed.

(2000)

The American President:
From Cincinnatus to Caesar

The great body of the nation has no real interest in party.
— JAMES FENIMORE COOPER, *The American Democrat*, 1838

The American presidency offers many fascinating questions for historical exploration. And by historical exploration I do not mean the all-too-common form of pseudohistory that puts the presidential office at the center of our experience as a people. That scenario in which presidential Lone Rangers—Abraham Lincoln, Woodrow Wilson, Theodore and Franklin Roosevelt, John Kennedy, Ronald Reagan—gallop in to save us from dark forces that threaten divinely ordained progress toward the universal triumph of "American democracy." (The dark forces are often discovered to be ourselves. The American people must be saved by presidential heroes from their ignorant prejudices against such things as foreign wars, affirmative action, and unlimited immigration.)

That scenario is not history at all but a part of the mythology of empire. Its origins can be traced to nineteenth-century Massachusetts when Calvinists lost their theology but none of their aggressive belief in their own chosenness, when the godly City upon a Hill was replaced by "American democracy" (that is, Bostonian arrogance) as the end goal of the universe.

No. I mean real historical questions to be explored. How did the chief magistrate of a confederacy of republican states evolve into the leader of the world? Historians of the remote future, should there be any such after the disintegration of Western civilization, will see this as a central factor in the rise and fall of the American empire.

But here let us take a more limited and manageable question. How did we come to the present system of choosing our elective monarch? Of determining what citizen has the qualifications necessary for an office which surely requires patriotism, intelligence and character of a high order? Or to put it another way, what could possibly cause an apparently normal person to stand on a chair and cheer at the prospect of an Al Gore or a George W. Bush assuming such grave responsibilities, as many did in the most recent election?

Part of the answer lies in the invention of the two-party political system, something utterly unknown to the Framers of the Constitution, and particularly to the invention in the early nineteenth century of the diabolically-devised political nominating convention. The intent of this nominating convention was to take the choice of candidates away from the people and insure control by professional politicians; that is, persons who seek profit and place by the pursuit of power rather than by honest, productive work.

There was a time when candidates for high office were expected to show their achievements and services for the commonwealth—successful leadership in arms, wise executive administration which met public necessities while relieving the burden of taxes, forethought and eloquence in the legislative hall in dealing with hard issues. Compare recent occupants and aspirants of the presidential office with this standard. What does the absence of this or any other standard from our electoral discourse tell us about our state as a people? In fact, presidential candidacy is and has been for some time a factor not of achievement or service but of celebrity, or what patriots who decried the emergence of this phenomenon in the nineteenth century called "availability."

One of those patriots, James Fenimore Cooper, wrote in his *American Democrat*:

Party is an instrument of error, by pledging men to support its policy, instead of supporting the [true] policy of the state. . . . Party leads to vicious, corrupt and unprofitable legislation, for the sole purpose of defeating party.

The discipline and organization of party, are expedients to defeat the intention of the institutions, by putting managers in the place of the people; it being of little avail that a majority elect, when the nomination rests in the hands of a few.

Party is the cause of many corrupt and incompetent men being preferred to power, as the elector, who, in his own person, is disposed to resist a bad nomination, yields to the influence and a dread of factions.

Party pledges the representative to the support of the executive, right or wrong, when the institutions intend that he shall be pledged only to justice, expediency and the right, under the restrictions of the Constitution.

When party rules, the people do not rule, but merely such a portion of the people as can manage to get control of party. . . .

The effect of party is always to supplant established power. In a monarchy it checks the king; in a democracy it controls the people.

Party, by feeding the passions and exciting personal interests, overshadows truth, justice, patriotism, and every other public virtue, completely reversing the order of a democracy, by putting unworthy motives in the place of reason.

It is a very different thing to be a democrat, and to be a member of what is called a democratic party.[25]

Cooper's hope was for a Washingtonian presidency who would be above party—Andrew Jackson. It was not an unreasonable hope in the beginning. But there were two problems with this appeal to a noble executive such as the constitution had designed the office to be. By the time anyone achieved the distinction necessary, he had more than likely reached the stage of declining mental powers. This was true of Jackson as it had been of George Washington. Though not in the same category as Washington and Jackson, it is likely that some of the worst mistakes of Wilson, FDR, and Reagan can be traced to this fact of life.

25. James Fenimore Cooper, *The American Democrat* (Baltimore, Md.: Penguin Books, 1969), pp. 226–27.

Those who hope to manipulate a powerful officeholder for their own ends are many, wily, and adept at raising plausible public clamor for their goals.

An even greater problem was the hope for a president above party, which both Washington and Jackson believed themselves, erroneously, to be. No sooner had the government been founded than Alexander Hamilton and his northeastern friends began to force through an agenda that boldly disregarded all the understandings that had been reached at Philadelphia, in the ratifying conventions, and in the first ten amendments—under the cover of Washington's prestige. The Jeffersonians managed to halt this initiative in mid-course and hold it in abeyance for a quarter century. But Thomas Jefferson should not be regarded as a player in the leftist scenario of presidential Lone Rangers. He did not regard the presidential office in that way, but as a consensual and restraining force. He walked to his inauguration rather than riding, like "plain" John Adams, in a carriage with white horses, sent his messages to Congress in writing rather than delivering them from the throne, and established Virginia country pell-mell as etiquette in the executive mansion. But he could not help being the leader of a party, however he wished otherwise.

Jeffersonians did establish for a time the dominance, at least rhetorically, of a limited collegial presidency, and more importantly, the dominance, at least rhetorically, of a confederal central authority restricted in its jurisdiction. This was the bedrock public feeling when Jackson was elected president. The majority was disgusted with John Quincy Adams's efforts at neo-Hamiltonian expansion of the government and regarded Jackson as honorable and safe. But, as Washington had his Hamilton, so Jackson had his Martin Van Buren, the American solon of party.

One may interpret Van Buren's motives in constructing the American party system in two different ways. He was a devotee of Jeffersonian principles who realized that under the conditions of mass democracy only a strong party organization could defend them. Or, as most observers at the time and later have believed, he was a shrewd pursuer of political preferment for its own sake, troubled no more by principles than was necessary to keep the hayseeds in line. Motive really does not matter. The effects were the same, either way.[26]

These effects were the substitution of party machinery and patronage for public opinion and the transformation of electoral contests into trials of celebrity rather than of issues. As an 1829 newspaper commented:

Mr. Van Buren seems disposed to take a conciliatory course. He looks forward to a higher station in the General Government, and his whole air and manners evince it. He desires, therefore, to make as many friends, and as few enemies, as possible.[27]

---

26. My interpretation of this period of presidential history differs greatly from that of Jeffrey Rogers Hummel, a very fine historian. Good historians, as honest men, may disagree, and that is all to the good. The reader may have his consciousness expanded in more than one direction and consider the options for himself.

27. Charleston, South Carolina *Courier*, April 14, 1829.

It would be hard to find a better description of the way our aspirants to the highest office have been addressing the issues most of the time since. Perhaps the most important issue of the late 1820's and early 1830's was that of free trade versus tariff protection. President Jackson took a bold and decided stand for "a judicious tariff." The Jeffersonian principle of free trade had become a party trick. One could be for or against free trade as long as one supported the party. Though it was assumed that Jackson's party leaned toward free trade, his supporters among Mr. Van Buren's friends in the northeast were free to vote for all the tariffs they wanted.

The key, of course, was organization. New York, because it had more patronage than other states, because political contests were close, and because Hamilton and Burr had left a legacy of competing organizations, provided the model for the nation. And federal patronage grew with the phenomenal expansion of the country in every measurable dimension. One need not be troubled with public opinion or issues. All you needed was to control the meetings. So appeared the party convention, which was actually thought of as an advance in popular control over the legislative caucuses which had previously nominated candidates, now decried as aristocratic evils.

So, if enough postmasters and pensioners and contractors and their friends and relatives and those who expect to be postmasters, contractors, etc. when their ticket wins, and their friends and relatives show up, that settles the matter. Whatever resolutions and platforms and nominations emerge from the meetings, already carefully designed by the managers, are, by definition, public opinion. The people have spoken. If you don't believe it, just ask the newspapers (who are getting most of their profits from public printing).

Meanwhile, you have been busy putting into place all those nice, new devices to better express the will of the people (that is, make the managers' job easier). Let us suppose that 20 percent of the electorate of Massachusetts is Democratic and 80 percent of that of Mississippi. But in the convention states are represented by population. Your Massachusetts Democratic voter is going to have several times the power per capita of my Mississippi one in writing the platform and choosing the candidate. The real effect, of course, is to allow a well-organized minority of a minority to choose the president. As Cooper pointed out: it is "of little avail that a majority elect, when the nomination rests in the hands of a few." And the minority which controls is a stealth minority, with a vested interest in disguising its agenda and avoiding any real public debate and decision of issues, since controversy might scare off voters. And have you noticed those new laws, unknown and unanticipated by the Constitution, which mandate that the party that wins New York by 51 percent or even by less in a three way race, gets 100 percent of New York's votes in the Electoral College? Thus do our leaders labor ceaselessly to bring us ever and ever greater democracy.

Despite historians' endless blather about "Jacksonian democracy," pro or con, there was now a president and party ruling by patronage and popularity with no principle in sight. True, there was much talk in the air about the common man, which meant that the party managers had learned to get his vote, after the options had been carefully culled down to the safest ones. (Rather, there were two Jacksonian principles in sight: an insistence on maximum presidential prerogative—and one the historians never mention in this context—firm opposition to abolitionism.) Even the vaunted war against the national bank—put forward as a campaign for hard money—actually resulted and probably was intended by the President's managers to result in a host of government-protected banks, inflating the currency happily for private profit.

It is true that Van Buren opposed this, as he did anything so decisive as to make enemies. As he reported unblushingly in his autobiography, he once missed a key vote because he had promised to accompany a friend on a cemetery visit. This method failed him at last when he lost the 1844 nomination by attempting not to take a stand either way on Texas annexation. Still, it made him president for a term. When elected in 1836 he was a veteran officeholder, but he had no real achievements to rank with Adams, Jackson, Clay, Calhoun, Webster, and many others. Cincinnatus had been called from the plow and turned out to look a lot like Uriah Heap rather than the natural aristocrat for whom the presidential office had been designed.

But the game was not over. Two could play. The Whigs, on the outs while Jackson was popular, had learned a few tricks from Van Buren. In 1840 their managers, who had been busy building up their own patronage network, devised a new strategy.

They found another quondam military hero, General William Henry Harrison, who was completely unburdened by any political opinions or record. They adopted no platform, thus reducing the chance of offending any potential voter. Instead of a platform there was a campaign—torchlight parades carrying log cabins, coonskin caps, and jugs of cider, to symbolize their candidate's identity with the common people, and whooping it up for "Tippecanoe and Tyler Too."[28]

A traveling circus had been sent to find Cincinnatus and had come back with his distinguished-looking but rather dimwitted cousin, who did not have a clue as to what he had been called for. This was just what the managers had in mind. The real leader of the party, Clay, announced that the electoral victory had been a mandate for the policies of the party (which had hardly been mentioned in the campaign)—a national bank, high protective tariff, distribution of tax money for internal improvements. For the moment the agenda stalled because Cincinnatus' cousin ungraciously died and was succeeded by a junior member of the electoral coalition, a "states' righter" who had opposed Van Buren without going for the Whig program.[29]

---

28. Harrison actually had been born in one of the best plantation houses in Tidewater Virginia, a fact lost on northern voters.

29. For years I hoped vainly I would be important enough to be asked to participate in one of those surveys where historians are asked to rate presidents, so I could nominate John Tyler as one of the Greats.

But the party men had managed to co-opt the process by which the people were to find their Cincinnatus and corrupt it beyond repair. The Whigs, soon to be Republicans, had designed a formula that they have clung to since. Never address a real issue if you can help it, and if you have to, redefine it till it's harmless. Serve big business (that is, safe, as opposed to entrepreneurial capital) but never mention it. Always be the party of the respectable middle class, a sure vote-getter everywhere outside the South. In pursuit of this goal the party has for more than a century and a half, with very rare interruptions of talent, produced a succession of presidential and vice-presidential candidates who have astonished the world with their mediocrity.

Calhoun, who shared Cooper's distaste for party and preference for an independent presidency and was in a much better position to assess the real state of affairs, described it thus:

the existing party organization[s] look only to plunder. The sole object of strife is to elect a President, in order to obtain the control through him of the powers of the government. The only material difference between the two parties is, that the Democraticks [sic] look more exclusively to plundering through the finances and the treasury, while the Whigs look more to plundering by wholesale, through partial legislation, Banks, Protection and other means of monopoly. The one rely for support on capital and the other on the masses; and the one tends more to aristocracy and the other to the power of a single man, or monarchy. Both have entirely forgot the principles, which originally gave rise to their existence; and are equally proscriptive and devoted to party machinery. To preserve party machinery and to keep up party union are paramount to all other considerations; to truth, justice and the constitution. Every thing is studiously suppressed by both sides calculated to destroy party harmony. . . . It is impossible for anyone, who has not been an eyewitness, to realize the rapid corruption and degeneracy of the Government in the last few years. So callous has the sensibility of the community become, that things are now not only tolerated, but are scarcely noticed, which, at any other period, would have prostrated the Administration of Washington himself. . . . It is time for the people to reflect.[30]

Calhoun's description of the end effect could serve as an epitaph for the late twentieth-century presidency:

When it comes to be once understood that politics is a game; that those who are engaged in it but act a part; that they make this or that profession, not from honest conviction or intent to fulfill it, but as the means of deluding the people, and through that delusion to acquire power; when such professions are to be entirely forgotten, the people will lose all confidence in public men. All will be regarded as mere jugglers— the honest and patriotic as well as the cunning and the profligate—and the people will

---

30. Clyde Wilson, ed., *The Essential Calhoun* (New Brunswick, N.J.: Transaction Publishers, 1992), pp. 341, 353.

become indifferent and passive to the grossest abuses of power, on the ground that those whom they may elevate, under whatever pledges, instead of reforming, will but imitate the example of those whom they have expelled.[31]

Remember George Bush and "Read my Lips." In some quarters there has been much emphasis on the disgrace brought on the presidential office by Bill Clinton and his obvious sleaziness. So what else is new? In fact, the Bush deception of the people is by far the worse of the two. Clinton's lies were mostly to cover up his misdeeds. Bush's lie was a deliberate deception of the people made publicly in presenting himself as an aspirant to their highest office, a corruption of the democratic process at its very root. But, of course, our sensibilities have become so callous that neither the deceiver nor the deceived thought much of it.

It is in fact possible to praise what Calhoun decried, to glory in the fact that American political parties present the people with no real alternatives. Freedom from ideological strife can be seen as a great boon when compared to the havoc wrought in Europe by struggles over irreconcilable visions of the political good. This has been a basic theme of left and right democratic capitalist penmen: for instance, respectively, Arthur Schlesinger in *The Vital Center* and Daniel Boorstin in *The Genius of American Politics*.[32] Instead of wasting themselves on class struggle, Americans have been busy manufacturing more refrigerators and automobiles for everyone. There is indeed much to be said for a nonideological regime that promotes peace and prosperity. One may wonder, however, if that accurately describes a country that killed 600,000 of its men in a civil war. Or if any number of friges, or even of guided missiles, can save a people with a leadership unable or unwilling to address honestly its real necessities.

Can a lack of principle—a refusal to contest real issues—be covered by an appeal to the evils of ideology? Would not a more accurate description suggest that since the Progressive Era of the late nineteenth century the driving force of American history has been a quasi-socialist ideology, whether it is called Progressivism, Liberalism, or Neoconservatism? There has not been an absence of ideology but rather a two-party agreement on one. For those who believe in Clinton's worldview, mistaken though they be, a vote for Clinton or Gore is a rational choice. In the same circumstances, a vote for a George Bush (junior or senior) is a vote for "Tippecanoe and Tyler Too" if it is thought of as a vote for an alternative.

The Whig frustration after 1840 was compounded by Calhoun's eloquent and intransigent stand for free trade, free banking, and strict construction, which had rallied the latent Jeffersonianism of the people. The Democratic Party, after

---

31. *Ibid.*, p. 101.
32. Boorstin was the original neoconservative, beginning as a Communist and ending as a spokesman for respectable conservatism (appointed director of the Smithsonian by President Ford). However, unlike Schlesinger and the giant minds that took up the cause of democratic capitalism after him, Boorstin was too good a historian not to see some of the ironies in such a position, as in his *The Image: A Guide to Pseudo-Events in America* (New York: Atheneum, 1975).

the breaking of Van Buren's power in 1844, returned to principle and held to it until principle was rendered irrelevant by blood and iron.

The economic centralists, whose drive had always since the time of Hamilton been presented as a moral imperative, needed other cards to play. The American presidency required two more steps to Caesarism. First, the party men must learn how to combine predatory patronage and predatory policy, which separated the Democrats and Whigs, into one power, something best accomplished in crisis. This Lincoln was able to lay the groundwork for in the midst of war, though the final consummation would not come until a century later when the Great Society discovered how to buy both sides by shifting the costs to posterity.

Ronald Reagan came to power, like Jackson, on a wave of protest over what the party men had done to the people's property and principles. He spoke like, and perhaps even believed himself to be, the Jeffersonian who would turn back to states rights and limited government. But as Jackson had his Van Buren, Reagan had a phalanx of handlers ready to reinterpret the revolution into a Hamiltonian form. The patronage thrown up by the Great Society was too great a temptation to be spurned. The bakery would not be closed; the cake would just be sliced a little differently. In order for the Reagan revolt to work, there would have to have been a real opposition party determined to take wealth and power from the federal government and give it back to the people.

The war allowed Lincoln to combine patronage and policy by eliminating effective political opposition. But a second step was needed before the presidential office metamorphosed from CEO to Caesar. This was the establishment of American history as a salvation drama. The groundwork for this had to be religious and cultural. It required a country in which superficial education emanating from New England schoolmarms had replaced, in a substantial part of the population, tradition and common sense.

Since the War of 1812, New England had declined severely in prestige and power. Its intellectuals had lost their religion but had retained their sense of themselves as The Elect. The Calvinist mentality, even without its theology, reasoned diabolically. That which stood in its way was by definition evil. By the time this impulse got to the hustings in the greater New England of the Burnt Over District of New York and the upper Midwest, it took on strange forms.

The New England clergy had preached rabidly that Jefferson was a tool of the Bavarian *Illuminati* who would set up the guillotine, kill Christians and declare women common property. A generation later came the belief that the harmless fraternal order of Masons was conspiring to subvert the country, and that fantasy was soon transferred to the Catholics. In the meantime, the religious dissolution of New England spun off many strange subcults including vegetarianism, feminism, communalism, Mormonism, Adventism. The underside edge of this great Age of Reform was the psychopathic gang of John Brown, in the same way that Charles Manson was the underside of the great Sexual Liberation of the Sixties. (Late bloomers of the latter include the Unabomber and Timothy McVeigh, whose crimes have been blamed by the intelligentsia on the "right wing Southern gun culture.")

The more respectable side of this phenomenon was a conflation of Christianity and Americanism, America as the fulfilment of God's plan for mankind, a seductive bit of blasphemy that has remained a strong motif in our national consciousness ever since. Out of this matrix came a thirst for vanquishing the devils that stood in the way, a thirst satisfied perfectly by the idea of the Slave Power. The South which stood in the way of Northern progress, economic and moral, was not simply a region defending its own interests within a federal system, it was a diabolic conspiracy of degenerate and imperious slaveholders to spread their evil ways to the North, threatening all things good and decent. Since domestic slavery had been a feature of American society from its first days, and since all American law and tradition forbade interference by one section with the internal affairs of another, this strategy could only work politically by the fantasy that the "Slave Power" was the aggressor. (And convenient forgetting of the fact that most of the most stalwart founders and defenders of American liberty and the American Union had been Southern slaveholders.)

It was the combination of economic agenda and cultural hysteria that brought Lincoln to power, thanks to the tricks that the party managers had played with the Electoral College. Lincoln was far too shrewd to really believe the conspiracy theory, but he was willing to allow it to benefit himself and his party. As long as the South remained a large, prestigious, and skillfully-led minority, there was an irreducible body of opposition to both economic nationalism and the cult of Americanism.

The trauma of war followed by the assassination provided the final missing ingredient in the drama of presidential salvation. The president had begun as the CEO of a federal republic, expected to have extraordinary republican virtue in the exercise of his powers. He was now the martyred savior in the world historical drama of American uniqueness. The Northern clergy and their business lobbyist allies were not slow to use the opportunity for all it was worth. There developed a huge literature in which Lincoln is literally a Christ figure who died for our sins. (They had tried this out on a limited scale with John Brown before the war, but it had not flown.) To read the Lincoln hagiography is to understand easily how the Romans came to grant divinity to their emperors (the difference being that those Romans did not claim to be Christians).

The conflation of America with God's plan for the perfection of human history was complete. And the president as savior was essential to the drama. It could not, of course, be used every day. But it would ever after be there as a potential to clothe dubious objectives with sacredness. And there would always be a portion of the people ready to follow. So Wilson could lead the country into the insane mayhem of the European war, kill and be killed in order to end killing, and make the world safe from democracy. Many would believe that Franklin Roosevelt had personally saved us from Depression and fascism.

Perhaps the strangest eruption of all in the salvation drama occurred after the assassination of the youthful President Kennedy. This dubiously elected, questionably competent, and churlish power-seeker became in death a sacrificed god. You have to be old enough to have been there to really remember what an orgy of adulatory hysteria was whipped up for that occasion.

It was that emotional eruption which provided the fuel for the Great Society, a salvation drama against the sins of poverty and discrimination, the chief result of which was to engross for the presidency ever more of the power and wealth of the country. Something which could not have happened, however, if there had been a real opposition party. The Great Society did not create the moral breakdown of the Sixties. Rather it was a product of moral breakdown in which the intelligentsia, through the grace bestowed upon them by the martyred president and their paternal egalitarianism, liberated themselves from morality and into irresponsible power and privilege to remake the world.

What was new about this was that the president no longer had to be even a dim copy of Cincinnatus. By the time we get to Clinton, the imperial office itself had become the object of worship. It does not matter how tainted the credentials of its occupant. In the drama of salvation, a sleazy prevaricator can be the saviour of the oppressed. It does not matter if this requires the murder of innocent women and children at home or abroad. The emperor can do no wrong.

This was in part because the presidency had become enmeshed in the public relations, advertising, and mass entertainment culture. It was no longer a debate on the business of the public, but a popularity contest. So the Republicans of my state were treated, during the 1996 presidential campaign, not to a declaration of Mr. Dole's principles and policies, but to a visit from his daughter who regaled us with the assurances of what a wonderful fellow he was.

I can recall as an undergraduate student the reiterated lesson that the American press was owned by big business, and therefore could always be expected to support the reactionary side in American politics. It was up to the working stiffs of the media to correct this terrible imbalance as best they could. A prime example of the corruption of American politics by public relations, I was taught, was the fact that Eisenhower had taken elocution lessons from a Hollywood actor. In a remarkably short time, the brave crusaders of the media became slavish lickspittles of the imperial Kennedys, who had pretended to regard them as wise and important.

The Federalists who designed the presidency at Philadelphia wanted a vigorous and independent power that could preserve the honor of the Union against all foes. In constructing the office, they violated all the wisdom of American experience. The Revolution had been in essence a struggle of the representative bodies of the thirteen colonies against the executive power, the monarchical prerogatives represented by the royal governor and his placemen. Because of these struggles, the colonies emerged from the Revolution with weak executive power, a governor elected annually by the legislature, a magistrate with very limited initiative in the vital matters of purse and sword.

The prevailing element at Philadelphia designed an office unlike any other in the world, a monarch with more than monarchical powers and in all respects except the requirement for election by the people of the states. (The Electoral College was designed not so much to take the decision out of the hands of the people as to guarantee weight to the states. If there was no majority, as might happen often, the House would choose, with each state having an equal vote. Party management once more triumphs over the intent of the Constitution in selecting the president.) Theory prevailed over experience.[33]

All three branches of the federal government, and thus the people too, are guilty in the transformation of America from a Constitutional federal Union to an empire. But it was the president who was meant to check evil tendencies in the body politic. This is why he was given the power to negate acts of Congress and to appoint the judges and generals. He was to be the hero of republican virtue who would represent all the people as a historic community of freedom rather than a coalition of interest groups and ideological agendas.

At the beginning of the new millennium, we can see only too well how misplaced was the hope. From Cincinnatus to Caesar was a long road. From Caesar to Caligula is but a few short and easy steps.

(2000)

---

33. This is why the theoretician James Madison is revered by every fake and superficial political philosopher in the land, because he provides a vehicle to translate the American regime from histori cal experience to the rationalization of power.

The Consent of the Governed

"When in the course of human events, it becomes necessary for one people to dissolve the political bands which have connected them with another. . . ." The necessity has occurred. The thirteen colonies have a long history as self-governing societies, a condition which is now threatened. The occasion calls for a statement of rights violated, in the good old English tradition of Magna Carta and the Glorious Revolution. Therefore "these United Colonies are, and of Right ought to be *Free and Independent States*." There you have it: the sovereignty and self-government of existing societies. Of course, as is always the case in human events, the declaration still had to be made good by the bayonet wielded by free men.

Mr. Jefferson was the drafter of a declaratory document to be adopted, or not, by the thirteen sovereigns. He was not Moses releasing a prophecy. Contrary to befuddled scholars, he did not get his fillip about Equality from reading French books. It came from his belief in the self-governing equality of Americans' primitive Anglo-Saxon ancestors before they succumbed to Norman centralism. "All men are created equal" meant that a Briton on this side of the water is just as damn good as a Briton on the other side, a second son is just as good as a first-born, and that no man is entitled, as the author said on another occasion, *by birth* "to ride booted and spurred over his fellows." Aristocrats were to be identified, as he said on yet another occasion, not by birth but by talents and services.

Every thoughtful American of the 19th century worried, and many said, that the unfortunate bit of language was a cannon that in the wrong hands might break loose on the deck and destroy everything in its path. Something had happened: the French Revolution, which endowed the minds of a large part of Western man with a vision of the Rights of Man bestowed by a centralized, self-justifying state.

On this side of the water, there were several effects. The disintegration of New England Puritanism spawned utopian and blasphemous Transcendentalism and various enthusiastic religious cults. The thrust of these phenomena was to create a popular ideology which confused together God's plan for the Universe and the New Man's destiny of perfection with America's destiny as the trailblazer for mankind (or rather the New England version of America). (In an 1844 public letter to American leaders, Joe Smith of the Mormons called upon the Declaration's alleged Rights of Man as justifying the federal government's authority to overrule the states on behalf of his beleaguered sect.)

The second thing that occurred in the United States was another consequence of the French Revolution. Among the Germans the Revolution left a bastard offspring: an ideology even more abstract, ruthless, and state-worshipping than the original. The human debris of the failed European Revolutions of 1848 poured into the free confederacy in America, which they assumed, mistakenly, was the embodiment of their version of the Rights of Man. It is easy to demonstrate that demographically, these Puritans and Forty-Eighters, along with ruthless economic exploiters, twisted politics out of its accustomed paths in the Midwest and made possible Abraham Lincoln's elevation to the Presidency by a 40 per cent vote.

Lincoln at Gettysburg declared that the Declaration had made not free and independent states, but a "nation." And specifically a nation dedicated to the proposition of equality, presumably justifying its pursuit by any means. The bigger battalions made the reinterpretation stick. Contrary to what countless mountebanks have proclaimed since, Lincoln was not proclaiming the equality of African-Americans, which was never a sincere goal and soon forgotten. He was proclaiming that the French Revolution had replaced the American Founding and would govern in the future. Anyone who will look honestly at the Union war will see that, aside from a few pretty speeches, it was justified in terms of blood and iron nationalism—an indestructible government.

Gone was the central idea of 1776, *consent*—that government required the consent of the people governed. Consent could be given only once and then was forever binding, not the recurrent process portrayed in the Declaration. The people were no longer the center, the government was. The plural United States was now an artificial singular. "American" which had meant the fellow feeling of related peoples now meant merely obedience to the same government.

Americans have never lost the idea of and the instinct for equality, which is a good thing. But we appear to have lost the idea and the instinct for freedom and independence. Can we recover them? The prospects are not good, but stranger things have happened in history.

(2001)

America as Idea

A testimonial for *Chronicles: A Magazine of American Culture*

America is an Idea and the First Universal Nation. So say the bedizened oracles and prancing shamans of the American Empire—empire, for what is universal cannot be a nation. But people don't live on an idea. They live on land—lush or dry, rocky or fertile, according to their fates. If they are lucky, it is land watered by the blood, sweat, and tears of forefathers and foremothers. Those other imperialists, the Romans, made a splendid empire, and lost it when too many of them forgot, or never knew, the *genius loci* and the *lares et penates*.

The one Universal Idea is not liberty or equality or fraternity. The one Universal Idea is Money. But no human being ever lived by Money alone. Remember Scrooge? As my little daughter, wise beyond her years, used to say: "Man does not live by bread alone. He must have peanut butter." Human man lives by song and story, custom and ritual, country and community. If you want to see the future of the Universal Nation, look at the cookie-cutter strip malls and nearly cookie-cutter slums of your nearest city. Or watch one of those near-future flicks like *Blade Runner* or *Starship Troopers*. Men and women, young and old, all races and faiths and nations, are equal—and indistinguishable. And all are rich—in gadgets of mass destruction. In contrast to the self-flattering public voices of American Empire, *Chronicles* has been a tireless, eloquent speaker for humanity. Even amidst all the cacophony of the Universal Nation, it has been heard by discerning ears. *Chronicles* has, from the first, known and spoken for the real America. It has not forgotten, as Bill Kauffman and others so movingly remind us, that we wake up every morning in real places, not in the Universal Nation; it has affirmed the reality of a Heartland that officially does not exist except in phony sentimentalized evocations of Utopia (No Place).

Chronicles has even remembered there is a Dixie, officially unknown except as a blemish to be eradicated, but always threatening to break through the stage makeup of the painted harlot of the Universal Nation. And Chilton Williamson, Jr., evokes for us beautifully a West which has set men's minds free with challenges. The West is a kind of idea, but far from a universal one.

Thanks to *Chronicles*, we know we are not alone as ciphers in the Universal Idea, but men and women in America. We know that America began not as the United State but as the States United. We know that our forefathers proclaimed an idea of liberty they hoped would encourage mankind, but that they pledged their lives, fortunes, and sacred honour to their own lands and liberties. Contrary to the marketing slogans and sophistic declarations of official public discourse, we know that America is not Anybody and Everybody, but many lovely lands for our children and our children's children.

(2000)

Chapter Five

Imperial Irritations

As a City Upon a Hill

A steady Patriot of the World alone,
The friend of every country—but his own.
— GEORGE CANNING

Books Reviewed: *The Tarnished Door: The New Immigrants and the Transformation of America*, by John Crewdson, New York: Times Books, 1983, 354 pages; *From Moscow to Main Street: Among the Russian Emigrés*, by Victor Ripp, Boston: Little, Brown, 1984, 247 pages; and *Refugee Scholars in America: Their Impact and Their Experiences*, by Lewis A. Coser, New Haven and London: Yale University Press, 1984, 351 pages.

I n 1629, during the crossing of the Atlantic, the prospective settlers of Massachusetts Bay heard a lay sermon from their chosen governor, John Winthrop. They had, he said, entered into a covenant with God. Provided the settlers kept their covenant of godliness, the colony they would found in the New World would become "as a Citty upon a Hill," a blessing to its inhabitants and a beacon to all mankind.

Winthrop's allusion has been a favorite reference in President Reagan's speeches, aimed at shoring up American morale and idealism. That America is a beacon to mankind and possesses a unique relation to divine favor is an idea of great comfort and appeal, and one for which there is a not-insignificant case from historical evidence. Yet there is a vast gap between what the "Citty upon a Hill" signified to Winthrop and the ideal invoked by Reagan. The difference, if I may express it musically, is approximately equivalent to the difference between "A Mighty Fortress Is Our God" and a rock music video. Within the gap lies most of American history.

Piety and exclusiveness were the heart of Winthrop's enterprise. Massachusetts was the retreat of that tiny minority of the elect called to godliness. Through a complicated historical process that included the destruction in the Civil War of an older and rather different Virginian ideal, this vision came to define America. Reagan's city is essentially secular. Not only is it secularized, but it is universalized in a way that would have been incomprehensible to Winthrop. As invoked by Reagan, the beacon upon the hill incorporates the 20th-century image of America as the successful melting pot of all races, nations, and faiths, in the cauldron of common ideals. By contrast, the Puritans were not only proudly Anglo-Saxon, they did not even like non-Puritan Englishmen. For almost three centuries their descendants considered themselves the elite of the elite and the benighted Anglo-Saxons from Pennsylvania southward as hardly within the pale of humanity, much less the rest of mankind. Their beacon was for the world to be guided *by*, not guided *to*.

What would Winthrop have made of a city upon a hill which beckoned as a cornucopia of worldly opportunity rather than as a strenuous struggle for a purified commonwealth? What would he have made of a utopia whose chief glory was in melting down all distinctions, in which any Hindu or Rastafarian could become a full member simply for the easy price of a vague allegiance to an undefined concept of democracy? (Of course, it would please the President if they would also believe in and practice "free enterprise.")

I do not mean to criticize the President, who is the most sincere, decent, and sensible we have had in many a day. He is, like the rest of us, caught up in a history of which we must make the best. There is nothing in Winthrop's city which *necessarily* leads us to the modern America of melting pot and high living standards. Yet, it is here. Reagan's formula, even if not historically sound in its use of Winthrop (historical allusions on the hustings never are), is a well-intentioned recognition of reality. America has had an astounding success, to this point, in incorporating a great variety of races, religions, and nationalities into a presumably workable society and one which has set the gauge for the world in living standards for its masses.

To an originally British (and African) base were added in the middle of the 19th century the Germans and Irish, and in the late 19th and early 20th centuries, the eastern and southern Europeans, all now proudly and patriotically American. Catholicism and Judaism have become full partners in what began as a thoroughly and consciously Protestant exercise. We have gloried in the strength of variety and weathered every crisis and strain.

The last third of the 20th century has brought the New Immigration—new presumably because it draws from parts of the world not before largely represented in the American population (Latin America and Asia), because its numbers surpass previous experience, and because a great deal of it is illegal and unassessed. Indeed, one of the characteristics of the New Immigration is that, while all sense that it is large and portentous, nobody really knows its dimensions. As Crewdson shows, no one knows or can possibly know how many foreigners have broken, are breaking, and will continue to break our laws by entering or overstaying. We have not lost control of our borders. Rather, in a sense we have lost control of our land. Responsible projections suggest that the dimensions of the New Immigration are such that within a few decades, by early in the next century, America will have a Latin American and Asian plurality and that the descendants of present U.S. citizens will be a minority.

It would seem reasonable to pose a question at this point in our history. Is the success of the melting pot something that is infinitely repeatable and expansible? One answer to this, seemingly the President's, is that of course it is. There have always been nay-sayers and prophets of doom, who have always been proved wrong. The creative, absorptive, and progressive power of American ideals and opportunities is unlimited. America will absorb the New Immigration and, as in the past, emerge the stronger.

There are many other answers that might be given. My own might go like this: We have been extremely lucky but there is no reason to gamble that the luck will hold forever. The economic, political, military, and moral problems we face are not like those of the past and will not be any easier to solve in a society even less stable and coherent in its values than that of today. It is true that America is in one sense an idea, an idea of universal appeal and inspiration and opportunity. But it is also true that America for many of us constitutes not an idea but a quite tangible land and tradition which we like to consider not everybody's and anybody's, but *ours*; and to which we relate not as an abstraction but as a link with our forebears and our posterity. I do not believe that this proclivity of some of us makes us fascists and racists. I think it stamps us indelibly as normal human beings and as quite in the spirit of the Declaration of Independence. Granted that all men and women are equal before God and before the law, it does not necessarily follow that all human societies are abstractions in which people are infinitely interchangeable. Human cultures are in some ways quite sensitive organisms, subject to disruption and debilitation in a variety of ways, many of them not well understood. Considering the changes that we face, would it not be simple prudence to pause and take thought of the morrow?

The two answers that I have suggested to the New Immigration by no means exhaust the possible range of responses. However, we are not, as a society, even posing the question, and our response is essentially that of fatalistic paralysis. The three books under consideration, for instance, take up different aspects of immigration. The authors do so ably but somewhat in the manner of the blind men examining the elephant. To none does it occur that there is anything to be done about the beast except to describe him and then to accept whatever bellows and kicks he chooses to give us. The democratic process may decide economic or military matters, but the future composition of the American population is something, apparently, which present citizens have no right to control, or even examine.

The stand of liberals seems to be that immigration is a moral question and one to which there is only one conceivable response. All morality (and also the entire meaning of democracy, the Constitution, ethics, and religion) is summed up for them by egalitarianism and compassion. It is unthinkable that a citizen might have rights which an illegal interloper (as opposed to an invited guest) could not also fully claim: It is unthinkable that, on prudential grounds, there might be some human beings who should not be welcomed and some who should even be expelled for the welfare of the commonwealth. Nor does it come within the realm of morals for present generations of Americans to consider whether they might be bequeathing to their descendants a society intolerably lacking in moral, religious, political, and cultural cohesion. Prior to about the year 1960, consideration of the welfare of one's posterity would have been the height of moral endeavor in the opinion of nearly all of mankind, but posterity has slipped from the consciousness of our present-centered society.

The approach of "conservatives," so far as one can tell, is like their approach to everything else: aside from an occasional verbal bone tossed out to quiet the moral concerns of yapping fundamentalists, it is all a matter of economics. The more people, the more prosperity. There is undoubtedly some connection between population growth and prosperity. But the bald proposition, without qualifying variables, though it seems to be enjoying a vogue, is too absurd to be taken seriously. Were it literally true, we would have to expect India to be all the more prosperous than Japan.

True, a high birthrate and a rising prosperity are historically connected. But does this apply to a welfare state or to a population increasing by immigration while the birthrate of citizens is actually declining? Conservatives are supposed to believe in tradition and community, but they appear to have given no thought to the impact of massive immigration on traditional and consensual values. Conservatives are popularly supposed to favor free enterprise, but appear not to have considered whether free enterprise might rest upon culturally determined habits rather than upon universally applicable abstractions. Conservatives, it is thought, believe in a strong defense and a vigorous foreign policy, but appear not to have reflected that the first requirement for these is morale, an effective domestic unity in which differences stop at the water's edge.

The works in hand are varied, each with a different approach and dealing with a different aspect of the immigration question. *The Tarnished Door* is contemporary reportage. *Refugee Scholars in America* is historical. *Moscow to Main Street* is sensitive cultural portrayal. Each work has the virtue of its genre. *The Tarnished Door*, which deals chiefly with the illegal flow across our southern borders, is the only one of the books centered on the New Immigration. Ripp's book is about the most recent wave from the Soviet Union (100,000 in the decade ending in 1981). There is nothing new about immigrants from Eastern Europe, unless one considers the newness to consist of the fact that these refugees are people who have lived their entire previous existence inside the Soviet system and have known no other.

The Soviet system, as the author shows, leaves its marks, and the encounter with America is for many far more ambivalent than Americans would like to believe. But then, Americans are the only people naive enough to expect new-comers to be completely satisfied and at home. In a series of well-drawn portraits of the experiences of Soviet refugees, Ripp, whose own background gives him a certain insider status among them, makes the ambivalence clear. One does not alter overnight a lifetime habit of suspicion and resistance painfully formed in a totalitarian society. Freedom itself is ambiguous and not self-limiting. It must be defined by other values, sometimes hard-won. Rejection of communism is not necessarily perfectly equivalent to allegiance to the United States. And present-day America, with its crime and formless hedonism, is not exactly the same country which once drew the abler spirits of Europe yearning for new opportu-nities and horizons. The escape to America, nevertheless, one feels, must be in some sense a gain for the Soviet refugees, or at least for their children. In what sense it is a gain for America is somewhat harder to fathom and must be reck-oned up in intangibles if at all.

Coser's book is a detailed and illuminating study of scholarly and literary refugees from fascist Europe between 1933 and 1945. The hard sciences are not covered, though the psychological fields, history, economics, political science, sociology, classics, philosophy, and theology are examined thoroughly, with some attention to creative literature.

It is clear, in retrospect, that the transfer of a substantial portion of European scholarship to this country was a revolutionary event for America. The Continent was the heartland of scholarly prestige while America was still, in most fields, the provinces. In Europe the modern disciplines were already hardened in the direction of their thrust, while in America they were still plastic. The impact of this vast transfer was varied and is not easy to characterize. However, it is per-haps fair to say that the refugees, not without a great deal of native help, were decisive, among other effects, in institutionalizing Marxism and Freudianism and in pointing the "social sciences," with the possible exception of history, in a pos-itivist rather than a humanist direction.

Coser's conventional research is thorough and able and is supplemented by personal acquaintance and interviews with many of the figures he treats or their associates. One of his merits is that he pays attention to those figures whose impact may be said to have been rightward—Voegelin, Strauss, Arendt, Von Mises, Wittfogel, Schumpeter, Nabokov—as well as to the much greater number of "leftists." His approach, if anything, is a bit too chummy and evenhanded. I am not convinced that Herbert Marcuse had a "winning personality," nor that his combination of nihilism and zealous pursuit of the stock market was merely an amusing foible.

Again, one is struck by the ambivalence for both sides of the encounter, in the final accounting. Are Voegelin and Mises sufficient to offset the permanent damage done by psychoanalysis, Marcuse, Adorno, Fromm, Lazarsfeld (and many others), and those writers who for a time turned a good deal of Hollywood into a Soviet propaganda mill? Such a question is impractical to ask about a rev-olution that is already over, and, at any rate, the answer can only depend upon one's scale of values—there are no scientific findings in history. It is clear, however, that in regard to American scholarship, the nature of the beast was changed forever. Considering that before the transfer the pinnacle of the American mind was regarded by many to be occupied by John Dewey, one may not regret the outcome. But what might have been the native developments had not the hardened categories of European thought impinged upon the New World in that way at that time? It would be interesting, also, to lay beside this account of the experiences and impact of the refugees from fascist Europe a comparison with those from post-1945 Communist Europe, but that lies outside Coser's scope.

Crewdson has investigated firsthand the day-to-day reality of the New Immigration. Much of his story has to do with the Border Patrol and the Immigration and Naturalization Service. It is largely a story of incompetence, fraud, corruption, and brutality, leavened by only occasional flashes of integrity and patriotism. But what else is to be expected when undertrained, underpaid, outnumbered young men are sent to do an impossible job under the demoralizing leadership of greedy, hypocritical, and irresponsible liberal appointees of the type with which we all became too familiar in the dreary years from Kennedy to Carter?

Crewdson, if I read him rightly, believes that the New Immigrants are changing America and that the situation we are in is a political and moral scandal, harmful to us and the immigrants. He also believes that given the present and prospective realities of Mexico, there is nothing short of a police state that we can do about it. He favors then, a mildly optimistic resignation to the inevitable. He sees the New Immigrants as, on balance, a plus. They pay income and social security taxes and engage in productive labor that otherwise would go undone, despite chronic citizen unemployment in some sectors.

If it is indeed inevitable and even mutually beneficial that a good portion of the population of Mexico, Central America, and the Caribbean take up residence in the United States, there are yet many creative responses that we could make. There is no historical or Constitutional reason, for instance, for the universalization of all the rights and benefits of American citizenship, which has led to a cheapening of the value of that citizenship more severe than that inflicted upon our currency before 1981. Such a universalization is an authentic American tradition only if one believes that American history began in 1962. Further, President Carter's refusal to enforce our laws during the Mariel boatlift and Congress's proposal to amnesty and reward those who have flouted them in the past would immediately have been recognized by the Founding Fathers as evidence of a deplorable fall from republican virtue and as far more impeachable offenses than poor Nixon's pathetic and absurd intriguings. What about the equally or more deserving immigrant who lost his place because he obeyed our laws? Nor is there any reason to make citizens out of students, because of marriage or procreation on American soil, when the skills they ostensibly came to acquire are desperately needed in their own countries. What would we think of Americans who abandoned their country for comfort if the situation were reversed? Are these the kinds of citizens we want in the next crisis?

Our present manner of universalizing citizenship, though regarded by nearly everyone as eternal and sacrosanct, is nothing of the kind. Citizenship, until very recently, has always been understood in historic and inherited terms. If not, there would have been no necessity for the 14th Amendment to formalize the admission of Black Americans into the body of citizens. Until the late 19th century, citizenship was in effect granted by the community. In a land where the work to be done far exceeded the available hands to do it, worthy immigrants were welcomed by their prospective neighbors. In many states they voted before receiving Federal naturalization, which was merely a kind of afterthought ratification of the fact that the immigrant had been accepted as a member in good standing of the community. Citizens of a democracy, in other words, were not interchangeable nonentities manufactured by the government, but grown and nourished by the people. Today hundreds of thousands are made citizens each year by government fiat who have given no sufficient evidence of a will to become members of an American community in good standing. Citizenship which is not earned, cherished, and tied to obligations is not the real thing.

Democracy requires civility and tolerance. It also requires honest deliberation of real issues and citizens with a full stake in their country. In some way or other, in the words of one of Crewdson's chapter titles, "We Are Going to Have to Say No." We do not serve democracy by evading realities, invoking taboos, and wallowing in sentimentality. Of all our modern qualities none would have been more foreign to John Winthrop than a supine yielding to the fates without responsibility for decision and action. Predestinarian or not, were he here today he would tell us straight out about the deadly sin of sloth, the peril of those who fecklessly stumble on into disaster.

(1985)

Flag Burning

Flags are a feudal phenomenon. Not until the French tricolor was the flag a focus of nationalism. Even during the 19th century, flags were used mostly in military, naval, and diplomatic contexts, and were seldom seen by civilians. Often there was not one national flag but a variety for different uses and occasions. Americans did not pledge allegiance to the flag, they swore to uphold and defend the Constitution—the swearing having definite overtones of Christianity and the Anglo-American legal tradition, unlike the secularist, imperial Pledge of Allegiance.

Not until the age of mass conscription—World War I for America—did the flag itself become a fixed focus of patriotism. Nevertheless, the Stars and Stripes are now firmly established as such, a symbol of American community in relation to the rest of the world, consecrated by the blood of free men. Most states, quite properly, have laws against desecration of this essential symbol.

The overturning of these laws by the federal Supreme Court, on the plea of freedom of speech, is thus a gratuitous strike at one of the few really binding elements of a large and diverse republic. No matter how many million-dollar Harvard lawyers are hired to develop sophistical arguments for the Court, their reasoning is puerile.

The Founding Fathers viewed freedom of speech as a prerequisite of majority rule, of that debate and deliberation of the public things that was necessary for consensus and decision. When Patrick Henry declared, "If this be treason, let us make the most of it," he was not engaging in a private fantasy. He was speaking as the delegate of the freeholders of Hanover County, in the councils of the Burgesses of the Commonwealth of Virginia. (The words were uttered, by the way, in the parish church of St. John's, Diocese of Virginia. Listen up, separation-of-church-and-state fanatics!)

The exercise of free speech is, then, evidence of participation in community, a desire to influence deliberation and decision. It cannot be absolute, since the equal right of others to speak and the rules of deliberation must be preserved. For the Founders, sedition, slander, and blasphemy were not protected by the right of free speech, though nearly all preferred to have offenses defined and punished by other than the central government, the restraint of which was the purpose of the First Amendment.

Such offenses demonstrate not a desire to participate in deliberation, but a contempt for the community and its processes. Thus there is no reason why Rushdie's infantile blasphemies have to be protected by the Western democracies (though, of course, the laws against murder and assault must be enforced), because such utterances are not an exhibition of deliberation and reason but of contempt for the process of reason.

I am not a Moslem, nor do I particularly wish to see Islam established in my country. Nonetheless, for any decent person, gratuitous slander of the historic faith of millions is a repulsive act, even if it is someone else's faith. It is something that no decent community tolerates, though it is perhaps better if such offenses are prevented by the community rather than by the state authorities. This would be true even if we were at war with Iran, for to discountenance blasphemy is a function of our own decency and self-respect, not of a phony pluralism.

But flag-burning does not even qualify for the protection offered to blasphemy in a doubtful case. Flag-burning is not speech, but an act. It is not participation in free deliberation but a demonstration of contempt for the community, the last step before an act of violence. It is, in this respect, analogous to a sit-in or painting a swastika on a synagogue. It is the instinctive understanding of this that creates the vast popular feeling against the Court's ruling.

But, alas, the clamor for a Constitutional amendment against flag-burning bears about the same relationship to real statesmanship as flag-burning does to real freedom of speech. It is a mere disingenuous and insulting gimmick. The problem is not flag-burning. The problem is judicial usurpation and a warped reading of the First Amendment. These are the ills that would be attacked by a statesman able to perceive and pursue the welfare of the commonwealth.

The Reagan Revolution had two possible accomplishments—the control of inflation and the rescue of the judiciary from left-wing extremism. We can only pray that the former will endure. The behavior of Justices Scalia and Kennedy in the flag-burning case must give us reason to wonder how solid the latter achievement really is. It will be a Pyrrhic victory if the justices continue to adhere to a disoriented legal tradition rather than exercising the courage and intellectual skill necessary to renew contact with the real Constitution.

(1989)

AIDS and Public Morality

The AIDS plague should be approached temperately because, like the Kennedy assassination, it is one of those universally frightening phenomena that is likely to ignite the pool of vulgarity, hysteria, and kookery that lie just below the surface, among the high as well as among the low. Having casually followed the pronouncements of the government and media on this issue, I had been bothered by a mild nagging sense of distortion, disproportion, and disingenuousness. I had noticed this and passed on, for we all automatically edit the information we receive from the official press. And, alas, we have come also to take for granted the Reagan administration's uncertain trumpet, a persistent background static created by the opportunists, rootless ideologues, and saboteurs the President has chosen as his instruments.

Viewing recently a televised press conference by one of these instruments, Surgeon General Koop, I was able to put in focus what I had found unsettling in the official sources reporting on the AIDS epidemic. The Surgeon General's performance on this occasion was virtuoso. He was calm, detached, factual, succinct, and informative, exactly as he should have been. The false notes were in what was implicit rather than what was overt. I had the sense that in the course of an apparently frank presentation, the points that were most important, to me at least, were being preempted rather than discussed.

Least among these false notes was the blithe assumption that society (presumably the government) is obligated to assume the projected costs of "care" for the afflicted. Perhaps we must, but it does not seem to me self-evident why this should be. And what exactly is meant? That we are without discussion and decision obliged to place an open-ended burden on our labor and our children's patrimony to provide heroic treatment and optimum comfort for persons who are doomed, in most cases by their own acts, is an assumption that needs more in the way of supporting argument. This is, in fact, merely a subspecies of the normal liberal delusion that resources can simply be created by the government infinitely. What about diversion of resources from the more deserving or the less hopeless? Indeed, what about the rights of the medical personnel who, after all, are entitled to be free of involuntary servitude? The Surgeon General is right to warn of impending economic problems, but his framing of the issue tends to convert a tough managerial question into an unexamined claim against the decent part of society.

I am disturbed also by the recurrent emphasis on the prediction that AIDS may be about to descend in epidemic proportions on the "heterosexual" population. (Note the terminology which makes the deviant and the normal equivalent.) Since our official information is all carefully pruned of qualitative judgment, it is difficult to know exactly what the apparent statistical increase of the infection beyond the high-risk groups signifies. But as far as we can grasp at this point, it would seem it is confined, like all venereal diseases, primarily to the most depraved part of the population which is in contact with the high-risk groups.

It is right that we should want to help our fellow creatures, however depraved, but there is no use denying that there are limits to what we can accomplish, individually or socially, in saving persons of legal age who are bent upon self-destruction. However, from the emphasis that is placed by the media and bureaucrats on the danger which the "heterosexual" population faces, one gets the impression that we can momentarily expect an epidemic outbreak to descend mysteriously upon the populations of Our Lady of the Sacred Heart or the East Carolina Christian Academy. I have a suspicious mind, which our forefathers considered a virtue in a republican citizen, but could this be a ploy to frighten the public into immense expenditures to save the affected population or to devise means to prevent the high-risk groups from suffering in the future from the consequences of their "life-style"? Or to remove the stigmas from abominable behavior by suggesting that "it could happen to anyone"? If these suspicions are justified, then the Surgeon General's zeal to thrust condoms upon grade-schoolers is a piece of gratuitous tyranny.

In ancient times and among primitive peoples, groups were held responsible not only for their explicit acts (as when the Romans put to death or enslaved rebellious tribes) but also for those less tangible transgressions which were thought to have offended the gods. Our more immediate forefathers progressed to a more reasonable and humane way of life in which groups were not blamed for the sins of individuals but individuals were held to be rationally responsible for their acts and the consequences thereof. (Such an assumption was an implicit *sine qua non* of democratic government.)

We have now progressed to a situation in which neither individuals or groups are held responsible for anything. Whether it is crime, AIDS, corruption, or economic backwardness, no one is to blame; instead, we have all been victimized by some disembodied social "problem." (Though groups as such cannot be held responsible, for instance, for an excessive crime rate, they can be considered as groups when benefits are to be passed around.) Responsibility is so diffused it is unlocatable, which among other things renders democratic decision-making impossible. Thus, disease brought on by an irresponsible group is to be handled not by taking appropriate action against the group responsible and protecting the innocent, but by spending money and an unseemly intrusion into the lives of the innocent. In other words, a superstitious shifting of guilt. The problem will not be solved that way. It will probably get worse. But we will all feel we have done our progressive enlightened best. One would like to lay this confusion at the door of ritualistic liberals, but it is so pervasive that we must begin to suspect that it is an irreparable defect in the national character.

The SG and his confreres seem to suffer, too, from the American confidence in technical solutions. It is not at all clear to me why anyone should necessarily expect a cure for AIDS (except possibly those people who are any day now expecting a cure for death to be announced). There are plenty of incurable diseases and even if a preventive vaccine were found, a mutant version might emerge all the more rapidly.

At any rate, it would appear that behaving oneself will provide far better protection than a vaccine. But encouraging people to behave themselves as opposed to invoking every possible means to save them from the consequences of misbehavior has a low priority in public discussion. The authorities are anxious to convince us that AIDS is the consequence of a virus and not a punishment for Sin. In fact, nothing in the last millennium so obviously and surely is a punishment for Sin—that is, *unless* the danger of infection by nonsexual means has been deliberately understated by our authorities.

By all means let us pursue scientific measures where they are promising. But what disturbs me and apparently many others is the ignorantly secularist and technological thrust of the official presentation. The SG, or our own physician, should offer us technical expertise, but we also normally and reasonably expect moral advice where it is relevant. (The SG sees no problem with this when it comes to cigarettes.) In fact, a physician is falling short of his full duty if he offers an easy technical solution for the pains brought on by a moral failure, or refuses to recognize a behavior problem. To his credit, the SG has endorsed chastity, but neither he nor anyone else in public life can bring himself to condemn aberrant life-styles, even when they endanger the entire society.

The real clincher in the SG's performance was the recurrent motif that, in thrust if not in tone, rose from clinical description to moral imperative. We *must* remove the *stigma* from AIDS infection, he said, again and again. Now, there may be sound practical reasons for this suggestion: To drive the infected underground might make the work of the epidemiologist more difficult. This was mentioned, but clearly the imperative went much further than that. The SG believes it is *wrong* to stigmatize people for deviant behavior. This conclusion is not science, for science does not dictate values one way or the other. This comes straight out of the bountiful cupboard of liberal sentimentality. Even if we admit a degree of practical usefulness in encouraging people not to hide their affliction, does not the right of the innocent to be warned and thus protected far outweigh it? We have no moral obligation, per se, *not* to condemn AIDS sufferers. On the contrary, there is a moral obligation not only on the part of the authorities but on the part of the diseased person individually to warn others. Here we come up against a new version of the mentality that finds punishment of the murderer more real and shocking than the incalculable sufferings of his innocent victims. In my state there is now in custody an AIDS-infected drifter charged with multiple rapes. It is only a matter of time until we see federal judges contorting the laws and candlelight vigils of liberals, both mobilized to interdict just punishment from falling upon this person.

The priorities of the public health establishment, who are after all bureaucrats as well as "scientists," would appear to be (1) to protect the "community" of deviants from public outrage and discrimination; (2) to pursue heroic curative and preventive measures to save the deviant "community"; and (3) to protect the decent public, insofar as it does not conflict with Priority 1. Deprived of unqualified support at both the executive and legislative levels, the decent public had better hope that the priorities get rearranged somehow, *before* the disaster.

We are all sinners and fall short of perfection, and we are enjoined to stand ready to extend our hand to our repentant fellow creatures. But I do not detect very much repentance, as opposed to regret and resentment, among the representatives of the "life-style" that has put us all in danger. In fact, in heeding the admonition not to stigmatize, we are actually throwing up obstacles to repentance.

We do not know and cannot control all the mysterious springs of human behavior, and misfortune stalks us all. For persons who succumb to an occasional act of perversion under an apparently uncontrollable compulsion, or for persons who carry on an unnatural but responsible relationship, most of us can indeed muster a degree of sympathy if not approval. But it seems that the plague has been brought on not by these, who have always been with us, but by people who have engaged exuberantly and persistently in abominable acts, contrary not only to every law of God and man, but even in disregard of that compassion for other individuals which our liberals and libertines invariably profess to honor.

Some of these persons lived respected and well-rewarded lives in the public eye while engaging in the most promiscuous, destructive, and exploitive debauchery. Where were our great heroic investigative journalists? I stand behind no one in my respect for the right of privacy. I even sympathize with the earthy realism that urges us to overlook a modest amount of sexual delinquency as inevitable. But this sanctity of privacy does not apply when the delinquency is rampant and aberrant, or in the case of persons like liberal politicians, whose public position is based upon aggressive pretensions to moral superiority over those who disagree with them.

Not too long ago, Rock Hudson was widely accepted among us as a proper person to represent pilots, police chiefs, and other exemplary masculine figures. And all the while he lived an exploitive, irresponsible, self-indulgent, deceitful life. Even setting aside the perversions, a society that was operating with normal, healthy mechanisms of self-preservation would have extruded such a person from its midst long before. In a decent society Hudson would not have been tolerated, much less lionized. (Among other things, his case should be a lesson to anyone naive enough to regard the 50's as a time of greatness.)

If our scale of values is so warped that a less than adequate movie actor—shameless in his private life—is entitled to the ritual sympathy of public figures and the awed respect of the masses, then civilization no longer exists in North America, and our country is nothing but a collection of bipeds whose only distinguishable characteristics are a fascination with gadgets and a respect for money.

It was not too many years ago that when a man misbehaved badly his neighbors and co-workers were able to discern it and to exert pressure for reform. It did not always work, but it kept many of us better than we might have been. This sort of social pressure is far removed from the police state. It is, rather, the only alternative to a police state. Our establishment has managed in the last few years to remove the *legal* sanctions against many forms of behavior that have been offensive to the law and order of every Western commonwealth for centuries, and to render punishment mild or unlikely for many other behaviors that they have not yet been able to redefine as harmless life-styles. On this point the Surgeon is exactly wrong: *Stigma* is the only means society has left to protect itself.

It is not, usually, the fear of punishment that keeps our hand out of the till when no one is looking—it is our sense of right and wrong and fear of shame, which, if we are fortunate, is constantly reinforced by our fellows. It is not, in the last analysis, a soldier's pay or his training or his advanced equipment that makes him fight—it is the awareness that cowardice and betrayal are *shameful*. Without our sense of shame and outrage we are lost. It is not an outmoded superstition that we moderns have got beyond—it is the voice of the Almighty and the adhesive of human society.

Unlike the Surgeon General, whose righteous indignation is reserved for his conservative critics and the criminals who seek the consolation of an occasional smoke, I hope that my righteous indignation will always be proportionate, discerning, and amenable to forgiveness. However, when confronted with people who flout Scripture, law, tradition, knowledge, common sense, and common decency, I intend to reserve the right to cry "Shame!"

(1987)

Two Prisoners

A tale of two prisoners. Nelson Mandela spent many years under arrest. Aleksandr Solzhenitsyn spent many years in a slave labor camp, as a fugitive and exile, and as a nonperson.

Mandela resisted a mildly repressive regime by terrorism. Solzhenitsyn resisted a brutal totalitarian state by heroism and eloquence.

Mandela sought the bestowal of benefits and privileges. Solzhenitsyn sought liberty to work, worship, and think.

Mandela was freed by bringing to bear the power of giant empires and media oligarchies on his own small country. Solzhenitsyn was freed by years of harrowing maneuver against an omnipotent but incompetent state, helped by the attention of handfuls of people in various free countries.

Mandela represents an alien, at bottom incomprehensible culture. Solzhenitsyn represents the deepest and noblest aspirations of our own culture.

Mandela is a very skilled politician. Solzhenitsyn is one of the greatest artists and most eloquent prophets of our age.

In America, Mandela is fawned on by Congress and the President. In America, Solzhenitsyn is avoided by Presidents and other politicians.

What does this tell us about America?

Think about it.

(1990)

Congress

That Congress has never been held in greater contempt at any time in its two centuries is something all available evidence, whether statistical or impressionistic, indicates. When our noble Conscript Fathers, a few months back, undertook to promote themselves a little pay raise, public outrage achieved its greatest negative unanimity since the Japanese hit Pearl Harbor. The unmistakable expression of the people's will has not fazed the people's representatives in the least, and the pay raise is back again.

The same public that regards our representatives as little more than matter for cynical jokes regularly reelects them to their posts at a rate in excess of 90 percent, also a two-century record. If we were any longer able to be surprised, we would regard this as a very startling paradox. Some attention has been paid to the excessive incumbency problem, but not enough. Political operatives blame it on gerrymandering and the advantages of incumbency in name-recognition, etc. Ralph Nader, strangely, blames it on PACs, though PACs, indeed, are the only powers in the land with enough strength to challenge incumbency.

None of these explanations even begin to get at the question. The existence of either aspect of the current situation, not to mention the paradox, would have been *prima facie* evidence to our Founding Fathers of a grave crisis in republican government—of defects and perversions so fundamental in the people and the principles as to call into question the whole foundation of representative government.

Our present situation is, in fact, merely the result of long-term changes that have been accumulating for some time but that have only recently become apparent—changes that have altered the essence of our government from republican to imperial. In government we must look at the thing itself, not at the name. Nothing could be more delusive than to believe that dead names and forms preserve something when its living essence is gone.

Our Congress as it stands is purely and simply the natural and normal spawn of the Great Society. While we have not quite reached the Utopia promised by Lyndon Johnson, we have achieved an immense patronage machine that extends with a thousand arms into every congressional district and every community and almost into every home. The federal government is now a great giant who presents us with endless goodies, but who also demands steady tribute and who might carelessly roll over and crush us to death.

Our congressmen have simply adapted themselves to function in natural harmony with the Great Society—itself a perversion of representative democracy. They are its creatures. They are not lawmakers—they do not go to Washington to give the law to Leviathan. Rather, they are brokers, or at best ombudsmen, who are in a position to coax and coddle the giant into throwing some of his goodies our way. To put it another way, they are not primarily the representatives of our communities to the government, but primarily the delegates of the government to our communities. They work for the government and not for us.

Only a minimal amount of cunning is needed in a congressman to sit atop the flow of largess from Washington and take credit for it. He need only make sure that a sufficient number of citizens are paid off, in some way or another, to guarantee reelection to infinity. It does not matter whether the representative is a Democrat or a Republican, a liberal or a conservative, an abortionist or a pro-lifer, a rake, a pervert, a thief, or a drunk. All he has to do is make sure enough of us get our share of the gravy, that the balance of those who *think* they are get-ting something from the government is maintained over those who know they are getting shafted. Thanks to the diabolical system of withholding, this is made much easier. We do not blame our representatives for the tribute we pay, but thank them for what we get back.

The very meaning of representation has been transformed into something our forefathers would not have recognized by the term.

In order to understand why representative government has been altered beyond recognition, we have to understand what it meant to our fathers. The executive branch of the government, especially of the federal government, was regarded by most people, except the lucky few of placemen and monopolists, as a necessary evil. The purpose of representatives was to protect the communities which they represented from the depredations of the government. This is why revenue bills had to originate in the House of Commons and the House of Representatives.

It was understood that the main job of the representative was to protect and defend the community—to give the law to its potential oppressor, the govern-ment; to make sure the government's impositions on the community were really necessary for the general welfare and were confined in strict and lawful limits.

Two-year terms were a way of making the representatives refer back to their communities frequently so that they would not be seduced away by the payola and honors that it was in the power of the executive to confer. Turnover was also an affirmation of government of the people in another sense. The representative was temporary. He came from the ranks of the people and when his term was done there he returned, to live as an equal citizen under the benefits or the bur-dens of the laws he had made.

But one of the things that has happened in recent years is that congressmen have been insulated from the consequences of their acts. Whether from malice, from ignorance, from irresponsibility, from cowardice, or from some combina-tion of these, they can decree for us war, taxation, inflation, crime, busing, abor-tion, and social decay, whatever they wish. They are largely immune—after all, the few who are unlucky enough to be turned out have their pensions, their appointments to the bench or the executive branch, nice jobs as lobbyists and "consultants," etc. etc. etc.

The traditional representative was not only a representative, he was also a leader. In the high original concept of Anglo-American democracy, the represen-tative was not a machine who registered the preferences of 51 percent of his constituents. He was, rather, an exceptional person entrusted with a high responsibility, along with which went the scope to exercise his own wisdom and ethics in pursuit of the long-term best interests of the community. That is, he was expected to be not a mouthpiece but a statesman. Until this century, nearly all the great and admirable political figures in the British and American tradition were parliamentarians—not those who promised the people everything, but those who showed the people what was needed.

Needless to say, we do not find many statesmen of this sort in our Congress, which is as much a reflection on our virtue as on theirs. In order to have such representatives again we would have to elect people with intelligence and moral determination to consider the interests and welfare of society in a larger timeframe than the next election or the next brown bag full of money. And people with a higher conception of their duty than constituent service or following the recommendations of their pollsters and publicity agents.

There is, then, in the minds of our congressmen no reason why they should not receive a raise, whether we want them to have one or not. They are the brokers who handle an immense transfer of wealth from hand to hand   and brokers are always entitled to a handsome percentage of what they handle. They do not work for us. They are the servants of Leviathan, and it is Leviathan that rewards them.

(1990)

☆☆☆

Congress, said H.L. Mencken, or perhaps it was Will Rogers, cost him about twelve dollars a year in taxes to support the institution, which was an unmatched bargain for entertainment. The statement was made during the raucous 20's, when things seemed to be going along pretty well, and the antics of our leaders did not usually result in inescapable and intolerable burdens. Congress, of course, costs a lot more today. Will Rogers was lost in 1935 and Mencken about the same time gave up political reporting for other interests. The whole thing has become a lot less funny, but we might as well get what enjoyment we can out of it—that's all the benefit we will get.

They are all funny, politicians, but perhaps the funniest are the establishment conservatives, who will provide us with many occasions for hilarity during the coming presidential campaign. The last time, during the Republican National Convention, they stridently demanded attention and representation. They got Dan Quayle, whom Bush and the media immediately identified as theirs, though most of them had never heard of him. Their one big payoff turned out to be a liability.

Probably the most amusing part of the whole campaign will be watching Bush, whose affirmative action quota bill was barely distinguishable from the Democrats' affirmative action quota bill, pose as the antiquota hero.

The knee-jerk conservatives rallied to the defense of Judge Clarence Thomas in the same fashion, because he was denominated the conservative candidate, though no one has ever explained whether or why this is actually so. If we are to take Thomas seriously in his intellectual positions, he is a "higher law" philosopher, something which is more alien and potentially more dangerous to what is left of our constitutional patrimony than even the fulminations of Justice Brennan. Let us hope we don't have to take it seriously. It is reported that Thomas's "higher law" writings were ghosted by a disciple of Professor Harry Jaffa, allegedly the author of the famous speech in praise of extremism that cost Barry Goldwater ten million votes.

But perhaps the establishment conservatives are not as dumb as I think. Maybe it is a fact that few of them have enough base to get reelected without the assistance of presidential glamour, since we now have an imperial rather than a representative government. That would explain why, except for Jesse Helms, none of them ever oppose their President, though the liberal Republicans do so whenever they want.

As one who spent an embattled youth as a "conservative" inside the academy, I feel I have earned the right to laugh at what "conservatism" has become. One must either laugh or cry.

And, of course, we can always fall back on the dubious consolation that the Democrats are worse. The Republicans have betrayed their middle-class constituency at every turn, which makes them ripe for revolt. But the Democrats are incapable of disengaging themselves from weirdness long enough to make any political capital out of it. Or perhaps they don't want to. Actually, the division of power between the Republican President and the Democratic congressional leadership, who disagree about nothing significant, makes the perfect arrangement for the imperial state. The most normal and logical thing for the Democrats to do is to nominate Bush for the presidency, in which case they would win the election—and get rid of Dan Quayle in the bargain.

It is impossible to find intellectual and ethical bankruptcy any greater than the turn the Democrats have taken on the Bush-Solarz war in the Persian Gulf. A great many voted against it, but now that it is over and popular, all we hear is the plaintive cry that they were not unpatriotic, they just wanted more time for the sanctions to work. I would submit that there is political capital to be made even yet out of honest criticism of the war—the cost in blood and treasure, the confused and dubious goals, the exposure of military technology that would have been better saved for a more important occasion. There remains something inherently foolish—and tragic—about using an artillery battery to kill a rat, a rat that was half dead already. But political capital totally aside, criticism of the war, now that the action is over, would be, for a principled opposition party, the right thing to do, which is why it will never happen.

And truly, if the Democrats had any spirit, any integrity, any faith in their own convictions, they would nominate for Bush's opponent the Reverend Jesse Jackson, who is far and away their most articulate, most charming, and most sincere leader. But this, of course, they will never do. Jackson at least has had the guts and the patriotism to complain about the loss of family farms and the ship-ment of American blue-collar jobs offshore—something no leading Republican has had the integrity to do, as far as I know.

Watch Jackson when the cameras go in close. He is a real human being—one who has suffered and thought. (I write completely without irony.) Though he is sometimes half-baked in his solutions—what leading politician isn't—he speaks from the heart about real problems, and once he has taken up an idea he does not retreat just because it's unpopular. That is, unlike Bush, he really repre-sents his constituency. Allowing for differences of style, he is in no rationally describable sense any more of a demagogue than Bush—and a lot more sincere. Beside him Bush looks like a preppie, and the other Democratic presidential con-tenders like pyramid scheme salesmen.

(1992)

Police Brutality

The now famous video of the Los Angeles police beating did not, for me, evoke the formulaic outrage that the media intended. Instead, strangely, it brought back a flood of memories from my misspent youth, a year of which was passed as a reporter on the "police beat" of a daily newspaper in a medium-sized city. Everyday I was in and around the station house, the courts, and scenes of crime and disaster (which, among other things, has made me a better historian than if I had spent the same time in a library).

In those days it was not a foregone conclusion that when there was a difference of opinion between a law officer and a felon, a reporter would always side with the felon. I had other advantages as well: I was the son of a fire captain who had more than once been subjected to sniper fire by "civil rights" activists while trying to keep their neighbors' houses from burning down. For these and other reasons, my liberal education had not taken and my sympathies were generally with the cops, humanly flawed as they often were.

One day off duty I saw an incident that crystallized a lifelong determination to always give the police the benefit of the doubt. I was on my way from lunch, walking across the main square of Charlotte, literally the busiest spot in the Carolinas, and thronged with the noon crowd. A young man was coming down the sidewalk toward me. He was white, about 19, clean-cut, and neatly dressed. Without warning, he began striking people in the face with his fist as he passed them.

The only authority in sight was a short, overweight policeman, well into middle age. He ran puffing down the block and grappled with the youth, trying to restrain him. The officer soon saw he was getting the worst of it. He gave the young man a tap with his nightstick—a quite gentle tap under the circumstances. That did not do the trick and was followed by a second.

Imagine the reaction of the passers-by who came upon the scene only at the end. They saw a nice-looking young man lying on the sidewalk with blood flowing from his head, an unprepossessing policeman hovering over him with a club. I noted the oohs and ahs issuing from three very well-dressed women, of the incorrigible upper-middle-class do-gooder type, who had just come up. It was clear where their sympathies lay.

For the policeman, it was a no-win. Suppose he had not subdued the aggressor? The same women would have been screaming at the failure of protection. For all I know he was chewed out the next day by the chief, who was much more interested in fitting in at the country club than in the welfare of his men. Lesson: Our reactions are often aesthetic and self-indulgent when they ought to be rational and ethical. Spoiled Americans want to rule the world and live in prosperity and safety, but we get in a dudgeon when reminded of the ugly details.

President Bush is a cultural type of exactly the same cut as the three women, who were undoubtedly the wives of transplanted Northern corporation executives, eager to believe the worst of a redneck Southern cop. The President avowed that what he saw of the Rodney King tape "sickened" him. I seem to recall a campaign clip of the President shoulder to shoulder in solidarity with the Boston police. But maybe that was only a campaign position, like being against taxes and affirmative action.

As far as I know, no one pointed out that this fastidious TV viewer had recently given orders by which 100,000 Iraqis were incinerated or otherwise had their lives terminated. Many of them doubtless were very decent human beings by comparison with Rodney King. They seem in most cases merely to have been trying to get away, and not contemplating a felony.

Aside from his irrepressible New England priggishness, which causes him to refer all public issues back to his private emotions, Bush is not that different from the rest of us. He is a victim of the moral obtuseness of what Richard Weaver called "the spoiled child mentality" and of the strange mental disconnections that afflict people whose idea of the world is formed by publicity and television. Of course, the President's military minions, unlike the police, did not have the media taping the more unseemly aspects of their mission, which was kept neat and upbeat for the viewers back home.

It is axiomatic that we can never—never—trust the media to tell the truth about these things. They will always make the police look as bad and the criminals as good as possible, suppressing essential facts and contexts to serve their agenda. There are still a few of us around who remember accurately the day of the Kennedy assassination. For the first few hours, Cronkite ("the most trusted man in America") was on the air reporting that the President had been shot by right-wing extremists in Dallas. The media have no basis for judging the merits or proportions of an issue except a liberal Pavlovian response. One of the givens of their world is that a criminal who is a member of a minority group is always unjustly treated and excusable.

The media people, far from being the paragons of wisdom and fairness that they portray themselves, are of quite mediocre intelligence and dubious ethics. They are selected by the same criteria used to choose actors for toilet paper commercials. Politicians, as despicable as they are, eventually must answer to rivals, voters, and prosecutors. The television news celebrities can lie endlessly without any responsibility, except to the few unknown old plutocrats who employ them, a system of irresponsible monopoly we call freedom of the press.

My time on the police beat coincided with the arrival of the Warren Court's edicts expanding the rights of defendants. The impact was palpable—demoralization of the cops, debasement of trials into the dishonest pursuit of technicalities over justice, and increased crime on the streets. There was a cause-and-effect relationship as clear and demonstrable as anything in the social sphere can be. Suddenly, the cops no longer had the discretion to carry out the most essential part of their job—stopping the criminals before their crimes.

Of course, there were and always had been police abuses, but they were not so widespread and major as to require the Supreme Court to tie the hands of the officers of the law. The restrictions were purely and simply the result of ideology and sentimentality—the feeling that crime could be cured by bribing and coddling the criminal. We now know beyond doubt what the fruits of that are, yet we are doomed to live with the institutionalized idiocy.

Surely the LAPD does not appear to best advantage in that tape, and where correction and punishment are called for, they should come—after careful proceeding and not in an atmosphere of political hysteria, and for discipline, not vengeance. But we should give the officers at least as much benefit of doubt and technicalities as federal judges and the ACLU bestow on the most heinous offenders. We do not know and can hardly imagine what those policemen may have gone through in the minutes—not to mention the hours, days, and months— before that videocam was pointed at them; nor what were all the experiences and dynamics that played into that incident.

The beleaguered policemen must subdue increasingly violent and numerous lawbreakers, protect the public and themselves, and be constitutional lawyers, all in the same instant. It is not too surprising that they will fall down on the job or even succumb to a little paranoia now and then, especially in the face of an uncomprehending and unappreciative public. All we asked of Schwarzkopf was to whip a greatly outnumbered enemy, with an unlimited purse and no real scrutiny. Thousands of policemen are asked every day to do things much more difficult.

We cannot let the politicians and mediacrats use a few instances of police excess to divert us from the real issue, as they would like. The real issue is an ever-escalating war against humanity by criminals who operate in America today on a scale and with a freedom unprecedented in human history. In the final analysis, we can survive well enough with a Rodney King roughed up now and then, though it ought to be discouraged. But what remains of Western civilization in this country cannot survive a half hour without officers of the law willing to risk life and limb on the front line of a war far more vital to our welfare than Mr. Bush's late glorious expedition amongst the Infidel. First things first.

(1991)

Capital Punishment

A legal execution occurred last summer in South Carolina, the first in about two years. Donald ("Pee Wee") Gaskins, a rural Bluebeard credited with 16 murders, was embraced by the electric chair amidst general public relief and the usual candlelight vigils by opponents of capital punishment. The public satisfaction, however, if it rests on a feeling that a rational system of criminal justice has finally been established, is sadly deluded. For the circumstances of Gaskins's capital sentence serve mainly to point up the absurdity of our federal courts.

Gaskins's first 15 murders, which included several children, were committed at a time when the learned and statesmanlike reign of Warren, Burger, Brennan, and Blackmun forbade us the right of carrying out our laws of capital punishment. (All the aforementioned are Republican appointees, by the way.)

So Gaskins was resting for life in our state prison when he made the mistake of killing *another murderer*. This individual, Rudolph Tyner, was also the guest of the state, courtesy of the Supreme Court, although he had cold-bloodedly gunned down an elderly couple in their country store. A relative of Tyner's victims (subsequently also sent to prison) hired Gaskins to carry out the justice that had been denied, and it was for this last murder that he was executed. In moments of provocation I am tempted to suggest that "Pee Wee," after a life of heinous crime, was executed for the only socially useful act he ever performed. No coherent principle of justice emerges from his fate, except perhaps this: that it is worse to kill one of the prisoners of the welfare-warfare state than to eliminate a dozen of us mere anonymous taxpayers.

Obviously, race should never become a question under the laws, and most especially the laws of capital punishment. But the opponents of the death penalty have made it an issue. A part of their case, and of the interference of federal courts into the processes of state law, has rested upon the claim that the death penalty has been racially discriminatory. I do not think the case was ever really proved, and it always involved a convenient ignoring of the fact that the crime statistics are also racially unbalanced. The purpose of the claim was clearly to garner for the anti-death penalty movement some of the emotional capital that always adheres to discussion of civil rights.

We in the South have many evils to answer for from the days before the civil rights revolution. Yet, contrary to civil rights mythology, our error in those days, broadly speaking, was not so much the oppression of excessive punishments to black criminals compared to white criminals, as it was the tacit failing of relative indifference to black-on-black crime. At any rate, those days are gone. No black person is convicted of any crime in the South, whether the victim is black or white, without a substantial black representation on the jury. Convictions not so obtained would be immediately overturned, nor do I think public opinion or the prevailing political powers would tolerate anything else today.

In our state, historically among the worst offenders in racial inequality, there are at present about forty individuals under capital sentence, awaiting the exhaustion of appeals: all but two or three of these are white. (I write from memory but the figures are broadly valid.) Obviously, the capital sentences are racially out of proportion, whether considering the general population or the population of convicted murderers, for those who are interested in such statistics. But if there is any discrimination going on in the application of the death penalty, it is just as obviously *against* white murderers.

I cite this unseemly matter merely to point out the dishonesty of the anti-death penalty movement in this respect. Having made an impact but not a decisive one, it has turned to other arguments. It has been contended (and I believe it is *sub judice* still) that the discrimination is in the race of the victim rather than the perpetrator, that the killers of whites are more likely to receive the death penalty than the killers of blacks. The kinds of liberals who advance these arguments are hardly noted for their careful veracity. They can be sure the media will never call them to account, and the official "conservative" spokesmen who reply invariably concede all the important points of the contest before they join battle.

So I would like to see the real data on this. But the contention is inherently implausible. "Pee Wee" Gaskins could not be executed for killing 15 people (all white). He was executed for killing one murderer (black). His last victim (black) could not be executed for wanton murder of two persons (both white). In one of the states thought most likely to be discriminatory.

But this does not begin to complete the catalog of the absurdities that have been forced upon the criminal justice system by the federal courts. It is not just that dangerous criminals are released or have their punishments mitigated. Even where there are convictions, the Supreme Court has surrounded the matter with rules that serve not only to make capital punishment difficult (which may be defensible) but to thrust into it a great deal more irrationality and inequity than was ever the case in the bad old days that were supposed to be reformed.

A relative of mine served on the jury at the trial of an individual who, on the day he was released from prison, killed five people, including a 13-year-old girl. (Criminal and victims in this case were all white.) The jury was sequestered for weeks, most of the time out of the courtroom while the judge decided nice points of what evidence they would and would not be allowed to see (as is now standard). A conviction and a death sentence were finally secured by the sensible people on the jury—no small achievement since defending attorneys these days routinely pack juries with the most ignorant available jurors, who are easily confused and intimidated—itself a travesty of the noble Anglo-American institution of the jury.

But under the rules of the Supreme Court, a mere wanton murder of five persons did not justify the death penalty, unless there were other circumstances. The "other circumstances" were that the killer had casually removed a change purse from one of his victims, making his killing one conducted "in the course of a robbery" and therefore subject to death. But it did not matter, since in a short time the sentence was overturned by a federal judge on the grounds of an alleged trivial error on the part of the prosecutor.

In another case in our state, a young woman (white) was kidnapped and murdered by three men (black) under circumstances so heinous that the death penalty was handed down for the ringleader by a predominantly black jury. Again, within weeks the sentence was overturned by a judge on grounds of a very minor technical violation in the conduct of the trial. Many, many similar instances have occurred.

I wonder if the opponents of the death penalty ever reflect on the damage done to the morale and ethics of the general public by this irrational frustration of the most basic and legitimate thirst for justice? And yet the same smarmy liberals who again and again facilitate the release of those who have broken the first rule of the social contract, lecture us on our moral failings when half of us don't bother to vote and don't show a sufficient amount of indignation about the homeless or South Africa.

And the worst of it is that we have created a field of opportunity for political demagogues. We now have before Congress a "crime bill" that provides the death penalty for a battery of federal crimes. This is nothing but fraudulent posturing. As Ronald Reagan was heard a few times to remark, though he was too smug and lazy to act on his insight: the federal government is not the solution, it is the problem. We have a proliferation of crime not because there are too few federal laws but because the federal courts have destroyed the rational functioning of the state criminal justice systems where the crimes that most affect us need to be punished. A federal crime bill does what does not need to be done and does not do what must be done.

We have even had a call, from so distinguished a statesman as Senator D'Amato, for the federal death penalty for drug dealers. The federal government regularly frees murderers but is it to prescribe death for dope peddlers? Under what principles of justice or public policy are those who sell narcotics to willing buyers more worthy of death than the wanton killers of innocent people? Are the lives of drug users more precious than those of murder victims? Such would seem to be the unstated assumption. And why should someone who kills a law officer in the course of drug business be any more or less subject to death than someone who kills an officer in the course of any other type of crime?

Here, as in so much else, our establishment, "liberal" and "conservative," has shown itself utterly unfit to rule. If we are to solve any of our problems, if we are "to secure the blessings of Liberty to ourselves and our Posterity," we must have a new agenda and a leadership that at least now and then will speak the truth.

(1991)

The Drug War

The lessons of history are never quite definitive. History repeats itself, but not exactly, and the trick is to know where the differences come in. Nevertheless, in the case of drug abuse and its control we have as good a lesson and as close an analogy as history ever provides—Prohibition. Unfortunately, our politicians have no historical memory, or perhaps the trouble is that memory serves reason and not appetite and hence is of no use to politicians. In any case, we have now reached the point where Prohibition was about 1930. What had begun as a misguided moral crusade in which many Americans had vast emotional investment had devolved into a scandal of hypocrisy, violence, and corruption. Sensible people knew all along that this was inevitable and that the problem should have been left where it could have been rationally dealt with. It should have been left to the states.

There are, of course, weightier arguments for the prohibition of most drugs than there ever were for alcohol. Alcohol was traditional and ineradicable, whereas drugs are relatively new or foreign and could have been stopped if vigorous and effective action had been taken early enough. It is too late for that now. A considerable portion of our population is beyond the pale, and it is useless to pretend that they will adhere to standards of behavior that have no meaning for them.

If we were to tackle the problem of drugs as a law enforcement problem, we might make some headway. But this has not happened, nor will it. Listen carefully to what the politicians *of both parties* are saying, and you will hear that for them, drugs are not a law enforcement problem, they are a welfare problem. People who buy and use illegal substances are not lawbreakers who ought to be punished. They are just another set of unfortunate victims of society who have to be saved by the government. If that's the case, how can we punish the users? Instead we blame the pushers and get tough with foreign exporters.

There is something ludicrous and contemptible about a powerful country blaming paltry neighbors for the misbehavior of its own citizens. It is as if the Bolivians had, like the British in China in the early 19th century, invaded California and *forced us* to buy the stuff. A little history and common sense would lead any person capable of reason and honesty to believe that given the nature of Latin American countries, it is childish to blame a poor country for selling its best product where there is a demand for it.

It doesn't help that the politicians who are now outraged that a tin pot dictator in Panama has been acting as a drug profiteer are exactly the same people who turned over the Canal to our noble Panamanian allies. Or that the people who are so exercised about the inability of the federal government to interdict boatloads of drugs from crossing the border are exactly the same people who are unconcerned that the government is also incapable of the much easier and more vital task of protecting the border from millions after millions of illegal aliens.

The latest fad is advocating a federal death penalty for drug pushers. This is, in fact, either hysteria or a sham. As far as I know there are no documented cases of drug pushers actually holding people down, forcing them to pay for the stuff and then ingest it. But in my state there is in prison a man who kidnapped an innocent young woman from a shopping center parking lot and subjected her to rape, torture, and murder. After two immensely elaborate trials, in the first of which the jury issued a death penalty, he is now serving a life sentence, which means 30 years. The reason this creature (and thousands like him) has not been executed is that the Supreme Court has contorted the process surrounding a capital verdict into an insane game that defies every tenet of law, reason, justice, and common sense. The death penalty for drug pushers? Maybe, but first let's return to the good old English common law of capital punishment for murder, rape, arson, treason, and first degree burglary, all crimes that damage the innocent irrevocably. Otherwise where is the logic in employing the death penalty to rescue us from evil profiteers and foreigners who have the effrontery to sell some of our citizens something they want?

I have no objection, in principle, to laws against sin. Even if they are not enforced they are often necessary or useful supports of society, for there certainly does exist an essential something known as public morality, even though a good proportion of Americans are now too much materialists to recognize it. I do not believe that liberty means anybody can do anything. But I am convinced that given the real world that exists now, the healthy and the conservative solution to the drug problem might well be a little laissez-faire. I am aware of the destructiveness of drugs and of the dangers of decriminalization. But I am also inclined to think that probably our best hope is to try it.

If I am certain of one thing, it is that the political and media fury now underway against drugs will never accomplish anything except to spend money. It is conservative wisdom which tells us that some things will always be with us and may as well be confined within bounds and left alone. It is liberal progressivism that tells us we have to save everyone from himself, whether he wants to be saved or not. Our cultural landscape is littered with the wreck and ruin of failed progressivism. Why not try for once getting the federal government and the liberal intellectual class and the pork-barrellers out of the way and allow the healthy forces of state law and community opinion to work?

The removal of the ban of law from drugs would at once undermine the huge profits and thus remove all the impetus and auxiliary criminality from the trade. There is evidence that the end of Prohibition was marked by a decline in the abuse of alcohol. It certainly put a dent in organized crime and cynical scofflawing and the corruption of public officials.

One of the many evils of Prohibition is that it accustomed our society to think of coercion by the federal government as a solution to every problem. The great destructive experiment was ended by turning the matter back to the states, where it should have been all along. Why not try that in our present situation? What have we got to lose? Many states would prohibit most drugs. Others would regulate them closely. Surely all would vigorously prohibit their sale to minors, and with reduced responsibilities they might, in fact, be able to do this job much more effectively than at present. And, of course, all would continue to educate on the evils of drug use, though there is not the least reason to think this does any good where direct personal experience does not work.

The supplies could be regulated, like alcohol, and taxed. We would have to be determined, of course, to punish people who committed crimes while under the influence of drugs, not for taking drugs, but for the crimes they commit. It is just possible that we might achieve an amelioration of the situation as great as can be hoped in an imperfect world. If not, one of the many virtues of states' rights is that it allows for learning and change and adaptation that the federal lummox has never been capable of. Possibly after a while our main "drug problem" will be to prevent the liberals in Congress and the courts from making the habit into an inalienable right and subsidizing it.

(1988)

✫✫✫

The Eighteenth Amendment, providing for complete Prohibition in the United States, was ratified in 1919 and repealed in 1933. That is fourteen years of attempted interdiction of alcoholic beverages, from which we learned nothing.

Prohibition was practiced by some states before and after the federal amendment, but it probably would never have been attempted on a nationwide basis except for an unusual conjunction of political circumstances. The Progressive Era's bent for efficiency, tidiness, and regimentation made a powerful combination with the old puritan desire to suppress indulgence and enjoyment.

Even so, Prohibition would not have passed if large parts of the public had not completely forgotten about individual liberty and states rights, looked automatically to coercion by the federal government as the answer to all problems, and had not become accustomed to World War mobilization.

Diehard prohibitionists have never given up, but the majority came to realize, after a time, that the cost of Prohibition in cynicism, crime, and corruption was too high. If it had actually worked, it might have been a different question. But of course it did not work, as any sane observer could have foreseen. As a result, Prohibition is the only federal intrusion in this century that has actually been pushed back.

Our current "war on drugs"—the attempt to prohibit the importation and sale of recreational narcotics—has been going on longer than Prohibition and is an even greater failure and a greater source of economic and social destruction. But it is not likely to end. There is a huge bureaucracy invested in it, for one thing.

But more importantly, the "war on drugs" must be kept going because its premises are absolutely essential to the liberal-statist world-view. There is, of course, really no drug problem—there is an addict problem (much as there is no gun problem, but only a criminal problem; no automobile problem but only an irresponsible driver problem). But to admit that there is an addict problem, as opposed to some mysterious disease of drugs which "society" has caused and must cure, would be to admit the possibility of individual volition and responsibility.

In order to take a realistic attitude toward the addict problem, our ruling class would have to abandon the notion that people are entirely shaped by their environment. For them the problem is not that some people choose to take drugs and to commit crimes in order to afford them. The problem is that some people are victimized by a vague but menacing "drug problem." A problem which society must solve—by a great dose of liberal compassion and government expenditure, of course.

The unfortunate people who, because society has failed them, have been "victimized" by drugs, must be saved by society. For the liberal-statist, no human action and decision ever enters into the question, except of course for evil persons like "drug dealers." There is no personal responsibility, only social guilt which is to them always profitable in power and perks.

Thus we have ever more hysterical proposals—the death penalty for drug dealers. Meanwhile, the federal courts have made it routinely difficult to inflict capital punishment on criminals who have murdered innocent victims. But we are to have capital punishment for the act of selling an illegal commodity to a willing buyer. What that means of course is that you and I, when murdered by a thug, are of no interest to our ruling class, while the unfortunate victims of the "drug problem" are objects of benevolence.

Andrew Lytle identified the basic liberal problem long ago as the heresy of devolved puritanism. The puritan insists on placing evil in the object—the gun, the deck of cards, the jug of whiskey—refusing to place the evil where it is really ineradicably located—in the human heart.

To do otherwise, the liberal-statist would have to recognize truths that have been known to all sensible people since the beginnings of the human race—the power of heredity and the power of Original Sin. They would have to drop environmental explanations and accept the fact that a certain number of people in all times and places will engage in destructive acts and that the human race is not perfectible.

Far better if we could end the federal drug war and turn the matter back to the states. They might prohibit drugs entirely, which they could do much more effectively than the federal government, the only competence of which is oppressing the innocent and expropriating the productive. Surely if we can prevent people from lighting up stogies in public places, we can prevent ingestion of more dangerous substances where they cause a public problem.

Or a state might make certain items available at specified times and conditions and quantities at legal market prices in state-owned or state-licensed stores, as is the case with alcohol. All states would certainly prohibit sale to the underaged, though the exact limit might vary. The drug problem would be reduced to the dimensions of the alcohol problem, which is the most we can expect.

Several things would have to change, though. We would have to be willing to punish people, not for taking drugs, but for actual real crimes committed under the influence. However, by legalization, we would cut the ground from under a vast criminal enterprise that is the greatest source of violence and corruption in our society, from the state-level to the corridors of power. Possibly we might even develop a new class of legitimate entrepreneurs who could raise themselves and their neighborhoods out of crime and poverty. The Kennedys, after all, started their rise to wealth on the basis of liquor.

We would also have to learn once more to respect the Tenth Amendment and enforce it. Otherwise, whenever a local policeman made an arrest for a drug crime, he would be hauled up before a federal judge for violating the civil rights of some Rastafarian illegal immigrant.

The repeal of Prohibition right now seems unthinkable, just as it did to many in the 1920's. Reality takes a long time to penetrate the political discourse of a ruling class as shortsighted and hypocritical as ours, but it does, sometimes, finally penetrate.

(1994)

Feds in My Back Yard

The Feds now control my backyard—in direct defiance of the Ninth and Tenth amendments. I have heard and read many stories over the years about imperial intrusions into private affairs, but I recently learned about these first-hand when I tried to refinance my mortgage to take advantage of lower interest rates. I immediately ran up against the benevolent wall of FEMA (the Federal Emergency Management Agency)—you know, those nice folks who take care of you when disaster strikes. (I wonder how folks got along before we had all these nice agencies to take care of us.) There is a tiny creek at the back of my property that has occasionally overflowed slightly into my back lot, which is quite large. The slight flooding has just about been eliminated since the county did some work up the line a few years ago. Flooding has never offered the slightest threat to my house, and all surveys have shown no reasonable possibility of it doing so. Neither I nor my neighbors have ever felt the need for flood insurance.

But it appears that the benevolent boys from FEMA made maps picturing my house potentially under water—a preposterous error. (What does this have to do with emergency management, by the way? And what were they doing in my back yard without permission?) As a result, the mortgage lender is now *required to require* me to take out flood insurance—or no loan. This requires a new survey and a "federal elevation certificate." So, profits for the surveyor, the lender, and the insurance company. For me, delay—nearly annihilating the benefits of low interest rates. (I find that several of my neighbors decided that the quest was not worth it.)

Will FEMA ever do anything for me? No. Do I want them ever to do anything for me? No. I will be grateful if heavily armed imperial storm troopers don't descend upon my house, as documented in the August *Chronicles* ("Desert Storm Troopers"). I am reminded of what happened in the aftermath of the major disaster we had here in South Carolina with Hurricane Hugo a few years ago. With great fanfare, Congress passed a $100 million relief bill, pushed by our two powerful senators. (The vote was 100-0 in the Senate, as I recall.) A while later we learned—in the small print—that we got almost none of the "victims' relief." It all went to Puerto Rico and the Virgin Islands, where nobody had any insurance.

It does no good to talk about "conservatives" and "liberals" in the context of such outrages, much less to complain endlessly about the evils of Clinton. (Does anyone really believe that the government terrorist/bureaucrats would have behaved differently at Waco if it had occurred on George Bush's watch?) The Republican "conservatives" have been promising to reduce government for a generation now. They lie. Two decades ago, I stood not far from candidate Ronald Reagan on the steps of our state capitol and heard him promise to reduce fraud, waste, expenditures, and regulation in every government agency. He lied. But we have a much deeper problem here than mere politicians' lies. The

Republican Party, in its very origins and *raison d'être*, was a vehicle for activist government. It was devoted to regulation and subsidy for the benefit of railroads, bankers, industrialists, and for suppression of "Rum, Romanism, and Rebellion" (i.e., the behavior of Southerners and Catholics). The "conservative" Bob Dole was completely in character and tradition when he sponsored a Disabilities Act that regulates every parking lot and building in every town and city in the land (including rural churches). He began his public career, after all, as the New Deal poster boy for "rehabilitation," part of the p.r. campaign to soft-soap the public about the sufferings of those citizens who were mangled in the "Good War."

The problem is more than one of efficient "public policy." It is a problem of national character. We cannot hope for any relief from the imperial state until enough people resume the habits of self-government, if that is possible.

I have just learned from a surveyor, by the way, that FEMA based its maps on an aerial survey, which has a large margin of error. What was FEMA doing *flying* over my back yard?

(1998)

The NEH

The NEH has provided me with several substantial (and highly competitive) grants, and so perhaps I should maintain a discreet silence in the current debate over the proposed abolition of the National Endowment for the Humanities and the National Endowment for the Arts. (Strictly speaking, I am not the recipient, but rather the Principal Investigator for grants received by my university.) But the media and politicians have so vulgarized and trivialized the issue (and when do they ever not?) that there are a few things that need to be said.

In principle, the federal government should not be in the business of subsidizing the arts (NEA). The argument is somewhat less conclusive in regard to scholarship. It is at least moot that there is a proper role for support of certain types of humanistic endeavor that have a "national" purpose. This is the same principle that justifies national parks, the Library of Congress, and the Smithsonian Institution. But in terms of both principle and the amounts of money involved, the NEA and NEH constitute a trivial issue (which is why it has interested the politicians). Doubtless there is more federal money stolen any Thursday in Chicago than the entire annual budget of the NEH and NEA. And considering all the things the federal government is doing that it should not be doing—consuming a third of the national income, inflating the currency, bombing Serbs, policing Haitians, incinerating members of obscure religious cults, interfering with schoolchildren, subsidizing the proliferation of illegitimate babies with low IQ's, subsidizing the murder of other babies, etc.—the arts and humanities subsidies are somewhere below number 200 on the list of things that need attention.

Egregious abuses have been perpetrated by the NEA, without any question. But it has not been pointed out that this was largely an administrative failure. The Republicans controlled the executive branch for 12 years. In this broad and goodly land are hundreds of people who are knowledgeable and dedicated in the arts, who are conscientious and talented citizens, and who even voted for Reagan and Bush. Instead of finding such people and getting them into management—the natural thing to do considering that the NEA was, for the nonce, established by law and not going to go away—the Republicans appointed Washington establishmentarians indistinguishable from Democratic appointees. It was under the execrable Frohnmayer, a Bush appointee, that the worst obscenities were perpetrated and defended.

Here, as in so much else, the failure was in the implementation of the "Reagan Revolution." Imagine if, as originally planned, M.E. Bradford, a great gentleman and a great scholar, had been put at the head of the NEH in 1981. Wonderful things might have happened, things that would have been good for the country, the administration, and the cause of scholarship. Instead, neoconservatives took over the NEH and made an effort to turn it into another patronage machine for themselves. They failed, largely due to a dedicated, professional, and honorable staff, and soon moved on to the Department of Education, where they had more luck. The NEH staff, in fact, has a good record of restraining politicization by both neocons and conventional leftists and adhering to responsible standards. Ethically, it certainly compares favorably to Congress, the federal courts, the armed services, the Department of Housing and Urban Development, etc.

Another aspect of the situation that has not been remarked on at all is the scandal of Indirect Costs. Indirect Costs originated with scientific grants which often required maintenance of extensive physical facilities. They were written into the arts and humanities law without rhyme or reason. This means that every time a grant is given to cover the costs of a certain project, the necessary amount is multiplied by a factor of the Indirect Cost rate. The I.C. rate for Harvard University is 200 percent. For my own institution it is 49 percent.

Without I.C., the same projects could be accomplished at much lower cost, or a greater number of projects could be supported with the same amount of money. I.C. constitutes an immense subsidy for the higher education establishment, a hidden agenda. These funds, moreover, are generally at the command of administrators with fewer controls than normally budgeted funds, which explains the famous Stanford University scandal of a few years ago. In addition, the intrusion of I.C. into budgets complicates every potentially worthwhile endeavor. Whatever the case for I.C. in the sciences, they seem unjustifiable in the arts and humanities.

None of us—not even the most knowledgeable Washington insiders—really know at this point what, if anything, will happen in regard to NEA and NEH. If the Republicans really want to dismantle the Great Society there are a couple of hundred better places to start.

(1995)

Abortion

The abortion question seems to have reached an unfortunate standoff. Just as the federal judiciary has seen fit to allow more scope for pro-life legislation, it would appear that public opinion, registered in the election returns (as interpreted), has turned against the pro-life position. If it is true that Americans are more pro-abortion now than they were before *Roe v. Wade*, then among other things this indicates how a corrupt government corrupts its people.

I have a modest proposal to help any governor or state legislator out of the ticklish position they are in as a result of having a controversial issue thrown back in their laps. I offer it freely. Were I governor of a sovereign state, I would do what I should have done all along. I would declare that *Roe v. Wade* was an illegal, unconstitutional, usurpative, and nonbinding decision. Therefore, the laws of my state in regard to abortion are still in force as written and on the books of 1973. There is no need for new legislation, unless the people, through their representatives, choose.

The only problem with this is that some states—I do not know how many—have doubtless changed their laws since 1973 to conform to *Roe v. Wade*. This in itself shows how far we have fallen from any proper conceptions of democracy, constitutional government, and the high and sovereign lawmaking power. States, on this and other questions, tamely pass the laws they are told by unelected authorities to pass, which is not lawmaking at all and not constitutional government, but pretty similar to what happens in the Supreme Soviet.

My own opinion is that the public hesitancy before endorsement of an unequivocal pro-life position does not reflect an approval of or a preference for abortion as a moral position or social policy. What it reflects is a suspicion of government. The "pro-choice" position that no one has any business interfering with a woman's private decision in regard to her body is intellectually and morally nonsense. The community clearly has an interest in life, which is why we have laws against prostitution and murder and why we permit the government to conscript men to die for the country. But, in my opinion, the people recognize that the state apparatus, especially the federal government, is not the community but is an alien, self-interested force. Therefore, they are quite reasonably suspicious of that authority thrusting itself into the most intimate private affairs. The main problem of our age is the overweening state, an even greater problem than the moral decay represented by "pro-choice."

As outrageous as it will doubtless seem to our global democrats to say so, the American constitutional system was primarily a creation of Protestant Christianity. Neither the liberal minority nor the Catholic minority can govern on this question. The only viable solution to the abortion issue will be a return to tradition. That means, first of all, state rights. Secondly, that means that public policy will generally come down to a position which says: abortion is a moral evil that shall not be allowed except under extraordinary circumstances—rape, incest, to save the life of the mother.

I realize that this position is not morally perfect and will not satisfy my pro-life friends. But I do not know of any law that is morally perfect. The purpose of law is to govern the daily affairs of men in as close an approximation of a moral order as we can manage in a flawed world.

(1990)

North of the Border

We know a kindly, mild-mannered old gentleman who works for an organization that receives "federal aid." The "federal aid" is only a small part of the organization's budget, but the organization, of course, has to be run according to the guidelines of Washington (which really means the guidelines of New York, since Washington has no ideas of it own).

The other day this friend of ours got a look at his federally mandated personnel file. He saw entered there the information that he was "White Non-Hispanic." It was a flash of revelation to him. "Do you realize," he said, "that as far as the Government is concerned, you and I are Nons? We are not important enough to have our own category. We are only noteworthy as *not* being a member of any privileged minority group."

"Maybe we Nons ought to band together. Maybe we ought to demand that the Government pay some attention to our welfare. Do you realize that if George Washington were alive today he would be a 'White Non-Hispanic' just like us? Maybe we Nons ought to demand that the history textbooks be rewritten to recognize our contributions. Maybe we even ought to demand that the television networks be made to portray our culture favorably."

(1982)

Drinking, Driving & Voting

A recent report by one of those relentless federal study commissions complains of the greater number of traffic fatalities in states with 18-year-old drinking limits compared to those with 21-year-old drinking limits. News didn't say how many million dollars per word this wisdom cost us. Wasn't it the feds who not too many years ago enforced 18-year-old voting nationwide (in a quite unconstitutional manner, incidentally)? Eighteen-year-olds can be trusted to vote, but not to take a drink? They can be trusted to drive the ship of state, but not Dad's new hatchback? Does this tell us something about the qualities the federal government looks for in voters?

(1982)

The Princes

Our free federal republic, once the envy of the world, is sinking ever further into the decadence of empire. We can scarcely call "republican" a regime in which oligarchical judges contravene law, common sense, and majority will, and yet are obeyed by 270 million "citizens" with barely a murmur; in which the media of education and information contract steadily into a uniform unthinking orthodoxy of ruler worship; in which artificial aristocracies of special privilege have become steadily more entrenched.

The best evidence of the decay of the Founding Fathers' republican virtues and principles is found in our two major presidential candidates. For the first time, the American people are presented with a choice between two princes of the imperial blood.

From the disappearance of the genuine aristocracy of the founding generation until today, at least one presidential candidate (and usually both) has been a self-made man that is, someone born of humble origins who has risen to high public office by achievement or, at least, by long and prominent service to the common-wealth. Think of the origins of Truman, Eisenhower, Nixon, Johnson, Ford, Reagan, Dole, Clinton. In fact, that one could be born in a log cabin and aspire to the White House was long regarded as the benchmark of American democracy.

But look at the contenders today: two preppie Ivy Leaguers born into pow-erful political families. Bush is the son of a president, and Gore, the son of a longtime powerful senator with insider connections to international capital.

There is little difference between them except, perhaps, that one appeals to jocks and the other to nerds. One is a presidential candidate from Connecticut with a running mate from the District of Columbia, while the other is from the District of Columbia with a running mate from Connecticut.

It seems that someone can now become president solely by virtue of being the son of a president—even a president who was rejected by the electorate. Indeed, the president voted out by the people is, along with his lackeys, set to return to power in his son's entourage.

The two pretenders, it is true, have been elected to public offices; they would not be a step from the White House if they had not been. But neither would have held any public office if he hadn't inherited his position. Both are of mediocre talent. Neither has any substantial accomplishment to his credit or any vision that could be called statesman-like. They are celebrities, which someone once defined as people who are famous for being famous.

They do not disagree more than marginally on anything that really counts: Both are dedicated to cultivating the metastasizing empire at home and abroad. We are left with the right to cheer for the prince of our choice and to acclaim one (and his entourage) into power.

(2000)

Whom the Gods Would Destroy
(Bombing Afghanistan)

*Such a decline in courage is particularly noticeable among
the ruling groups and the intellectual elite, causing an
impression of loss of courage by the entire society. Of course
there are many courageous individuals but they have no
determining influence on public life. Political and intellectual
bureaucrats . . . explain how realistic, reasonable as well as
intellectually and even morally warranted it is to base state
policies on weakness and cowardice. And the decline in
courage is ironically emphasized by occasional explosions of
anger and inflexibility on the part of the same bureaucrats
when dealing with weak governments and weak countries . . .
which cannot offer any resistance.*
— SOLZHENITSYN, Harvard Address, 1978

"The Afghan air defences still pose a threat to the United States." So
Secretary of Defence Rumsfeld, the latest in a long line of robotic technocrats
who have held his post (remember McNamara?), informed the world on the air-
ways recently. If you resist Americans bombing you, then you are a threat to the
United States. To resist the U.S. government is to embrace prima facie evil and
to deserve destruction. Doubtless, General Sherman is smiling through the sul-
phur fumes. You can hear "The Battle Hymn of the Republic" in the background.

And the President himself is so incoherent that he can nasal on about enemies that are "cowardly," "faceless," and to be understood simply and only as
"evil" attackers of "freedom." The first moment of clear thought tells anyone that
the perpetrators were not cowardly, whatever else may be said about them. And
they were not "faceless" either. They were known to the government and had
been operating freely in our country. September 11 was a vicious attack on life
and property. It was an attack on freedom only if we allow it to be. To miscon-
ceive your enemy is a dangerous fault.

Words are not everything, and can be used for evil (remember Clinton).
However, Bush's crippled style indicates more than a problem of articulation. It
indicates a lack of thought, a lack of focus, a disconnection between the words
and the realities for which they are counters. And that betrays an inability to
encompass the big picture, to grasp the essential elements of the situation, which
is the sine qua non of good leadership and administration. Every successful
statesman (and soldier) that I can think of in history has been eloquent (though
often laconic) in crisis, for eloquence is simply clear thought. In the President we
have not a lack of articulateness, but a lack even of simple plain-speaking

shrewdness.

Was ever so much deadly power at the command of one so lacking in wisdom and gravitas?

After briefing by his handlers, the President shifted from describing the situation as terrorism to describing it as "war." In law, international and domestic, "war" has a rather exact meaning. Constitutionally, that grave evocation can come only from a declaration by Congress of the existence of such a state between the United States and another state.

But the rhetorical "war" allows a shift from hunting terrorists to a war against the institutions and civil population of another state alleged to have sheltered the terrorists and one that is surely not on board the "New World Order" proclaimed by George Senior.

George Senior had the same disconnect. I recall his fuming about Panamanian rowdies harassing the wife of an American officer. There was an unacknowledged racist implication, but the disconnect was that, thanks to the federal government, such incidents occur a thousand times a day in the United States. And Senior was "sickened" by the video of Los Angeles police officers' tactics in subduing a muscular felon high on PCP. At the same time he was authorizing the "turkey shoot" that murdered thousands of unresisting non-felonious Iraqi soldiers (not to mention the civilians).

And then, our born-again leader proclaims "Operation Infinite Justice." One would think that a Christian would understand that there is only one Source of infinite justice. But America and God are the same thing in minds like those of our leaders. We had to get rid of that slogan, not because it offends a Christian majority but because it offends Muslim sensibilities.

And while fighting a war against Muslim terrorists, we must be so obedient to ethnic sensibilities that airport security must body search little old ladies whose families have been in the country since the 1600's—to avoid "profiling." And how about the disconnect between fighting Muslim terrorists in the East while killing Christian men, women, and children in the Balkans in aid of Muslim terrorists?

A few weeks ago, our long-time member of the U.S. House of Representatives from my district in South Carolina, Floyd Spence, passed away. He was, as politicians go, a pretty plain and honest man. He left instructions that a Confederate flag be displayed and "Dixie" be played at his funeral in the country town near which I live. However, one of the princes, Vice Emperor Cheney, refused to make his ceremonial appearance at the occasion if anything reflecting the South appeared. So, the family, the community, and the wishes of the dead must defer to the ideology of an imperial government that, with billions in treasure, cannot fend off murderous mass attacks on the population. One would think that in a crisis, some of the best American symbols of courage and loyalty would be celebrated (as they were in World War II).

Instead of correcting and punishing the incompetence and failures of the bureaucrats, Congress rises to the crisis by voting them still more billions. And our solons, in peacetime, blithely vote away personal liberties against search and seizure that are the products of a millennium of struggle, in pursuit of an illusory security.

I hope I am wrong, but so far as one can tell, the people at large have not displayed much reason or morality in their responses to the crisis. Enthusiasm to get the enemy (never mind which) resembles the fervor displayed for the favorite athletic team—a stupid but potent force. (In my area lots of people now have two flags on their vehicles—the Stars and Stripes and the banner of their favorite college team.) In decadent Rome the citizens engaged in bloody battles over the respective merits of the Blue and Green chariot racing teams with the same zeal they held against the foreign enemy.

"The increase in barbarity goes on until everything is dissolved in blind violence . . . and the pleasure of destroying and punishing," wrote Richard Weaver in contemplation of World War II. The end result, he said, is nihilism, the loss of all humane values. Long before Weaver it was common wisdom that: Whom the gods would destroy, they first make mad.

(2001)

Chapter Six

Cons and Neocons

The Conservative Identity

C arlyle defined history as "the essence of innumerable biographies." This is only one of the many inadequate but suggestive definitions of history, numerous enough to fill a small volume, that have been put forward, but perhaps it is sufficient to excuse a bit of auto-biography as pertinent to the last quarter century of American conservatism. That phenomenon has been with us long enough now to allow a degree at least of historical perspective. A once resilient Goldwater Youth has begun to feel the preliminary twinges of mortality in his bones, and therefore perhaps can review usefully the history and thus the present status of that intangible but real phenomenon, conservatism, which has been a significant determining influence as he has gone about his personal and professional life.

I believe that it is descriptively accurate to say that most of us who regarded ourselves as "intellectual conservatives" before 1964 are in a state of demoralization and discouragement at the status of conservatism in 1986. I think this is true both of those who have entered the government in recent years and those who are, like me, merely perplexed observers on the fringes of public life. The degree of disappointment may vary with situation and temperament, but it is the predominant mood—notwithstanding the apparent flourishing of "conservatisms" on every hand and the common agreement that we have a great deal to be thankful for in the present condition of the commonwealth, compared to what might have been.

The Goldwater campaign, for those who came of age about the time I did, was the central public event (though not, I think, the formative influence) of the time. For those who had eyes to see, it revealed for all time the arrogant deceitfulness of the media lords and lackeys and the intellectual and moral bankruptcy of the Republican establishment of that day. More importantly, it revealed, in retrospect, how far we had to go to translate into popular and political success ideas that we knew in our hearts would appeal to the majority of the American people, properly heard.

Those of us who regarded ourselves as intellectual conservatives came from a variety of regional, ethnic, and ideological backgrounds, as was only fitting in a large and various republic. We had our differences (more significant than we, or at least I, realized at the time) which we argued heatedly but usually with chivalrous respect. We were united by common enemies. In these somewhat more relaxed times it is difficult to recall the embattlement of conservatives within the academy—where we could expect to meet usually hostility, sometimes vicious, and the best we could hope for was amused condescension. It took, I will not say courage, but a certain stubborn perversity to make one's way, and allies were welcome. But we had positive sources of unity as well. We might differ in our primary heroes, but we could share a general and eclectic admiration for the mentors of the movement—Kirk and Buckley, Burnham and Weaver, Kendall and von Mises, Molnar and Meyer, and many others. This consensus was captured by the Intercollegiate Studies Institute, which on some campuses provided the only evidence of an intellectual dialogue that in tone and quality was respectable in the light of the best traditions of the West. The working platform was summed up neatly enough by George Nash as agreement (allowing for differences of emphasis) on tradition, the free market, and anti-Communism.

And despite our differences we can, in historical perspective, be accurately seen as one movement. And not only that, but as a movement that was in some sense or other, a success. While there has been an entrenchment and institutionalization of totalitarian radicalism, in some places, in the last quarter century, it is also true that the academic dialogue is today more open to ideas from what might be loosely described as the Right than at any time since the 1920's. In the voting booth, which alas is no longer sovereign (if indeed it ever was), the rejection of institutionalized liberalism has been resounding and today represents the view of the overwhelming majority of decent Americans. The extent to which that mandate has been translated into policy ought not to be under-estimated. The control of inflation and taxes—which is another way of saying the expansion of the liberty of the citizens; the firming up of defense; the first hints of reform in the degraded judiciary—these are limited but quite real successes. Nor should we discount the value of the revolution wrought in Presidential style. We have a Chief Magistrate whose dignified informality, whose candid and good-natured simplicity (in the best sense of that word) reflect some of the best of the national character and who has restored some badly needed poise to the public life.

Why then, the malaise that I mentioned among the Old Guard? There are many reasons. Conservatism, despite heroic efforts to put a different face on the matter, must always involve some pessimism and skepticism. That might even be a virtue in a society in which public demeanor is often a compulsive optimism. We can also attribute something to the unavoidably imperfect connection between ideas and the public sphere. It is a truism that those who launch ideas into the world often see them come back in unrecognizable form. John Dos

Passos observed that in setting about to correct evils, the liberals of his generation forgot that man is an institution-building animal, that their ideals would be
codified and bureaucratized by others. The consolidator and preserver is a different kind of man from the thinker and creator. The disciple inherits and con-
verts to his own. There is no getting around this. Madison subverted Jeffersonian
democracy, as Martin Van Buren did the Jacksonian variety, and as Sumner and
Stevens did Lincoln's Reconstruction.

Still, when all is said, this does not exactly describe what has happened to
the conservative intellectual movement. We ought to have had more success than
we have had in translating ideas into a regime. The ball has been dropped too
many times. There have been too many weak stands and too many unnecessary
retreats. The other side did it far better than we have done. Perhaps because they
had a head start; perhaps because they have learned to use the vast leverage provided by the conservative virtues of our Constitution and fellow-citizens to keep
the load rolling in the direction they want it to go. Put it another way: Has no
more been accomplished because it was impossible, or because the effort was not
made or was not made in the right way? Whichever way the question is
answered, a certain degree of disappointment is our reward.

But I do not believe we have yet uncovered the two main reasons for the
alienation of the conservative intellectual from the conservatism of the day. First
of all, we have simply been crowded out by overwhelming numbers. The offen-
sives of radicalism have driven vast herds of liberals across the border into our
territories. These refugees now speak in our name, but the language they speak
is the same one they always spoke. We have grown familiar with it, have learned
to tolerate it, but it is tolerable only by contrast to the harsh syllables of the bar-
barians over the border. It contains no words for the things that we value. Our
estate has been taken over by an impostor, just as we were about to inherit.

A Confederate soldier, who when captured preferred to serve in the Union
army rather than face prison, was referred to as a "galvanized Yankee."
Galvanized conservatives (as well as Georgia snake-oil salesmen) are numerous
and flourishing now that we seem to be the winning side, and the Old Guard cannot help but catch on the wind from the Potomac a faint but unmistakable odor
of opportunistic betrayal. Of course, it is exceedingly natural for a party in pursuit of victory and consolidation of power to welcome newcomers, and even to
take its old faithfuls for granted. Yet the relative degree of influence which each
shall be allowed is a choice. That we have lost this decision, for whatever reason,
says nothing about the merits of our claims. And tactical decisions can yet be
amended, to some degree at least. In this there is hope.

But the conservative intellectual must grapple with something even more
daunting than an enemy salient in his territory. In the early 1960's it was possible to take for granted that the social fabric of the West, in its American form,
was relatively intact. And that, therefore, a change of leadership and emphasis
and a firm dealing with the foreign foe would put us right. I do solemnly wish
that I will be proved wrong here, but history has moved on and the signs of the

times suggest that we must come to grips with the much more serious and difficult crisis of the unraveling of the social fabric itself. For if our original stand,
our old conservatism, meant anything at all, it meant, on its bottom line, a
defense of the traditional social fabric of the West, which we deemed to be
threatened.

Civilization is primarily a spiritual phenomenon, though it may have material expressions. Civilization begins with the successful combining of the universal with the particularities of a time, place and people. Such a combination
results in forms of behavior, standards, which are the substance of civilization.
These are revealed in both high culture and folk culture, neither of which can
exist without them. The standards are a great and providential achievement—
nothing less than the imposition of order on the chaos of existence, an order that
rests not upon outward coercion but upon inward apprehension of its beauty and
fitness. Tradition concerns itself with the preservation and transmission of this
achievement. A conservative, a.k.a. a traditionalist, is one who understands the
importance and difficulty of this task. Far from being preoccupied with a dead
past, he is the most forward looking of men, for his function is to understand,
adapt, preserve, and transmit the essence of civilization to future generations. He
must save it from wanton destruction, from deadening inertia and inflexibility,
and from indifference. One of the most successful exercises of this function in
history was the American Revolution, an inspired adaptation which preserved the
essence of British liberty.

Since the life of man is here and now, and since culture can only be trans-
mitted in the forms in which it has been cast, traditions are necessarily particu-
larist. One cannot be a traditionalist in general, as one can be a liberal or a
Communist. A traditionalist can only be so about a particular tradition. American
conservatism can mean nothing else but preservation of the traditions of Western
civilization. There is wide room here, since proliferating variety and independence of judgment are hallmarks of the Western tradition. But there is an irreducible core of givens: religion, implying at the least a demeanor towards the
universe, our fellow man, and ourselves that can be summed up as reverence or
piety; concepts of manhood, womanhood, and family—by which is meant not
niches in which people are to be confined, but ideals that people aspire to fulfill
in realization of their highest ethical potential; liberty—by which we mean not
aimless and arrogant nonconformity, but freedom of thought and action tempered
by responsibility to community and obedience to lawful authority.

It is possible, of course, to become so obsessed by the forms of a tradition
as to lose its essence. The dustbin of history is full of societies which died in an
inflexible worship of forms. This is not a danger that besets Americans, even
American conservatives. It is also possible for tradition to be violently interrupted. That is exactly what the radical wishes, so that he can create the world anew.
We need only to mention the names of Lenin, Hitler, and Mao to make this point.
But this, too, is a danger from which America, relatively at least, is immune.

Our danger is indifference. The liberal, who is a most characteristic type of

American, relates to civilization as a fish relates to water. He is unconscious of its existence and therefore of its need to be cherished, cultivated, and handed down. It will never occur to him that endless attrition by criticism, pollution, indifference, and the introduction of innovations and eclectic elements could damage it. The liberal lacks all reverence toward, even awareness of, the universal and the forms which symbolize it. In the simplest terms, he is a man incapable of making the connection between what he regards as a happy liberation from outmoded repressions and the proliferation of divorce, pornography, rape, perversion, child abuse, abortion, and callousness.

The conservative, considering himself to be in touch with the tradition of the West, faces in 1986 a society in which the everyday virtues of honesty, loyalty, manners, work, and restraint are severely attenuated. So far as one can tell, millions of people are so cut off from all standards of value that they actually believe that Walter Cronkite is wise, Edward M. Kennedy is a statesman, Mr. T is a model for youth, and Dr. Ruth is a guide to the good life. We have a society in which educated and apparently decent mothers join their subteen daughters in viewing musical "performances" by obscene and tasteless degenerates, which degenerates become millionaires. A society in which a "serious" book is represented by the vulgar and trivial memoirs of Lee Iacocca, and in which aspirations to culture are satisfied by government subsidies to untalented and decadent poets and artists. A society in which the appointed guardians of the Constitution are so far out of touch with the essence of ordered liberty they are sworn to uphold that they have cavalierly taken a Constitutional provision whereby the States forbade the federal government to interfere in the exercise of religion and warped it into a grant of power to the federal government to interfere with the exercise of religion in the States.

The task of the conservative intellectual remains the same as it has always been, though acquiring new urgency. It is not primarily a political task, although it has unavoidably political dimensions. That task is to keep alive the wisdom that we are heir to and must keep and hand on—something more and higher than equality, a high standard of living, and a good sex life—as fine as these things may be in their place. The liberal cannot help us here, even if he now dwells on our side of the border and at times calls himself a conservative. None can do the job but those who know what needs to be done. Among the proliferation of conservatisms, let us discriminate. Let us nourish as kinsmen those who will help in the essential task, no matter how outlandishly provincial their accents and clothes. As for the rest, let us go to the marketplace of ideas as honest traders, aware of the quality of our goods and determined not to be taken in by any interloper, no matter how plausible, finely turned out, and full of seductive promises.

(1986)

Moments in the Sun

A Review of *The Neoconservative Mind: Politics, Culture, and the War of Ideology*, by Gary Dorrien, Philadelphia: Temple University Press, 1993, 500 pages.

One can no better describe the subject of this book than by quoting the publisher's press release:

> Once there was a group of liberals and Leftists. They were Democrats, they were radicals, they were freedom riders. But they became disillusioned by the Left. They moved toward the Right, they opposed the anti-war movement, they made socialist arguments for electing Richard Nixon. They claimed to be the true American liberals, and they attacked their former friends who continued to identify with the Left. . . . They went on to campaign for Cold War objectives of "exporting democracy," and to support Ronald Reagan and his crusade for "family values." . . . What can explain such a reversal in ideology?

Most of what has been written about the strange band called neoconservatives has been written either by themselves and their admirers or else by persons, to the right and to the left, who bear the bootmarks of their climb to power. The author of *The Neoconservative Mind*, however, seems to have no axe to grind, but to be motivated by genuine intellectual curiosity about the phenomenon in question. He is a man of the moderate Christian left and has written a dispassionate, seriously researched, and historical account. At the level of intellectual history and public discourse, he has answered the question "What can explain such a reversal in ideology?" very well—as far as it goes.

A more important question, however, remains to be answered: How did a group of New York Trotskyites come during the 1980's to assume the ideological management of the Middle American Reagan revolution? The answer to this question lies in the realm of intellectual logistics and political factionalism, not in that of the history of ideas. A fascinating account remains to be written, and the answers may be looked for in the neoconservatives' proximity to the media and large capital of the Northeast, well documented here, and in the intellectual and ethical shallowness of the decision-makers of the Reagan era.

In his attempt to capture the "neoconservative mind," Dorrien has written thorough, respectful, but candid intellectual biographies of four of the leading lights of the movement: Irving Kristol, Nonnan Podhoretz, Michael Novak, and Peter Berger. He has traced the development of their public thought and related it to the right and left and to the larger questions of the 20th century. This is a useful exercise, though one of the things it proves is that, with the exception of Berger, none of these writers has any real claim to being a serious scholar or important thinker (as opposed to political polemicist), though Kristol has undoubted talents as an editor and intellectual logistician. That is, most of the neoconservatives would be of no importance at all in a public discourse that was less vulgarized and commercialized than that of the present day.

Dorrien has not neglected the questions of intellectual logistics mentioned above or the neoconservative accomplishments in this area; his description does not differ greatly from the critical assessment made by paleoconservatives, and I will resist the temptation to quote more than a couple of his best bits: "The supreme irony of his [Kristol's] attacks on the self-promoting opportunism of the New Class intellectuals was that they were most convincing as descriptions of the career he knew best," and, "Novak moved further left. For the next two years, when such attitudes were most fashionable, he epitomized the social type of the liberal-bashing New Leftist."

One of the most interesting parts of the book is the author's careful treatment of the particular variety of Marxism that he sees as the seedbed of neoconservatism. It will surprise many conservatives to learn that Dorrien judges James Burnham to have played a large role in the neoconservatives' journey from Marxism to an equally ideological Cold War liberalism. Here is a fascinating chapter in American intellectual history, though I have to enter something of a demurrer. Burnham, after he escaped from the belly of the beast, was motivated chiefly by the desire to preserve Western civilization. It is not clear that the neoconservatives who adopted a similar stance did so from a similar motive. Basic to Burnham's view was the idea that the *gestalt* of the left had imperiled the West by disarming it. In my youth a favorite barroom game of conservatives was to test oneself and others against Burnham's 39 theses of liberalism as set forward in *Suicide of the West*: the fewer of the insidious, plausible lies of liberalism one agreed with, the better. I do not think the neoconservatives would score very high on Burnham's test.

Dorrien would have done much better to search for the intellectual antecedents to neoconservatism in the strange cult of Straussian political science. Though the personal connections are not as direct, and though the Straussians represent a higher level of scholarship than do the neoconservatives, the affinities between the uncritical pursuit of "global democratic capitalism" and the Straussian universalization of equality are clear. If the Straussians had not succeeded in putting 19th-century German left-wing Romanticism into American conservative discourse in place of the chaste and cool republicanism of the Founding Fathers, the neoconservatives would never have achieved their success as philosophers of the pseudo-right. But the name of Leo Strauss appears in the index of this book only a few times and that of Allan Bloom not at all, which is a real limitation. The author does provide full accounts of his subjects' controversies with the paleoconservatives. This is a useful survey, though at a superficial journalistic level, that by no means exhausts the subject.

Dorrien finds the neoconservatives' positions shot through with contradictions—a judgment made from the left but one with which no conservative not on the neoconservative payroll will disagree. The history of this "movement," in the final analysis, is a history of opportunism: of leftists, that is, who used their clout with the major media to form a very profitable alliance with the corporate elites. At the very moment that the American economy was deteriorating at its base, the American social fabric was unraveling, and the American middle class was threatened by decimation, the neoconservatives formulated an abstract democratic capitalism that appealed, with plenty of well-funded publicity, to some of the more superficial aspects of the public discontent.

Though Dorrien seems to believe that, despite all, the neoconservatives are in a position to offer powerful opposition to the "reconstructed progressive politics" for which he hopes, I am inclined to disagree. Their moment, I believe, will not be prolonged—the ever-changing tides have shifted. The neoconservatives may well ride out the next big wave, but it will be in some other guise than that to which we are accustomed, and in the long perspective of history they will rate but a footnote.

(1994)

Treasury of Virtue

A Review of *The New Jacobinism: Can Democracy Survive?*, by Claes G. Ryn, Washington, D.C.: National Humanities Institute, 1991, 102 pages.

"Contrary to widespread belief, evidence is accumulating that Western democracy is in continuous and serious decline," writes Claes Ryn in the opening of this eloquent, concise, and hard-hitting manifesto that goes immediately to the heart of our times. "Many commentators proclaim democracy's triumph over evil political forces in the world and hold up today's Western society as a model for all humanity. They do so in the face of glaring symptoms of social decay," he continues, and adds, a little later: "Although the difficulties of Western democracy are manifold and have no single source, the most important can be seen as directly or indirectly induced by a deficiency at the ethical center."

Though written against a background of rich scholarship, *The New Jacobins* is not an academic book. Nor is it one of those volumes of semi-fashionable "conservative" journalism that appear from time to time and are hyped for their marginal empirical criticisms of the reigning establishment. Rather, Professor Ryn's work resembles one of those great political pamphlets that have appeared occasionally at points of crisis in Western history to mobilize the decent and thinking into a recognition of peril. So apposite to our present situation is the book that I am tempted to turn this notice into a string of striking quotations, but let two or three suffice:

Nationalism, by contrast [to patriotism], is an eruption of overweening ambition, a throwing off of individual and national self-control. Nationalism is self-absorbed and conceited, oblivious of the weaknesses of the country it champions. It is provincialism without the leaven of cosmopolitan breadth, discretion, and critical detachment. It recognizes no authority higher than its own national passion. It imagines itself as having a monopoly on right or as having a mission superseding moral norms. . . .

Of those in the West today who are passionate advocates of capitalism and want it introduced all over the world, many are former Marxists. The shift from being a Marxist to becoming a missionary for capitalism may be far less drastic than commonly assumed. . . . The Jacobin spirit can align itself with that set of potentialities in capitalism that are most destructive of the ways of traditional society. . . . A certain kind of advocacy of capitalism turns out to have much in common with the Jacobin passion for an egalitarian, homogeneous society. . . .

It is indicative of the influence of the Jacobin spirit in the Western world that a fondness for abstract general schemes and utopian visions should today have attraction even for people said to be "conservative" or "on the right." This development says a great deal about the scope and depth of the Western flight from reality.

Constitutional democracy and Jacobin democracy are two different things. Constitutional democracy consists of a healthy social order with dispersed power. Like a healthy individual, constitutional democracy lives by prudence and moderation and with a set of ethical rules (a constitution in the case of a state) that govern the pursuit of prudent ends by ethical and restrained means. Jacobin democracy is egalitarian and plebiscitary, but also, of course, centralized and elitist, and aggressive both at home and abroad. It is the burden of Professor Ryn's alarum that we are fast inclining into an advanced state of that latter condition—that loud hosannas to the beauty and success of democracy portend not its triumph but its end. And that our real problem is ethical, not political or utilitarian—the substitution of self-congratulatory abstract political goals for a decent and ordered life and state. He is, of course, right, and nowhere has the argument been better stated in short compass.

Ryn makes his case admirably, especially in those passages in which he shows the neoconservatism to be a symptom of the problem and not a cure; as well as in the chapter, worth a book, that shows us that today's trumpeters of capitalism are talking about something that is as different from our forefathers' love of private property and freedom of trade as their "democracy" is from the constitutional order of our Framers. It would be well if this work could be widely dispersed, and I wish I could be as optimistic as Professor Ryn that a reaffirmation of traditional principles will serve. But I am not, for several reasons.

It may be that the social fabric no longer exists in which good principles can find root. We need to be able to produce young men who want to ride hard, shoot straight, speak the truth, and revere their ancestors, and not to imitate Michael Jackson, lust after the fast buck, and crow over the skill of lobbing high explosives accurately onto alien women and children from a safe distance. We do, indeed, still turn out such young men, but given the existing regime, their virtues are quickly perverted to bad ends or degraded into cynicism.

It is healthy and wholesome to appeal to tradition and to try to enshrine it in our education. But, as Allen Tate pointed out long ago in his criticism of Irving Babbitt, we are already at so great a level of disconnection from tradition as a living reality as to render our achievement in that regard doubtful. Alas, why appeal to the need for a leavening of aristocracy and constitutionalism in the life of democracy? That question was settled at Appomattox, a century and a quarter ago, in favor of aggressive and self-congratulatory democracy. If Americans had any real connection with their constitutional traditions, then the Straussian sophistries (which Ryn skillfully skewers as the source of neoconservatism) would not be officially enshrined. They would be regarded merely as silly, eccentric, and inconsequential German abstractions with no relevance to American history or principles.

And, I fear, we suffer not only from bad doctrine, but from defects of character. The kind of spirit that compels me to buckle my seat belt and forbids me to smoke, that finds virtue in subsidizing my private decision to kill my unborn child while forbidding me to criticize any favored foreigner or minority group from fear of hurting tender feelings—that kind of spirit is not Jacobinism only. It is, rather, the natural reflection of what has come to be the predominant and normal strain of the American national character. And it is so far from what our fathers regarded as the rights and duties of constitutional liberty as to render their spirit unrecoverable. The absentee, abstract, and artificial moralism that Professor Ryn so eloquently exposes is not anything new. It was already evident a century and a half ago in what Robert Penn Warren called, in his book on the legacy of the Civil War, "the Treasury of Virtue."

The great political pamphlets of the West that this work resembles (and I mean political pamphlet as a complimentary term) were addressed to the independent gentlemen of every community who were capable of thought and action. But who is to read and act upon this eloquence in a society of bureaucrats, proletarians, hedonists, and con artists calling themselves politicians? Yet I should not allow my pessimism to blight Professor Ryn's accomplishment. He has identified for us, as well as it can possibly be done, our malady and the course of treatment we must follow to survive. The rest is up to us.

(1991)

Contemporary Liberalism

The difference between socialism and liberalism is the difference between a doctrine and a fashion. Viewed from the standpoint of the Western political tradition, both are heretical. Socialism may be likened to the Christian heresy of Socinianism and liberalism to that of Catharism. Behind socialism can sometimes be discerned a genuine though misguided aspiration to reason and justice in the community—behind liberalism, never.

Prior to the nineteenth century, Western men understood human history in the light of Greek philosophy, or of the Bible, or of organic metaphor. The great advances in industrialization and technology in the nineteenth century led to an aberrant application of mechanical analogies to human society—to talk of "inevitable forces" and to the reification of certain words thought to describe historical realities into absolute descriptors and predictors of society. (Thus the likeness to Socinianism, which mistook words for things.) The most systematic and sophisticated form of the aberration was Marxist socialism, which became a historical tradition among a good deal of the new class of intelligentsia in the West and its liberated colonies and which was institutionalized in a totalitarian state, thanks to the evil genius of V.I. Lenin. Thus, though its shoddiness as a means of understanding reality has long been evident, socialism in its institutionalized forms remains a potent force in history.

To describe liberalism is much more difficult, if by "liberalism" one means a certain intangible force in Western public life in the twentieth century that we all recognize as a pervasive influence. It is clear that this liberalism is not the same thing as certain specific "liberalisms" in the past—such as the doctrine and political movement for free trade in nineteenth-century England—even though its development may have some derivative relationship to earlier liberalism. It is also true that modern liberalism has drawn upon socialism, and many other sources and tendencies, usually unacknowledged, but it is something other than the sum of its influences.

One may write a detailed and satisfactory history of socialism, both as a doctrine and a movement. It is, however, as nearly impossible to write a history of liberalism as it is to write a history of women's hairdos, and for the same reason. Liberalism is a fashion, a style; it involves elements of perpetual mutability and subjectivism. One of its essential features is that it is constantly changing. In recent years, good liberals have believed in rapid succession that (1) budget deficits are unimportant and that (2) budget deficits are among the most serious problems we face; that (1) all persons must be treated as individuals, whatever their ethnic background, and that (2) some individuals must be given special privileges because of their ethnic background; that in the interests of world peace (1) sanctions must be imposed on South Africa and (2) sanctions on Nicaragua must be lifted. The list could be expanded ad infinitum. We run into great difficulties in trying to describe liberalism as a doctrine and in establishing a pattern to its history.

We will do better by attempting to understand what function liberalism serves in modern society. James Burnham, in *The Suicide of the West* (1964), described the *end results* of liberalism. Let us attempt to understand its sociological function. A group of ideas does not exert force upon society unless it serves some purpose, acknowledged or unacknowledged, in the functioning of that society. It will not help us much in such an examination to take liberalism at face value. Not only would we have difficulty in establishing its doctrinal clarity, but we would be required to assume, against all reason and evidence, that Earl Warren, Jane Fonda, Teddy Kennedy, and Howard Metzenbaum are capable of systematic thought and social responsibility.

Liberalism can be better grasped by description than exposition. We can find in modern English literature an adequate description. Americans have seldom managed this because they have been less aware than some Englishmen of older and better traditions in the light of which liberalism might be judged. One of the successes of liberalism is that it is its own standard; rather than being judged, liberalism is so pervasive that it provides the standard by which all things are judged—and a very conveniently flexible standard it is. Evelyn Waugh's *Basil Seal* is a superb portrait of one type of liberal; Kenneth Widmerpool in Anthony Powell's *A Dance to the Music of Time* provides another illustration. We can mention also the scientific progressives in C.S. Lewis's *That Hideous Strength*. The essence of these characters is not a doctrine but a style—unscrupulous opportunistic individualism under the cover of a vague sentimentality of collective progress and kindness.

We might consider how one becomes a liberal. Imagine a youth down on the farm in Iowa. In the normal course of events, this youth might aspire, as youth will, to various things. He might aspire to be an athlete or an aviator, a mathematician or a mechanic, a millionaire or a mass murderer, because these activities appeal to him. Under certain circumstances, he might even aspire to be a socialist. But why would he aspire to be a liberal? Because, through the mass media, he has learned that to be a liberal is glamorous, fashionable, and potentially rewarding in social prestige. To become a liberal will bestow upon him the aura of elitism, of liberation from mundane conventions and petty consistency. He need only be clever enough to keep up with the ever-changing standard.

The role of the mass media reminds us that liberalism is a relatively recent phenomenon that depends entirely upon certain artificialities in the intellectual discourse of modern society. Prior to the nineteenth century, men took their ideas and standards of behavior from blood ties, local and traditional mores, the Bible, and classical learning. Where these standards were not fully available, as sometimes on the American frontier, men reverted to an earlier Western style of heroic individualism. In any case, it was understood that a man was his beliefs, his ideas. Wrong religious or political ideas might, indeed, lead him to the stake. He might disguise or repudiate his ideas, but it would never have occurred to him to change his ideas constantly in the manner of fashion.

In the nineteenth century, however, a considerable portion of men came to enjoy an abstract relationship with their work and sources of income, to have the luxury of creating their social identity for the occasion. This development was contemporary with the appearance of mass media with a mass audience and, thus, of a realm of public discourse that differed from all earlier politics in that it was abstracted from day-to-day reality and characterized by incessant superficiality and inconsistency. In the mid-nineteenth century, it was possible to become a public figure of moral celebrity in Massachusetts by decrying Southern slavery, without being required to take any responsibility for the squalid conditions in which one's own factory workers labored.

No one is a liberal about the things that affect him directly. One may be a liberal about criminals in general but not about the particular criminal who bashes one's own skull. Liberalism, like feminism, is a luxury of the abstractness of urban life and mass communications. Thus, persons who are superficially educated often aspire to be liberal. People with no education but strong common sense or persons with great learning are much less likely to do so.

Both socialism and liberalism, functionally, are attempts to come to terms with the terrifying feelings of impotence and insubstantiality that we all experience among the massive, impersonal institutions of modern life. The same is true, of course, of ideologies of the Right, including the nastier forms of nationalism. Socialism is a *doctrine* that claims to be the key to history. By contrast, liberalism is a *style* that provides its devotees with a sense of moral righteousness without corresponding responsibility in their personal relationships.

(1987)

The Disappearance of Conservatism

The defeat and disappearance of what has been known as conservatism in the 20th century is a subject worthy of a large book. What would be said in such a book would depend on whether we took a historical focus of a few years, a few decades, or a larger span. And on whether we looked at political parties and mass politics, intellectual movements, or far-reaching social change.

It is possible that the most recent American experience in international adventurism has effectively finished off what we have known as conservatism, and also what has been known as liberalism—both swallowed up by the imperial state, for which ideas, principles, and even material interests are expendable. For the latest adventure (the Gulf War), unlike earlier ones, has not occurred because of unavoidable conflict, but by deliberate choice.

It would be interesting to pursue Roman analogies and what they suggest about the long-term perils of bankruptcy and proletarianization for the state that undertakes the imperial role. But it is perhaps enough to point out that the bill is not in for the economic and psychic costs, and they cannot be discussed until the present euphoria has passed. And that politicians will be able to obfuscate the costs for a long time.

It would also be interesting to chart the course of movement of intellectual conservatism into the terminal state of vulgarity and triviality in which George Will can be regarded as a leading intellectual. However, I will focus in this brief space on the strange and almost unnoticed failure and betrayal of conservatism as a domestic political movement, despite three resounding national election victories.

The chief reason for this failure is that conservatism allowed itself to be captured within the contaminated vessel of the Republican Party. Our President, who was elected three times on an anti-affirmative action platform, is for affirmative action. And who can gainsay the Great Emancipator of Kuwait? He was elected by millions concerned about the Willie Hortons of the world. We have no evidence that he has done anything about the Willie Hortons. We have no evidence that he wishes to do anything. The only evidence we have is that he wants the votes of those who are concerned.

He was elected, after an explicit promise, by the votes of millions of middle- and working-class Americans who sought some remedy for the government burden on their earnings. They now face increased government spending and greater taxes, to bailout the bureaucracy, the bankers, and the sheiks. Northeastern yuppies who voted for Dukakis may take a tax deduction for the interest on their vacation homes. The millions of middle-class people who voted for Bush cannot take a deduction for the interest paid to buy a car needed to get to work and support the government.

The difference between the Democratic and Republican parties—and this dichotomy can be found in earlier periods of the history of the vile American two-party system—is that the Democrats serve their constituency. The unions, minority groups, bureaucrats, and assorted social enemies who support them can expect to profit by their victory. And also by their defeat, since the other party neither wants to nor can provide effective opposition to their agenda.

The Republicans have been talking about the Emerging Republican Majority, Middle America, the Silent Majority, etc. for more than two decades now. Some pundits have wondered why this Majority has not emerged. The explanation is simple. It has been betrayed by the Republican Party, which wants its votes but not its platform. The only effective conservative movement in recent history in mass politics was that of a non-Republican, George Wallace, which made a far profounder change in American politics than the so-called Reagan Revolution. If Wallace had not badly scared the leaders of both parties, they would not now be giving even lip service to the concerns of Middle America. The function of the Republican Party is to capture and contain those concerns.

Many political movements and tendencies emerged in postwar America— those of Johnson, Nixon, Wallace, Reagan, and others. But the winner has been that tendency that had the least popular support: Nelson Rockefeller's. His Liberal Republicanism of the 1960's postulated that the Republicans could do everything the Democrats could do, but could do it better. (Meanwhile minimizing impact on the inherited wealth of the Northeast.) Thanks to the nature and history of the Republican Party, despite unfailing rejection at the polls, that regime is now triumphant.

(1991)

Pat Buchanan

A Review of *Right From the Beginning*, by Patrick J. Buchanan, Boston and Toronto: Little, Brown, 1988, 392 pages.

My grandmother, the daughter of a Confederate "high private," always said that if someone had done something particularly good, you could be sure he had Southern ancestry somewhere. I first heard this during the latter days of World War II in connection with General Patton, who at that time, with the help of a couple of uncles, was spectacularly chasing the Hun across his own territory.

Like everything else my grandmother told me, this has nearly always proved to be true. Therefore, I was not surprised to learn from Pat Buchanan's memoirs that he—the favorite TV personality at our house—was descended from the Buchanans and Baldwins of Mississippi. In *Right From the Beginning*, Buchanan has given us a lively and good-spirited account of his background and early career, up to the time he went to work for Richard Nixon in 1966, describing by the way how he was on the "right from the beginning."

Pat Buchanan is not ashamed of these Southern origins and knows that he owes something to them (would that a few more of his tepid fellow conservatives had the same Southern "Celtic" spirit), yet the predominant, immediate force in his background was the confident and principled Irish Catholicism of the post-World War II era. One of nine children of an upper-middle-class Catholic family, Buchanan grew up in what was then the sleepy, decent Southern town of Washington (the one our forefathers called "the federal district"), a town which has now disappeared beneath the weight of the cosmopolitan capital of the flabbiest empire in world history.

His education was entirely Catholic (except for one year at the Columbia Journalism School), academically and morally religious, and reinforced by a robustly healthy and uncomplicated family life in which tradition, faith, common sense, and patriotism were reflexive values. To this he attributes his ability to cut through the multiplying webs of cant and pseudo-sophistication that tie down modern public discourse and to rely upon fundamental principles in his columns, speeches, and television appearances. For this we should be eternally grateful. Buchanan tells us that while serving in the White House he ghostwrote Nixon's "Silent Majority" speech and Vice President Agnew's famous illumination of the sinister power of the media. These, so far, were certainly the high points of American rhetoric in the second half of the 20th century, though they have as yet borne no fruit in policy.

Buchanan gives us occasional tidbits like these from his years seated near the mighty. His recollection of his first two meetings with Nixon, for instance, should be of interest to every future student of that phenomenon. However, those who hope for a political insider's memoirs of 20 years (on and off) in the Nixon and Reagan White House—including the explosions of Watergate and Iran-Contra—will be disappointed by *Right From the Beginning*. That, Buchanan tells us, is for the next book. This is not a politician's show-and-tell but a conservative's *Bildungsroman*.

He does give us two concluding chapters of political prescription for the future, beginning with an account of his brief presidential precampaign in 1987, humorously entitled "Is That Churchill Under the Bed?" Buchanan withdrew, he tells us, because he could not hope to win and would only have detracted from the strength of Kemp and Robertson. Those words were written before Pat Buchanan's beloved conservative movement was left with a choice between a Rockefeller Republican and a Ford Republican (both, as he comments in another context, cowboys who are all hat and no cattle).

I wonder if he thinks differently now? What might a principled and hard-hitting conservative candidacy have done to transform the campaign into something from which some hope or value might have been salvaged? Buchanan, it is true, has no political base in the traditional sense. He has made his career in the media, and as an appointed official in the executive branch. He does not come, except spiritually (which is after all the most important way), from the grassroots. It is amazing how old-fashioned and backward our political party system is. Our society is now almost totally centralized and consolidated in every sphere, and it is nearly impossible to rise or to have any influence unless you begin near the top, whether in business, professions, culture, or communications. Only in the instance of the political parties (and organized crime) does one still have to begin near the ward-heeler level to build a "base."

Without such a political base, Pat Buchanan was justified in his hesitation. On the other hand, as he clearly recognizes, the key to political leadership today is communication. Buchanan is certainly able to communicate, not because of some magic articulateness, but because he has something honest and deeply felt to say (like Ronald Reagan before he began to sound like Ike or Gerald Ford).

He is probably the only person in sight who could really carry out his prescription for the next Republican President: to accept the need for a continuing principled confrontation with the media and their Democratic allies. We do not know if this will work because it has never been tried with perseverance. Why is it that whenever it has been tried and seemed to work it was hastily abandoned for a policy of "go along and get along"? That—the avoidance of principle except on the hard left—is, I suppose, a part of the much-touted "genius of American politics."

These are my conclusions, not Pat Buchanan's, but he ought to agree with them. He is loyal to his former bosses, Nixon and Reagan, a loyalty quite old-fashioned and commendable under the circumstances. I would not have it any other way. But it takes only a little reading between the lines to cull out of *Right From the Beginning* an indictment of stupendous and tragic failures of principle by these flawed leaders, despite protestations to the contrary.

Our era is not like the 50's, he observes, rightly. "Our political and social quarrels now partake of the savagery of religious wars because, at bottom, *they are religious wars*. The most divisive issues of American politics are now about our warring concepts of right and wrong, good and evil. In a way the Kerner Commission never predicted, we have indeed become 'two nations.'" Not much headway will be made, Buchanan implies, until we accept that. But, alas, it seems as if the whole history of American politics is made up of the avoidance of issues, not their confrontation.

If he ever had any future aspirations to elective office, he probably abandoned them with this book. *Right From the Beginning* is personally frank. Not only frank about youthful admiration for Joe McCarthy and Goldwater but frank about his own hell-raising youth and young manhood. Frank, but not graphic: Ladies are referred to respectfully and mostly only by first names. I am nearly of Pat Buchanan's age, and I find his hell-raising youth familiar and refreshing. Those of us who grew up through the 50's and early 60's can remember when hell-raising was exuberantly barbaric and enjoyable, but not mean-spirited and decadent. Those days left a lot to be desired, but we are justifiably nostalgic comparing them with the pall that began to descend on American life when Kennedy and his "best and brightest" took over, shortly followed by the blossoming of drugs, promiscuity, and perversion. My chief regret is that my hell-raising career did not last as many years as apparently did Buchanan's.

This is not a great memoir, but an interesting one that does succeed in invoking, vividly and memorably, a real segment of American life in the 50's and 60's. It ought to be enjoyed by those who had similar experiences and to have a minor but secure place as a historical document. We all know a great deal more than we need to about the heroic youth of that era and their noble struggle for civil rights, peace, freedom, snottiness, drugs, degeneracy, terrorism, and treason. It is good to have on record some account of those who were young in that day and on the other side of the barricades.

Pat Buchanan suggests that the young conservatives of the period can be understood in terms of the aftermath of World War II. I think he is right and would carry the observation even further. How we split in the 60's depended upon which war we inherited. If our people were in the trenches in order to make the world safe for decency, we became "conservatives." Those from Washington bureaus who saw the war as a great social welfare project—to make the world safe for Eleanor Roosevelt and Uncle Joe—begat the radicals of the 60's. James Gould Cozzens foresaw it all in *Guard of Honor*. The same fault line decided Vietnam and will dictate the loss of Central America. There are too many Americans in high places who cannot accept an effective, reasonably decent, anti-Communist regime. They have to have an imaginary and impossible "democracy" in places where it never has nor ever will exist.

Perhaps *Right From the Beginning* was originally to be a campaign autobiography. If so, it evolved a great deal. It ends where such a biography would begin, with Buchanan at 28, about to start his career as a draftsman for the mighty. His last two chapters, however, appear to be a campaign platform, full of worthwhile plans for specific action.

He is, however, neither shallow nor optimistic enough for the hustings. He begins with T.S. Eliot's observation, almost a half century ago now, that democracy is not enough. Democracy is fine and necessary (and the only possible arrangement for Americans, Mr. Buchanan adds), but it is only a method—it does not have enough content to sustain us. "If you will not have God (and He is a jealous God)," said Eliot, "you should pay your respects to Hitler and Stalin."

"The hard truth," glosses Buchanan, "with which conservatives must come to terms is that the resolution of America's social crisis may be beyond the realm of politics and government, in a democratic society." "Democracy really has no answer to decadence. . . ." "Naiveté is not our problem; the West's problem is willful self-delusion. The reason that we do not learn from history is that we do not wish to learn from history."

Nevertheless, the government must do what it can. Buchanan proposes a 10-plank platform, which is as much populist as Republican, and therefore will never be adopted by any party politician. Aside from the balanced budget, much of it has to do with repairing the havoc wrought by the Supreme Court in the issues of unborn life, religion, reverse discrimination, and the like. The only social concern omitted is immigration. Yet Pat Buchanan should know that there is no point in getting tough with the Chinese government while they are busy *colonizing our country*.

Buchanan is ready to go for national initiative and referendum, repeal of the two-term amendment, and limited terms for federal judges including the Supreme Court. The standpat conservatives will be shocked by his willingness to push this program through a new constitutional convention. This goes against the accepted wisdom, but as Buchanan points out, all proposed amendments would have to be approved by three fourths of the states—as good a guarantee as we could hope for. I agree. Constitutionally speaking, we could not be any worse off than we are. The work of our Founding Fathers cannot be endangered by a Constitutional Convention. It has already been destroyed. Such a convention might work, especially if there were a concerted effort to elect decent citizens to it and to ratifying conventions—people who had not been previously corrupted by public office.

All in all, Pat Buchanan's ideas would have made a great agenda for a Reagan administration in 1981—if there had ever been one.

(1988)

Murray Rothbard

Murray is no longer with us in the flesh, but the fireball of his mind and spirit will be giving us light and energy deep into the 21st century.

Two characteristics—in addition to genius, integrity, and courage—distinguished Murray from the official libertarians and conservatives of the Manhattan editorial towers and Washington foundations. First, a consummate comprehension of Misesian praxeology. He always understood economics as social and ethical human action in the fullest sense. Thus he was never taken in by slogans like "capitalism" and "free trade" when they were used as cover for special arrangements for special interests. Murray believed in economic liberty, pure and simple, an economic liberty to be practiced by genuine human beings, not by statistical abstractions.

Second, Murray was deeply learned in American history. His *Conceived in Liberty* is as good a libertarian history of the foundations of America as can be written. His works on *America's Great Depression, The Panic of 1819*, and the tortured history of banking and currency make these difficult and crucial matters comprehensible in a way that no other historian has even approached.

It was the clarity of his historical vision that gave Murray his inimitable grasp of the events of the day. A typical Rothbard essay (like "the November Revolution and its Betrayal" in the January 1995 Rothbard-Rockwell Report) cuts through propaganda, cant, and trivia to the heart and substance of the matter. The thing really at issue at that historical moment is left starkly naked in all its aspects. No shred or corner of the enemy's smokescreen is left to obscure the vision. This was intellect, ethics, and inspiration at work in perfect harmony.

Unlike the official libertarians and conservatives—the warfare wing of what Murray so aptly dubbed the "welfare-warfare state"—and like all great conservatives and libertarians, Murray did not advocate a particular version of the state. He knew America as a living proposition and a historical reality, not as a group of abstract slogans about equality and freedom. His analysis always centered on what a particular phenomenon portended for that real America.

Unlike any of the official theorists, as his works show, he deeply understood the religious dimension of the American character, and he deeply understood, and identified with, the rebellious populist streak that makes for what in the national character is truly and distinctly American. It was this, above all else, that deeply offended establishmentarians: the irreverent refusal to accept their elevated self-image at face value.

So Murray has gone on into the Valhalla of happy warriors, preceded by those other chieftains of American liberty, M.E. Bradford and Russell Kirk. They differed on much, but they shared much. They were all stiff-armed by the official libertarian/conservatives. They all knew and represented an America that extended beyond the Hudson River and before 1932. They all inspired thousands of the thoughtful and were—the word is not too strong—beloved. Beloved only as leaders of wisdom, truth, and courage can be in a time starved for genuine leadership.

We perhaps should forgive the official libertarian/conservatives for their endless offenses to these great men. The establishmentarians are products of World War II and the 1960's, both periods of radical deformation. They see themselves as the anointed mandarins of the New World Order to be imposed by the American state. They draw their models not from American history, of which they know nothing, but from the British imperial class; though they fall far short of being as bright or as tough as the Brits at their best.

So let them enjoy their wealth and power. They have seduced many but have inspired none. They are sometimes obeyed but never loved. Unlike Murray, they will be forgotten before the heat has vanished from the television screen.

(1995)

Russell Kirk

A Review of *America's British Culture*, by Russell Kirk, New Brunswick, New Jersey: Transaction Publishers, 1993, 122 pages.

For more than two centuries the English-speaking world has been occasionally graced by the appearance of a man of letters of a particular type not known elsewhere (though there is a distant model, perhaps, in Cicero). Dr. Samuel Johnson is the great exemplar of the phenomenon I have in mind. This man of letters, though broadly learned and capable of a scholarly exposition or a philosophical argument, is not a pedant. Capable of turning out a craftsmanlike story or poem, yet he is not a self-conscious artist. Able and willing, if the times are so disjointed as to demand it, to pen a scathing political polemic, he is definitely not an ideologue of the kind only too prevalent on the Continent (and in recent years, alas, in America).

The particular type of the man of letters of whom I speak graces his times because he preserves and renews the culture—man being in his primary aspect a culture-bearing animal, which is an attenuated modern way of saying he is made in the image of God. As a preserver and renewer of genuine culture, our true man of letters is immune from the curses of specialization, utilitarianism, trendiness, and conformity that dominate the public discourse in our times. He constitutes in himself a bridge between the everyday and the eternal, between life's shifting sensations and the essence of things known for truth. We think of, in this century, the examples of Chesterton and Belloc and C.S. Lewis. And on our side of the Atlantic in the second half of the twentieth century, of Russell Kirk.

The great man of letters, unlike the scholar or the artist or the politician, must necessarily be, like Russell Kirk, a Christian and a conservative. A Christian for the simple reason that the culture he preserves and renews is Christian. (Even the magnificent heritage of the ancients, as Kirk recounts in an interesting afterword to *America's British Culture*, is of use to us only through its Christian transformation.) A conservative because to preserve and renew—the great Burkean calculus—is to adhere to the essence, whatever adjustments the endless flux of this world requires in inessentials. And not a mere conservative, but, like Russell Kirk, a radical conservative. For to discern and adhere to the essence is always a radical act in a world where rulers and majorities sometimes or often mistake shadows for things. Such a conservative is not, cannot be, a mere standpatter and vested-interest defender. Though he is, paradoxically, able to appreciate the much-neglected virtues of standpattism and even vested interests in an age when innovative sophists and calculators have caused infinitely more harm than has mere stupid resistance to change. As Dr. Kirk puts it: "Modern men and women live in an age in which the expectation of change often seems greater than the expectation of continuity."

Or, in other words, a barbarous and inhumane age. That our culture is in a parlous state is hardly debatable, at least for anyone who grasps what a "culture" is. (Dr. Kirk defines it for us in his first chapter, "The Necessity for a General Culture," an exposition too thorough and penetrating for my synoptic powers.) A parlous state we are in, but how much worse off we would be if it had not been for Russell Kirk and his gallant fight for the moral imagination that is the essence of our civilization. A fight carried out for decades now in countless battles and skirmishes on many fronts. We have no better example of resourceful defense of unchanging principle, through bad times and worse.

And of all the battles, it is possible that none has been more serious than that which calls forth *America's British Culture*. The occasion is always grave when it is necessary to defend obvious truths. The obvious truth, for instance, that what we know as America was and is British in culture. It is a truth that our forefathers seldom remarked upon for the same simple reason that a fish does not notice the water he swims in. The powers that be have banished the obvious truth and proclaimed as an operative principle an obvious untruth: multiculturalism. Multiculturalism is, as Dr. Kirk argues beyond dispute, not many cultures but no culture, or, in fact, an anti-culture. For a true culture is, of course, an inheritance, an achievement, a tradition, grown not made. Not a decree of the state but a seamless web of the everyday and the eternal, the high and the low.

In four concise, deeply and broadly learned, hard-hitting chapters, Dr. Kirk ranges over the centuries and brings home pointedly the obvious truth: the Britishness of our culture. Chapters devoted to the magnificent English language and its unparalleled literature; the unexampled heritage of Anglo law that accomplishes the impossible reconciliation of liberty and order; the great evolved achievement of representative, deliberative, constitutional government; the theological, moral, and educational patrimony in the peculiarly British form which makes our tradition. Things in the absence of any of which there would be no America.

America's British Culture is a great exercise in the man of letters' unending task of the renewal of culture. It is one of the best and most lasting of Kirk's many books. It is a splendid handbook for teachers of history, literature, and government. More, it is an example of the moral imagination at work. Our official culture is made by people who have neither morals nor imagination—who, indeed, hardly believe in the existence of what these words represent.

They believe not in culture but in schemes and manipulations, of which multiculturalism is only the latest and one of the worst. They have given us, as Kirk shows, "communication skills" in place of poetry, sociological statistics in place of history, "critical legal studies" in place of jurisprudence, ideological constructs in place of right reason. They have convinced many, including many who fancy themselves to be conservatives and defenders of culture, that America is not a living heritage but merely a notion, infinitely malleable.

And, possibly worst of all, they have destroyed the real possibility of multiculturalism, of a harmonious coexistence of cultures. Who is grounded well in his own civilization can appreciate the unique characteristics and virtues of another. What the multiculturalist wants is not multiple and mutually respectful cultures but a monolithic anti-culture of his own devising.

Having shown us what we stand to lose, are already losing, our man of letters outlines in his last chapter, "Renewing a Shaken Culture," the beginnings of a program for recovery: "If America's British culture is to be reinvigorated, its roots must be watered."

(1993)

Richard Weaver

Books Reviewed: *The Vision of Richard Weaver*, edited by Joseph Scotchie, New Brunswick, New Jersey: Transaction Publishers, 1995, 245 pages; and *Richard M. Weaver, 1910–1963: A Life of the Mind*, by Fred Douglas Young, Columbia: University of Missouri Press, 1995, 224 pages.

Richard Weaver once wrote that it was difficult to perceive the decline of civilization because one of the characteristics of decline was a dulling of the perception of value, and thus of the capacity to judge the comparative worth of times. Weaver, I think, did not have us common folk in mind, for whom it is not at all hard to see when things are getting worse. When the rich flee to guarded enclaves; when the middle class dissolves into the proletariat; when the distinction between citizen and foreigner is lost; when savage criminals go free; when populai culture is reduced to brutal trivialities with no vestige of Christian civilization—then we know that something is wrong.

Weaver's remarks were addressed rather to the post-World War II intelligentsia who were busy laying out plans for a New World Order. We have grown accustomed to Weaver's accomplishments and have to be reminded of the heroic context in which they were made—how out of step he was with the glorious dawn of global democracy that formed the stuff of public discourse in the 1940's. The intelligentsia, after all, spent World War II safely in the United States, gaining in pay, prestige, and power. They did not see the war as the nadir of Western civilization but as a gloriously elating opportunity.

That many of us are able to perceive the moral reality of our times in our materially obsessed culture is due in no small measure to Richard Weaver, the monkish scholar who died at 53, leaving a legacy of eight slim books, half of them published after his death. The scenario of Western decline that Weaver analyzed in *Ideas Have Consequences* and *Visions of Order* is confirmed by every day's news (both its content and its form). He is now accepted as a prophet and one of our keenest social observers. He has attracted considerable attention (nine Ph.D. dissertations so far) and will attract more. Besides the volumes in hand, there are at least three other scholars preparing works on the North Carolinian philosopher.

Mr. Scotchie's collection, the most valuable contribution to Weaver scholarship so far, should have been published long ago. It gathers 16 previously published (from 1964 to 1992) commentaries on Weaver's individual works, Weaver as rhetor, Weaver as Southerner, and Weaver's legacy. The authors include Chilton Williamson, Jr., M.E. Bradford, Marion Montgomery, and Thomas Landess. The many-faceted treatment confirms our sense of Weaver's enduring importance. (How many celebrated and highly rewarded intellectuals of his time are now utterly and justly forgotten! So it ever has been and is.)

Mr. Young has written a thorough and detailed biography from letters and interviews. He has also elaborated on the background to and influences on each of Weaver's works, giving them a context that we previously had only in fragments. The influences are clear—the Southern Agrarians, in particular John Crowe Ransom's "unorthodox defense of orthodoxy," and Donald Davidson's teaching of "language as a covenant." We learn how Weaver felt about the moral ambiguity of war, and how his deep thinking differed from the gibbering Chicago intellectuals with whom he was thrown.

Out of this heritage and a lifetime of hard study, the reclusive scholar fashioned, as Thomas Landess writes, "a splendid vision of order that no crew of sleek upstarts can ever tear down."

(1996)

James Burnham

A Review of *Power and History: The Political Thought of James Burnham*, by Samuel T. Francis, Lanham, Maryland: University Press of America, 1984, 141 pages.

Without presuming to provide a definitive list of the elements that make up that phenomenon or tendency known in the second half of the twentieth century as conservatism, one can state with certainty one that is essential—a realistic concept of the limitations of human nature and human potential, based upon both history and practical experience. No American political thinker of our era has better exemplified this stern and hallowed dictum than James Burnham. It was, as Dr. Samuel T. Francis shows, one of the unifying themes of Burnham's various books and of his *National Review* column (1955–1978).

Francis's respectful examination of Burnham's thought is an exemplary piece of intellectual history in its succinctness and precision and in the insight with which it discerns and portrays recurrent and characteristic themes. Burnham's writings were all to some degree entangled in the issues and events of their own day. By looking at them systematically and in retrospect, as a completed corpus, Francis has given Burnham's thought a consistency and a depth that do not self-evidently emerge from particular works.

By this analysis Burnham's realism has its roots in a Western tradition going back to antiquity and usually associated with the great Renaissance realist Machiavelli. In Burnham's case the influence was refined through the medium of the two modern social thinkers who figured in his 1943 book, *The Machiavellians: Defenders of Freedom*—Vilfredo Pareto and Gaetano Mosca. Machiavelli's sincere republicanism did not prevent him from looking candidly, some would say cynically, at men and motives. In fact, one might argue, only through such toughness of mind could the hope of republicanism be kept alive. By the same token, Burnham's very allegiance to Western liberty forced him to look realistically at its weaknesses and saved him from that easy and sentimental faith in the certainty of its endurance that characterized his time. His apprehension of the vulnerability of the West could only have been reinforced by his personal experience before 1940 inside the communist beast and his intimate acquaintance with the merciless efficiency of Marxist dialectics. In the final analysis, few Americans were better equipped to look this frightful century unflinchingly in the face.

Burnham thus had a unique immunity to the two most characteristic failings of his countrymen—sentimentality and superficiality. Pareto and Mosca, as well as Marx, taught Burnham that the study of politics is the study of elites and that elites must be understood in a functional rather than an ideological sense. While the attention of the fashionable opinion leaders was focused on emergent liberalism as a set of enlightened policies, appropriate to the day, Burnham almost alone was asking what the liberal worldview and its characteristic purveyors portended for the West in a functional sense. Using Pareto's concept of the circulation of elites between lions and foxes, he was able to describe the changes taking place in American society in a deep historical perspective. *The Managerial Revolution* (1941), though wrong in many details and not quite emancipated from Marxist vocabulary, did make the essential point that the nature of leadership—the attitudes and characteristics of the elite and therefore its capacity to meet crisis, internal or external—was changing. This was bound to lead to a change in the Western position in the world. At the end of this chain of analysis was a natural conclusion in *Suicide of the West: An Essay on the Meaning and Destiny of Liberalism* (1964). Functionally—stripped of its subjectivities and sentimentalities—liberalism was the ruling foxes' ideological rationalization for dallying with grave threats to domestic tranquility and the common defense.

In between *The Managerial Revolution* and *Suicide of the West* were works that filled out descriptive aspects of the revolution, like *Congress and the American Tradition* (1959), or works that illuminated how the new elite was facing and should face its greatest challenge: *The Struggle for the World* (1947), *Containment or Liberation?* (1952), *The Web of Subversion* (1954), *The War We Are In* (1967). In these books and by his fortnightly exposure in *National Review*, Burnham not only positioned himself as a major figure in the conservative alternative; he also added a new dimension to that alternative. While approving the free market and tradition, Burnham always stressed the gravity of the present threat to Western liberty and therefore the insufficiency of pleasant and traditional nostrums. In other words, he continued to remind a rather feckless folk of the hardness of historical choice. His distaste for the managerial elite, that is, the regime of liberalism, never led him into nostalgia for its predecessor, the entrepreneurial elite. It was the inadequacy of their predecessors that had left the field to the liberals. One could not look back. One could only look forward, bleak as that prospect might be.

Perhaps the one unsatisfying aspect of this study is its lack of a comparative perspective. In order to appreciate fully the stature of Burnham's achievement, we need to compare his thought with that of the men who passed for the best thinkers of the West at the same time. This comparative perspective would perhaps have taken the study beyond the author's purposes, and there is a virtue in Francis's narrow, unwavering focus on his subject. However, Burnham would have appeared at his best by contrast with his pretentious contemporaries. The concept of the "managerial revolution" stands tall in comparison with the naive faith in democratic technocracy that formed the public gospel of 1941. (This faith in utopia to be brought by a combination of mass sentiment and manipulation by a technical elite remains to this day the central tenet and lowest common denominator of the liberal mentality. Part of Burnham's virtue was to discern that this was no more nor less than the rationalization of the substitution of oligarchy for a republic of self-governing citizens.) And Burnham's assessment of the Red menace, again, looks best in comparison with the fetish for cultivation of "world opinion" that largely governed at the same time.

One could make a long list of pompous nincompoops who flourished in the last three or four decades, who were awarded with media adulation, office, and money for no greater achievement than mouthing the superficial analyses of the day. In any state one prospers by serving the ruler. In a democracy one flatters the people (or the media, which usurp the voice of the people). But democracy can only survive if it can continue to turn out from time to time men willing to tell what is true rather than what is flattering or comforting. Burnham is one of such in a time in which they have never been rarer.

One finds in his stern and solitary figure only one missing element—another of those elements which, along with realism, constitutes an indispensable element of conservatism. That is an awareness of a divine presence in the universe. His later writings give an intellectual obeisance to this awareness, but nowhere does it shine through with a spiritual conviction. Not himself, perhaps, completely attuned to the spiritual essence of Western civilization, he was still able to think as realistically and honestly as any man about the necessary conditions for its preservation.

Much of the writing by conservatives about conservative thinkers falls into one of two types. Either it is excessively (though understandably) adulatory, or it constitutes an exercise in exclusion: the promotion of one style of conservatism over its competitors, the competitors to be read out of the faith. To both these approaches Francis has supplied an alternative worthy of imitation. While he clearly admires Burnham, he has examined his ideas with the same hard, classical detachment with which Burnham has examined the world, and in a prose as austere and lucid as that of his subject. The result is a model analysis: a serious mind pondering and assessing a serious mind. As such, this book constitutes a benchmark on the path to maturity of conservative scholarship. We can only hope that it will inspire similar succinct and hard-hitting studies of other giants among our fathers—Weaver, Kendall, Meyer, Kirk, Molnar, and others.

(1984)

Sam Francis

"A Day With Sam Francis," Willie Pie's Store, Crozier, Viriginia, December 26, 1992.

It is a great pleasure and honor for a mere Carolinian to be here on the hallowed soil of the Old Dominion to take part in the wonderful tradition of Willie Pie's Store—this celebration of the best intellectual and moral heritage of the South. I have often said that if we had one impresario like David Bovenizer in every state in the South, we could take back our country from the interlopers who now control it. If we had one David Bovenizer in every county in the South, we could take over the world—though of course we would not want to do anything so silly.

If our country is to be saved, the initiative will have to come from the South. John C. Calhoun said: "You know that it is an axiom with me, that every revolution in favor of liberty in our system, must be effected by the South, and, I may add, the South headed by Virginia." He repeated the same idea many times. I propose it as a motto for our gathering today.

So it is fitting that our conversation celebrates a strong, clear Southern voice in the cause of republican liberty: Dr. Samuel T. Francis, the distinguished syndicated columnist for the *Washington Times* and contributing editor of *Chronicles*. Dr. Francis has raised American public discourse to a new high of intelligence and realism and historical scope in a time when the discussion of public affairs has never been more trivialized and lacking in integrity. For which point I call to witness the juvenilia of the present presidential campaign.

Sam Francis is a Tennessean. He was graduated from Johns Hopkins and holds a doctorate in history from the University of North Carolina at Chapel Hill. I was fortunate to know Sam in our graduate school days when he was the spearhead of a conservative group which was the intellectual and ethical highpoint of my education, as it was for others.

I had published a few small pieces in *Modern Age* and *National Review*, and I remember well Sam calling me up and flattering me into attending the meetings by telling me I was "the best known conservative writer on campus." I had a full-time graduate load, a full-time job, and a family, and was not inclined to take on any more activities, but I attended, and kept on as long as I was at Chapel Hill. The Chapel Hill Conservative Club was the germinating point for a proliferating circle of friendships and careers. You would recognize immediately many of the names. The circle is strongly reflected in the books *Why The South Will Survive* and *The New Right Papers* and in the present board of editors of *Chronicles* magazine.

On leaving UNC Sam worked for the Heritage Foundation as a foreign policy analyst and as national security advisor for our lamented friend Senator John

P. East. He then joined the editorial page of the *Washington Times*, in its early days. As deputy editorial page editor he won twice in succession the prestigious writing award of the American Society of Newspaper Editors, an unprecedented achievement. He is now a syndicated columnist for the *Times* and also widely known for his monthly columns in *Chronicles*, a brilliant collection of which will soon appear in a book. Those who have survived the famous Lost Weekends of *Chronicles* editors in Rockford know also that Sam is a man of infinite jest and a great raconteur. He is the author, as well, of *Power and History: The Political Thought of James Burnham*, and a contributor to other books.

Dr. Francis's stature has been increasingly recognized of late. He was selected by Patrick J. Buchanan to take over his column when Mr. Buchanan was diverted by other activities recently. Just last month Sam was described by the *New Republic*, in an analysis of contemporary conservatism, as the "guru" of the Paleoconservatives. I am delighted to think that I know a guru, as I have never known a real one before.

Without presuming to provide a definitive list of the elements that make up a true conservatism, we can state with certainty one essential—a realistic conception of the limitations of human nature and human potential in this fallen world—a sense of limitations based upon history, upon practical experience, and upon Revelation.

Amidst the fatuous petty utopianism that pervades American public discourse, Sam Francis's strong clear voice of realism rings above the babble. The peculiar failings of the predominant American mind since the war (and I do not need to tell this group which war I refer to) are these—superficiality and sentimentality. Dr. Francis's writings have shown a rare immunity from these failings. To avoid superficiality we need to look at what is, not at what is said to be. To avoid sentimentality we must take men as they are. That is what our Founding Fathers did.

That is what Dr. Francis does in his commentary. Trenchantly and often humorously he conveys the deeper structure of the world and the larger meaning of the passing hubbub of the day's events. (As to the humor, my favorite is the image of Old Dutch being strapped to his pony to be sent home to California at the end of his reign, to the consternation of the swarm of patronage artists who had fattened off his regime.) No one does this better. This immensely gifted commentator has a range that covers history, economics, political power, sociology, and culture with equal ease. He has raised public commentary in the syndicated column to heights of seriousness and intelligence not reached in a long time. I was about to say since Walter Lippmann. But Walter Lippman was not really as good as he is supposed to have been, and Sam is much better.

One of the most pleasing things about Sam's career is the way in which he has continued to grow in depth and scope. Unlike the babble of commentators that clutter the press and the airwaves, he keeps getting better. It is one of the characteristics of American commercial communications that when someone succeeds, the overwhelming temptation is for them to keep on repeating over and over the same thing. Commentators become celebrities for repeating and caricaturing themselves. I offer in evidence the tragic denoument of William F. Buckley's career. Unlike these others, Sam keeps learning.

There is somewhere the silly idea grown up—stemming from willful misinterpretations of the Declaration of Independence spread by New Englanders and solidified by Lincoln's disingenuous cant about government of, by, and for the people—that tough realism is undemocratic, that we have to be naively stupid and optimistic to be supporters of a government of the people.

This was not true, emphatically, of our Founding Fathers. It was not true of the great thinkers from whom Sam Francis has drawn his lessons about the realities of power and elites in human society. His great teachers Machiavelli, Pareto, and James Burnham, were realists in defense of the liberty of the West. Let us not forget, despite Machiavelli's bad reputation, that he was a republican—his interest was not in promoting cynicism and ruthlessness for its own sake, but in preserving the safety of self-governing commonwealths by making their leaders tough and effective. Machiavelli was a republican who knew that republics could not survive in a hostile world by sentimentality and shallowness.

Likewise James Burnham, whose analysis of the managerial state Dr. Francis has applied, extended, and deepened. Burnham's experiences within the belly of the Communist beast taught him to study the nature and function of power without sentiment. Burnham's very allegiance to Western liberty, once he had won to it, forced him to look realistically at its weaknesses and kept him from too soft and easy a faith in the effortless triumph of democracy.

After World War II sentimental Liberalism was triumphant in the public discourse, from which no deviation went unpunished. Burnham alone was asking what the Liberal worldview and its characteristic purveyors portended for the West—truly, in a long range and functional sense. His answer was in his 1964 book *The Suicide of the West: The Meaning and Destiny of Liberalism*. Nothing has happened since, not even the fall of the Soviet Union, to change Burnham's sad predictions about the self-immolation of the West. If anything, the new challenges to the weaknesses of Liberalism are more deadly than communism because they are much more diffuse and less easily grasped and responded to.

Like Burnham, Francis knows that self-government and the free market and tradition are great things, but they do not in themselves spare us from the perils of a contingent world and the hardness of historical choice. Today Francis alone among the complacent conservatives and liberals calls us to these truths. When we look back and compare Burnham's thought with that of what passed for the wise men of his day, we can easily see who stood above the herd. The same will be true in the future. When the Safires and Buckleys and Tyrrells and Krauthammers and Wickers and all the other pretentious pundits are long forgotten, perceptive historians will be able to get a true reading of our own times from Dr. Francis.

Now in a time when third-raters occupy the seats of power and the forums of intellectual prestige and prattle on about New World Orders and The End of

History, even as the social fabric of the West unravels before our very eyes, we need badly a voice of truth and realism. Republican self-government can only survive if it can produce from time to time men who are willing to tell what is true rather than what is comforting and flattering. We are fortunate to have such a man in Sam Francis.

Clinton, Bush, et al.

The Reagan Revolution is dwindling down in its latter days into something that in the final analysis differs in only a few details from its predecessors. In fact, Reagan may have established that no Administration, no matter what its will or the size of its majority, can survive the push of the media and the pull of the bureaucracy.

Consider: An honorable nominee for Chief Justice of the United States is subjected to a marathon impugnation by Senators whose private moral character is such that no prudent man would leave them alone in a room with his female relatives or portable valuables. The Administration responds to this outrage by a policy of passive resistance.

Consider: An egregious interference into the complicated internal affairs of a remote country which has never expressed the slightest hostility toward us is promoted as a great moral victory. (Remember that this interference could not have been consummated without massive aid from the President's own party; that, though sought for decades, this interference never before occurred under even the most leftist administrations; and that it is as *certain* as any empirical prediction can be that our new South African policy—if it has any effect at all—will be disastrous for all parties in that country.)

Consider: Under the guise of "tax reform," some of the last remaining protections are stripped away from the property of the beleaguered middle class which surely constitutes the President's only real constituency.

Consider: The Strategic Defense Initiative, hailed as a means of breaking out of the mad equilibrium of MAD, bodes to become just another bargaining chip in the long-running "detente" pursued by previous Administrations.

And most egregiously, in my opinion, an Administration which took office with promises to get the government "off the people's backs" and to return to personal and community responsibility now spearheads a campaign of harassing citizens with "drug tests." With the President's example and precept, this practice is now being extended through the Federal bureaucracy and is inspiring a host of imitators in the corporate, state, and local governments.

It is tempting—especially as we hear the usual chorus of liberals, professional civil libertarians, and union bosses screaming opposition—to assume that "drug testing" must not be such a bad thing. However, even a blind hog will stumble over an acorn now and then, and we must be clear about what the President's policy means when viewed in the light of principle and as a stage in the historical devolution of his Administration.

The drug testing stunt, first of all, takes on the character of a random and arbitrary invasion of the privacy of citizens who have committed no offense. Its basic unexpressed assumption is authoritarian. The government does not, as we thought, belong to the citizens. Rather, the citizens are the property of the government, interchangeable nonentities who differ only in that they are more or less troublesome property. In a republic, the citizen is free and immune in his person and property unless he has compromised his rights by an offense against society, an offense established by his peers after due process. In an authoritarian government, on the other hand, we are only potential "social problems" who are to be handled by the government in whatever way it deems convenient.

Further, such a campaign is a reflection of the irrelevance and disingenuousness of an overextended and incompetent government—a government seeking to divert the attention of the people from its inability to perform the ends for which it was established. The government is unwilling to punish violations of the border—so it is proposed that 10th-generation Americans be forced to carry cards to prove they are not illegal aliens. The government is unable to curb violent criminals—so it is proposed to take all weapons away from law-abiding citizens. The family is falling apart—so let the government celebrate and subsidize "the alternative family." The government is unable to control the importation, vending, and abuse of illegal and dangerous substances—therefore present an illusion of concern and action by forcing a scientific test on everybody. Surely if such measures had been proposed in 1976 or 1980, Ronald Reagan would have ringingly declared that government ought to get on with prosecuting criminals and leave honest citizens alone.

The craze for drug testing tells us honest citizens, who try to obey the laws and stay as much as we are able within the bounds of decency, that our efforts at self-government are worthless and without reward, that we are in the eyes of the government that was once our property nothing except statistical raw material, with no more rights than the worst of our fellows. And what does the craze tell us about the state of management and leadership in our society? In every part of the Federal bureaucracy we have well-paid supervisors. Do these supervisors not know when those who work under them are abusing drugs to any degree that interferes with normal performance? Are they inattentive? Do they not know normal performance when they see it? Do they lack authority to act without the deceptively "hard" evidence of a urinalysis?

And this is the same President who sent his condolences to Rock Hudson. We do not wish to quarrel with an act of individual kindness to the dying. However, a consistent moral position does not emerge from the data. If it is the President's duty to shepherd us into the paths of clean living, should he not be consistent?

In fact, it would appear that this rather un-Reaganish Reagan policy, when its origins are closely scrutinized, is a result of what our ancestors, in a very wise prejudice, would have decried as "petticoat government." I hasten to affirm that I heartily rejoice that many fine wearers of petticoats have won elections and served ably in public office. But why should we suffer under policies made by persons whose only qualification is that their petticoats were purchased by someone who has won an election? Our ancestors, who are now spinning in their graves at approximately the speed of sound, would have regarded this as one of the contemptible defects of *monarchy*, and gloried that their republic was free of such abuses.[1]

Meanwhile, Rome burns. Our politicians, too often, lack the talent to fiddle. Yet even if they dare not even mention any of our real problems for fear of offending some segment of the electorate or media, they can call a press conference and congratulate themselves that they are virile enough to p--s in a bottle.

(1987)

✫✫✫

Cui bono? That is the question to ask now that the fur and feathers have settled from the celebrated January match between gamecock Vice President Bush and wildcat Dan Rather. Clearly the answer is George Bush. Before the encounter Bush had two serious liabilities: a general impression of wimpishness and a lingering taint (at least among grass roots conservatives) of Liberal Republicanism.

All that, it would appear, was turned completely around in less than 10 minutes. The Vice President is now the hero of 10,000 American barrooms, where people are slapping each other on the back and saying: "How about ole Bush? The first guy to tell off Rather since George Wallace!" And the conservatives, always ready to grasp at a straw, are telling themselves that if CBS wanted to get the Vice President that bad, he must be better than they feared.

Paranoids on the old right suspect that the whole thing was an orchestrated affair. Imagine what's going on in the minds of the CBS brass: The American rubes are no longer buying the Democrats. Since even a replay of Watergate didn't work, the next President will be a Republican. Which one of those guys can we live with? Obviously Bush. If we put Rather on his tail, we can kill two birds with one stone: Wipe out the wimp image and get rid of Rather, whose behavior is increasingly bizarre.

Stranger things have happened. The TV bosses have always, in fact, tried to orchestrate the Republican Party. In 1964, during their stop-Goldwater phase, they promoted the ineffably forgettable Governor Scranton into a national folk hero in a matter of a few days. They kept alive the hopeless presidential candidacy of the late Governor Rockefeller for 20 years. (If I recall rightly, some of them were still touting his inevitable victory right down to the second day of the Republican National Convention in 1968.)

With Bush, they have something to work with. It has always, actually, been unkind and unfair to consider the Vice President a wimp. He has more courage and integrity than most politicians. His real weakness is not in his character, it is in his intellect. George Bush has never had an *idea* that was a genuine solid con-

---

1. The world had hardly yet heard of Hillary Rodham Clinton when these words were written.

viction learned in the school of real life. That is, he has never taken a public stand that had behind it anything more than pleasant plausibility and vague good intentions. Duking it out with Dan Rather over whether or not he was asleep at what meeting does not change this a bit.

In this, he is simply nothing more and nothing less than the legatee of Liberal Republicanism. Viewed over the long haul of its history, the Republican Party (like the Democratic) is a strange, strange entity. Now, nearing the end of the Reagan revolution, the Republican Party finds itself with no capacity to move constructively into the future, or to do anything but fade reflexively back into its past. Its leading candidate is a throwback to Rockefeller and Scranton, and its second chance, Senator Dole, is a throwback to Nixon and Ford. Some revolution. (Of course, I am forgetting Representative Kemp, who is a throwback to Horace Greeley. The most positive force in the party, Mr. Robertson, brings back happy memories of William Jennings Bryan, who was, alas, a Democrat.)

If Bush could somehow dedicate himself to continuing the Reagan program, there might be some hope. We knew, in 1980, or thought we knew, what the Reagan program was. The trouble is, now, nobody has the slightest idea what the "Reagan program" means. There are many, many reasons why this is so, but one of them is that what Mr. Reagan stood for has been hopelessly blurred and diffused by the former Bush supporters with whom the President has stocked his administration.

Reaganism is over, whoever is nominated. I am betting that within hours after President and Mrs. Reagan take off for the ranch next January, no one will even remember it, not even professional Republicans and commentators with a slow news day.

(1988)

☆☆☆

The phenomenon of popular movements of protest succeeding and then being swallowed up by the Establishment is not a new story in American history, but the fate of "conservatism" in the last decade or so gives a remarkable case study. Not long ago, after ages of liberal dominance, conservatism seemed to be in the ascendancy both intellectually and at the grassroots level. Somewhere between the election of 1980 and now, a vast popular demand for reform was captured and emasculated by party politicians and literary spoilsmen, so that conservatism has ended up as nothing more than a vague rhetorical label for a very slightly modified form of Liberal Establishment.

These reflections are ignited by the sad fate of two erstwhile fighting conservatives, Jack Kemp and William Bennett. Both these gentlemen were youthful (as national politicians go), energetic, and articulate. Both have ended up in petty administrative posts in a "moderate" Republican administration—posts from which they cannot possibly draw any credit. In fact, I will bet a bound volume of, say, the last good year of *National Review* (1968) that they are politically dead.

That Kemp accepted the post of Secretary of HUD and Bennett that of "Drug Czar" speaks well for their honorable desire for public service. It speaks poorly indeed for their political judgment. In fact, only a very slight and healthy bit of paranoia would suggest that they have been deliberately tricked into corners where they could be finished off as rivals and critics of Bush. Can one detect the quick and dirty hands of Mr. Atwater and Mr. Baker at the bottom of this smooth and barely noticeable coup?

Maybe so or maybe not. We won't know for a long time, maybe never. The media don't notice intraparty dirty tricks (quite as common as the interparty ones) because they would take too much work to ferret out, and they are really only interested in dirty tricks against liberals. If neither Kemp nor Bennett can possibly emerge from the present posts except as weaker public figures than they were, then *cui bono*? The party operatives have disarmed youthful, energetic, articulate, and potentially troublesome figures, and we are left with the Vice-President, who is a handpicked man and who is, well, youthful. Not long ago there were half a dozen solid aspirants to the leadership of "conservatism" in the Republican Party. Now there are no conservatives at all, just Republicans.

It is a shame to see useful men destroyed by their own virtues. Both of them have accepted the major premises of the Liberal Establishment, which they have attacked only on marginal and instrumental questions. Both have been fairly popular with the media, which is a certain sign that they are not too serious a threat to the Establishment. But they had the virtue of standing for *something*.

Mr. Kemp seems an honorable man, no small accomplishment for someone who was a denizen of the House of Representatives for so long. His arm-waving invocations of 19th-century egalitarian mythology disgust conservatives, but they energized the Republican electorate, or at least three percent of them. (When a Kemp-for-President rally was held in my very conservative area, no one showed up except some fraternity boys looking for free beer, and two very rustic libertarians from the Pee Dee Swamp.)

The appropriate thing for Mr. Kemp to do was to go back to New York (or even his native Southern California, where earnest superficiality would be an asset) and run for senator or governor. He would have lost but gained credit. There must be some strange defect in judgment in a free marketeer who takes on a government boondoggle in the hopes of transforming it by the spirit of enterprise. (His assumption seems to be that the spirit of free enterprise can be created by government subsidy.) Surely every public figure in Washington on Kemp's level knew the HUD scandals had to break soon. Even if guiltless of wrongdoing, his name will hereafter be indelibly associated with a scandal from which he cannot possibly gain any credit, especially after his naive and premature defense of his predecessor.

(Since HUD exists totally and entirely for the purpose of bribing contractors, white collar "experts," local politicians, and the more clever and less scrupulous members of minority groups, how are we to distinguish the illegal graft that is supposed to have taken place from the legal graft that goes on as a matter of course?)

Mr. Bennett, for all his eloquence and wit, has fallen into the same trap. Does he or anyone really believe that the drug-taking portion of the American public can be educated into giving up their hobby with exhortations to "democratic values"? There are only two ways that drug-taking will be stopped: effective local enforcement against users, with swift, long, and certain prison terms; or the return of a very muscular form of Christianity to the hells of the streets. Neither of these things is going to happen. There is no way Mr. Bennett can win his war, and he will go down as a failure who met none of his promises.

In a sense both of these gentlemen deserve their fate, but it would have been much better if they had been overcome by superior ideas rather than by political operatives utterly devoid of idea and principle.

(1989)

☆☆☆

Governor Clinton's candidacy for President, plagued as it's been by charges of marital infidelity and draft evasion, has brought to the fore once again the question of whether personal character is relevant to fitness for public office. There are those to whom it is obvious that private behavior is relevant to public office. Others contend that public officials should be measured by their public acts and their private lives left alone. The latter position may have had some validity in older and better days of the Republic, when private life and public affairs were distinct spheres of life. The fact that the bachelor Grover Cleveland had possibly, as a young man, fathered an illegitimate child did not affect his capacity to execute the duties of Chief Magistrate of the Union, because he did not aspire to be anything more than a chief magistrate. That is, he sought nothing more than to execute the laws in keeping with his office, just as he had done as sheriff of Buffalo, where his duties had included that of hangman, and as governor of New York.

But the case is very different now, because the separation of state and society has completely broken down. When the state has its hand in our pocket, tells us with whom we may associate, threatens to regulate our spiritual life, and generally superintends us from cradle to grave, the private virtues of public officials, or lack thereof, become significant to us. This is especially true of those who put themselves forward upon a politics of moralism. Martin Luther King's lying and lechery might not invalidate his public position, but when his public position rests upon his role as a religious and moral leader whose chief business is to break down the barrier between private morality and public policy, then it does indeed become highly relevant. No one is entitled to be a saint until they have been examined by the devil's advocate.

Imagine the misery the Republic would have been spared if the private defects of character of John Kennedy and Lyndon Johnson had been widely known. Certainly neither would have been elected had the public been aware of what is readily known now. We have had, since Kennedy, a politics in which public figures have tried to carry the day by the glamour of high moral purpose—in which case private character becomes extremely relevant. Since the Kennedys have prospered largely through celebration of their glamour and virtues, we are entitled to know the other side of the story. Think what would have been saved to the Treasury if the people had known in advance about Senator Cranston's methods of campaign finance. But, of course, our great crusading media hid all these things from us, not considering them relevant. Imagine the barrage of sensationalism we would have received if poor Nixon, or Goldwater, or George Wallace had been guilty of 1 percent of the *private* malfeasance of Kennedy or Johnson. We can always count on the media to pursue their own agenda. Which is why we have seen a sudden rehabilitation of Dan Quayle, as the media have realized his usefulness in putting down a really dangerous conservative like Pat Buchanan.

In the meantime, we must insist that we have complete information about those who put themselves forward for public trusts. We want to know if our surgeon drinks or is a homosexual, if our accountant gambles, or our clergyman lives too well, and we are entitled to know what we need to know that is relevant to judging the character of those who seek to be entrusted with the fate of the Republic. It is reasonable to assume that the people are smart enough to distinguish between a youthful indiscretion, which few have escaped, and a real character problem, or whether a particular failing is relevant to public performance. When we judge Mr. Warren Beatty as an actor or Mr. Magic Johnson as an athlete, we should perhaps pay attention to their professional performance and not their private lives. But if they endorse a presidential candidate or are held up as a model for our youth, then we are entitled to enquire into questions of character.

In the old Republic private and public life were distinct, but it was also understood that a successful government of the people depended upon private virtue, in the people and the leaders. The office of the presidency, after all, was designed with George Washington in mind.

(1992)

Clinton-bashing is a tempting sport, as indicated by the phenomenal popularity of Rush Limbaugh. But like everything that is too easy, it has its pitfalls. It will be a fruitless enterprise if it merely succeeds in tearing down Clinton to make way for a lackluster Republican administration only marginally better on the critical issues.

Clinton's band of lowlifes does provide a good target—his awful wife, his zoo of appointees (Trachtenberg, Shalala, Elders, Bentsen, Reno, Christopher, *ad infinitum*). Yet these indicate not so much the evil of Clinton or of the Democratic Party as what American society and the American political system have become. The Republican Party, after all, gave us Justices Brennan, Blackmun, and Souter; "Condom" Koop; Packwood of the wayward tongue; Frohnmeyer of the NEA; proscription of serious Christians from policy-making; double prosecution of the L.A. cops; NAFTA; Somalia; and "no new taxes." The distinction is nothing to get excited about.

Despite his public and private shortcomings, it is not apparent to me that Clinton is of a quality significantly below the general level of American leadership. He is more intelligent than any Republican of recent history except Nixon. There is no reason to believe he is less sincere or competent or more prone to lust and greed than many other politicians.

My friend Murray Rothbard has complained that Clinton is "an Arkansas peckerwood in the White House." Would that it were so. That would be cause for rejoicing. But he is not: He is a typical Southern liberal—i.e., a horrible opportunist but also generally less dangerous than a real liberal. It is a peculiar feature of the mainstream American public consciousness that an evil and bumbling Southerner seems even more evil and bumbling than his mainstream counterpart. Thus Clinton, like Carter, makes an easy target for demagoguery. Even more peculiarly, reflecting the ambiguity and love-hate with which the South has always been regarded, a Southerner also seems more decent, which made it possible for Carter and Clinton to be elected when a real liberal could not.

I have never been able to get exercised about the harm Clinton could do. More opportunist than George Bush? Dumber than Jack Kemp? Meaner than Bill Bennett? Clinton seems to have a core of authenticity, measured by the fact that he has made no effort to change his native accent (unlike Albert Gore, Jr., who is a museum-quality specimen of the Southern rich boy who went away to prep school in the East and came back sounding and acting like a complete phony).

I have always thought that given Clinton's naturally cautious and compromising style, and his election as a minority candidate (something he owes entirely to Pat Buchanan and Ross Perot and not to the Republican Party), he would not be able to accomplish anything very significant—despite his execrable company and symbolism—and would therefore be less dangerous than an effective George Bush.

At least the Democrats, unlike the Republicans, actually try to represent their constituency, which is what they are supposed to do in a democracy. This seems to me a moral advantage over the Republican Party, which has been repeatedly elected to represent the middle class, limited government, and traditional values, to none of which it has any honest commitment. It has basically perpetrated a fraud, thus promoting a cynicism and despair among decent Americans that is much more destructive than any watered-down socialist schemes Clinton may be able to get through.

The Republican Party is not and never has been able to meet a challenge such as our times present. The best it can do is call out Dan Quayle to defend the family and to promote semisocialist schemes of "empowerment." Conceived in greed, hypocrisy, and fanaticism, the Republican Party has never performed any positive role, except tacitly. It serves two functions in the American body politic: defending the interests of American business, which it does incompetently (in regard to legitimate small business, though competently with respect to the illegitimate demands of big business), and ratifying and consolidating previous Democratic programs (thus, the Kemp-Bennett empowerment program provides a final prop and validation for Lyndon Johnson's failed Great Society). There are a number of good young Republicans in Congress. But, witness my point, it has been the young New Democrats who have taken the effective lead on budget reduction, anti-NAFTA, and immigration control—a lead that Republicans by their nature are incapable of taking.

If we care for the fate of our dispirited and decaying Republic, if we want to mobilize the good qualities of the American character and not just reap temporary benefit from the natural public revulsion to Clintonism, then our first order of business must be to find a vehicle other than the Grand Old Party.

(1994)

✫✫✫

The November election revealed a populist upsurge of repugnance against Washington. In the current two-party system, this upsurge could only take the form of support for the Republicans.

If the Republicans are interested in real reform, they will act as statesmen and not politicians. A statesman is one who understands and pursues the long-range best interests of his people—not one whose range of vision is limited by the next TV interview, poll results, or brown bag of unmarked bills. If the Republicans were statesmen, the following is what they would do.

Cut taxes. As Edmund Burke said, the revenue is the state. It is all well and good to talk about welfare reform and cutting the paltry millions of the NEA. But nothing will be done about reforming the bloated federal government until its funds are squeezed off. They should also follow the lead of Representative Dick Armey, who is pushing for a middle-class tax cut.

Return to federalism. It may well be that the protest in many states against unfunded federal mandates is the most constructive development on the scene today, and let us hope it portends a real constitutional revolution. But the states should not only be resisting unfunded federal mandates—they should be resisting *all* federal mandates: That is what self-government is all about. True federalism is not when the federal government allows the states to do things. True federalism—as spelled out in the Constitution—is when the states forbid the federal government from doing things.

Curb illegal immigration and rethink legal immigration. It is the responsibility of Congress to look after the well-being of the American people and our posterity—not to provide jobs for the world's surplus population of Mexicans, Chinese, and Hindus. What is the point of preserving an economy and government if they are not ours? Republicans often act as if they thought the purpose of government was to keep the shopping malls full of warm bodies.

Eliminate the power of the federal courts to thwart majority will. As things now stand, any moral or mental cretin appointed to the federal bench 30 years ago by Lyndon Johnson can, by the stroke of a pen, overturn the democratic will and invalidate the results of any election. Until the national leadership undertakes serious, fundamental constitutional reform of the enormity of judicial usurpation, it is useless to talk of any other reforms. In fact, willingness to curtail the courts should be our measure of the seriousness of the Republican agenda during the next two years, since the black-robed deities will undoubtedly impose their will to thwart any genuine reform.

(1995)

☆☆☆

Myths are part of what makes us human; all peoples live by myths, some healthy, some destructive. Among the unhealthy beliefs that have been propagated amongst Americans are that the Constitution came from the gods; that the conquest and destruction of the Southern states was noble; that the Americans who fought and died in World War II were starry-eyed devotees of global democracy. And, worst of all, that the 1960's generation was the most idealistic and love-filled of all generations. In fact, that generation was the most spoiled, selfish, and vicious generation ever produced by America. I know. I was there and saw them first hand. Their destructiveness, irrationality, and irresponsibility were evident to anyone who looked. Their behavior has been blamed on Doctor Spock's doctrines of permissive child-rearing. But there already had to be some widespread defect of character for Spock to gain entry into so many homes.

The late undeclared war in the Balkans (like urban crime and the drug culture) is merely the natural outcome of the 60's. The Flower Child generation happily sends cluster bombs to destroy innocent people who have caused them frustration. It is not a reversal of character for them, but a natural expression of their customary self-righteousness, irresponsibility, and viciousness.

(1999)

The presidential election is still one year away, but now is the time for American patriots of all stripes to reconsider their political attachments. Since the end of World War II, domestic opponents of the American Empire have struggled fruitlessly to contain its growth. As a philosopher friend recently remarked, we have no politics today in America. There is no significant contest of issues, policies, or principles, merely an imperial party line adhered to by the media, the two-party cartel, and much, though certainly not all, of the vast American middle class.

The anti-imperialist movement has failed, most obviously because it has used the wrong vehicle—the Republican Party. The Democratic Party of the 1960's and 1970's was hopeless, and anti-imperialists accepted the only alternative available in the two-party system. But the Republican Party, in its origins, its predominant interests, and its natural ideology has always been a vehicle of the imperial state—even before the Democratic Party succumbed early in this century.

It is truly astounding that "conservatives" who have been betrayed over and over again by the empty rhetoric of shallow, cynical politicians should still, at this late date, be attached to this failed vehicle. But there are signs that the unnatural attachment is beginning to wear thin.

Third parties have no chance of winning—so goes the conventional wisdom. Very well, but the purpose of political action is not necessarily to win, but to influence the outcome. The most constructive antiestablishment influence exercised in recent history has come from the grassroots movements organized by George Wallace and Ross Perot. If Wallace had not built a large movement, the Republican Party would still be in rhetoric, as well as in actuality, the party of Rockefeller. And whatever may be said about Perot, he reduced the Democrats and Republicans both to minority parties in two presidential elections. If Pat Buchanan had run an independent campaign in 1992 or 1996, he would today exercise much more influence over events.

Even in my limited, mostly apolitical acquaintance there are numerous former stalwart Republican activists who have finally defected and are now without a home. What if dissidents—the Constitution (formerly U.S. Taxpayers), Reform, Southern, and Libertarian parties—could be united behind a presidential slate of integrity and articulateness—say, Sen. Bob Smith and Rep. Ron Paul? The object would not be to elect a President, but to change the terms of public discourse, to turn the press conferences called presidential "debates" into the real thing. Given a forum, men of character could easily uncover the empty suits of creatures like George W. Bush and Al Gore. The candidates would, of course, have to ignore the media and polls and speak directly to the people in every way possible.

Ideally, such a coalition would also field candidates in some states for the House of Representatives and governor, with the same object of education in view. There are plenty of articulate, attractive, and principled young conservatives around. In a three-way race with a strong ticket at the top, a few people might even be elected in the states. A long-range goal would be to get a balance of power in the U.S. House so that the two-party cartel would be unable to organize the process without concessions to the swing vote.

Here's a suggested platform that should appeal to all of the dissident parties: an immediate, real, and substantial middle-class tax cut; an immediate enforcement of immigration laws and a moratorium on legal immigration; an immediate end to affirmative action and a reduction of business regulations like the Americans With Disabilities Act; an investigation of the government atrocities at Waco and elsewhere and punishment of those responsible; defeminization of the military; an end to imperial military actions like Kosovo; legislation to enforce the Tenth Amendment by removing all state domestic concerns from the jurisdiction of federal courts, including criminal law and abortion; and an end to all federal expenditures and regulations regarding education.

I would advise setting aside the issues of Social Security, Medicare, and the federal debt for the nonce simply because the opportunity for two-party lies and confusion is too great. Other than that, add your own ideas, and I'll vote for them. Does anybody have a better idea?

(1999)

✭✭✭

It was Mencken, I think, who defined democracy as the system of government in which the people get what they deserve. In a similar spirit, I confess to having a grudging admiration for our retiring Chief Executive, Mr. Clinton.

Yes, I know he is a rake, a liar, and probably a psychopath. And he has advanced the centralization of corrupt power in Washington far more effectively than the "compassionate conservatives" are able to do with their best efforts. Limbaugh and the other Republican radio demagogues have not needed much wisdom or insight to convince a goodly portion of the American people that Clinton is an evil force.

But his depravity is not what distinguishes Clinton from the general run of politicians. Politics in our imperial system is the realm of vanity, greed, lust, lies, and exploitation. The politician in our system is one who holds you in contempt and picks your pocket while persuading you he is your friend and benefactor. In some misspent years in youth as a newspaper reporter, I saw this pervasively in operation even in the paltry strivings of mayors, police chiefs, and county officials.

Clinton is not notable because of his depravity. He is notable because he is so good at it! I am old enough to remember when Governors of Arkansas were regarded by the federal government and respectable opinion as fit for nothing except suppression by paratroopers.

Here is a governor of Arkansas, without money or inherited position, twice elected to the most powerful office in the world. What a performance! He beat the great lights of Northeastern Liberalism—Kennedy, Cuomo, etc.—on their own turf, and then whipped the best that Skull and Bones and country club Republicanism were able to match against him. And he kept the bicoastal Hollywood and media celebrities and financial tycoons, who normally should have despised him, eating out of his hand!

Without even bothering to change his accent! (Yes, I know it is better to have a man of good character as President than a man of high intelligence. But do we really have to settle for the astonishingly mediocre alternatives which the "opposition party" has fielded against Clinton and his successor?)

Clinton is too intelligent to believe the Maoist claptrap he spouts so smoothly. He is probably too depraved to believe anything. (Unlike the new Senator from New York, who is a museum quality specimen of the Deep North self-aggrandizement and fanaticism that has bedeviled the United States for two centuries.) But he understands better than anyone ever has how to cover imperial coercion and corruption with a seeming sincerity that bedazzles and flatters the do-gooder and racketeering part of the American public.

True, Clinton has "damaged the Presidency." For this alone he deserves the thanks of patriots. Not being an admirer of the imperial office, I am always encouraged to see it damaged in the affections of the people. The important question about Clinton is the one raised by Mencken. Did we, or at least a lot of us, deserve him?

(2000)

Five Minutes With Governor Bush

Through the good offices of a friend who is a large contributor to Republican causes, *Chronicles* was able to secure a brief exclusive interview with George W. Bush—the likely next President of the United States. We caught up with Governor Bush in Des Moines a few minutes before he was to address the annual joint convention of the Midwestern Association of Funeral Directors and the Funeral Cosmetologists of America.

Chronicles: *Governor Bush, you have promised tax cuts. Many people remember your father's famous promise of "no new taxes" and may be afraid that such promises can't or won't be kept. A related concern is that the middle- and working-class incomes are declining while the rich are getting richer.*
George W. Bush: America is the land of opportunity for everybody. We have to cut taxes to make sure people take advantage of the great entrepreneurial opportunities—like oil, and baseball, for instance.

C: *Many Americans feel deeply that abortion is a sin and a crime and that its widespread acceptance is a sign of a sick society.*
B: I am deeply concerned about abortion. That is why I passed a parental notification law in Texas that is a model for the nation—to make sure teenagers notify their parents when they're going to have an abortion—and *vice versa*.

C: *Many Americans are concerned about the militarization of the federal police and incidents such as Ruby Ridge, during your father's administration, and Waco, which happened in your state. Do you think measures should be taken to identify those responsible and punish them, and to restrain such incidents in the future?*
B: I am the law-and-order candidate. As President, I will make sure the police have all the tools they need to handle dangerous criminals. When I am President, you won't have dangerous bigots like this John Rocker prowling the streets shooting off his mouth. He makes me sick. I wish we could have him at Yale for just one week, but he probably couldn't pass the entrance exam.
And I want to assure my friend Charlton Heston and members of the NRA that I admire the Bill of Rights, and when I am President there will not be a lot of bad people owning guns who are not NRA members.

C: *Governor, nearly everybody realizes that public education is failing. Is it possible that the problem is too much federal intervention and that the government ought to cut back its involvement?*
B: I will be the Education President. I will make sure all our teachers are held to high standards and all our students have equal opportunity to the highest quality education so that they are prepared to be part of the global economy in the New World Order—which, by the way, my Dad invented.

C: *Governor, our readers feel that American military intervention in foreign situations has been too frequent and aggressive and that we ought to scale back toward a national interest policy.*
B: I am a conservative, a bold, compassionate conservative. America must always be ready when democracy is threatened anywhere in the world—like those people that invaded Albania. As President Kennedy said, you must bear any burden.

C: *Many people are concerned about the high levels of immigration, as well as apparently unrestricted illegal immigration, which may be drastically changing our country. Do you think one million immigrants a year is too many, not enough, or about right?*
B: America is a nation of immigrants. We need immigrants with their talents and skills to take advantage of those entrepreneurial opportunities that I said before. That is why I sponsored bilingual education in Texas—to help all those immigrants we need to have a strong, healthy economy.

C: *Many of our readers are concerned about what could be called judicial tyranny, that the federal courts have usurped the role of the people and lawmakers in deciding major issues, How do you feel about that?*
B: I am the bold conservative candidate for compassionate conservatism! I will appoint great Republican Supreme Court justices like Earl Warren, Harry Brennan, Clarence Blackmun and Ruth Bader O'Connor. And I will make sure we have diversity on the Court.

At this point, we were interrupted by staff members reminding the governor of his next engagement.

C: *Thank you, Governor. This has been most enlightening for our readers.*
B: Remember to tell them I am the conservative candidate, the true, the bold, the compassionate conservative. That's how we will win the Republican victory.

(2000)

Chapter Seven

History and Historians

Tocqueville Redivivus

A Review of *Outgrowing Democracy: A History of the United States in the Twentieth Century*, by John Lukacs, Garden City, New York: Century, Doubleday, 1984, 423 pages.

Were some power, either republican or princely, to entrust me with a classroom of promising youth who were to be educated to become the best possible historians of the future—well, I would find the works of John Lukacs indispensable. Why? Simply because I can discover in our time no better example of creative historical thinking and practice.

One of Lukacs's themes has been the defense, at the same time innovative and reactionary, of history as a form of knowledge—distinct from other forms of apprehending the world and uniquely characteristic of the West. He has also practiced what he has preached. Each of his books—*A New History of the Cold War*; *The Passing of the Modern Age*; *The Last European War: 1939–1941*; *1945: The Year Zero*; *Philadelphia: Patricians and Philistines*, and the latest—has provided a working example of how to apply historical thinking to the understanding of some part of the awesome and overwhelming experience of our century.

Many of our best historians, after their first few insights, have tended to repeat themselves. (This, perhaps, is more a criticism of national standards of discourse and the degradation of American publishing than it is of historians.) By contrast, Lukacs has in each book set himself a new challenge. Purposes and themes recur, of course, but each book has been an exhibit in creative historical practice, and *Outgrowing Democracy* is no exception.

Basic to Lukacs's performance was his realization, early on, that the canons of historiography created in the 19th century were not fully applicable to the historical reconstruction and understanding of the 20th. History, by these canons, was to be written from a thorough and thoroughly detached examination of the documentary record. This was and is an eminently sound doctrine, but the secret of all good rules is in knowing when to apply them. (For instance, computers are marvelous aids for accounting and for analysis of empirical data, but to apply them more than incidentally to matters such as education or warfare merely reveals that the researcher does not know what he is doing. This, Lukacs would say, is a characteristically American error.)

The canons of historical research simply do not fit our century. Our century is the century of inflation (another of Lukacs's themes), including inflation of the documentary record. Like dollar bills, there are more and more documents worth less and less (not to mention the shift of large segments of communication and consciousness away from the written word to electronic and pictorial media). To write the history of the 20th century from documents alone is both impossible and irrelevant. Historical understanding must, rather, be an imaginative act—faithful to the factual record but embodying a process closer to that of creative literature than scientific investigation. Lukacs has dramatically demonstrated the utility of this approach successfully once more in *Outgrowing Democracy*, though the book has received less favorable attention than some of his other works.

The challenge that Lukacs has set himself in *Outgrowing Democracy* is Tocquevillian—the interpretation of the nature and status of American democracy as it has evolved through our century. For his purpose, the title is perhaps unfortunate, for it gives an unjustified authoritarian connotation to his analysis. What Lukacs's analysis seeks is not the abandonment but the maturing of American democracy. It is just such a work as Tocqueville himself would have written—could he have added to his knowledge of the Jacobin revolution a sad wisdom acquired by observing the Bolshevik, National Socialist, and sexual revolutions. *Outgrowing Democracy* is the work of a European, friendly to the aspirations of the American people, but distant enough and culturally conservative enough to observe the blemishes as well as the accomplishments of America. That is, the work examines us sympathetically, but with historical perspective and from outside rather than inside the accepted conventions of American thought.

It is just such an approach that finds Americans, and probably any people, most resistant. Large numbers of Americans will accept any totalist rejection of their society that can be invented, because that is compatible with their categories of thought. To be required to examine and expose the flaws in these categories of thought themselves is an uncomfortable and unwanted experience. But this kind of examination and exposure is just what historians should supply. We may argue forever about the merits of internationalist or anticommunist policies. That is for politicians and journalists. What the historian can and should give is the underlying pattern. For instance, Lukacs points out tellingly that in 1942 the Luce publications declared Lenin to be perhaps the greatest man of the century, but in 1953 they theologized that Communism *per se* was mortal sin. Lukacs's point is that both positions fell short of an intelligent assessment of reality and of a prudentially responsible patriotism, and that the flipflop is characteristic of the American way of going about things.

To tell Americans that their sentimental celebration of the family has been demonstrably accompanied by a massive breakdown of sound domestic relations; that their vast expenditures and pretensions in education and culture have been largely counterproductive; that their national feeling has often served ideology rather than patriotism, and that their generous internationalism has been merely a naive nationalism; that their prosperity has often been synonymous with rootlessness and declining standards and their equality with conformity; and that their religion has been more sociology than faith; or to point out the obvious truth that the American national character has been at least twice destabilized by massive immigration, and that each ethnic group has brought negative as well as positive additions to the melting pot—none of this is what we want to hear, whether we are radicals dedicated to a vision of endless tampering with the social fabric or "conservatives" who think the sufficient ends of life have been found in the marketplace and anticommunism, perhaps held together by a synthetic "civic religion."

Many of Lukacs's familiar historical themes have been worked into *Outgrowing Democracy*: the immateriality of materialism and especially of economics, the destructive Wilsonian straitjacket of American thinking about the outside world, the passing of the bourgeois age, the falsity of "public opinion." There are many new (at least to me) themes as well. These, I suspect, are intended to offer historical perspective on the emergent establishment of "conservatives" and "neoconservatives" and are not apt to please its leaders. For instance: The Eisenhower era was not the halcyon time of American goodness, but a tragedy of missed opportunities and the seedbed of later disasters and degradations; bureaucratization of mind is as endemic in and characteristic of the American private sector as the public; our anticommunism has sometimes been as shortsighted as our international do-goodism—that is, that Americans have often exhibited nationalism rather than that older and better sentiment, patriotism.

My recapitulation badly slights the subtleties of Lukacs's account of American history in the 20th century, for nearly every page is freighted with subsidiary insights. Now and then, naturally, the American who is largely persuaded will yet be provoked to an objection. In picturing, correctly, the pernicious effects of the devolution of American Puritanism and the dilution of American Catholicism, for instance, Lukacs has left out of the picture the continuing widespread vitality (obvious in the South) of a healthy, non-Puritan Protestantism. And American literature, one can argue, despite the decline perceptively identified by Lukacs, has in some ways reflected the Western tradition better than has that of jaded Europe. True, there is not much doubt about the American obsession with physical comfort—but I have never heard of a single other nation that has not shown the same tendency when it could be afforded. There might even be something to be said for American naiveté and "exceptionalism" (as long as it is not messianic), when one considers how regularly the wisdom and maturity of Europe has stumbled over the brink of disaster.

I happen to think Lukacs is correct on nearly every point. But even if he is not, he has fulfilled the historian's duty in the highest manner by expanding our ability to understand ourselves and our situation. He is the friend who loves us enough to be objective when we need objectivity. I began by indulging in the fantasy that I was charged with the education of the best of future historians. Allow me the teacher's ultimate fantasy: that I am charged with the education of future statesmen. The first thing would be to make sure that the promising youth learned to ride hard, shoot straight, and tell the truth. Then, I would set them to master the ancient and English classics (including the Bible) and the Founding Fathers. When that had been accomplished, it would be time for them to begin to understand their century, their nation, and the task demanded by their future—which Lukacs correctly formulates as the development of a mature American conservatism, aimed at the intelligent adaptation and preservation of the substance of the West. For this stage of the education of future statesmen, I can think of no better place to start than *Outgrowing Democracy*.

(1986)

Historical Consciousness

A Review of *Historical Consciousness, or The Remembered Past*, new edition with a new introduction and conclusion, by John Lukacs, New York: Schocken Books, 1985, 409 pages.

In the introduction to the new edition of his *Historical Consciousness* (first published in 1968), Professor John Lukacs observes of the body of academic historians, circa 1960's: "They were interested in their profession, without paying much, if any, interest to the *nature* of their profession." If there were some way that the historians to whom Lukacs refers could, like a class of recalcitrant undergraduates, be required to read *Historical Consciousness* and be tested on what they had learned, I am certain that the results of the exercise would confirm the continuing accuracy of Lukacs's observation.

Historical Consciousness is an inspired attempt by a writer both passionate and disciplined to come to grips with the nature of historical thinking and what it means to us as *men*. A great many academic historians would be either unable or unwilling to make *any* response, positive or negative, to the book on its own level. For they do not grapple with ideas: they label and classify them; and they would be very hard put to find a familiar label for *Historical Consciousness*. It does not fit into any classification scheme that will cover the rest of the groaning shelf of books on the "philosophy of history" published in the last few decades. Lukacs has broken the rules. He has written, and even had the audacity to update and republish, a book about history that says something. Such a book is not supposed to be alive with ideas or to make connections with real life and authentic culture. It is supposed to be a ritual totem, known only to the Elect and by them to be labeled, not responded to.

I do not want to make my generalizations about academic historians too sweeping, for to do so would wrong many good men and women who do not deserve the characterization. It would also, unhistorically, ignore the differences of generations: Both older and younger historians are better than the generally execrable group that came to maturity in the sixties and is now early middle-aged. Nevertheless, in general, Lukacs is, if anything, too kind in his observations on the bureaucratization of the academic professionals. Not only are many of them not interested in the nature of history, a lot are not even interested in history—they either lack historical consciousness and imagination altogether or else consider it unimportant. Often, "history" at their hands reduces to a preoccupation with what historians have said—or even worse, what historians have said about other historians. That is to say, a good deal of what passes today for historical scholarship has as much relation to the real life of man as what Mrs. Smith reported under the hair dryer that Mrs. Jones said about Mrs. Green.

Thus, as the author remarks in his assessment of developments since the original publication, we have a strange paradox. On the one hand, historical thinking is in the blood of Western man, an inescapable part of his nature. Further, there is evidence of an increasing public thirst for history—history, in fact, is one of our few remaining means of making contact with reality amidst the frenetic vulgarity of American culture. (Witness the change that Lukacs points out in the standing of the concept of "old-fashioned." Not long ago it was the sign of something not "with it," to be shucked off. Now "old-fashioned" is a prestige term denoting the solid and real in a shoddy world that is remade daily.)

The paradox is that, on the other hand, despite the thirst for history and the centrality of historical thinking in our consciousness, academic historians have never been more irrelevant, incestuous, and unreadable. The public thirst must be satisfied by trashy novels or even trashier docudramas. Or by tours of government-managed historic "sites" overlaid with the canned patter of professional guides, who do for historical understanding exactly what the Big Mac does for good dining. This debacle is not in the least relieved by the periodic fads of fashionable "relevance" that sweep over the field.

What the author's analysis holds up to an unflattering light is not scholarship; even the most esoteric and pedantic scholarship can serve a purpose and express a commitment. What is condemned is a lack of moral vision, a lack, to use a traditional term, of "vocation." "They were interested in their profession" not "in the *nature* of their profession." And, in this respect, history is only one example among many in a bureaucratized society where institutions progressively lose sight of their function as they increase their wealth, power, and consciousness of group interest.

It does not do to be too pessimistic. So far as history is concerned, there are hopeful signs that the creativity of the Western mind has not atrophied, but is rather seeking new channels. Lukacs has been early, though not alone, in pointing to and describing the re-assertion of historical vision that is taking place within literature. There are other examples, of which the works of Solzhenitsyn are perhaps the most conspicuous and persuasive. But this development is taking place outside of and even largely unknown to the academic historical enterprise.

Another hopeful sign for historical understanding, perhaps, is the republication of *Historical Consciousness*, which will increase the chances for the book to get into the hands of young scholars who are still capable of an earnest pursuit of meaning. In most cases their teachers are unlikely to go out of their way to bring this unclassifiable and unbecomingly passionate work to their attention.

Historical Consciousness deals fruitfully with most of the problems (sources, causation, generalization, objectivity, to mention only a few) that confront anyone who considers seriously what it is or should be to write history. Such a person will get answers, not pre-classified and conventional answers, but answers that will have to be wrestled with. If this review has meandered a bit, it is John Lukacs's fault. His is guilty of having written a rich and promethean work in which almost every page has a tendency to send a responsive reader off on extended explorations of his own.

(1990)

Forrest McDonald

A Review of *Requiem: Variations on Eighteenth-Century Themes*, by Forrest McDonald and Ellen Shapiro McDonald, Lawrence: University Press of Kansas, 1988, 216 pages.

The best historical writings, whatever their subject matter, have certain characteristics in common. All display a deft mastery of primary sources, building up from a solid base of fact without allowing the data to drag them down into pedantry. They also bear on their faces both an open and honest viewpoint *and* objectivity. That is, the best historian is a writer of conviction and values who is yet able to view all sides of a question and to state opposing arguments honestly, the rarest of all faculties in modern discourse. Then, the best history must deal with high and not trivial matters. Finally, the best histories are relevant, not in the sense of pandering to the fashions of the moment, but in the sense that they give any intelligent reader food for thought about his own times.

These virtues are all splendidly marshaled in *Requiem*, the McDonalds' collection of occasional pieces on the early years of the American federal republic. Each of the 11 essays takes up a familiar and problematic question of those days—Shays' Rebellion, John Dickinson, the "middle party" in the Philadelphia Convention, the relation of the Framers to capitalism, the ambivalent evolution of the doctrine of separation of powers, the rituals of 18th-century war in relation to the American War of Independence, the role of Alexander Hamilton, the legacies of Washington and Jefferson to the office of the presidency, and others. And each is a gem of historical analysis, interpretation, and nonsuperficial relevance, from which the Founders emerge as neither plaster saints nor archaic curiosities, but as real, flawed, and extraordinary human beings.

It is probably true that all good history is sober, if not indeed somber; such must be the usual reaction of any honest student of the human condition. Few experiences are more sobering than being regularly compelled to compare the achievements of our Fathers with what 20th-century Americans have made of those achievements, which perhaps justifies the melancholy title of this collection. The respectful realism of these essays provides a good antidote to the mindless sentimentality of sunshine patriots and the compulsive hectoring of self-appointed re-Founders under whom we have suffered during the Constitution's bicentennial celebration.

The last essay is a masterful historical exposition of "Federalism in America" and concludes with the wisest and saddest words of the bicentennial: "Political scientists and historians are in agreement that federalism is the greatest contribution of the Founding Fathers to the science of government. It is also the only feature of the Constitution that has been successfully exported, that can be employed to protect liberty elsewhere in the world. Yet what we invented, and others imitate, no longer exists on its native shores."   (1989)

The Imperial Penman

A Review of *The Imperial Presidency*, by Arthur M. Schlesinger, Jr., Boston: Houghton Mifflin Company, 1973, 504 pages.

The title gives us a fleeting but instructive glimpse at the curious rhetorical operations which flourish in this as in Mr. Schlesinger's other writings. "Imperial," from the pen of a historian and linked with "Presidency," disposes the reader to expect a carefully descriptive comparison of the institutions of past empires with the American Presidency. But nowhere in the book is "imperial" defined, nor is there a single significant reference to any historic empire or emperor. Dressed up as dispassionate, denotative, scholarly, the title is actually a propaganda epithet for the impassioned moment. In the sub rational milieu of *kitsch* where the book will be most commonly received and read, "imperial" has a pejorative connotation akin to "imperious." It is a slogan against the "imperial," *i.e.*, imperious, dictatorial, contrademocratic administration of Mr. Nixon. The term is an ideological sword disguised as a scholarly plowshare, attention being diverted from the demagogic cutting edge by a seemingly objective glance down the centuries.

The text confirms our glimpse of the title. Superficially a historical review of the accretion of presidential power, the book is actually a partisan attack upon the Nixon Presidency. Two uncongenial rhetorical operations, analysis and philippic, are, as usual, carried on simultaneously but with such disarming equability that much vigilance is required to keep each distinctly in view. In the dexterity with which the combination is effected lies the secret of Professor Schlesinger's celebrity.

The occasion for *The Imperial Presidency* is the Liberal Establishment's need to cover its historical flank while it reverses party line on the question of presidential power. The book carries in itself ample evidence that the reversal is temporary and expediential, for it provides for an easy return to the old position when necessary. The Liberals have for more than a generation favored (and exercised) the widest latitude in presidential (and executive generally) initiative and authority. They have portrayed the Presidency as "the central instrument of democracy," and continuing additions to its prerogatives as desirable and inevitable. However, Mr. Nixon has evinced a need to curtail presidential power in non-Establishment hands. In an over-modest apology the author counts himself among the scholars who, "over-generalizing from the prewar [World War II] contrast between a President who was right and a Congress which was wrong," lent themselves to "an uncritical cult of the activist Presidency." But unlike Andrew Jackson's deathbed chagrin that he had not shot Henry Clay and hanged John C. Calhoun, there is no genuine regret or repentance here. When in his last chapter Schlesinger comes to discuss concrete proposals for shifting the balance of power back toward the Congress, he finds none of them satisfactory, being unwilling to tie the hands of any future Liberal President. And in more than four hundred pages of historical discussion of the growth of executive power in such respects as war-making, treaty-making, spending, and privilege, the only power grabs that arouse his unmitigated indignation were committed either in the remote past or by Mr. Nixon. All this is to say that Professor Schlesinger does not intend to give up the "cult of the activist Presidency," only the "uncritical cult of the activist Presidency."

The real thesis of *The Imperial Presidency*, nowhere unambivalently stated, is that pre-Nixon accretions of presidential power were essentially natural (and therefore good) developments, while Nixon's exercises of authority have been unnatural (and bad). Not that the rationalization of all non-Nixonian aggrandizements is explicit. Rather it is a matter of tone and weight, of carefully selected and artfully arranged connotations. A close attention to language shows us that in Schlesingerian history accretions of executive authority under Democratic Presidents have occurred with a kind of blameless inevitability. In the case of FDR, for instance, there was "extraordinary power flowing into the Presidency to meet domestic problems." Again, prior to Nixon, "a generation of foreign and domestic turbulence had chaotically delivered [power] to the Presidency." And if Kennedy exercised great initiative in foreign affairs it was chiefly because of "the prevailing atmosphere" when he became President, and because the Cuban missile crisis "*really* combined all those pressures" which made presidential initiative uniquely necessary (Schlesinger's italics). Before Nixon then, Presidents had not sought power so much as had it thrust upon them! Mr. Nixon, however, is denied the comfort of rowing with the currents of history. With him there has been a deliberate, unprecedented, malevolent seizure of power, "a scheme of presidential supremacy," "a drastic reorganization of national authority," an attempt to govern in defiance of Congress, people, press, and even of most of the executive branch. Because of peculiar defects, Mr. Nixon has flouted Constitution and consensus to gather powers that were previously only potential into an "imperial Presidency." It is encouraging to be assured, however, that he has had to wrench history out of its channel in this, for if "a more traditional politician" like Humphrey, or a "more conscientious politician" like McGovern had been raised to the presidential seat, they "would doubtless have tempered the tendency to gather everything into the White House."

Again, it must be stressed that in Schlesingerian history these insinuations are not so much directly and consistently made as they are sneaked upon us in the midst of apparently temperate accounts of events. The Schlesinger technique is to have it both ways, to shift from determinist to moral critic and back again as occasion requires, and as the following passage will illustrate:

Nixon's Presidency was not an aberration but a culmination. It carried to reckless extremes a compulsion toward presidential power rising out of deep-running changes in the foundations of society. In a time of the acceleration of history and the decay of traditional institutions and values, a strong Presidency was both a greater necessity than ever before and a greater risk—necessary to hold a spinning [sic] and distracted society together, necessary to make the separation of powers work, risky because of the awful temptation held out to override the separation of powers and burst the bonds of the Constitution. The nation required both a strong Presidency for leadership and the separation of powers for liberty.

Examples might be multiplied endlessly, but by making his own comparison of the treatment of FDR's destroyer deal of 1940 (pp. 106 ff.) with the account of Nixon's "Cambodian incursion" of 1970 (pp. 189 ff.), the reader may obtain a sufficiently detailed understanding of how these maneuvers work, of how carefully constructed portrayals of situations, which on the surface are merely descriptive accounts, can seduce us down the primrose path to unwarranted generalizations. Stripped of its comely rhetorical camouflage, Schlesinger's defense of Roosevelt on this occasion reduces to two incompatible points: 1) Roosevelt did not stretch presidential power, necessity did. 2) When Roosevelt stretched presidential power it was a good thing because he was a good man. To put It another way, presidential aggrandizements which meet Mr. Schlesinger's standards of necessity and virtue are by definition not usurpations. Presidential aggrandizements for purposes or from necessities with which he does not agree are, by definition, usurpations of power. This tells us what Professor Schlesinger (and the Liberal Establishment) likes and dislikes, but it does not lead us to any objective principles, valid for all occasions, by which to identify, either technically or morally, abuses of executive power. One may agree with Schlesinger that Nixon acted with deviousness, historical ignorance, and constitutional insensitivity, and that his conduct would seem foreign and reprehensible to the Founding Fathers. But we still have nothing but Professor Schlesinger's preferences— immaterial evidence—to prove that Nixon's acts differed in kind or degree from those of his predecessors. It depends simply on who is defining necessity and virtue. At best the author's main point is a shallow subjective judgment, at worst an Orwellian stratagem.

There is nothing new about this trick of being at the same time determinist and moral critic—it is a Schlesingerian stock-in-trade, and most convenient in disguising the partisan behind the historian. In his *Partisan Review* article in 1949 on "The Causes of the Civil War: A Note on Historical Sentimentalism," Schlesinger argued 1) that the antislavery movement did not cause the Civil War, and 2) that the anti-slavery movement was morally justified in causing the Civil War. This article is still considered by many as the definitive putdown of historians whose views of causation are more complex ("sentimental"?), which only goes to prove that tricks are not too hard to pull off if a large part of your audience yearns to believe in magic. In the celebrated *The Age of Jackson*, Schlesinger began with Jeffersonian democracy, *i.e.*, Southern planter agrarianism, transmogrified it through something which he labelled "Jacksonian democracy" but which more precise students have identified as anti-Jacksonian reformism, and ended up with Lincolnian Republicanism. All these incongruous elements were tied together with a golden ribbon of rhetoric and the package bequeathed as the exclusive inheritance of the New Deal. *All* the angels are on Professor Schlesinger's side, *all* the time.

Mr. Nixon's real offense was not that he soiled the splendid mantle of his predecessors; rather, with a pathetic lack of fashion sense and aplomb, he has clung to the rags and tatters of his Liberal predecessors' garments long after they have seen their best days. But it may be that Schlesinger too has made a fashion blunder, which will explain why this latest book has not been very cordially received, even among ideological confréres. Many of those who share his tastes and distastes no longer care to argue by artful historical plausibilities. They prefer more direct and violent rhetoric. While he still pines for Augustus, they are ready for Caligula and Nero. Certainly there is nothing here that would cause us to doubt that when the usurper is laid low and the true imperators return to claim their throne, Mr. Schlesinger's pen will be once more at their service. Meanwhile, we must look elsewhere to be enlightened and armed against them.

(1975)

The Banality of Banal

*An autobiography is the truest of all books, for while it
inevitably consists mainly of extinctions of the truth . . . the
remorseless truth is there, between the lines.*
— MARK TWAIN

A Review of *A Life in the Twentieth Century: Innocent Beginnings,
1917–1950*, by Arthur M. Schlesinger Jr., Boston and New York: Houghton
Mifflin, 2000, 557 pages.

I first thought I would title this review "Memoirs of the Imperial Jester." The
Jester being one who is of no importance but is always present at the imperial
court, it seemed to fit the author. However, after looking into the pages, I saw I
was wrong. A jester should occasionally be amusing and show some shrewd
insight and exercise his special license for candor.

Inevitably, Schlesinger's memoirs get the big publisher and the big hype. Mr.
Schlesinger is "the finest historian of our age," according to dust jacket celebrities like the erudite Mr. Tom Brokaw and the judicious Mr. Norman Mailer (how
would they know?). The same authorities tell us that this fat book, which takes
Arthur Jr. up to age 33, is "an eloquent and insightful history of the 20th century" and also "a fabulous journey through the first half of the 20th century."

The fact is, Schlesinger is not and never has been a historian, but a writer of
clever political tracts, a press agent for the left wing of the Democratic party
(now the only wing). In *The Age of Jackson*, his Harvard M.A. thesis, with no
fear and insufficient research, he gave us a supposedly definitive interpretation of
the most complicated period of U.S. history. In contrast to all previous (and subsequent) understandings of serious historians, Jacksonian Democracy, it
appeared, was centered in Boston and New York and uncannily resembled the
New Deal coalition of progressive intellectuals and labor radicals.

His own, blow-by-blow and rather gee-whizzy account of his research herein, confirms what I have always thought. The case in *The Age of Jackson* was
made by slim research, artful elaboration of out-of-context quotations, ignoring
of contrary evidence, and making plausible but non-existent connections
between various movements.

A serious historian would have put forth Schlesinger's interpretation of the
period in a tentative essay to be explored and tested. Years of serious research and
thought would occupy a serious historian before setting forth so sweeping a historical interpretation. Schlesinger chose a different route, a well-rewarded one:
penman for the imperial state. (It is a curious phenomenon I have often noticed,
that academic historians as a group, while giving lip service to professional stan-

dards, give their admiration to the writers who rise above professional standards to celebrity.)

Schlesinger qua historian went on to provide us with the definitive middle-brow apologiae for FDR and JFK. Among his other services was *The Vital Center* (1949) which justified the Cold War liberals in kicking their erstwhile Communist allies out of the citadel of power and provided the real starting point of the noisy and pernicious phenomenon of neo-conservatism. And all this accomplished while facing the challenges of a *Playboy* interview and the Kennedy swimming pool.

Our memoirist's quality as a historian is conclusively defined by his *The Imperial Presidency* (1973), in which he pointed to the dangerous ambitions of executive power under Nixon while suavely justifying the far worst usurpations of Nixon's predecessors as necessary and good.

OK, so he is not the finest historian of the age. But he has known a lot of important people and been in a lot of important places, so this is surely an interesting, if not a "fabulous" look at our times just passed? Would that it were so. But, alas, it is hard to believe anyone could plow through this trivia except a New Deal junkie or a collector of celebrity anecdotes. Autobiography at this level of exhaustive but essentially unrevealing detail might possibly be mildly interesting for a really important historical figure, though I doubt it. For a merely self-important figure it is an excruciating bore.

Does the world really need to see a picture of stalwart young Arthur busy preparing to interpret history for us all at his pre-school desk in Iowa City? Or to savor the boyhood experiences of his father in Xenia, Ohio? (Though Schlesinger Sr. actually was a serious historian of sorts, despite ending up at Harvard.) Do we really need to know faculty room gossip at Cambridge among historians now, mostly justly, forgotten?

One bit of gossip does not appear. It can't be proved now but was told to me years ago by an honest man who had been a visiting professor at Harvard: Once Mrs. Schlesinger Sr. got up and fled when a black man sat down beside her in a theatre. Here we have the true nature of Boston liberalism revealed in all its naked glory.

Young Arthur never lets us forget that his doings are a part of history even before he was born. "Nineteen twelve was the exciting year of Wilson's New Freedom and of Roosevelt's New Nationalism." (13) The events in his life are historical watersheds. "My formal education now began." (41) "In September 1931 I traveled forty miles north from Cambridge to boarding school." (81) "Boredom arose in my third undergraduate year." (176) "The war was everywhere," (249) concluded the young war lord at Harvard in 1939. "The war rumbled on," (283) still for our hero as he labored on his first book.

"When we wanted sandwiches, we had to use a knife to slice the bread; sliced bread was still in the future." (109) "That summer of 1935 was the last totally relaxed time," (117) for then the noble Arthur began his career of writing the words that would make our times comprehensible to all. "The variety was exciting" (267) in the papers that flowed across Arthur's desk in the Office of War Information while thousands of better men of Arthur's age were dying for their country. And so on.

Is there nothing good to be said at all? Well, there are a lot of big and medium-sized names dropped, for those that like that sort of thing. The main virtue is as primary research material for the future historian of the smug, self-aggrandizing Boston/New York intelligentsia which has been a curse to the American people for two centuries and more now. I'll give that future scholar a working title for his research: "Pseudo-Intellectualism as a Force in American History."

(2000)

The Presence of the Past

This was written, on request, for a symposium of the Gallatin
Review *and never published by that journal.*

I am obliged to you for sending me the "New Millennium Issue 1," containing the essays on "The Presence of the Past." Being charged with teaching introductory historiography to graduate students, and having written a modest bit
about some of the questions your writers address, I have read the collection with
profit and pleasure. Most especially the pieces by Webb, Neusner, and "Janus."
Their assessments of our present troubles and discontents in historianship seem
to me right on target. The whole issue is an example of tough historical thinking
(than which nothing is more truly "relevant" to the present) such as we would
have taken for granted half a century ago as widespread among those training in
the vocation. But it is rare in this day when a weird combination of determinis-
tic social science, on the one hand, and uncritical romanticism toward favored
causes, on the other, dominates historical writing and teaching, particularly in the
most prestigious academic institutions.

One dimension your writers do not address is the strange paradox, elucidated
by John Lukacs, that never has there been such a widespread thirst for historical
knowledge and never have so many resources been devoted to historical thinking,
yet never have those charged with slaking the thirst been so unable and uninterest-
ed to address an eager audience. In my own observation the corps of professional
historians are far gone in esoterica and onanism, perhaps too far to return. Certainly
it will take a long time, given the slowness of institutional change (in no academic
discipline slower than in history) and the tendency of academic mediocrity to nur-
ture and reproduce itself. If the daring initiatives of "Janus" are to be taken, they
are likely, it seems to me, to occur outside the academy.

The appeal of "Janus" is bold and stirring. His call for intellectual honesty,
for energy, ingenuity, and initiative, for broad sympathies and interests, for
respect without adulation toward the past, for relevance without trendiness, seem
to be just what we need. What will work if anything will. But "Janus" and your
other writers are heirs of the intellectual ambitions, energies, and ethics, and the
social and cultural cohesion of the 19th century. I see no evidence on the present
scene that this inheritance will survive in more than scattered pockets. And even
if it survives, I see no evidence that there will be any market for it among the
shallow, frenetic, polyglot subjects and the callous bureaucracies of the American
empire of the next generation. However, I have always had a weakness for lost
causes. "Janus," if you have need for a rather tattered but still game recruit, then
enter me on your muster roll. Let us occupy the high ground and make the bastards take it, foot by bloody foot.

(1993)

Chapter Eight

Restoring the Republic

What might have been and what has been
Point to one end, which is always present.
— T.S. ELIOT, "BURNT NORTON"

A history textbook used by thousands of college freshmen for the last twenty years tells fledgling citizens that democracy is the system of government which "trusts the average man to free himself from tradition, prejudice, habit, and by free discussion come to a rational conclusion." This tissue of sophistry encapsulates the derailment of republican self-government in our time. Most certainly democracy has something to do with the "average man," the common people, the many. But one of the numerous defects of the modern and artificial definition above is that it leaves out three-fourths of the moral and historical context that was taken for granted by the Framers and Founders of the American federal republic when they talked about a government of the people. The definition, in fact, subtly shifts democracy away from substance to procedure, from ethics to instrumentality. The pins have been kicked out from under democracy, leaving it balancing precariously on one leg.

The definition, to begin with, abandons virtue for reason. Our forefathers took it for granted that virtue was necessary in a ruler—whether it be the one, the few, or the many. And where in the definition do we find the ends and limitations of government? In other words, where is the Constitution? What tells us which things men in the collective are entitled to come to "rational conclusions" about, and what things are they to leave alone? What restrains the 51 percent from coming to a "rational conclusion" to expropriate, enslave, or exterminate the 49 percent? And why is it necessary for the common man to divorce himself from "tradition, prejudice, habit"? In fact, the average man at all times and places (and the wise man too) is fond of tradition, prejudice, and habit, and rightly so. If we believe in the rule of the many, are we not obliged to respect their traditions, prejudices, and habits as well as what we deem to be their rational conclusions? What, after all, are our liberties and democratic forms—freedom of the press and assembly, fair play, parliamentary procedure, due process of law—if not traditions, prejudices, and habits handed down by our forefathers over centuries, which owe their survival to inheritance as much as to abstract argument.

Most assuredly "free discussion" is indispensable to democracy. That is, free, candid, and tolerant deliberation among differing opinions and interests in the process of arriving at decisions—decisions on those things which the public is entitled to decide. But free discussion divorced from "tradition, prejudice, habit" rather leads us away from the common man. It describes a type of society loved by the few, not by the many. Who exactly is it that is "trusting" the "average man" to arrive at a "rational conclusion"? "Rational" according to what system of values? According to whose views and interests? Here is the most insidious part of this peculiar modern democracy—the rationale for a hidden elite. If the average man perversely refuses to come to a "rational conclusion," what happens?

What happens is a government of the few who decide, against the will of the many, that "free discussion" requires a foreign-born pornographer be subsidized to create obscenity; a government in which the few enforce "rational" social policies (such as busing, affirmative action, coddling of criminals) overwhelmingly considered unjust and oppressive by the many; a government in which schools, local authorities, and even the taxing power (immemorially reserved to the people) are taken over by unelected and untouchable judges. Democracy suddenly requires the people to submit to their betters, whether they will or not. This, of course, is not democracy at all, but oligarchy, as our Fathers would have immediately recognized.

Again and again, we have seen the self-government of the American people frustrated by the few, the oligarchy, in the name of "rational democracy." This is the problem of republicanism in our time—our chief dilemma in society and government—the consolidation of power in the hands of the few. It explains that, while sophisters (whenever they raise their snouts from the public trough long enough) shout hosannas to the triumph of democracy, the American people, everywhere, have ceased to believe that the government they elect is really theirs or that they will be allowed to make the institutions ostensibly theirs respond to their will. Everywhere an ideological construct mislabeled "democracy" has triumphed. And everywhere the people feel powerless.

For those who really value the rule of the people, as well as the special constitutional heritage of American federal republicanism, the task of the day is not to spread democracy about the world while we congratulate ourselves on our success. The task is to restore the federal republic at home. In order to carry out this task we will need the spirit of liberty that animated generations of our forefathers—not an obeisance to their forms, but an imitation of their spirit. For forms may survive when the soul is fled from them.

What we need is a return of power to the many. Not a concentration of power in the hands of the few for the alleged benefit of the many, abstractly conceived. That way lies Hitler and Stalin. Rather a dispersal and deconsolidation of power. Only power can check power. And self-government is in its nature local and individual. Only then is it real.

For our Fathers, liberty consisted in a negative upon government. It was not a boon bestowed by government, but something that must be asserted against government. It will not increase the power and liberty of American families in the least for the government to bestow upon them a voucher to spend on a limited choice of schools under stipulated requirements. It will rather further consolidate power and further intrude the government into as yet unregulated spheres of life. The only way to increase the power and liberty of the family is not to collect the taxes and not to lay down the regulations to begin with. Both our governing parties agree on the consolidation of power—they argue only over marginal aspects of administration.

Unlike us, the attitude of our Founders toward democracy was not ideological and not self-congratulatory. They believed in the right of those who were capable of governing themselves to do so. They were pleased that Americans had the fortunate opportunity to live under self-government at a time when, unlike today, most of the world was hostile to the very idea. They hoped they might set an example for oppressed mankind. They did not entertain a duty to spread democracy about the world by fire, sword, harangue, and money. They were the opposite of self-congratulatory and arrogant. Their demeanor was cautious, monitory, and self-demanding.

"Well, gentlemen," Dr. Franklin is supposed to have said at the Philadelphia Convention, "you have made a republic—if you can keep it." If republican self-government was to survive, if Americans were to go on governing themselves, then government must be watched. Republican liberty could always be subverted by lust for power on the part of the cunningly ambitious few and by the decay of those strenuous and demanding virtues among the many that made self-government possible. When our Fathers spoke of America as an experiment, they did not mean a glorious mission of revolution. They meant an experiment in the exercise and preservation of republican virtues.

"Power is always stealing from the many to the few," was the motto of a Washington democratic newspaper in the early days of the republic. It was a paraphrase of Mr. Jefferson's "the price of liberty is eternal vigilance." Mr. Jefferson also said that the tree of liberty must be watered from time to time by the blood of tyrants, and of patriots, that a little revolution now and then is a good thing.

Because Jefferson has been, since the mid-19th century, enveloped in a dense fabric of lies woven by Jacobin democrats and made the symbol of consolidated power in the name of equality, it is difficult for us to see what he meant. But what he meant was exactly what I have described above as the task of the day—the occasional need to restore the republic. He was not suggesting the overturn of society, a perpetual revolution for ever greater consolidation of power in the name of equality. Jefferson is nothing if not the enemy of consolidated power. It is not society that is to be overthrown—it is society, as in the American Revolution, that is to assert itself and overthrow those rulers who have usurped the power of society.

Jefferson's democracy ran thus. No one can be trusted with power. Government, though necessary, must be confined within narrow limits and dispersed. The average man, the many, is the least dangerous receptacle of power, lacking the opportunities for usurpation that afflict the few. But the essential point is the limitation of power. As he asked Adams: "If man cannot be trusted to govern himself, how can he be trusted to govern others?" That was his answer to the Federalist contention that the weakness of human nature required popular government to be restrained by checks and balances and the deference of the "average man" to his betters. Jefferson put his finger immediately on the hidden elitist assumption, the hidden elitist agenda, that lurked in the contention—as it lurks in our guardian democracy today.

Trusting or not trusting the common man to arrive at a "rational conclusion" was the wrong way to put the problem. It was Jefferson's point that the "betters" are just as corruptible, probably more so, than the popular mass—that is, more likely to abuse the limits of power, which are the essential thing. Jefferson is here exactly in agreement with C.S. Lewis's Christian defense of democracy. That democracy makes sense exactly because of original sin—precisely because man (all men) cannot be trusted to govern himself, much less others. But the Federalist idea has prevailed since the War Between the States, and in this century, given the consolidating tendencies of the modern form of society, it has become overwhelming.

Jefferson's little revolution now and then is not, then, revolution but reaction. Not a new utopia, but something radically conservative—a radical returning to the roots, to old virtues and old principles lost by the dilutions of time and the distortions of usurpation. In the American system this can only happen by the revival of states' rights, the only true force for limiting power. Which is exactly what Jefferson's own "Revolution of 1800" meant to him and his generation.

What we need is a reaction, a renewal, a true return to roots. We should approach our constitutional heritage and our governing establishment in exactly the spirit of our forefathers—with both deep respect and intelligent flexibility. To conserve is to save the essence, not the dead form, as true conservatives have always known. Our heritage is something to be understood and used by us to meet our present dangers. As Calhoun said, constitutions are human contrivances, and what man does and his reasons for it surely ought not to be beyond man's capacity to fully comprehend.

Let us contrast such an attitude with that of our current oligarchy. They want us to treat the Constitution with mystical awe and submission, but their Constitution is not the one handed down by our forefathers for our use. Rather, it is whatever the oligarchy mysteriously discovers it to be, by the alchemies of natural rights and evolution, which can justify any abuse of power on their part. On the other hand, they twist and distort the plain historical sense in the most petty and deceitful ways. Thus we get the worst possible combination of a phony tradition and destructive innovation. What we need is a real tradition and constructive innovation.

Many of the constructive innovations are already known at the grass-roots level, and others will emerge in the course of popular revolt. They seek to recover the spirit of the Constitution, to return power to the people. These would include term limits, for the federal judiciary as well as the Congress; a balanced budget amendment with inviolable restraints upon taxing and spending power; a line-item veto for the executive to check legislative irresponsibility, with balancing devices in the Congress to check executive warmongering; and the restoration of the Tenth Amendment to what Madison, the Father of the Constitution, said it should be, the cornerstone of our government. We have nothing to fear from a new constitutional convention, if necessary. Such a convention cannot destroy the handiwork of our Fathers. That has already been destroyed and must be restored. Whether we are able to accomplish this will be the measure of whether we have enough moral and social substance left to be a self-governing people.

Another area that will require creative work of restoration is that of "free discussion" so essential to self-government. For self-government to work we must have public deliberation that is free and honorable. Due to the consolidation of modern economy and government, freedom of the press has come to mean the right of a few giant media monopolies to define for us what we may and may not discuss, what we may and may not decide. Despite what our masters in the media think, the American people are perfectly capable of hearing all sides of all issues and coming to a reasonable conclusion (not the same thing as a pre-defined "rational conclusion").

The struggle between politicians on the one hand, and giant media monopolies on the other, has nothing to do with freedom of speech. We do not further the power of the people when a few media organizations and their hirelings harass the elected government and manipulate the public discourse. Even if the media occasionally serve as a check on some of the usurpations of government, it is a sham battle. They are always on the side of Leviathan. There is no liberty of the press involved in the right of CBS and NBC, Ted Turner and the *New York Times*, to tell us what we may think. Liberty of the press, like all liberties, rests upon the dispersal of power—a multiplicity of free voices rather than a few government-granted, or even market-granted, monopolies. It should not be too difficult to break the power of the media moguls and restore real debate. There is no reason why we cannot, if we choose, have many television networks rather than a few.

There is a deep cultural question here as well as a question of power. The tendency of American democracy, as its best friends have always pointed out with concern, has been, unfortunately, to sink to a low common denominator. Related to this is a progressive inability to distinguish between the public and the private, so that the private becomes ever more subject to the illegitimate authority of public "rational conclusions." Thus our public deliberations suffer not only from controls laid down by the oligarchy, but also from debasement, a pervasive mediocrity and triviality. We should remember that our forefathers' conception of liberty was essentially aristocratic—they believed in levelling up, not levelling down, and for them liberty meant precisely the freedom of the private sphere from manipulation by the state.

The necessary freedom of the public debate about public things is not enhanced by the licensing of obscenity and blasphemy on the part of the irresponsible. This is a deep error related to the confusion of the public and private. Freedom of speech is damaged, not enhanced, by the Supreme Court's licensing of obscenity and flag-burning. Our liberty of speech depends a great deal more on Roberts Rules of Order and on good manners than on the ACLU. Real liberty is inseparable from decorum, responsibility, and that respect for others that should be given by all to all in engaging in mutual deliberation.

There was something necessarily aristocratic in the republican spirit of our forefathers. Democracy did not mean reducing all to the equality of the lowest common denominator. It meant, rather, the right of the common man to aspire to the liberty previously deemed fit only for the few. This meant the restriction of the artificial aristocracy of birth and privilege so that the natural aristocracy of merit might rise. Jefferson's educational system did not seek to promote equality, but rather quality, to remove the barriers from the rise of obscure talent. Nothing could be further from his spirit than the complacent and vulgar egalitarianism of education and culture that America suffers today. Measured by our literature, arts, public discourse, current American democracy has nothing to leave to posterity. And will not until we revive the aristocratic Jeffersonian spirit that Faulkner had in mind when he said that the "pursuit of happiness" did "not mean just to chase happiness but to work for it." And by happiness our Founders meant "not just pleasure, idleness, but peace, dignity, independence and self-respect."

So we have not one problem but two—the consolidation of power and the decay of virtue. But from the viewpoint of the classical republicanism of our Fathers these are but one and the same, two inseparable evils that feed upon each other. Consolidation of power breeds the decay of virtue in the people, and decay of virtue in the people breeds consolidation of power.

Our forefathers were neither economic determinists nor, like us, materialists. But they realized that, as Burke put it, the revenue is the state, that the power of taxation and expenditure is the master of all other powers. There is no clearer principle established in the American Revolution and the whole heritage of British liberty that preceded it. Put another way, the restoration of power to the people can only come with limitations on the taxing and spending power of the federal government, which has become autonomous and limitless. We despise our representatives and yet we reelect them at the greatest rate in history. This paradox is a key to our times. Our forefathers would have recognized this condition immediately as a symptom of decayed republican virtue. Our politicians buy us, with our own money. The habit of spoils is so deeply ingrained that only the most radical remedy will cure it.

The government takes from all and gives to all, in the meantime performing magic tricks that shift the burden to posterity and bemuse enough of us into thinking that we might be getting something. And, of course, the politicians are afloat in a sea of money and scoop up the lion's share for themselves and their clients. It does not take much cleverness for a Congressman to take credit for the flow of manna back to his district and thus be re-elected forever. The system puts a premium upon chicanery and irresponsibility. We are disgusted with our leaders because we now, at last, realize that while they profit from the system, it has escaped from control. And we have been forced to realize that an overweening government is not only unjust. It is inefficient and destructive of true prosperity.

The munificence of our land and the hard work of our people have, until now, sustained the system of plunder, extortion, and redistribution. But we show signs of exhaustion. So much debt has been piled up and so many unearned entitlements have been loaded onto the shoulders of the productive that catastrophe threatens. The politicians are unable to make necessary decisions. The public has correctly concluded that this is the fault of the Democrats *and* the Republicans, the Congress *and* the President. And I believe, also, that the public realizes that it bears some of the fault and is willing to bite the bullet given a leadership in which confidence can be placed.

The Cold War has ended, making possible a great decrease in the burden of expenditure carried by the American people for more than a generation. A responsible republican government would do two things in this situation—reduce taxes and retire debt. That is, the people would enjoy a great boon in the lifting of burdens, a peace dividend. It is a measure of our degradation that neither of our ruling parties has considered either alternative. Instead both parties and both branches of government have conspired to raise taxes. They have considered only the opportunity to broker funds in new ways and buy new allegiances. The peace dividend is not ours, but theirs. Like all economic questions, this is at bottom a moral question, which our leaders evade by seeming to see only a technical question. So accustomed are we to the evil system that we hardly notice the unreality of the debate.

The hope of the "Reagan Revolution" was that this system would be reversed and ultimately dismantled. Such was the was the rhetoric of 1980. We must face the fact that the revolution has failed, utterly, or as Patrick Buchanan has put it, we can no longer blame the liberals. We must face the fact also that in many respects the situation is worse. The conservative victory which should have led, by carefully considered measures, to restoring the wealth and liberty of the middle orders has instead ended only in enriching international speculators and exporting productive capacity. The Silent Majority is now more powerless, if not more silent, than before, after twelve years of rule of the party they raised to power.

The system works for the benefit of the rich and the unproductive, an unholy alliance, at the expense of the vast unorganized middle, and of posterity. The privileged always take care of themselves. The benefit of government spending and debt always accrues chiefly to the rich and the politically well-placed, as Jefferson knew—which was the reason for his counter-revolution against

Hamilton's economy. "There is, indeed, no uglier kind of state," wrote Cicero in a passage very familiar to our Founders, "than one in which the richest men are thought to be the best."

If the election of 1980 meant anything it meant the desire of the many to throw off the burden of the unholy alliance of the rich and the unproductive classes to profit through government spending. This mandate was never fulfilled. Rather, it was co-opted and reinterpreted by servants of the existing establishment (called "moderate Republicans" and "neo-conservatives"). In part this was human error and weakness, in part it demonstrates merely the immemorial ability of establishments to capture protest and preserve themselves. We needed an Andrew Jackson and got a Calvin Coolidge.

Reflect that Reagan was brought to power by a populist-conservative revolt of the Heartland, West, and South against the establishment. But not only did he fail to take on the establishment, he bequeathed his movement to a wealthy New Englander who was a lifelong insider of the establishment and who had no sympathy with the movement. And that heir made his heir another wealthy establishmentarian from the New England area of the upper Midwest, the region of obsolescent vigor.

And reflect that for more than a century, when protectionism was beneficial to rich Northeasterners and harmful to the American people, we had protectionism as the central plank of the Republican party. And now that "free trade" is beneficial to rich Northeasterners and harmful to the majority of the American people, "free trade" has become sacred to the Republican party and to the swarms of lickspittle publicists and politicians who follow in the wake of wealth.

The "genius" of the American two-party system has, alas, always been in its ability to blunt protest by avoiding and reinterpreting issues. Thus our public deliberations except in extraordinary times always fail to make a true diagnosis and reach our real discontents. A new refinement has been added to flim-flam politics to protect the reigning powers from revolt, by the Bush candidacy. He ran on the program and platform of a movement as a publicity stunt, without any allegiance whatever to the sentiments of the movement. This trick has now worn thin.

There have been a lot of complaints, thoroughly justified, about American corporate moguls and the stupendous salaries they make even while running their companies into the ground. This is only one part of the vast consolidated system in which we have been busily divorcing reward from effort, productivity from profit. Such people hold positions of power and profit for exactly the same reason that Bush and Quayle were chosen to head a movement with which they had no sympathy. We are governed by yesterday's men, the type who are able to receive honors very gracefully in quiet times, but who have no capacity or desire to adapt to new challenges.

The car executives got where they are because of the politicization of our society. Our forefathers' republican philosophy recognized explicitly that wealth and government corrupted each other—that an overweening government which monopolized rewards by politics rather than merit tended to corrupt social virtue and productivity. The car executives are not engineers, not entrepreneurs, not managers, not inventors, not even speculators. They are politicians. They achieved their position through politics—that is, through the manipulation of existing power relationships, not through accomplishment. Anyone who has observed closely the present generation of American leadership in government, in business, in education, in the armed forces, and in every other area, cannot have missed the endemic phenomenon of manipulators rising to the top over achievers.

But it is not just at the higher levels. Affirmative action is a product of the very same mindset at work, the same politicization of society. We do not give scholarships and prestige admissions to the most gifted students—we give them to the well-connected and the officially-privileged minorities. And such is true in every part of our society. We do not publish and promote the best books, but rather the books that are politically correct or politically connected. Our society is in conspiracy against talent and innovation, led by the very people who tout themselves as "progressive" and champions of "equality of opportunity."

Such a state of affairs is exactly what our forefathers wished to repudiate in the American Revolution—aristocracy, that is, artificial state-granted advantage not related to talents and services. Such a state of affairs is destructive for any society, but especially so for Americans, whose morale rests more than any other people on a belief in opportunity, that performance and effort can overcome barriers, that talent can rise. Politicization of rewards is also a sure-fire formula for economic and cultural stagnation and mediocrity. Every society, and especially America, depends upon the energy and creativity of rising talent. When the criterion for success becomes politics rather than performance, creativity dies.

And then we wonder why there is demoralization and cynicism. We wonder why we are not competitive with societies which reward talent, effort, and productivity rather than status. The only solution, that our leadership can offer is to rev up once again Leviathan, to absorb more and more of the product of society, in order to "invest" in America—meaning profits for politicians and bureaucrats—and programs which talk about merit and competitiveness but are strangled in egalitarianism. We will restore morale only by restoring real liberty and real opportunity.

The people must not only put limits on government. They must break their own dependence upon the corrupt system, give up the expectation that things will be done for them, and demand the return of our resources to ourselves, to dispose of in our own way. For liberty plain and simple is the ability to decide and dispose. This is even less easy than it sounds, because demands upon the Treasury always come disguised as public benefits; because we have as a people almost lost the ability to distinguish between public necessity and private subsidy; and because we have created an immense clamoring clientele that exists only on and for ever increasing patronage.

The answer will be the hardest reform of all. To restore the federal republic we will have to begin to level up rather than level down, to substitute liberty for equality as our chief goal. Ideological equality is the enemy of republican citizenship. It is in its guise as the imposer of equality that the overweening state has taken most power to itself, even more so than in war, and become the arbiter of society. Government programs for preferential groups must be ended, and all citizens become equal under the law. In no way else can we restore morale and productivity, belief in fairness and opportunity. We must take away from the oligarchy the brokering of how differing groups of a pluralistic society live together. Also, in order to restore the value of republican citizenship, it will have to be restricted. That means that immigration has to be reduced to a small number determined specifically by the future and current interest of the American people, not by any philosophical or economic consideration. We must end the system by which any respiring creature who manages to sneak under the fence becomes immediately entitled to all the rights and privileges of citizenship. To say that everyone in the world who can manage to get here is an American citizen is to say that there is no such thing as an American citizen in any meaningful sense, to cheapen our citizenship beyond toleration. The restriction of immigration and citizenship rights will make American citizenship more valued and viable, not less so.

Democracy, as our forefathers clearly recognized, is not a group of people living under common procedures and economic exchanges. It is a social fabric of tradition, habit, and prejudice that makes self-government possible in a way that no proclaimed set of procedures or even carefully balanced interests can. A miscellaneous collection of people are not citizens of a republic but interchangeable ciphers of imperialism. The aspiration of a globalized citizenship is not the vision of republicanism but the dream of empire. In order for American society to begin to feel its power and reassert itself against government, it must have a period of stabilization. We must have time to absorb the great immigration we have received in the last three decades. Otherwise we will have a society increasingly fragmented rather than pluralistic, divided into hostile groups competing for advantage, a situation in which democracy cannot long survive, as the history of the world shows. Unlimited immigration serves the rich and the government, not the people.

Here we find the deep moral problem of modern society. Our unrestricted immigration, the celebration of constant and endless social transformation, does not result from allegiance to democracy or liberality of spirit. It results from the same state of mind as our economic irresponsibility—an inability to care about posterity and act for the future. A healthy society, like that of our forefathers, will automatically take account of the welfare of its posterity when it makes decisions. There can be no posterity in a society whose citizens are merely interchangeable parts of a politico-economic machine.

How we got to be the way we are would take a long historical explanation. The explanation falls under two headings. One is the intrusive do-gooder mentality described by Nock. The other is the natural consolidating tendencies of modern society, which should not be under-estimated. Since the middle of the 19th century we have developed huge organizations and concentrations of capital, of population, of dependency and interdependency, of collectivization of technology, welfare, public health and warfare, and reliance on experts. All these have concentrated power. More importantly they have made us think in terms of universalist and technical solutions rather than political wisdom and self-government.

It is true that we live in a very different world from our Fathers and that our solutions cannot always be the same as theirs. But our problem is the same—the harnessing of power. They solved the problem for their time, and the problem is solvable in our time, given sufficient will and political genius. There is much in modern society that makes convenient the dispersal and devolution of power as well as its consolidation. The computer can serve decentralization as well as centralization. There is no reason why we cannot have many small humane factories or schools rather than a few large ones. As Edward Abbey observed in one of the wisest insights of our time: "Growth is the enemy of progress." Consolidation of power is not so much inherent in our current state of society as it is the product of choices made and institutions constructed in the past that showed a bias in favor of gigantism over humane scale, centralized control over freedom, and elitism over democratic rule. In imitation of our Fathers we may solve the problem of consolidated power.

Allen Tate observed that our Founders "had a profound instinct for high style, a genius at dramatizing themselves at their own particular moment of history. They were so situated economically and politically that they were able to form a definite conception of their human role; they were not ants in an economic anthill, nor were they investigating statistically the behavior of other ants. They knew what they wanted because they knew what they, themselves, were."

It may be that this sense of self-determination of free men enjoyed by our Fathers is an impractical goal, not fully realizable in the modern world. But unless we recover it at least as an ideal and a point of reference toward which we direct our collective selves, the American experiment has failed. The restoration of the federal republic will not in itself solve all our problems because the ends of human life do not rest in government and because modern society is in deep spiritual crisis, as every great thinker of our century has observed. But the restraint of power is a necessary first step for all progress—moral, economic, political, cultural. Leviathan has gotten loose from the harness our forefathers so skillfully fashioned for him. He has knocked over the fence, laid waste our gardens, and waxed fat on our substance. We must begin to look to our husbandry, but first we will have to chain the beast. In this task we have one great advantage—the preponderance of the American people are still republican at heart.

(1992)